Four Degrees of Glob

At the UN Climate Conference in Copenhagen in December 2009, the international community agreed to limit global warming to below 2°C to avoid the worst impacts of human-induced climate change. However, climate scientists agree that current national emissions targets collectively will still not achieve this goal. Instead, the 'ambition gap' between climate science and climate policy is likely to lead to average global warming of around 4°C by or before 2100. If a Four Degree World is the *de facto* goal of policy, we urgently need to understand what this world might look like.

Four Degrees of Global Warming: Australia in a Hot World outlines the expected consequences of this world for Australia and its region. Its contributors include many of Australia's most eminent and internationally recognized climate scientists, climate policy makers and policy analysts. They provide an accessible, detailed, dramatic, and disturbing examination of the likely impacts of a Four Degree World on Australia's social, economic and ecological systems.

The book offers policy makers, politicians, researchers, students and anyone interested in climate change access to the most recent research on potential Australian impacts of global warming, and possible responses.

Peter Christoff is a political scientist and Associate Professor who teaches Climate Change Politics and Policy and Environmental Policy at the University of Melbourne, Australia. From 2005 to 2013 he was also the Vice President of the Australian Conservation Foundation, Australia's largest national environmental NGO.

This is an important book that addresses the defining question of the 21st century: Can we really afford to let the world slip down the warming slope – towards the 4 degrees mark or even beyond? The authors provide compelling evidence from the Australian perspective that the answer reads "no". Peter Christoff should be praised for initiating and editing this colossal intellectual effort.

–Hans Joachim Schellnhuber, Director of the Potsdam Institute for Climate Impact Research (PIK) and Chair of the German Advisory Council on Global Change (WBGU), Germany

'Four Degrees' reveals what might become of Australians and their country if global average temperatures are allowed to increase by 4 degrees above that of 200 years ago. It paints a 'bleak vision of a continent under assault.' And that will be out future if we do nothing – just keep going along as we are today. Thankfully the book is also full of clear and realistic solutions, which makes it a must-read for all caring Australians.

–Tim Flannery, Chief Commissioner, Climate Commission, Australia

This important book, though ostensibly about climate change, raises profound and personal questions about the type of world we wish to bequeath our children. Setting out stark and scientifically informed choices, the authors provide a cogent framing of the challenging issues facing Australian policy makers, businesses and civil society.

–Kevin Anderson, University of Manchester, UK

Despite a generation of talks, the international community has failed to stem the global increase in greenhouse gas pollution that is causing climate change. Consequently, the earth is set to get hotter, and Australia is in the eye of the storm. In this important new book, Peter Christoff brings together the insights of distinguished scholars, scientists and analysts. They explore the ecological, social and economic impacts for Australia of a much warmer world, in the process providing a valuable guide to the future.

–Paul G. Harris, Hong Kong Institute of Education

Four Degrees of Global Warming

Australia in a hot world

Edited by Peter Christoff

LONDON AND NEW YORK

First published 2014
by Routledge
2 Park Square, Milton Park, Abingdon, Oxon, OX14 4RN

and by Routledge
270 Madison Avenue, New York, NY 10016

Routledge is an imprint of the Taylor & Francis Group, an informa business

© 2013 Peter Christoff, selection and editorial material; individual chapters, the contributors

The right of Peter Christoff to be identified as author of the editorial material, and of the individual authors as authors of their contributions, has been asserted by him in accordance with sections 77 and 78 of the Copyright, Designs and Patents Act 1988.

British Library Cataloguing in Publication Data
A catalogue record for this book is available from the British Library

Library of Congress Cataloging-in-Publication Data
Four degrees of global warming : Australia in a hot world / [edited by] Peter Christoff.
p. cm.
Includes bibliographical references and index.
1. Global warming--Australia. 2. Global warming--Social aspects--Australia. 3. Global warming--Economic aspects--Australia. 4. Global warming--Government policy--Australia. 5. Social change--Australia. 6. Australia--Environmental conditions--Forecasting. 7. Australia--Social conditions--Forecasting. 8. Australia--Economic conditions--Forecasting. I. Christoff, Peter.
QC981.8.G56F68 2013
363.738'740994--dc23
2013018665

ISBN13: 978-0-415-82457-6 (hbk)
ISBN13: 978-0-415-82458-3 (pbk)
ISBN13: 978-0-203-37047-6 (ebk)

Typeset in Goudy by
Fakenham Prepress Solutions, Fakenham, Norfolk NR21 8NN

Contents

Figures and tables   vii
Contributors   x
Acknowledgements   xv
Acronyms and abbreviations   xvi

Introduction

1   Four degrees or more?   1
    PETER CHRISTOFF

PART I
Climate science and four degrees   15

2   Australia's climate in a Four Degree World   17
    PENNY WHETTON, DAVID KAROLY, IAN WATTERSON, LEANNE WEBB,
    FRANK DROST, DEWI KIRONO AND KATHLEEN MCINNES

3   Changes in extreme weather   33
    KARL BRAGANZA, KEVIN HENNESSY, LISA ALEXANDER AND BLAIR TREWIN

PART II
Ecological impacts   61

4   Changes to Australian terrestrial biodiversity   63
    LESLEY HUGHES

5   Australia's marine resources in a warm, acid ocean   84
    OVE HOEGH-GULDBERG, ELVIRA POLOCZANSKA AND ANTHONY
    RICHARDSON

6   Agricultural in an even more sunburnt country   101
    MARK HOWDEN, SERENA SCHROETER AND STEPHEN CRIMP

7   Compounding crises: climate change in a complex world   121
    WILL STEFFEN AND DAVID GRIGGS

PART III
Social and economic impacts   139

8   Compounding social and economic impacts: the limits to adaptation   141
    ROSS GARNAUT

9   Health impacts in Australia in a Four Degree World   155
    ANTHONY J. MCMICHAEL

10 Hot in the city: planning for climate change impacts in urban Australia   172
    JAN MCDONALD

11 No island is an island: security in a Four Degree World   190
    PETER CHRISTOFF AND ROBYN ECKERSLEY

PART IV
Adaptation   205

12 Challenges and opportunities for climate change adaptation in
    Australia's region   207
    ANDREW HEWETT

13 Can we successfully adapt to four degrees of global warming? Yes,
    no and maybe ...   216
    JEAN P. PALUTIKOF, JON BARNETT AND DANIEL A. GUITART

Conclusion

14 Avoiding a Four Degree World – Australia's role   235
    PETER CHRISTOFF

    Appendix   261
    Index   263

Figures and tables

Figures

2.1	Projected warming over Australia at +4°C GW for summer and winter and for selected percentiles of the GCM-based uncertainty range	18
2.2	Projected changes in rainfall for summer and winter and annual mean temperature for northern Australia, southern Australia and south-western Australia	19
2.3	Central Victorian temperature (a) and rainfall (b), observed (solid) and model-based projections	20
2.4	Annual totals and 11-year moving averages of 1-in-20 year hot or cool months in south-eastern Australia, modelled for 1910–99	21
2.5	Likelihood of increase in annual rainfall across Australia	22
2.6	Projected precipitation change (in per cent) over Australia at +4°C GW for summer and winter and for selected percentiles of the global climate model-based uncertainty range	23
2.7	+4°C GW climate analogues for three selected sites – Melbourne (top), Nuriootpa (middle), and Dubbo (bottom) – based on annual maximum temperature and precipitation	27
2.8	Australian Alps: Current and projected future days of snow cover	29
3.1	Area-averaged Australian annual mean temperature, 1910–2011	36
3.2	Frequency of record high and low maximum temperatures in Australia, 1910–2011	36
3.3	Frequency of record high and low minimum temperatures in Australia, 1910–2011	37
3.4	Trend magnitude in annual total Forest Fire Danger Index (FFDI)	38
3.5	Daily maximum temperature extremes for 7 February 2009	39
3.6	Rainfall deciles for the period 1 September 1996 to 31 August 2009	40
3.7	Rainfall anomalies (departure from 1961–90 average rainfall) in mm for December 2010 to February 2011	43
3.8	Sea surface temperature anomalies (departure from 1961–90 average) for September to December 2010	44

3.9   Annual numbers of major tropical cyclones for the 1981–2 to   45
       2006–7 cyclone seasons, with linear trends
3.10   Projected changes for 2070 in risk of large hail   50
3.11   Estimated increases in the frequency of extreme sea-level caused   55
       by a mean sea-level rise of 50cm
5.1   Key chemical and physical changes in the atmosphere and oceans   87
       as a result of climate change
5.2   Locations where marine climate change impacts have been detected   88
5.3   Sea temperature data on coral reefs at the northern end of the   91
       Great Barrier Reef from 1860 and projected to 2100
5.4   Analogues from extent reefs on the Great Barrier Reef of the state   94
       of coral reefs under ocean warming and acidification in the future
6.1   Global annual population growth and growth in global cereal crop   103
       production from 1961–2010 shown as 10-year running means
6.2   Coefficient of variation (%) of annual global cereal crop   103
       production 1961–2010 shown as a 10-year running average
6.3   Growth in annual wheat yield (%) with 1961–2010 shown as a   104
       10-year running average
6.4   Global drivers of change, their impacts on earth systems and   105
       sustainable agriculture
6.5   Frequency of days per month unsuitable for spraying for Emerald   112
       (Queensland) and Kellerberrin (Western Australia) for the
       historical baseline, 2030 and for 2070
7.1   Changes in the global environment, 1750–2000   124
7.2   Changes in the human enterprise, 1750–2000   125
7.3   Tipping elements in the Earth System, overlaid on the human   127
       population density on Earth
7.4   Unwanted social outcomes resulting from the interactive effects of   130
       both biophysical and social drivers in the Earth System
7.5   The nine planetary boundaries and estimates of the current value   135
       of the control variable compared to the boundary estimate

Tables

2.1   Projected climate changes for eight selected sites at +4°C GW   25
3.1   Average number of days per year above 35°C at selected sites for   48
       the current climate (average for 1971–2000) and for 2070
3.2   Percentage change in the intensity of 1-day rainfall totals with a   49
       20-year return period for the 2090 climate relative to that of 1980
3.3   Average number of extreme fire weather days per year for 26 sites   52
       in south-eastern Australia
3.4   Projected changes in total tropical cyclone numbers, cyclone days,   54
       duration of a given cyclone, genesis latitude and decay latitude
       for seven simulations, downscaled using CCAM to 65km grid
       spacing, for the period 2051–90, relative to 1971–2000

4.1 Regions in Australia considered most vulnerable to   68
     transformational change and biodiversity loss
4.2 Examples of methods used to project the impacts of future climate   74
     change on species and ecosystems, summarizing some of the
     advantages and disadvantages of each
6.1 Increases (%) in mean annual potential evaporation (Penman-   110
     Monteith; Allen 1998) for Emerald (Qld), Birchip (Vic.) and
     Kellerberrin (WA) for 2030 and 2050
6.2 Catchments in the Murray–Darling Basin and the prospective   110
     changes in water availability under 'dry', median and 'wet'
     scenarios for 2030
6.3 A subset of the adaptation options available to adapt farming   114
     systems to climate change
7.1 Vulnerability of tipping elements to a 4°C global warming   128
9.1 Infectious diseases likely to be introduced or reintroduced to a   164
     +4°C warmer and institutionally stressed Australia, or have their
     current Australian rate and range extended
13.1 Examples of recent storyline type scenarios across different scales   218
13.2 The drivers of adaptation and characteristics of the sectors   222
     adapting in the three storylines for the future of Australia with
     4°C warming, as described in this study
14.1 Australia in a Four Degree World   237

Contributors

Lisa Alexander is a Senior Researcher at UNSW Climate Change Research Centre and a Chief Investigator in the ARC Centre of Excellence for Climate System Science. Her primary research focuses on understanding the variability and driving mechanisms of climate extremes. Of particular significance is her ongoing work assessing global changes in temperature and rainfall extremes.

Jon Barnett is Professor and Australian Research Council Future Fellow in the Department of Resource Management and Geography at Melbourne University. He is a political geographer who researches the impacts of and responses to environmental change on social systems in Australia, East Asia and the South Pacific.

Karl Braganza is the manager of the Climate Monitoring Section at the Bureau of Meteorology's Climate and Water Division. This section is responsible for collecting and analyzing climate data for Australia and the region. It provides sector-relevant climate information related to drought, bushfires, extreme events and climate change. His research has focused on understanding climate variability and change using climate modelling, instrumental observations and palaeo-climate evidence.

Peter Christoff is an Associate Professor and political scientist in the Department of Resource Management and Geography at Melbourne University. His research focuses on Australian and international environmental and climate policy, and his recent publications include *Climate Law in Australia* (co-editor, 2007) and *Globalization and the Environment* (with Robyn Eckersley, 2013).

Steven Crimp is a Senior Research Scientist within the CSIRO Agricultural Systems Research Program, working on identification and evaluation of management practices that provide resilience to climate variability and climate change. Over the last 15 years his research focus has been on mixed cropping/grazing enterprises across Australia.

Frank Drost was a Research Fellow in the School of Earth Sciences at the University of Melbourne comparing global climate model simulations of variations over the last 100 years with observed climate variations. He is currently employed in the Australian Bureau of Meteorology.

Robyn Eckersley is a Professor of Political Science in the School of Social and Political Sciences at the University of Melbourne and a Fellow of the Australian Academy of the Social Sciences. She has published widely in the fields of environmental politics, political theory and international relations, with a focus on the politics of climate change. Her recent books include *Special Responsibilities: Global Problems and American Power* (co-author, 2012), *Why Human Security Matters* (co-editor, 2012) and *Globalization and the Environment* (with Peter Christoff, 2013).

Ross Garnaut is Vice Chancellor's Fellow and Professorial Fellow in Economics at the University of Melbourne. He is also Distinguished Professor of Economics at The Australian National University, a Fellow of the Australian Academy of Social Science, Distinguished Fellow of the Australian Economics Society and Honorary Professor of the Chinese Academy of Social Sciences. He is the author of the two Garnaut Climate Change Reviews, prepared successively for Prime Ministers Rudd and Gillard.

David Griggs is Director of the Monash Sustainability Institute, which delivers sustainability research and education solutions. In 2008 he created and became CEO of ClimateWorks Australia, focused on action to reduce green-house gas emissions. Previous positions he has held include UK Met Office Deputy Chief Scientist, Director of the Hadley Centre for Climate Change and Head of the Intergovernmental Panel on Climate Change (IPCC) scientific assessment unit. Dave is a past vice-chair of the World Climate Research Programme. He is a Fellow of the Australian Academy of Technological Sciences and Engineering and was awarded the Vilho Vaisala award (World Meteorological Organization).

Daniela A. Guitart works at the National Climate Change Adaptation Research Facility (NCCARF), Griffith University, where she has managed the production of two edited volumes on climate change adaptation and coordinates Adaptation Research Network activities. Her research interest focuses on urban agriculture and its contribution to food security and agro-biodiversity conservation.

Kevin Hennessy is a Principal Research Scientist at CSIRO Marine and Atmospheric Research. He leads the Impacts, Adaptation and Vulnerability team in the Climate Variability and Change Program. Amongst over 200 publications, he has looked at the impact of climate change on drought, fire, snow, extreme temperature and extreme rainfall. He was a Coordinating Lead Author of the 'Australia and New Zealand' chapter of the 2007 IPCC assessment of 'Climate change impacts, adaptation and vulnerability'. In 2011, he wrote a chapter on 'Climate change impacts' for the CSIRO book *Climate Change: Science and Solutions for Australia*.

Andrew Hewett was Executive Director of Oxfam Australia, the Australian member of the Oxfam International network, from 2001 to 2012. He began working for Oxfam (then known as Community Aid Abroad) in 1991 to establish its national advocacy program. He was a member of the Executive Committee of the Australian Council for International Development for over a decade. He frequently visited Oxfam's development and relief programs in Asia, the Pacific, Africa and Central America.

Ove Hoegh-Guldberg is a marine biologist who has worked extensively on coral reefs (www.coralreefecosystem.org), particularly on their response to ocean warming and acidification. He is also Director of the Global Change Institute at the University of Queensland.

Mark Howden is Leader of the Adaptive Primary Industries Theme in the CSIRO Climate Adaptation Flagship. He is also an Honorary Professor at the University of Melbourne. He works on adaptation to climate variability and climate change, cost-effective emission-reduction options, sustainable agriculture and adoption of innovation across various industries. He assesses climate change impacts and effects of climate extremes on urban and rural systems, and works to link science with policy outcomes. Mark has been a key contributor to the IPCC Second, Third, Fourth and Fifth Assessments, IPCC special reports and international and national greenhouse gas inventory development.

Lesley Hughes is a Professor and ecologist in the Department of Biological Sciences, Macquarie University who researches the impacts of climate change on species and ecosystems. She is a lead author on the IPCC Fourth and Fifth assessment reports, a member of the Australian Government's Land Sector Carbon and Biodiversity Board and Commissioner on the federal Climate Commission.

David Karoly is Professor of Climate Science in the School of Earth Sciences and the ARC Centre of Excellence for Climate System Science at the University of Melbourne. He is an internationally recognized expert in climate change and climate variability, including greenhouse climate change, stratospheric ozone depletion and interannual climate variations. Professor Karoly is a member of the new Climate Change Authority in Australia and the Science Advisory Panel to the Australian Climate Commission. He was heavily involved in preparation of the Third and Fourth Assessment Reports of the Intergovernmental Panel on Climate Change (IPCC), in several different roles.

Dewi Kirono is a Senior Research Scientist at CSIRO Marine and Atmospheric Research. Dr Kirono's work focuses on interfaces between climate change and adaptation sciences. Examples are the Murray–Darling Basin Sustainable Yield Project and the assessment of impact of climate change on the nature and frequency of exceptional climatic events.

Jan McDonald is Professor of Environmental Law and Associate Dean (Research) at the University of Tasmania. Her research spans the legal and policy dimensions of climate change adaptation, including urban planning and coastal management, liability and insurance issues.

Kathleen McInnes' research expertise lies in understanding how climate change will affect weather events and coastal sea levels. She was a lead author on the IPCC Special Report on Extremes and is currently a lead author on the IPCC Working Group 2 Fifth Assessment Report chapter on Coastal Systems and Low-Lying Areas.

Anthony McMichael is Professor Emeritus (Population Health) at the ANU. Since 2001 he has developed the ANU's research program on population health risks of climate change. He is an elected member of the US National Academies of Science and Honorary Professor of Climate Change and Health, University of Copenhagen. He has contributed substantively to scientific assessments by the Intergovernmental Panel on Climate Change (IPCC); advises WHO on climate change risks to health; and chairs an expert group for WHO's Tropical Diseases Research Programme on interactions between environment, climate, agriculture and poverty in the emergence of infectious diseases.

Jean P. Palutikof is the Director of the National Climate Change Adaptation Research Facility (NCCARF), Griffith University, where she has built a national programme of adaptation research, communication and partnerships. Prior to joining NCCARF she managed the production of the Intergovernmental Panel on Climate Change (IPCC) Fourth Assessment Report for Working Group II (Impacts, Adaptation and Vulnerability). Her research interests focus on climate change impacts and responses, and the application of climatic data to economic and planning issues.

Elvira Poloczanska is a climate change ecologist focused on impacts of climate variability and climate change on species and ecosystems at both global and Australian scales and investigating potential adaptation actions for conservation and marine industries.

Anthony Richardson is a climate change ecologist focused on observing and understanding climate variability and change in marine pelagic systems. He is most excited when using quantitative approaches for explaining patterns in large datasets.

Serena Schroeter is a recent science graduate currently working with the Adaptive Primary Industries Theme in the CSIRO Adaptation Flagship. She collaborates with research scientists across a range of disciplines involved in the study of the impacts of increased climate variability and extremes on Australian agricultural systems.

Will Steffen is a climate and global change researcher and Professor at the Australian National University (ANU), Canberra. He served on the

Multi-Party Climate Change Committee (MPCCC) in 2010–11, and is a Climate Commissioner. From 1998 to mid-2004, Steffen served as Executive Director of the International Geosphere-Biosphere Programme, based in Stockholm, Sweden, and is currently a guest researcher at the Stockholm Resilience Centre. His research interests span a broad range within the fields of climate and Earth System science, with an emphasis on incorporation of human processes in Earth System modelling and analysis, and on sustainability and climate change.

Blair Trewin has been a climate scientist with the Bureau of Meteorology since 1998. He is a member of the World Meteorological Organization's Expert Team on Climate Change Detection and Indices, and is currently President of the Australian Meteorological and Oceanographic Society. He is also editor of the *Australian Meteorological and Oceanographic Journal.*

Ian Watterson has, from a background in dynamical meteorology, contributed to climate modelling and analysis at CSIRO over the past 23 years. He has had a significant role in the communication of climate change through research reports and papers, and as an IPCC Lead Author. His work on climate projections led to the results used in this paper.

Leanne Webb has worked in the climate impacts field with CSIRO, the University of Melbourne and the University of New South Wales over the past decade, using spatial tools to link biophysical metrics with climate data. Exploration of the impact of projected climate change has been undertaken for many sectors, though particularly focusing on the wine industry, agriculture and health.

Penny Whetton is a Senior Principal Research Scientist with CSIRO's Climate Adaptation Flagship. Dr Whetton has worked on projecting regional climate change and its impacts for over 20 years and taken a leading role in Australian climate change scenarios released by CSIRO in 1992, 1996 and 2001, and by CSIRO and the Bureau of Meteorology in 2007. She was also a lead author of the regional projection chapters of Third and Fourth Assessment Reports of the IPCC and is currently a lead author of the forthcoming Fifth Assessment Report. Her research group was a recipient of a 2003 Eureka Prize.

Acknowledgements

This book owes its existence to a chain of events that began at Oxford in 2009. David Karoly, a friend and colleague from Melbourne University, is a renowned climatologist and a significant contributor to Australian climate science and policy. At a pub after the Oxford Four Degrees conference, he and I talked about the value of something similar occurring in Australia. David provided encouragement, wise advice and help on the path from Oxford to the conference in Melbourne and then to this book.

The Melbourne conference provided a significant opportunity for substantial intellectual collaboration between some of Australia's finest climate scientists and other thinkers grappling with different elements of Australian climate policy. That work became the substance of this book. The conference could not have occurred without the generosity of the Vice Chancellor's Office at the University of Melbourne, and of the Melbourne Sustainable Societies Institute, the Melbourne Energy Institute and the Monash Sustainability Institute, as well as the strong support of their respective directors at that time – Professor Craig Pearson, Professor Mike Sandiford and Professor Dave Griggs. The conference also received generous assistance from Rob Purves and the Purves Environmental Fund.

This book has been greatly enhanced by the critical input of its anonymous academic and scientific reviewers, including those within the CSIRO. For its editorial development and passage to publication, profound thanks are also due to the skilful nurturing, assistance and advice of Khanam Virjee and Helen Bell at Earthscan from Routledge.

Acronyms and abbreviations

4AR	Fourth Assessment Report of the IPCC
+4C	Four degrees or more (Celsius)
ABARES	Australian Bureau of Agricultural and Resource Economics and Sciences
ABS	Australian Bureau of Statistics
ACF	Australian Conservation Foundation
ACORN	Australian Climate Observations Reference Network
ACOSS	Australian Council of Social Services
ADB	Asian Development Bank
ADF	Australian Defence Forces
AIMS	Australian Institute of Marine Science
AOSIS	Alliance of Small Island States
ARI	Average recurrence interval
BAU	Business as Usual
BCC	Brisbane City Council
BoM	Bureau of Meteorology (Australia)
CC	Climate Commission (Australia)
CCA	Climate Change Authority (Australia)
CDM	Clean Development Mechanism
CFCs	Chlorofluorocarbons
CHS	Commission on Human Security
CMIP	Coupled Model Intercomparison Project
CO_2	Carbon dioxide
CO_2e	Carbon dioxide equivalent
COAG	Council of Australian Governments
CSIRO	Commonwealth Scientific and Industrial Research Organization (Australia)
DCC	Department of Climate Change (Australia)
DCCEE	Department of Climate Change and Energy Efficiency (Australia)
DFAT	Department of Foreign Affairs and Trade (Australia)
EAC	East Australian Current
EEA	European Environment Agency

ENSO	El Nino-Southern Oscillation
FAO	Food and Agriculture Organization (United Nations)
FAR	Fourth Assessment Report (IPCC)
FFDI	Forest Fire Danger Index
GBR	Great Barrier Reef
GBRMPA	Great Barrier Reef Marine Park Authority
GCMs	Global Climate Models (atmospheric/oceanic)
GDP	Gross Domestic Product
GEF	Global Environmental Facility
GFDI	Grass Fire Danger Index
GHG	Greenhouse gas
Gt	gigatonne (billion tonnes)
GW	Global warming
GWP	Global warming potential
IEA	International Energy Agency
IPCC	Intergovernmental Panel on Climate Change
LDC	Least Developed Countries
LULUCF	Land Use and Land Use Factors
m	metre
MDB	Murray-Darling Basin
MEA	Millenium Ecosystem Assessment
Mha	million hectares
mm	millimetres
NASA	National Aeronautics and Space Administration (US)
NDRC	National Development and Reform Commission (China)
NOAA	National Oceanic and Atmospheric Administration (US)
NRDC	National Resource Defence Council (US)
OECD	Organisation for Economic Cooperation and Development
PCMDI	Program for Climate Model Diagnosis and Intercomparison
QFCI	Queensland Floods Commission of Inquiry
QRA	Queensland Reconstruction Authority
RAMS	Regional Atmospheric Modelling System
R&D	Research and development
SEI	Stockholm Environment Institute
SIDS	Small Island Developing States
SLR	Sea level rise
SoE	State of Environment
SPP	State Planning Policy
SPREP	Secretariat of the Pacific Regional Environment Program
Tmax^{99}	99th percentile of maximum temperature (hottest 1 percent of events)
UN	United Nations
UNDP	United Nations Development Program
UNESCAP	United Nations Economic and Social Commission for Asia and the Pacific

UNFCCC	United Nations Framework Convention on Climate Change
UNGA	United Nations General Assembly
VBRC	Victorian Bushfires Royal Commission
WA	Western Australia
WCRP	World Climate Research Program (WMO)
WGBU	German Advisory Council on Global Change
WHO	World Health Organization
WMO	World Meteorological Organisation
WWF	World Wide Fund for Nature

1 Introduction

Four degrees or more?

Peter Christoff

This book is based on a simple premise. Public debate and policy choices about climate change should be based on the best available evidence about the risks we face. Decisions about how much and when we should cut our emissions, and how much we should spend on adaptation, should be determined by what we understand and accept are the costs and consequences of *failing* to take sufficient action.

Australia has committed itself to trying to help limit global warming to 2°C. Yet there is widespread agreement that current mitigation efforts – including Australia's – will lead to global average warming of 4°C or more from pre-industrial levels by the end of this century ... to a Four Degree World.

The central aim of this book is to make us aware of the likely social, ecological and economic implications of catastrophic climate change for Australia and its region. If 4°C of global warming is the outcome – the *de facto* goal – of present policy settings, we should look at what we will encounter in a Four Degree World. If we don't like these prospects, then perhaps this book may encourage us to think differently about our current commitments and to choose an alternative future.

A heat like no other

Summer in Australia is often marred by hellishly hot days. However, the summer of 2013 was exceptional in several ways. January 2013 produced the hottest month on record. It started fires and broke temperature records across the country. It prompted international media coverage.

Following four months of very warm temperatures, an 'extensive dome of heat' hung over the continent (Braganza, in Hannam, 2013). Successive days of extreme heat covering most of the continent are rare and isolated. Yet for seven days, from 2 January to 8 January, the continental average temperature exceeded 39°C. Previously, Australia had only once seen four days in a row over 39°C, in 1972.

On Monday 7 January the continental average temperature rose to 40.3°C (105°F), the hottest maximum on record, breaking the previous high of 40.17°C on 12 December 1976. The next day, Sydney reached 42.3°C, and on 18 January,

45.8°C – almost 20° above the monthly average and breaking the previous record of 45.3°C set in 1939. Hobart hit 41.8°C, its highest temperature on record, while in Perth, suffering its fiercest heatwave in 80 years, hospitals experienced a wave of admissions of people suffering from heat-related symptoms.

These days also created extreme wildfire conditions across the country. The New South Wales fire service issued 'catastrophic' fire warnings – the highest level on the scale – in four areas of the State. In Victoria, the Country Fire Authority's fire warning website crashed under unprecedented community demand for information as temperatures rose above 40°C in parts of that state.

Across Australia, over 500 wildfires were ignited. Towns and lives were lost. When 100 homes in Dunalley, Tasmania, were incinerated, 2,700 people sheltered on beaches and were stranded at community refuges on the Tasmanian Peninsula, many later evacuated by sea. Images of the aftermath and stories about tragedies of individual and community loss appeared in media footage.

Climate scientists stress that while the cause of an individual weather event, including heatwaves, is always linked to specific weather conditions, 'it is possible to determine the influence of climate change on the frequency of occurrence of such an event' (Plummer et al., 2013). Changes in the frequency and intensity of extreme events are the most obvious manifestations of a changing climate. The extreme weather events of January 2013 in Australia – and others elsewhere – display the influence of a warming world. Plummer et al. (2013) report that 'Australia has warmed steadily since the 1940s, and the probability of extreme heat has now increased almost five-fold compared with 50 years ago.'

Recent research has shown Australia's preparedness for even gradual, low-level climate change is poor. In Canberra in 2003, fires killed 4 people and destroyed 500 homes. In Victoria, the Black Saturday fires in 2009 killed 173 people and more than a million animals, destroyed over 2,000 homes and caused over $4.4 billion damage (VBRC, 2010). Much is required to adapt to even low levels of warming.

Prime Minister Gillard, touring the fire-ravaged ruins of towns in Tasmania, warned that 'we need to prepare for more scorchers' and that extreme bushfires were a part of life in a hot and dry country, and that 'we do know over time that as a result of climate change we are going to see more extreme weather events' (Darby, 2013).

But for what exactly should we prepare?

*   *   *

Our planet now is only some 0.8°C warmer than it was in pre-industrial times. This change seems slight, especially when considered against the fluctuations in temperature we experience daily. Yet, even with such a small increase, since the start of the twenty-first century we have already witnessed many climate change-related impacts. These include record-breaking weather events in both the southern and northern hemispheres, such as the hottest summer on record in Europe in 2003, in which some 70,000 are estimated to have died (Robine et al.,

2007) and the wettest summer in England and Wales in 2007. In 2010, the worst recorded flood in Pakistan directly affected the lives of some 20 million people. It was accompanied the hottest summer in Russia, which caused massive wildfires and led to the deaths of an estimated 56,000 people. Record-breaking heatwaves occurred in a number of states in the United States in 2011, and 2012 was its warmest year on record. Australia too just has had its longest and most severe drought on historical record, a series of devastating fires, floods and damaging cyclones, and now an unprecedented national heatwave.

Scientists agree that these events are highly unlikely to have occurred without the influence of global warming. What, then, if global warming reaches much higher levels? In this coming century, extreme events and significant underlying changes in temperatures, rainfall, storms and to the productivity of our oceans and landscapes will challenge our ability to live comfortably on this continent.

Negotiating blindly

Until relatively recently, the idea of a Four Degree World seemed fanciful – the stuff of alarmism, a genre of horror–science fiction. Scientists, science journalists and climate commentators increasingly talked and wrote about critical systemic thresholds and global tipping points and the risks of 'dangerous' and runaway climate change (e.g. CACC et al., 2002; Schellnhuber et al., 2006; Lynas, 2007; Pearce, 2007; MacCracken et al., 2008). But until the failure of negotiations at Copenhagen, these discussions remained peripheral to the mainstream debate over the prospect of global warming in the twenty-first century, the carefully phrased reports of the InterGovernmental Panel on Climate Change (IPCC) and slow progress with international climate negotiations.

When the international community adopted the United Nations Framework Convention on Climate Change (UNFCCC) in 1992, it committed itself to preventing 'dangerous anthropogenic interference with the climate system' (Article 2). Defining what such dangerous interference or 'dangerous climate change' might be depends on a value judgement about danger and impact, which will vary geographically (with climate change threatening earlier and more 'dangerous' consequences in northern latitudes, low-rainfall and low-lying areas, and for poorly adapted communities [e.g. Crowley, 2011]). Concerted action depends on reaching consensus about these definition.

Parties to the Convention agreed they would accept their 'common but differentiated responsibilities' in reducing greenhouse emissions and dealing with adaptation. Under the treaty, developed industrialized countries – the major contributors to greenhouse emissions and historical beneficiaries of fossil fuel use – would act first.

In 1997, the Kyoto Protocol was established to enable implementation of the UNFCCC's goals. It required developed countries to adopt mitigation targets during its first commitment period. These targets, determined through political agreement in a multilateral forum, reflected neither scientific advice nor principles for equitable burden-sharing between nations. The agreement was criticized by environmental NGOs for doing too little in this first period: the developed countries' targets lacked ambition; aggregate reduction of global emissions during the first commitment period would have been about one per cent of the total.

The Protocol was immediately rejected by the United States, which refused to ratify it because the Protocol failed to set emissions reductions targets for major developing economies, notably China (despite this claim being explicitly at odds with the requirements of the UNFCCC). Although the US failed to destroy the Protocol, it managed to delay the agreement coming into force until 2005 and thereby postponed concerted international action to reduce emissions. The Protocol's first commitment period only began in 2008 and ran until the end of 2012.

Once Kyoto was in force, the prospect of its second commitment period – or of a successor post-2012 agreement – loomed. This new arrangement would be conditioned by changing global conditions, including China's growing global economic role and ecological footprint. In 2006 China overtook the United States as the world's largest annual aggregate emitter of carbon dioxide, (although the United States' cumulative and per capita emissions remain much greater). This reflected both its rapid internal economic development and growing wealth and the effects of economic globalization, which since 1992 had turned China into the manufacturing hub of an ever more intensely trade-oriented and carbon-intensive world (see Davis and Caldeira, 2010). Along with other major emergent developing countries, such as India and Brazil, China's growing contribution to aggregate global emissions, along with that of other major emergent developing countries such as India and Brazil, could not be overlooked.

From 2007 onwards the prospects for timely and effective international climate agreement improved and then faltered. In 2007, the 13th Conference of Parties (COP) to the UNFCCC decided on the Bali Action Plan, a roadmap for developing a successor to the Kyoto Protocol's first commitment period and its targets. The Plan would be developed over the next three years and finalized at Copenhagen in 2009.

By 2007 there was emergent agreement in policy and scientific circles that 2°C warming above the pre-industrial global average was the highest level that could be endured before the risks of dangerous climate change, including abrupt and catastrophic climatic shifts, became too high.

In response, the IPCC's Fourth Assessment Report (4AR, published in 2007) suggested that developed countries need to reduce their emissions by 25 per cent to 40 per cent below 1990 levels in 2020, and by -80 to -95 per cent by 2050, with developing countries contributing 'a substantial deviation from their baseline', if we are to stabilize long-term levels of greenhouse gas concentration levels at 450 parts per million (ppm) CO_2 equivalent (Box 13.7) (IPCC, 2007b). Even so, this concentration level would merely offer around a 50-per cent chance of limiting global average warming to 2°C (Meinshausen. 2006a, 2006b).

The *Copenhagen Diagnosis*, produced by an eminent body of climate scientists to update the IPCC's 4AR (Allison et al., 2009), confirmed that global emissions would need to peak between 2015 and 2020 and then decline rapidly if warming was to be limited to a maximum of 2°C. Greenhouse emissions – if stabilized at 2009 levels for 20 years – would mean the planet had less than a one in four chance of staying below 2°C.

The climate negotiations in 2009 in Copenhagen spectacularly failed to produce a new agreement containing legally binding and targets that reflected best scientific advice and equity principles. The story of Copenhagen is well known: its failure – involving a standoff between the United States and China, the overwhelming influence of national political constraints on ambitious international commitments and the occluded decision-making processes of the UNCCC – threatened the very future of ongoing multilateral climate negotiations.

Nevertheless, last-minute wrangling between the heads of state of the major emitters produced an informal political statement – the Copenhagen Accord – that saved the conference from collapse (Christoff, 2010). Signatories to the Copenhagen Accord for the first time formally agreed to a definition of dangerous climate change, 'recognising the scientific view that the increase in global temperature should be below 2 degrees Celsius' (Para 1, UNFCCC, 2010). They also agreed that 'deep cuts in global emissions are required according to science ... so as to hold the increase in global temperature below 2 degrees Celsius' (Para 2, UNFCCC, 2010).[1]

The Accord process also produced non-binding 'unconditional' and 'conditional' pledges from most developed and some major developing states for 2020 emissions targets but it failed to deliver longer-term targets for 2050. Rather than being the product of a negotiated agreement reflecting scientific advice and equity-based formula to produce a robust and defensible target, these 'bottom-up' pledges were what individual nations decided they could manage based on their domestic political circumstances and economic capacity.

This has generated a crisis for international climate negotiations. In effect, expedient unilateralism has replaced concerted multilateralism. Negotiators continue to hope that this 'bottom-up' process of target setting will somehow manage to stagger slowly and blindly towards a collective goal capable of meeting the objective of averting dangerous climate change, at a time when the time available for effective action is rapidly diminishing.

The targets pledged included some within the range suggested by the IPCC (Norway's, Germany's and the EU's are in line with the IPCC's conservative reduction range of −25 to −40 per cent), but most were not. In all, the aggregate reduction pledged would make achieving the aggregate global reductions necessary to keep below 2°C impossible.

Following Copenhagen, most Annex I countries pledged an unconditional national target and also a more ambitious conditional target dependent on other countries pledging comparable reductions. The Netherlands Environmental Assessment Agency and consultancy Ecofys noted that the unconditional ('low') pledges would result in a total Annex I emission reduction target of 4 per cent to 18 per cent below 1990 levels by 2020. The conditional ('high') pledges amount to a reduction target of 9 per cent to 21 per cent (den Elzen et al., 2010: 11). In all, these pledges fall well short of the cuts suggested by the IPCC.

Even if current pledges are fully implemented, global total greenhouse gas emissions in 2020 are likely to be between 53 and 55 billion tonnes CO_2 eq per year (Schellnhuber et al., 2012: 6).

In all, there is a substantial ambition gap of about 14 billion tonnes CO_2 eq per annum between current commitments and what is required in 2020 to stay on an emission reduction pathway consistent with meeting the 2°C target (and more if the target is 1.5°C). This gap is approximately the equivalent of the emissions of the USA and China combined.

Since Copenhagen, climate negotiations at Cancun, Durban and Doha have sought to restore faith in the multilateral negotiation process and cautiously to re-establish momentum toward a successor to Kyoto's first commitment period. But progress has been slow and tentative.

At Durban in 2011, the parties to the UNFCCC agreed to a new negotiating process – the Durban Platform for Enhanced Action – for 'a protocol, another legal instrument or an agreed outcome with legal force', to be finalized in 2015, to include all major emitters, and to be implemented from 2020 (UNFCCC, 2012). The parties also formally amended the Kyoto Protocol to include the 2020 pledge targets from Copenhagen. Significantly, major developed and developing countries – including the US, China and India – accepted that the new agreement would contain targets for them all. Crucially, the Durban conference also formally noted the 'ambition gap' between these targets and what is needed to limit warming to 2°C or 1.5°C above pre-industrial levels – but no adjustments to the pledges are expected before 2015 at earliest.

There are different interpretations of value of this new process, which can be seen optimistically as getting the negotiations on the road again or, pessimistically and more realistically, as an agreement to produce an agreement on a timetable that ignores the urgency of the problem.

The ambition gap – and the contrast between the glacial pace of international negotiations and current commitments and the need for rapid emissions reductions outlined by recent climate science reports – is threatening to become a chasm. Despite pledges and commitments, global aggregate greenhouse emissions have remained above the highest projected range under the IPCC's modeled scenarios, bouncing back to a new annual record in the period following the Global Financial Crisis in 2008.

The Netherlands Environmental Assessment Agency reports that, instead of progress since the start of this century, we are slipping further behind:

> Global emissions of carbon dioxide (CO_2) – the main cause of global warming – increased by 3% in 2011, reaching an all-time high of 34 billion tonnes in 2011 ... With a decrease in 2008 and a 5% surge in 2010, the past decade saw an average annual increase of 2.7% ...
>
> In many OECD countries, CO_2 emissions in fact decreased – in the European Union by 3%, in the United States by 2% and in Japan by 2% ...

[However] CO_2 emissions from OECD countries now account for only one third of global emissions – the same share as that of China and India, where emissions increased by 9% and 6%, respectively, in 2011.

(Olivier et al., 2012)

Clearly, to ensure adequate emissions reductions which do much more than leave the planet with a 50/50 risk of exceeding 2°C, and to have a chance of meeting safer lower targets, developed and developing nations and economies will have to adopt far more aggressive emissions reduction paths than those currently conceived – and do so before 2020.

Further, international action undertaken from 2020 onwards will have to be particularly substantial if we are still to achieve the goal even of remaining below 2°C . Analysis suggests a reduction in global emissions of between 3.7 per cent and 9 per cent per annum is required between 2020 and 2050 if this goal is to be achieved, depending on when global emissions peak (WBGU, 2009, Figure 3.2-1).

In the absence of concerted and effective multilateralism, and in the absence of effective international limits on emissions, there is an increasing urgency for more immediate, more powerful and unilateral mitigation action from every country that can do so. The implications of this prospect will be considered for Australia at the conclusion of this book.

A Four Degree World?

Interest in what would happen when the planet warms beyond 2°C has grown only slowly, as if considering the consequences of such a world is one traumatic step too far for human imagination.

Successive IPCC reports have underlined the contribution of human activities to global warming through the production of greenhouse gas emissions. As a consequence of such activity, atmospheric greenhouse gases have increased from pre-industrial concentrations of 260–80 ppm to around 400 ppm in 2013.

The observed increase in global average temperature over the past century can be largely attributed to human influences (IPCC, 2007a). This warming, and the increase in atmospheric greenhouse gases, has also begun to contribute to rising sea levels, warming oceans and ocean acidification, increasing melting of ice from Greenland and Antarctica and loss of Arctic sea ice (Allison et al., 2009) and – as already discussed – to new records for heat waves, extreme temperatures and other forms of extreme weather (Trenberth, 2010).

Climate modeling undertaken since the start of this century has provided a guide to the probable consequences of increasing emissions, including from fossil fuel use. While successive IPCC reports remain the most authoritative summary of this work, they have also proved to be conservative in their assessment of likely trends and impacts.

Without effective action to mitigate anthropogenic (human-induced) green-house gas emissions, it is likely that atmospheric CO_2 concentration will double (from pre-industrial levels) sometime this century (IPCC, 2007a). Global CO_2 emissions have risen by 1.9 per cent per year in the 1980s, 1.0 per cent per year in the 1990s and 3.1 per cent since 2000 (Peters et al., 2012). These growth rates are at the high end of the emissions scenarios used by the IPCC.[2] They would lead to a global-average warming of 4.2–5.0°C by the year 2100 (Peters et al., 2012). While some of the changes associated with this warming would be gradual, others could be abrupt and non-linear, catalyzing changes in the state of the planet that would be largely irreversible and sometimes dramatic.

In 2006 the Stern Review commented on the likely impacts of increasing levels of warming for different ecosystems, geographical regions and for human growth and development. It highlighted the increased risks of four degrees of warming to vulnerable communities, with potentially 30–50 per cent decrease in water availability in Southern Africa and the Mediterranean; agricultural yields declining by 15–35 per cent in Africa; and entire region out of production (e.g. Australia); up to 80 million more people exposed to malaria; and 7–300 million more people affected by coastal flooding each year (see Stern, 2007: 57 [Table 3.1] and Figure 2 [Executive Summary]).

In the following year, science journalist Mark Lynas spent several months in the Radcliffe Library at Oxford. He reviewed the scientific literature on the impacts of warming and produced a degree-by-degree guide to our planet's future (Lynas, 2007). Lynas reported that, based on geological evidence, at 4°C of global warming, the whole planet would be without ice cover for the first time in 40 million years. Over time sea levels would rise by some 65 metres, but well before then oceans would threaten deltaic cities from Mumbai to Shanghai, submerge a third of Bangladesh, and displace tens of millions living coastal regions and the inhabitants of low-lying islands. Such warming would cause agricultural production to crash, including in highly populous countries such as China. New deserts would spread in Southern Europe, while droughts would be the norm across parts of the north. Summers would be dreaded and the extreme temperatures of 2003 would seem normal, perhaps cool. The book was well received but hardly created a stir.

The Hadley Centre and British Met Office also addressed the question of 'When could global warming reach 4°C?' (Betts et al., 2009). Its authors concluded that:

> While much political attention is focused on the potential for global warming of 2°C relative to pre-industrial, the [IPCC's] AR4 [Fourth Assessment Report] projections clearly suggest that much greater ranges of warming are possible by the end of the 21st Century in the absence of mitigation. The centre of the range of AR4 projected global warming was approximately 4°C …
>
> (Betts et al., 2009: 1)

The report went on to examine the consequences of emissions continuing along the high (A1FI) trajectory, which was one used by the IPCC – and which currently is slightly less than the emissions trajectory occurring in reality. It concluded that:

> our best estimate is that the A1FI emissions scenario would lead to a warming of 4°C relative to pre-industrial times during the 2070s. If carbon feedback cycles are stronger, which appears less likely but still credible, then 4°C warming could be reached by 2060.
>
> (Betts et al., 2009: 1)

Four Degrees and Beyond: Implications of Global Climate Change of 4+ Degrees for People, Ecosystems and the Earth-system was a scientific conference held at Oxford University, late in 2009, The Oxford Conference was driven by concern about the growing gap between the emerging target of 2°C and languid emissions reduction policies. It provided further insights into impacts for specific ecosystems, water, agriculture and the growing risks of reaching 4°C (New et al., 2011), and received some international media coverage. Nevertheless, its findings were reported as 'fringe science' – a side-note of disciplinary concern to be registered while the international community moved to seal an agreement to deal with just such a problem ... at Copenhagen.

Since Copenhagen, however, with momentum towards effective mitigation faltering, the potential for catastrophic climate policy failure has become a tangible reality and anxiety. This shift in perspective was reflected in the national and global media coverage received by the *Four Degrees or More?* Conference in Melbourne in 2011, and by the recent report *Turn Down the Heat: Why a 4°C Warmer World Must be Avoided*, written for the World Bank in 2012 (Schellnhuber et al., 2012).

The report for the World Bank concludes that even if the current Copenhagen/ Cancun commitments and pledges are fully implemented, there is roughly a 20 per cent likelihood of exceeding 4°C by 2100. If they are not met, then there is a much higher likelihood – more than 40 per cent – of warming exceeding 4°C by 2100, and a 10 per cent chance of this occurring in the 2070s (Schellnhuber et al., 2012: 23). It also reminds us that on the IPCC's high fossil fuel intensive pathway (SRESA1F) – the trend we are currently pursuing – warming exceeds 4°C earlier in the twenty-first century. Moreover:

> Warming would not stop there. Because of the slow response of the climate system, the greenhouse gas emissions and concentrations that would lead to warming of 4°C by 2100 would actually commit the world to a much higher warming, exceeding 6°C or more, in the longer term, with several metres of sea-level rise ultimately associated with this warming.
>
> (Schellnhuber et al., 2012: xiii)

This Four Degree World is one of almost unimaginable social, economic and ecological consequences and catastrophes. The report confirms that, at 4°C, there is a greater risk of rapid, abrupt and irreversible change associated with loss of Arctic sea ice, rising seas caused by melting of ice from Greenland and the

West Antarctic Ice Sheet, increasing drought and aridity and extreme temperatures in many regions (Africa, Europe, the Middle East, Americas, Australia and South-East Asia), increasing ocean acidification and decarbonization of large-scale ecosystems like the Amazon forest. It also notes that the risk of global impacts on food supplies would be great, with greater-than-predicted adverse impacts associated with warming already being observed in crop production (Schellnhuber et al., 2012: 15).

Four Degrees and Australia in a hot world

Currently, international economic and energy policy settings make a Four Degree World an impending reality. So we must ask: what does this mean for Australia? This book reflects research, discussions and debates that occurred before, during and after the conference *Four Degrees or More? Australia in a Hot World*, held at Melbourne University in 2011 and inspired by the Oxford conference held two years earlier. It is divided into four parts.

Part One lays the scientific foundations of the book. It introduces the climate science that frames our understandings of what our continent will be like in a Four Degree World. This section clarifies the assumptions and understandings which underpin the book, and provides scientific reference points for the sections and chapters that follow.

Chapter 2 considers the implications of four degrees of warming for longer-term shifts in the continental incidence and distribution of temperature and rainfall, and the prospects for drought.

Chapter 3 considers historical patterns and projected changes to events such as intense rainfall and hail, storms and floods, extreme temperatures, droughts and heatwaves, and extreme sea-level events.

Part Two then presents an overview of what these climatic changes might mean for Australia's physical environment – its terrestrial and marine ecosystems and its plants and animals, and its farmed landscapes and agricultural productivity.

Chapter 4 examines impacts on Australia's land-based plants and animals. It considers the resilience that has been 'built' into Australia's ecosystems by previous periods of climate-related hardship and whether this resilience might serve it well in a future in which rapid climate-related transformations and impacts place significant demands on species and systems.

Chapter 5 looks at the impacts of warming seas, sea-level rise and ocean acidification for the survival and productivity of Australia's marine ecosystems, with special attention to coral reef systems – such as the Great Barrier Reef – already stressed by human activity.

Chapter 6 examines how Australian agricultural systems, which have developed robust productive responses to already highly variable weather and challenging landscapes, might be affected by projected substantial changes in temperature and rainfall. The chapter considers the effect of the relocation of some agricultural landscapes, and the transformation or loss of others, on Australia's food industries and future food security.

Chapter 7 focuses on the compounding crises that will emerge as global warming affects interlocking ecological, social and economic systems. The high level of global integration of each of these systems will ensure that even if wealthy states such as Australia are able to engage in a relatively high level of investment in domestic adaptation, their global interdependency will lead to additional and probably unpredictable difficulties for which it is hard to plan and to adjust.

Part Three considers the implications of a Four Degree World for Australia's social and economic systems. Chapter 8 takes up the theme of compounding effects specifically in relation to social and economic impacts. The chapter raises the issue of timing in relation to mitigation and adaptation effort. It also raises the question of possible limits to effective adaptation as temperatures rise and complex systems begin to change.

Chapter 9 examines potential impacts on human health and also on Australia's healthcare system as climate change and extreme weather generates new pressures associated with shifting disease vectors, increases in vulnerability associated with deteriorating circumstances and diet, and deteriorating infrastructure and services.

Chapter 10 shifts focus to the built environment and the major cities where the bulk of Australia's population lives. Impacts associated with temperature and rainfall changes, and changing trends in extreme weather, have implications for infrastructure, service provision and patterns of human habitation. The chapter critically reviews preparation for these changes as embodied in current adaptation planning.

Chapter 11 returns to the issue of Australia's global integration by looking at the implications of catastrophic warming for Australian security, a term which the authors extend beyond the conventional frame of militarized security and defence to a broader definition of human security. The chapter examines projected implications for Australia of climate impacts on regional neighbours, and it looks at Australia's obligations in a region distressed by coastal flooding, food insecurity and forced population movement.

Part Four extends these arguments – considering, in Chapter 12, the regional pressures for adaptation, and then in Chapter 13 the question of successful versus failed adaptation. It envisions the different possible places Australia could become by posing three quite different scenarios for adaptive policy responses to rapid and extreme climate change.

Finally, Chapter 14 considers what might be required of Australia if we are to contribute meaningfully to avoiding a Four Degree World.

It is not the task of this book to predict the immediate political future of Australian climate policy – although this appears to be dire. Rather, the book is intended to highlight our real challenges, and suggest that we need much greater action both in mitigation and adaptation than appears to be contemplated by Australian politicians and policy makers. The World Bank writes that 'it is clear that assessments to date of the likely consequences of 4°C global warming are limited, may not capture some of the major risks and may not accurately account for society's capacity to adapt'. This is also the case for Australia. Despite best attempts, there are significant gaps in our understanding of the likely outcomes of a Four Degree World. For instance, since the Garnaut Report in 2008, no significant modeling has been undertaken to assess the likely impacts of substantial global climate-related changes to the Australian economy – for instance, to tourism, trade and agriculture, and to the welfare state as it struggles to cope with the increasing costs of climate-related impacts to Australia's infrastructural and social fabric. One hopes that this book will provoke further work to refine future goals and policy settings.

Notes

1   AOSIS, the Alliance of Small Island States, had pressed for consideration of a lower 'guardrail' temperature of 1.5°C, recognizing that 2°C would lead to sea level rise which ultimately would threaten their survival. This too was inscribed in the Accord.
2   Between SRES A1B and A1FI, and close to the new RCP8.5.

References

Allison, I., N. L. Bindoff, R. A. Bindschadler, P. M. Cox, N. de Noblet, M. H. England, J. E. Francis, N. Gruber, A. M. Haywood, D. J. Karoly, G. Kaser, C. Le Quéré, T. M. Lenton, M. E. Mann, B. I. McNeil, A. J. Pitman, S. Rahmstorf, E. Rignot, H. J. Schellnhuber, S. H. Schneider, S. C. Sherwood, R. C. J. Somerville, K. Steffen, E. J. Steig, M. Visbeck and A. J. Weaver. 2009. *The Copenhagen Diagnosis, 2009: Updating the World on the Latest Climate Science*. The University of New South Wales Climate Change Research Centre (CCRC): Sydney, Australia.
Betts, R., M. Collins, D., Hemming, C. Jones, J. Lowe and M. Sanderson. 2011. When could global warming reach 4°C? Hadley Centre technical note 80. December 2009. [Republished as Betts, R., M. Collins, D. Hemming, C. Jones, J. Lowe and M. Sanderson. 2011. When could global warming reach 4°C?. *Philosophical Transactions of the Royal Society A* 369: 67–84.
CACC (Committee on Abrupt Climate Change), Ocean Studies Board, Polar Research Board, Board on Atmospheric Sciences and Climate, Division on Earth and Life Studies, National Research Council. 2002. *Abrupt Climate Change: Inevitable Surprises*. National Academies Press: Washington, DC.
Christoff, P. 2010. Cold climate at Copenhagen: China and the United States at COP 15. *Environmental Politics* 19 (4): 637–56.
Crowley, P. 2011. Interpreting 'dangerous' in the United Nations framework convention on climate change and the human rights of Inuit. *Regional Environmental Change* 11 (Suppl. 1): S265–74.
Darby, A. 2013. Prepare for more scorchers, Gillard warns. *The Age*, 8 January: 2.
Davis, S. J. and K. Caldeira. 2010. Consumption-based accounting of CO_2 emissions. PNAS, 23 March 2012, 107 (12): 5687–92.

Den Elzen, M. G. J., A. F. Hof, M. A. Mendoza Beltran, B. J. van Ruijven, J. van Vliet, D. P. van Vuuren, H. Hohne and S. Moltmann. 2010. *Evaluation of the Copenhagen Accord: Chances and Risks for the 2°C Climate Goal.* Netherlands Environmental Assessment Agency (PBL)/Ecofys. PBL publication number 500114017. At: http://www.ecofys.com/en/publication/evaluation-of-the-copenhagen-accord/ [accessed 12 January 2013].

Hannam, P. 2013. 'Dome of heat' covers the continent. *Sydney Morning Herald*, 7 January. At: http://www.smh.com.au/environment/weather/dome-of-heat-covers-the-continent-20130107-2ccno.html [accessed 20 July 2013].

IPCC. 2007a. *Climate Change 2007: The Physical Science Basis. Contribution of Working Group I to the Fourth Assessment Report of the Intergovernmental Panel on Climate Change.* S. Solomon, D. Qin., M. Manning, Z. Chen., M. Marquis., K. B. Averyt, Tignor, M. and H. L. Miller (eds). Cambridge University Press: Cambridge, and New York.

—2007b. *Climate Change 2007: Mitigation of Climate Change. Contribution of Working Group 3 to the Fourth Assessment Report of the Intergovernmental Panel on Climate Change.* B. Metz, O. Davidson, P. Bosch, R. Dave, and L. Meyer (eds). Cambridge University Press: Cambridge, and New York.

Lynas, M. 2007. *Six Degrees: Our Future on a Hotter Planet.* Fourth Estate: London.

MacCracken, M. C., F. Moore and J. C. Topping Jnr. 2007. *Sudden and Disruptive Climate Change: Exploring the Real Risks and How We Can Avoid Them.* Earthscan: London.

Meinshausen, M. 2006a. *<2°C Trajectories – a Brief Background Note.* Kyoto Plus Papers 3. At: http://www.kyotoplus.org/www2.kyotoplus.org/uploads/meinshausen_fin_rev.pdf. [accessed 26 September 2008].

—2006b. 'What does a 2°C target mean for greenhouse gas concentrations? A brief analysis based on multi-gas emission pathways and several climate sensitivity uncertainty estimates', H. J. Schnellnhuber et al. (eds). *Avoiding Dangerous Climate Change.* Cambridge University Press: Cambridge.

New, M. G., D. M. Liverman, R. A. Betts, K. L. Anderson and C. C. West (eds). 2011. *Four Degrees and Beyond: The Potential for a Global Temperature Increase of Four Degrees and its Implications.* Theme issue. Phil. Transactions. R. Society A 369. 1934.

Olivier. G. J., G. Janssens-Maenhout and A. H. W. J. Peters. 2012. *Trends in global CO2 emissions.* 2012 Report. PBL Netherlands Environmental Assessment Agency: The Hague/Bilthoven.

Pearce, F. 2007. *With Speed and Violence: Why Climate Scientists Fear Tipping Points in Climate Change.* Beacon Press: MA.

Peters, G. P., R. M. Andrew, T. Boden, J. G. Canadell, P. Ciais, C. Le Quere, G. Marland, M. R. Raupach and C. Wilson. 2012. The challenge to keep global warming below 2°C. *Nature Climate Change.* doi: 10. 1038/nclimate1783.

Plummer, N, B. Trewin, D. Jones, K. Braganza, K. and R. Smalley. 2013. What's causing Australia's heat wave? *The Conversation*, 18 January 2013. At http://theconversation. edu. au/whats-causing-australias-heat-wave-11628 [accessed 2 February 2013].

PBL (PBL Netherlands Environmental Assessment Agency). 2007. China now no. 1 in CO2 emissions; USA in second position. At: http://www.pbl.nl/en/dossiers/Climatechange/moreinfo/Chinanowno1inCO2emissionsUSAinsecondposition. [accessed 10 January 2013].

PWC (Price Waterhouse Cooper). 2013. *Business Resilience in an Uncertain, Resource-Constrained World.* Carbon Disclosure Project. At: https://www.cdproject.net/CDPResults/CDP-Global-500-Climate-Change-Report-2012.pdf [accessed 20 July 2013].

Robine, J.-M., S. L. K. Cheung, S. Le Roy, H. Van Oyen, C. Griffiths, J.-P. Michel and F. R. Herrmann. 2008. 'Death toll exceeded 70,000 in Europe during the summer of 2003'. *Comptes Rendus Biologies* 331 (2): 171–8. doi:10.1016/j.crvi.2007.12.001. ISSN 1631-0691.

Schellnhuber, H. J., W. Cramer, N. Nakicenovic, T. Wigley and G. Yohe (eds). 2007. *Avoiding Dangerous Climate Change.* Cambridge University Press: Cambridge.

Schellnhuber, H. J., W. Hare, O. Serdeczny, S. Adams, D. Coumou, K. Frieler, M. Martin, I. M. Otto, M. Perrette, A. Robinson, M. Rocha, M. Schaeffer, J. Schewe, X. Wang and L. Warszawski. 2012. *Turn Down the Heat: Why a 4°C Warmer World Must Be Avoided.* A Report for the World Bank by the Potsdam Institute for Climate Impact Research and Climate Analytics. November 2012.

Stafford Smith, M., L. Horrocks, A. Harvey and C. Hamilton. 2011. Rethinking adaptation for a 4°C world. *Philosophical Transactions of the Royal Society* A 369: 196–216.

Stern, N. 2006. *Stern Review on the Economics of Climate Change.* Cambridge University Press: Cambridge.

Trenberth, K. E. 2010. Changes in precipitation with climate change. *Climate Research* 47: 123–38.

UNFCCC. 2010. *Report of the Conference of the Parties on its fifteenth session, held in Copenhagen from 7 to 19 December 2009. Part Two.* UNFCCC/CP/2009/11/Add.1. 30 March 2010.

—2012. *Report of the Conference of the Parties on its seventeenth session, held in Durban from 28 November to 11 December 2011. Part Two: 1/CP. 17.* UNFCCC/CP/2011/0/Add.1. 15 March 2012.

VBRC (Victorian Bushfires Royal Commission). Teague, B., R. McLeod and S. Pascoe. 2010. *2009 Victorian Bushfires Royal Commission Final Report – Summary.* July 2010. Government Printer: State of Victoria.

WBGU (German Advisory Council on Global Change). 2009. *Solving the Climate Dilemma: The Budget Approach.* Special Report: Berlin, Germany.

Part I

Climate science and four degrees

2 Australia's climate in a Four Degree World

Penny Whetton, David Karoly, Ian Watterson, Leanne Webb, Frank Drost, Dewi Kirono and Kathleen McInnes

Introduction

What climate change would Australia see if global warming reaches 4°C on average (+4°C global warming) above pre-industrial levels? This chapter describes projected changes in temperature, rainfall, potential evaporation, drought, snow cover and regional sea level with a focus on mean changes, ranges of uncertainty and the possible time evolution of the changes under such a scenario. As well as providing maps of changes and describing their limits and uncertainties, more detailed projections are shown for a set of selected localities. Together, this chapter and the next – on projected changes to extreme events in Australia (Braganza et al., 2013) – form the scientific foundation and provide the regional climatic backdrop that is then considered, in terms of potential impacts on species, farming, cities and so on, in the remainder of this book.

Data and methods

The projections presented here are based primarily on the Australian regional results from more than twenty Global Climate Models (GCMs), supplemented in some places with high-resolution statistical and dynamical downscaling (Christensen et al., 2007) and some other techniques. Results are either directly drawn from earlier publications or have been produced for this book (mostly by adapting available results and methods for the four degree case), as described in the Appendix. A more recent climate model ensemble is now available (Taylor et al., 2012), but projected changes over Australia differ little from results shown here (Irving et al., 2012).

These results[1] – often indicating high, medium and low chances of being exceeded – are presented in a number of ways: as maps, as ranges for selected localities, and as scenarios which combine changes in temperature with changes in rainfall to create hot-dry, warm-wet, and mid-case scenarios for the selected localities. Current analogues for the projected future climate for the selected localities are also identified (using a simple technique, introduced later), thus illustrating the projected climate in terms of the move of climate zones across the landscape. Furthermore, some time series results are shown for individual climate models, selected for projecting global warmings approaching four degrees or more by 2100 or earlier. Finally, other relevant results are drawn from the literature, including some commentary on recent observed climatic trends, to form some context for projections about a Four Degree World.

Temperature change

Figure 2.1 shows projected Australian warming at +4°C global warming for the summer and winter seasons, and for high, medium and low chances of being exceeded (Watterson, 2008). Table 2.1 shows ranges of warming for selected sites.

In inland regions in summer, warming is typically above the global average and ranges between 3.5°C and 7°C; in winter, it is centred more on the global average with a range of 3°C to 5°C. Southern and northern coastal areas warm at close to the global average rate (range of 3–5°C). However, in southern areas in winter, the warming range is around 2–4°C. Warming at +4° C from a different

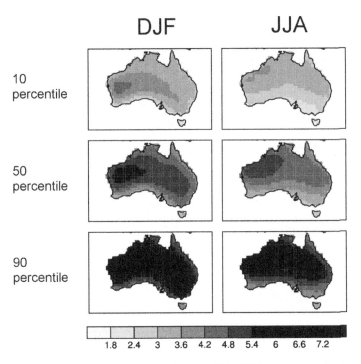

Figure 2.1 Projected warming over Australia at +4°C GW for summer and winter and for selected percentiles of the GCM-based uncertainty range

Notes
a Summer = DJF; winter = JJA.
b Developed using a climate model ensemble and the method of Watterson (2008).

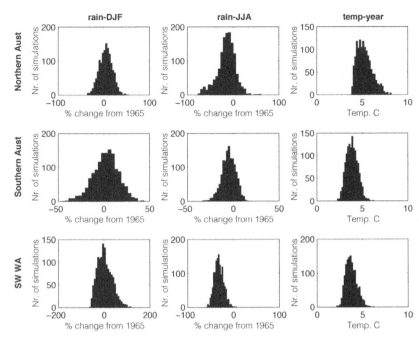

Figure 2.2 Projected changes in precipitation for summer and winter and annual mean temperature for northern Australia, southern Australia and south-western Australia

Notes
a Precipitation (pr); summer (DJF); winter (JJA); temperature (tas); northern Australia (nau); southern Australia (sau); south-western Australia (swa).
b Figure using all members of a perturbed-physics ensemble of simulations that reach +4°C GW by 2100.

set of climate model simulations[2] averaged over northern Australia, southern Australia and south-west Western Australia (Figure 2.2) shows broadly similar projected warming. The reduced warming in the southern region would arise due to the large ocean area included in the regional average. These projected warmings can be compared to observed warming over Australia of around 0.9°C since 1910 (Fawcett et al., 2012).

Projected regional warming is very large compared to natural decade-to-decade variability of the climate, meaning that by mid century most or all years are warmer than the average of the 20th century. Figure 2.3a shows the time series of observed temperature over Central Victoria (with decadal smoothing) compared with the range of projected warming to 2100 under a medium emission scenario. (Note that the global warming for the scenario used in this figure is only 2.8°C.)

In a Four Degree World, projected warmings in our region will be accompanied by a large increase in the frequency of high-temperature extremes and a decrease

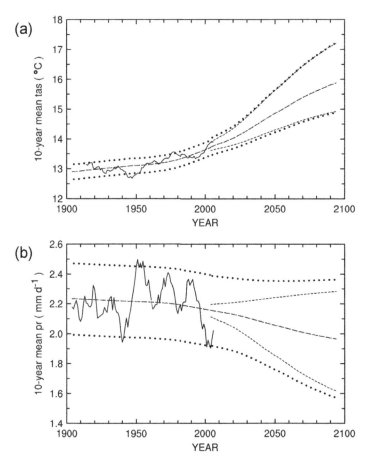

Figure 2.3 Central Victorian temperature (a) and rainfall (b), observed (solid) and
model-based projections

Notes
a Shown are the multi-model median (long dashed line) and the inner envelope (short
   dashes) giving the spread of model projections based on the CSIRO&BoM (2007)
   projections for a mid emissions scenario.
b The outer envelope allows for decadal scale variability..
c Method of constructing these is described in Watterson and Whetton (2011).

in the frequency of low-temperature extremes. Daily extremes will be considered
in detail in Chapter 3, but here we consider the change in occurrence of cool
months and hot months (defined by a 1-in-20 year frequency in the historical
period) in south-eastern Australia[3] in a simulation which reaches +4°C global
warming by 2100 (see Figure 2.4). Cool months are very rare after 2040, and hot
months occur most of the time after 2070.

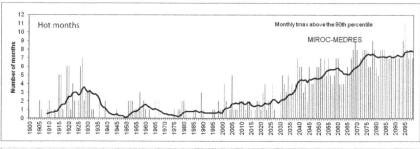

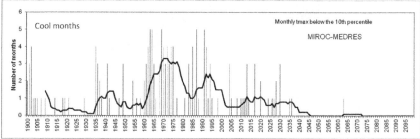

Figure 2.4   Annual totals and 11-year moving averages of 1-in-20 year hot or cool
months in south-eastern Australia, modelled for 1910–1999

Notes
a Annual totals (bars); 11-year moving averages (lines).
b The MIROC-MEDRES model exceeds a global warming of 4°C (relative to 1990)
late in the 21st century.

Rainfall change

Global climate models project significant changes in Australian rainfall under
enhanced greenhouse conditions. However, the projected patterns of change
(including areas of increase and decrease) differ considerably between models.
Figure 2.5 indicates the extent to which the climate models agree on the
direction of annual rainfall change over Australia. In the southern third of
continental Australia, at least two thirds of models point toward a decrease in
rainfall, and in the far south west and southernmost parts of the south east, this
trend is evident in 90 per cent of models. Elsewhere (mainly for the summer
rainfall-dominated zone), models range from increase to decrease without a
clear direction of change. A similar analysis by seasons shows that models
disagree about summer and autumn change throughout Australia, but show some
consistency on projected decreases in winter and spring rainfall.

Consequently, projected seasonal rainfall changes for Australia[4] show very
broad ranges of change at +4°C global warming (see Figure 2.6 and Table 2.1).
Summer rainfall changes range from −50 per cent to +50 per cent across most
of Australia. The range is also broad in winter, but in southern areas is skewed

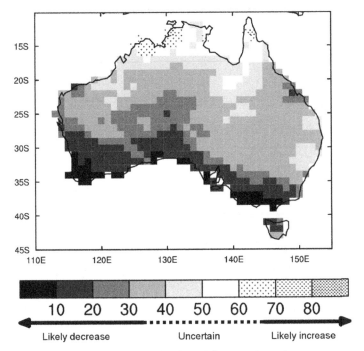

Figure 2.5 Likelihood of increase in annual rainfall across Australia

Note
a As indicated by the fraction of climate model experiments in a multi-model ensemble showing increase (re-drawn from CSIRO and BoM, 2007).

to decrease and the range is typically around −40 to +10 per cent. Annual changes (which factor in rainfall seasonality) can be seen for the selected sites in Table 2.1.

The range of change in Perth is from 0 down to −50 per cent, Melbourne from 0 down to −35 per cent and in Adelaide from +5 per cent down to −40 per cent. On the other hand, projected change in Brisbane is from −45 to +25 per cent and in Cairns from −35 to +30 per cent.

In the case of rainfall in Central Victoria (Figure 2.3b), the projected changes (for global warming of around +2.8C only, not +4°C) are comparable in magnitude to current decadal variability, and thus may be masked by this variability for some decades.

These rainfall projections are consistent with the rainfall projections from the perturbed physics model ensemble (Figure 2.2), which also show no clear direction of change in summer rainfall, but a bias to decrease in winter rainfall. The latter tendency is very strong in the south-west region, where almost none of the 1,000 simulations considered show an increase in winter rainfall.

In addition to these large ranges of uncertainty in projected rainfall change

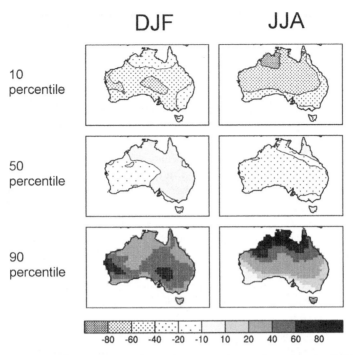

Figure 2.6 Projected precipitation change (in per cent) over Australia at +4°C GW for summer and winter and for selected percentiles of the global climate model-based uncertainty range

Notes
a Summer = DJF; winter = JJA.
b Based on the method of Watterson (2008).

provided by the climate models, it needs to be noted that local rainfall changes can be significantly modified by mountain ranges not adequately represented by the models. A recent application of high-resolution modelling to Tasmania (Grose et al., 2010) led to significant differences in simulated rainfall change from those in the coarser resolution climate model.

Combined temperature and rainfall scenarios

What, in real terms, might these trends and shifts in climate mean? To illustrate the potential environmental significance of the changes to average temperature and precipitation described above, we consider places that provide spatial analogues based on Australia's current climate for +4°C global warming for selected sites: in other words, where in Australia at present is most like – in terms of temperature or rainfall – what we can expect in a Four Degree World for, say, Melbourne or Sydney.

Three scenarios were defined for each location: 'least hot, wettest', 'mid case' and 'hottest, driest'.[5] Spatial analogues for the three scenarios were sought based on current climate matches to the projected annual maximum temperature (tolerance of $\pm 1.0°C$) and annual precipitation (± 15 per cent) for the target site.

Examples of analogous sites based on climate are shown for Australia's major cities in Table 2.1, while Figure 2.7 maps the location of all analogue localities obtained for selected towns in southern inland agricultural areas.

In the mid and drier cases, there is a clear tendency for Perth, Melbourne, Adelaide and Canberra to have climates more typical, at present, of the semi-arid interior. Furthermore, for these two scenarios, inland agricultural sites 'move' into the arid zone (for instance Dubbo 'moves' to Hermannsburg).

On the other hand, in the least hot, wet case, sites in this zone move towards the east coast (for example, Nurioopta in the Barossa Valley goes to Muswellbrook in the Hunter Valley). Melbourne's analogues range from the WA wheat belt in the driest case through eastern NSW in the wettest case. There is a strong tendency for the east coast sites of Sydney and Brisbane to adopt climates from at least 1,000 kilometres northwards on the coast (or a little inland in the drier cases).

In some cases, analogues for the new climates of Alice Springs and Cairns can only be found beyond Australia (see Table 2.1). Those for Darwin (not shown) are unlikely to exist anywhere on the planet.

Perth was assigned analogues in western Queensland, but if a winter rainfall maximum is maintained (as it should be), it too would have a new climate not currently present anywhere on earth. Globally, no winter rainfall region is as warm as Perth is projected to be by the end of this century.

Drought and changes in rates of evaporation

Moisture in the environment is affected not just by changes in rainfall but also by changes to rates of evaporation. Potential ranges of evaporation have been recalculated[6] for $+4°C$ global warming and presented for each of our selected localities (Table 2.1). In all cases, potential evaporation is projected to increase, with the range being 10 to 20 per cent greater on the east coast and between 0 to 20 per cent greater in the south and inland.

Where average rainfall decreases, drought is likely to increase in frequency, and this will be exacerbated by the projected increase in potential evapo-ration. By 2040, exceptionally dry years are likely to occur more often and over larger areas in the south and south west (i.e. south west of Western Australia and Victoria and Tasmania regions) (Hennessy et al., 2008a).[7] With greater relevance to $+4°C$ global warming, Kirono et al. (2011) extended this analysis to 2070 and also included potential evaporation change in a drought index they used. They show changes in drought frequency in the south and west that ranged between little change and five times more frequent droughts than current rates. Changes in the north ranged between a halving and around two to three times greater occurrence. The implications of these changes for farming and agricul-tural output are considered in Chapter 6 (Howden et al., 2013).

Table 2.1   Projected climate changes for eight selected sites at +4°C GW

	Sydney area	Brisbane area
Annual temperature change	3.2 to 5.2 C warmer	3.0 to 4.0 C warmer
Annual precipitation change	−35% to +12%	−45% to +25%
Annual PE change	+10% to +19%	+10% to +18%
Current climate	22.7 C, 1180 mm, moderate summer-autumn peak	25.8 C. 1070 mm, moderate summer peak
Mid case scenario, and analogue	26.8 C, 1030 mm Bundaberg, QLD	29.5 C 970 mm, Ayr, QLD
Hottest, driest scenario, and analogue	27.8 C 760 mm Rockhampton, QLD	30.3 C 670 mm Collinsville, (Charters Towers area) QLD
Least hot, wettest scenario, and analogue	25.8 C 1330 mm Tewantin, QLD	28.7 C 1330 mm Proserpine, QLD

	Melbourne area	Canberra area
Annual temperature change	2.8 to 4.4 C warmer	3.3 to 5.1 C warmer
Annual precipitation change	−35% to 0%	−40% to +10%
Annual PE change	+3% to +22%	+7% to +20%
Current climate	20.0 C, 610 mm, year around	20.0 C, 625 mm, year round
Mid case scenario and analogue	23.6 C, 510 mm Wyalong, NSW	24.2 C. 545 mm, Dubbo, NSW
Hottest, driest scenario, and analogue	24.4 C, 420 mm Leeton, NSW	25.1 C, 405 mm Cobar, Western NSW
Least hot, wettest scenario, and analogue	22.8 C, 610 mm Cowra,, NSW	23.4 C, 690 mm Tamworth area, NSW

	Cairns area	Perth area
Annual temperature change	2.8 to 4.4 C warmer	3.1 to 4.8 C warmer
Annual precipitation change	−35% to +30%	−50% to 0%
Annual PE change	+10% to +18%	+5% to +16%
Current climate	29.1 C, 2010 mm, summer peak	25.8 C. 1070 mm, winter peak

	Cairns area	Perth area
Mid case scenario, and analogue	32.6 C, 1925 mm Weipa, QLD	28.6 C, 555 mm, St George QLD, (but summer rainfall peak)
Hottest, driest scenario, and analogue	33.5 C 1350 mm Jabiru, NT	29.4 C, 395 mm Quilpie, QLD (but summer rainfall peak)
Least hot, wettest scenario, and analogue	31.9 C 2580 mm None in Australia Mumbai, India (but summer peak too strong)	27.7 C 800 mm Rockhampton, QLD, (but summer rainfall peak)

	Adelaide area	Alice Springs area
Annual temperature change	2.7 to 4.6 C warmer	4.1 to 6.3 C warmer
Annual precipitation change	−40% to 5%	−60% to 20%
Annual PE change	+4% to +17%	+1% to +19%
Current climate	21.0 C, 510 mm, winter peak	29.1 C, 305 mm
Mid case scenario and analogue	24.6 C, 405 mm Cobar, western NSW	34.3 C, 230 mm Roebourne, WA
Hottest, driest scenario, and analogue	25,6 C, 305 mm Kalgoolie, WA,	35.5, 125 mm None in Australia this hot and dry Sudan area
Least hot, wettest scenario, and analogue	23.7 C, 525 mm Forbes, NSW	33.2, 370 mm Winton, QLD

Notes

a The range of changes in annual mean temperature, precipitation and potential evaporation is formed from the 90th and 10th percentiles. The three scenarios combine the 50th percentiles changes of temperature and rainfall ('mid case'), the 90th temperature and 10th rainfall percentiles ('hottest, driest') and the 10th temperature and 90th rainfall percentiles ('least hot, wettest'). Climate data are from gridded BoM data for 1976–2005, the list of localities from Geosciences Australia and (partial) analogues for the three scenarios are based on current climate matches to the projected annual maximum temperature (±1.0°C) and annual precipitation (±15 per cent).

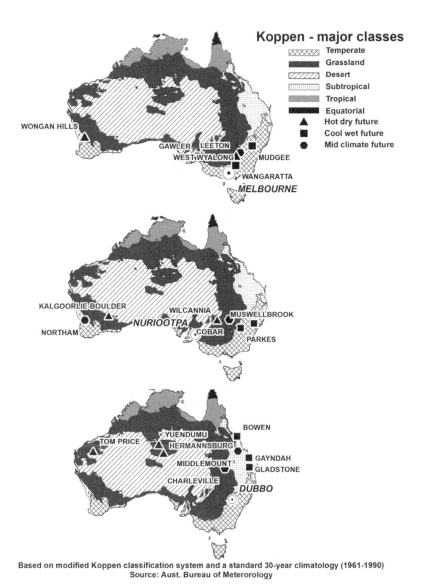

Based on modified Koppen classification system and a standard 30-year climatology (1961-1990)
Source: Aust. Bureau of Meterorology

Figure 2.7   +4°C GW climate analogues for three selected sites – Melbourne (top),
Nuriootpa (middle), and Dubbo (bottom) – based on annual maximum
temperature and precipitation

Notes
a Shown for each target site (dotted circle) are analogue sites for the hottest, driest
scenario (triangles); the mid-case scenario (hexagons); and the least hot and wettest
scenario (squares).
b Koppen climate zones for Australia are also shown.
c See text and Table 2.1 for more details of method.

Snow

Nicholls (2005) has observed declines in maximum snow depth in the Snowy Mountains, with spring snow depth declining by 40 per cent between 1962 and 2003. Hennessy et al. (2008b) modelled projected impacts of climate change on snow cover in the Australian Alps using a range of scenarios for 2020 and 2050. Their worst-case climate change scenario for 2050 (+2.9°C, −24 per cent in winter precipitation) is at the extreme low end of the warming likely to apply at +4°C global warming and a mid case for precipitation change, so this scenario would represent a conservative estimate of Australian snow cover at 4°C global warming. Figure 2.8 shows their calculated length of snow season for this scenario across the Alps, compared to current season length. In most regions currently with a significant snow season on average, annual snow cover goes to zero. Only in the very highest locations does a snow-season persist, but this is greatly shortened (for instance, at 2,000 metres in the Snowy Mountains, the season length is cut to one third its present length).

Sea level rise and coastal impacts

Over the period 1920 to 2000 sea level rise around Australia was 1.2mm a year (Church et al., 2006). This has accelerated to a rate of 5.9mm a year between 1993 and 2009 (Church and White, 2011). Australia will be affected by the rise in regional sea levels projected for a Four Degree World (see Chapter 5: Hoegh-Guldberg et al., 2013). For a number of reasons, regional sea level rise can proceed at a different rate from the global rate. In particular, where ice-sheet loss is a significant contributor to sea level rise – and this is likely as we approach a Four Degree World – sea level rises least in the area closer to the areas of ice loss and most further afield, in areas such as the Australian region (Church et al., 2011). DCC (2009) estimated a sea level rise of 1.1 metres by 2100. Irreversible melting of the Greenland ice sheet is likely to be initiated at +4°C global warming and would lead to a sea level rise of seven metres, although this will take many centuries to be realized (Ridley et al., 2010).

The coastal impacts of sea level rise potentially include increased inundation of low-lying terrain and recession of soft shorelines (DCC, 2009). Severe episodes of coastal inundation and erosion occur during severe storm events, during which high waves and storm surges may beset the coast. Patterns of change in high waves and storm surge may be inferred from changes in circulation patterns that affect mean and extreme wind patterns. Over Australia, a distinct pattern of wind change has been projected for 2081–100, relative to 1981–2000, in the climate model ensemble for the more moderate temperature increases associated with a medium emission scenario. This shows an increase in mean winds in coastal regions between 25–35°S in summer and north of 25°S and over the Victorian coast and Tasmania. In winter, wind speed declines occur between 38–44°S in summer and between 25–35°S south in winter. A decline in strong winds is seen around much of coastal Australia in summer and all but Bass Strait and Tasmania in winter (McInnes et al., 2011). This

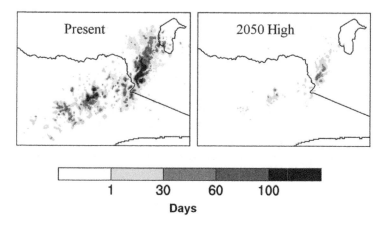

Figure 2.8 Australian Alps: Current and projected future days of snow cover

Source: Hennessy et al., 2008b

Note
a The 2050 high case is an underestimate of the +4°C GW case.

response is associated with the southward movement of the southern hemisphere storm track (Frederiksen et al., 2011). Changes in wave climate on the east coast of Australia have been found to reflect the changes seen in winds along this coastline and show a small decline in mean and storm waves for 2081–100 relative to 1981–2000 (Hemer et al., 2011).

Conclusion

In a Four Degree World, the effects of climate change in Australia will be dramatic. They are projected to include:

- temperature increases of about 3°C to 5°C in coastal areas and 4°C to 6°C in inland areas;
- likely declines of annual rainfall in southern Australia, particularly in winter, of up to about 50 per cent but uncertain rainfall changes in other regions;
- marked increases of potential evaporation of about 5 per cent to 20 per cent;
- snow cover duration falling to zero in most alpine regions; and
- sea level rise of up to about 1.1m in 2100, increasing to more than 7m over subsequent centuries even for no further global warming.

In the broader region (South-East Asia and the South Pacific), large changes in climate would also be expected at four degrees of global warming, although the tropical and mainly maritime climates of this region would lead to slightly less warming than over continental Australia. Perkins et al. (2012) give climate model-based projections for much of this region (for a case approaching 4°C global warming). Projected regional warmings were around 2.5°C to 3°C and rainfall increases of up to around 60 per cent in the vicinity of major regions of heavy rainfall, such as the inter-tropical convergence zone.

Acknowledgements

We acknowledge the modelling groups, the Program for Climate Model Diagnosis and Intercomparison (PCMDI) and the WCRP's Working Group on Coupled Modelling for their roles in making available the WCRP CMIP3 multi-model dataset. Support of this dataset is provided by the Office of Science, US Government Department of Energy.

Notes

1   Analysis of the climate models employs the probabilistic method developed by Watterson (2008) and Watterson and Whetton (2011) and used in the most recent national climate projections for Australia (CSIRO and BoM, 2007). Based on this approach, a probability distribution is fitted to the projected local changes for 4°C global warming from across the 23 climate models. This provides the 10th, 50th and 90th percentile thresholds for each case, with 90, 50 and 10 per cent (high, medium and low) chances of exceeding these thresholds.
2   Assessment derived from a large perturbed-physics climate model ensemble.
3   Defined as mainland Australia south of 33.5°S and east of 135.5°E.
4   Based on the climate model ensemble (using the Watterson [2008] method).
5   'Least hot, wettest' combines the 10th temperature and 90th rainfall percentiles. 'Mid case' combines the 50th percentiles for changes in temperature and rainfall. 'Hottest, driest' combines the 90th temperature and 10th rainfall percentiles. These combinations are consistent with the tendency for drier conditions to be linked with greater warming over Australia (Watterson, 2011) and also highlight cases of greatest interest to many affected systems (such as ecosystems and hydrology). Note that this process ignores potentially very important seasonal differences in rainfall occurrence, but it nevertheless should indicate sites of broadly similar annual maximum temperature and water balance. Also note that the results presented here are for +4°C of global warming relative to 1990, not the pre-industrial period, and thus represent a slight overestimate (by around the equivalent of 0.5°C of global warming) of the +4°C GW case.
6   Using CSIRO and BoM (2007), which gave projected changes in potential evaporation based on the climate model archive and the method of Morton (1983).
7   Based on Hennessy et al. (2008a), who assessed changing drought occurrence in 13 climate models by examining trends in annual dry events that occurred once in 20 years in the twentieth century.

References

Braganza, K., K. Hennessy, L. Alexander and B. Trewin. 2013. Changes in extreme weather. In Christoff, P. (ed.), *Four Degrees of Climate Change: Australia in a Hot World*. Earthscan: London, ch. 3.

Christensen, J. H., B. Hewitson, A. Busuioc, A. Chen, X. Gao, I. Held, R. Jones, R. K. Kolli, W.-T. Kwon, R. Laprise, V. Magaña Rueda, L. Mearns, C. G. Menéndez, J. Räisänen, A. Rinke, A. Sarr and P. Whetton. 2007. Regional Climate Projections. In

S. Solomon et al. (eds), *Climate Change 2007: The Physical Science Basis. Contribution of Working Group I to the Fourth Assessment Report of the Intergovernmental Panel on Climate Change*. Cambridge University Press: Cambridge and New York.

Church, J. and N. White. 2011. Sea-Level Rise from the Late 19th to the Early 21st Century. *Surveys in Geophysics* 1–18.

Church, J. A., J. M. Gregory, N. J. White, S. M. Platten and J. X. Mitrovica. 2011. Understanding and projecting sea level change. Oceanography 24 (2):130–43. doi:10. 5670/oceanog. 2011. 33.

Church, J. A., J. R. Hunter, K. L. McInnes and N. J. White. 2006. Sea-level rise around the Australian coastline and the changing frequency of extreme sea-level events. *Australian Meteorological Magazine* 55: 253–60.

CSIRO and BoM. 2007. *Climate change in Australia.* CSIRO Bureau of Meteorology: Melbourne.

DCC. 2009. *Climate Change Risks to Australia's Coast: A First Pass National Assessment.* Commonwealth Department of Climate Change, 168 pp.

Frederiksen, C. S., J. S. Frederiksen, J. M. Sisson and S. L. Osbrough. 2011. Changes and projections in Australian winter rainfall and circulation: Anthropogenic forcing and internal variablilty. *International Journal of Climate Change Impacts and Responses* 2: 143–62.

Grose, M. R., I. Barnes-Keoghan, S. P. Corney, C. J. White, G. K. Holz, J. B. Bennett, S. M. Gaynor N. L. and Bindoff. 2010. *Climate Futures for Tasmania: General Climate Impacts.* ACE CRC, Hobart, Tasmania, 67 pp.

Hemer, M. A, K. L. McInnes and R. Ranasinghe. 2011. Climate and variability bias adjustment of climate model derived winds for an east Australian dynamical wave model. (Submitted to Ocean Dynamics.)

Hennessy K. J., R. Fawcett, D. G. C. Kirono, F. S. Mpelasoka, D. Jones, J. M. Bathols, P. H. Whetton, M. Stafford Smith, M. Howden, C. D. Mitchell and N. Plummer. 2008a. An assessment of the impact of climate change on the nature and frequency of exceptional climatic events. In DAFF CSIRO BoM: Canberra.

Hennessy K. J., P. H. Whetton, K. Walsh, I. N. Smith, J. M. Bathols, M. Hutchinson and J. Sharples. 2008b. Climate change effects on snow conditions in mainland Australia and adaptation at ski resorts through snowmaking. *Climate Research* 35: 255–70.

Hoegh-Guldberg, O., E. Poloczanska and A. Richardson. 2013. Australia's Marine Resources in a Warm, Acid Ocean. In P. Christoff (ed.), *Four Degrees of Climate Change: Australia in a Hot World*. Earthscan: London, ch. 5.

Howden, M., S. Schroeter and S. Crimp. 2013. Agriculture in an even more SunBurnt Country. In P. Christoff (ed.), *Four Degrees of Climate Change: Australia in a Hot World.* Earthscan, London, ch. 6.

Irving, D., P. Whetton and A. Moise. In press. Climate projections for Australia: a first glance at CMIP5. *Australian Meteorological and Oceanographic Journal.*

Kirono, D. G. C., D. M. Kent, K. J. Hennessy and F. Mpelasoka. 2011. Characteristics of Australian droughts under enhanced greenhouse conditions: Results from 14 global climate models. *Journal of Arid Environments* 75: 566–75.

McInnes, K. L., T. A., Erwin and J. M. Bathols. 2011: Global Climate Model projected changes in 10 m wind due to anthropogenic climate change. *Atmospheric Science Letters.* DOI: 10. 1002/asl. 341.

Meehl, G. A., C. Covey, K. E. Taylor, T. Delworth, R. J. Stouffer, M. Latif, B. McAvaney and J. F. B. Mitchell. 2007a. THE WCRP CMIP3 multimodel dataset: a new era in climate change research. *Bulletin of the American Meteorological Society* 88: 1383–94.

Morton, F. 1983. Operational estimates of areal evapo-transpiration and their significance to the science and practice of hydrology. *Journal of Hydrology* 66:1–76.

Nicholls, N. 2005. Climate variability, climate change and the Australian snow season. *Australian Meteorological Magazine* 54: 177–85.

Perkins, S. E., D. B. Irving, J. R. Brown, S. B. Power, A. F. Moise, R. A. Colman and I. Smith. 2012. CMIP3 ensemble climate projections over the western tropical Pacific based on model skill. *Climate Research* 51: 35–58.

Ridley J., J. Gregory, P. Huybrechts and J. Lowe. 2010. Thresholds for irreversible decline of the Greenland ice sheet. *Climate Dynamics* 35: 1049–57

Sanderson, B., R. Knutti, T. Aina, C. Christensen, N. Faull, D. J. Frame, W. J. Ingram, C. Piani, D. A. Stainforth, D. A. Stone and M. R. Allen. 2008. *Constraints on model response to greenhouse gas forcing and the role of subgrid scale processes, Journal of Climate* 21: 2384–400.

Taylor, K. E., R. J. Stouffer and G. A. Meehl. 2012. An Overview of CMIP5 and the experiment design. *Bulletin of the Amererican Meteorological Society* 93: 485–98.

Watterson, I.G. 2008. Calculation of probability density functions for temperature and precipitation change under global warming. *Journal of Geophysical Research* 113: D12106.

Watterson, I.G. 2011. Calculation of joint PDFs for climate change with properties matching Australian projections. *Australian Meteorological and Oceanographic Journal* 61: 211–19.

Watterson, I.G. and P. H. Whetton. 2011. Distributions of decadal means of temperature and precipitation change under global warming. *Journal of Geophysical Research* 116: D07101.

3   Changes in extreme weather

Karl Braganza, Kevin Hennessy, Lisa Alexander and Blair Trewin

Introduction

Extreme weather events, interacting with exposed and vulnerable systems, can lead to disasters (IPCC, 2012). In Australia, vulnerability to extreme weather events has been recently highlighted by:

- the south-east Australian heat wave in late January 2009, which resulted in 374 excess deaths in Victoria over what would be expected (Vic DHS, 2009);
- the Victorian bushfires in early February 2009, which killed 173 people and more than a million animals, destroyed more than 2,000 homes, burnt about 430,000 hectares, and cost about $4.4 billion (Victorian Bushfires Royal Commission, 2010);
- the floods in Queensland in 2010–2011, which killed 33 people and affected more than 78 per cent of the state and over 2.5 million people, with 29,000 homes and businesses suffering some form of inundation, and a cost in excess of $5 billion (Queensland Floods Commission of Inquiry, 2011).

Changes in such weather events, and changes in exposure and vulnerability, will alter the impact of disasters. Recent observational evidence shows changes in the frequency of extreme weather events that are consistent with a warming climate. Most of the global warming since the mid-20th century is very likely due to increases in greenhouse gases from human activities such as burning fossil fuels. Further increases in greenhouse gases are expected due to human activities, leading to more warming and changes in extreme weather events.

This chapter first provides a global perspective on observed changes in extreme weather. It then reviews changes in extreme weather that have already been observed in Australia over the twentieth century and concludes with a discussion of projected changes to Australian weather extremes in a Four Degree World.

A global perspective on observed changes

A changing climate leads to a variety of changes in the frequency, intensity, spatial extent, duration and timing of many extreme weather and climate events.

Some regional climate extremes – such as the south-east Australian droughts from 1997–2009 – may be the result of an accumulation of weather or climate conditions that are not extreme when considered independently. While all extreme weather events can be said to result from intrinsic climate variability, such variability is now influenced and altered by the effect of human-induced warming of the climate system (IPCC, 2012).

The most robust observed evidence of changes in extreme events comes from changes in the frequency of their occurrence, and particularly the increase in extreme heat events. The Intergovernmental Panel on Climate Change report *Managing the Risks of Extreme Events and Disasters to Advance Climate Change Adaptation* (IPCC, 2012) concluded that it is very likely that global warming has caused changes in the frequency of some extreme weather events observed since 1950. It is very likely that there has been an overall decrease in the number of cold days and nights, and an overall increase in the number of warm days and nights, at the global scale (IPCC, 2012). It is also very likely that these changes have occurred at the continental scale in North America, Europe and Australia (IPCC, 2012). There have been statistically significant increases in the number of heavy precipitation events in most regions (IPCC, 2012).

Determining the extent to which an *individual* extreme event is influenced by a specific cause, such as increasing greenhouse gases, remains difficult. This is due to a number of factors. Specifically, extreme events themselves are rare, thereby providing small sample sizes for studying and determining change over time. Additionally, and equally importantly, extreme events have a very large range even in an unchanging climate, which also contributes to difficulties in determining significant changes (IPCC 2007: FAQ 9.1). Many types of extreme weather events are complex, with many different antecedent drivers in the weather and climate system. Hence, for instance, larger changes in global mean temperature are likely required before changes in the magnitude of individual extremes are clearly distinguishable from background variability.

Nevertheless, advances are being made in determining the 'fraction of attributable risk', which links a particular extreme event to specific causal relationships (Stott et al., 2004). These techniques have allowed us to determine that the occurrence of some recent individual extreme events, notably the 2003 European heatwave, 2010 Russian heatwave, and the extreme Australian summer of 2012–13, would be very much less likely without global warming (Stott et al., 2004; Rahmstorf and Coumou, 2011; Otto et al., 2012; Lewis and Karoly, 2013).

According to the IPCC (2012):

- it is likely that human influences have already led to warming of extreme daily minimum and maximum temperatures at the global scale;
- there is medium confidence that human influences have contributed to the intensification of extreme precipitation at the global scale;
- it is likely that there has been a human influence on increasing extreme coastal high water due to an increase in mean sea level;

• there is only low confidence that human influences have contributed to changes in tropical cyclone activity.

Historical changes in Australian weather extremes

Extreme temperatures

Among the most statistically robust observations of changes to Australian climate have been changes in maximum and minimum temperatures. Most of the observed trend in temperatures has occurred since 1950, with both maximum and minimum temperatures increasing by around 0.9°C (Fawcett et al., 2012). Over the entire twentieth century, the increase in minimum temperatures has exceeded that of maximum temperatures by 0.35°C. Australia's warmest year was in 2005. The ten warmest years occurred after 1980, with six of those ten years occurring after 1998.

This has been accompanied by a shift in both warm and cool temperature extremes. Averaged over the entire continent, the frequency of extreme high temperatures, in both daytime maximum and night time minimum temperatures, has increased while the frequency of extreme low temperatures has decreased.

The frequency of days with maximum temperatures above the 90th percentile, after remaining fairly stable until about 1980, has increased by about 40 per cent in the last three decades, while the frequency of minimum temperatures below the 10th percentile has declined steadily after 1950, and is now about 40 per cent below pre-1950 averages (Trewin and Smalley, 2013).

Across Australia, there has been a slight increase in the duration of heatwaves (defined as consecutive days above the 90th percentile of daily maximum temperature) since the 1950s (Alexander and Arblaster, 2009). There have, however, been marked regional variations in the occurrence of multi-day heatwaves over that time, with decreases in parts of southern coastal Australia (especially south-western Western Australia), and strong increases further north (Trewin and Smalley, 2013). The decreases in southern coastal Australia contrast with increases in the frequency of single-day high temperature extremes at many of the same locations over the same period.

Figure 3.1 shows the increase in Australian annual mean temperature since 1910. Figure 3.2 shows the frequency of record high (black) and record low (grey) maximum temperatures from station data for 1910–2011. Figure 3.3 shows the frequency of record high (black) and record low (grey) minimum temperatures from station data for 1910–2011.

While warming trends in mean temperature are well established over the second half of the twentieth century, it was not until after 1990 that strong trends emerged in the frequency of record high maxima and minima, with particularly large numbers in the decade from 2001 onwards. Over the 2001–11 period record high maxima outnumbered record low maxima by a ratio of 2.8 to 1, while for minimum temperatures the ratio was 5.2 to 1 (Trewin and Smalley, 2013).

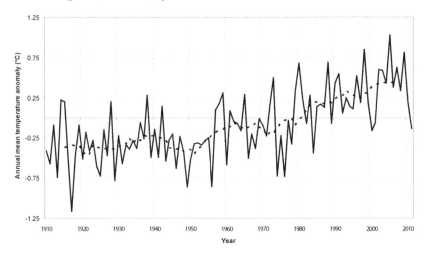

Figure 3.1   Area-averaged Australian annual mean temperature, 1910–2011

Source: Bureau of Meteorology (Australia)

Note
a Dashed line is 11-year running mean.

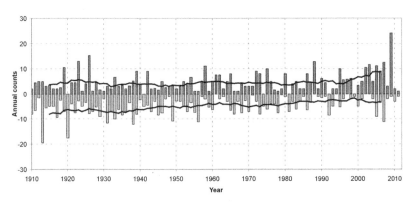

Figure 3.2   Frequency of record high and low maximum temperatures in Australia,
           1910–2011

Source: Trewin and Smalley, 2013

Notes
a Black bars represent high temperature maxima.
b Grey bars represent low temperature maxima.

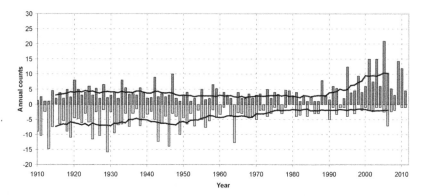

Figure 3.3 Frequency of record high and low minimum temperatures in Australia, 1910–2011

Source: Trewin and Smalley, 2013

Notes
a Black bars represent high temperature maxima.
b Grey bars represent low temperature maxima.
c Data are taken from a fixed and well-spread observational network. Records refer not to progressive record setting (as a function of time) but records broken relative to the entire distribution of events. Yearly counts represent the number of monthly station records broken across the network in a calendar year.

Fire weather

Many parts of Australia are prone to large bushfires. Southern and eastern Australia are particularly vulnerable to both forest and grassland fires occurring in close proximity to populated centres. For example, in Canberra, fires in January 2003 killed 4 people and destroyed 500 homes. In Victoria, fires in early February 2009 killed 173 people and more than a million animals, and around 430,000 hectares of land were burnt, destroying more than 2,000 homes and costing about $4.4 billion (Victorian Bushfires Royal Commission, 2010).

In most Australian states, fire weather risk is quantified using one of two indices: the Forest Fire Danger Index (FFDI) or the Grassland Fire Danger Index (GFDI) (Luke and McArthur 1978). The Fire Danger Rating system is used by fire agencies to reflect the fire behaviour and the difficulty of controlling a particular fire.

Annual cumulative FFDI, which integrates daily fire weather across the year, increased significantly at 16 of 38 Australian sites from 1973–2010 (Clarke *et al.* 2012). The number of significant increases is greatest in the south east, while the largest trends occurred inland rather than near the coast (Figure 3.4). The largest increases in seasonal FFDI occurred during spring and autumn, while summer had the fewest significant trends. This indicates a lengthened fire season.

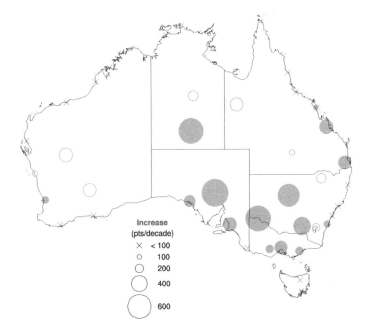

Figure 3.4 Trend magnitude in annual total Forest Fire Danger Index (FFDI)

Source: Clarke et al., 2012

Notes
a Marker size is proportional to the magnitude of trend.
b Reference sizes are shown in the legend. Filled markers represent trends that are statistically significant.
c The marker for Laverton has been moved west to avoid overlap with Melbourne Airport.
d Days of extreme heat are often associated with bushfires. The Black Saturday bushfires around Melbourne in February 2009, for example, were preceded by a record-breaking heatwave across south-eastern Australia (Figure 3.5), with Melbourne and Adelaide breaking records for consecutive days above 43°C during this period, while Mildura set a Victorian record with 12 consecutive days of 40°C or above.

Melbourne had a record sequence of temperatures of 43°C, 44°C and 45°C between 28 and 30 January. The average temperature in Melbourne was nearly 36°C between 27 January and 7 February 2009. Combined with prolonged drought, these conditions provided extreme fire weather and very dry vegetation across the state. Melbourne hit a record of 46.4°C on 7 February, the day of the initial firestorm, with more than 400 fires burning across the south east of the continent.

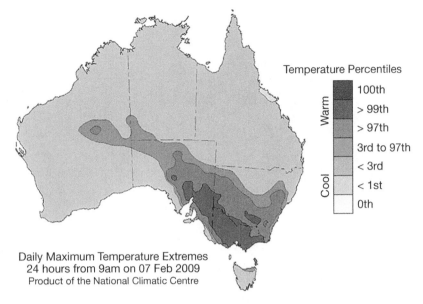

Temperature Percentiles

Warm

100th
> 99th
> 97th
3rd to 97th
< 3rd
< 1st

Cool

0th

Daily Maximum Temperature Extremes
24 hours from 9am on 07 Feb 2009
Product of the National Climatic Centre

Figure 3.5   Daily maximum temperature extremes for 7 February 2009

Source: Bureau of Meteorology (Australia)

Note
a Temperatures are displayed as percentiles. Percentile analysis is a way of determining
   how unusual a temperature event is. To determine whether a temperature observation
   is unusual for a particular month, it is compared with all other rainfall and
   temperature daily observations in the same month in the climate record (1950 to
   present for daily analyses). All the observations for that month are ranked in order,
   from coolest to hottest for temperature, and driest to wettest for rainfall and then
   broken into 100 equal groups. The first group is the 1st percentile, the second group
   the 2nd percentile and so on. Red shows the area over which the day was the hottest
   February day on record.

Extreme rainfall and drought

Changes in average rainfall have been observed across parts of Australia since
1950, but trends are less clear than for increases in temperature. The most statistically significant changes, those clearly discernable from background rainfall
variability, have been observed declines in late autumn and winter rainfall across
southern Australia, in particular south-west Western Australia. Declines in
rainfall have also been observed across the eastern half of Australia, particularly
the south east of the continent. The large inherent variability of rainfall across
Queensland and the northern and central Murray–Darling Basin means that a
pattern of change cannot be assumed from apparent rainfall declines with little
statistical significance (Le Blanc et al., 2012). Similarly, monsoonal rainfall
increases across the tropical north and north west have occurred against a
background of large natural variability.

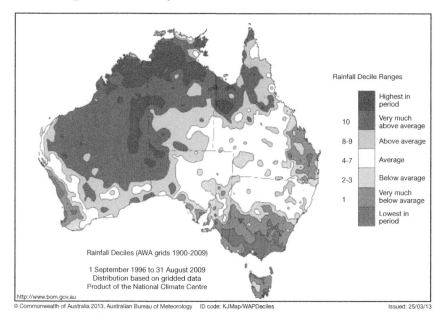

Figure 3.6   Rainfall deciles for the period 1 September 1996 to 31 August 2009

Source: Bureau of Meteorology (Australia)

Notes
a Deciles are calculated with respect to the 1900–2009 period.
b South-eastern and south-western parts of the continent experienced driest on record
   conditions during this period.

Very high year-to-year and decade-to-decade rainfall variability, and an association between rainfall and the El Niño–Southern Oscillation over large parts of the continent, mean that periods of extended drought are common on the mainland, interspersed by occasional periods of very heavy rainfall (Power et al., 1998; 1999).

Changes to the duration and severity of drought periods can be characterized as changes in local climate extremes. In this context, the noteworthy changes in rainfall that have occurred across south western and south eastern parts of the continent (Figure 3.6) have likely impacted on the severity of episodic drought. In the south west, the rainfall changes have been characterized by a seasonal decline in winter rainfall of around 15 per cent since 1970, as well as an absence of very wet years altogether. In the south east, similar declines in autumn and early winter rainfall have occurred since 1996, with a similar absence of wet years ended abruptly by heavy spring and summer rainfall in 2010/2011.

To date, many studies have noted the possible impact of both the timing of rainfall changes and of highest on record temperatures on recent periods of extended rainfall deficits, with the tendency toward amplification of hydrological drought. In particular, autumn and winter rainfall deficits (of around 10–20 per cent) across the south-eastern and south-western corners of the continent have been a characterized by large losses (of up to 60 per cent) in subsequent streamflow and water storage (Potter et al., 2011).

The south-east and south-west corners of the continent traditionally have a Mediterranean-type climate, with relatively dry hot summers and relatively cool wet winters (although the south east does receive high summer rainfall on occasions, such as during a La Niña event). The relatively high rainfall during the winter half of the year has historically supported large forests and, more recently, significant agricultural areas. Any potential long-term loss of rainfall, or change in the seasonality of rainfall, has significant implications for agriculture and natural ecosystems (Dunlop et al., 2012).

The recent decline in rainfall has been attributed, in part, to a number of dynamical changes, and with possible links to anthropogenic climate change (Hope et al., 2006; Frederiksen et al., 2010; Timbal et al., 2010; Timbal and Drosdowsky, 2012; Cai and Cowan, 2012). A significant decrease in storminess has occurred over the south east, coinciding with the period of rainfall decline (Alexander et al., 2011). More generally, future declines in mid-latitude rainfall driven by global warming have been consistent feature of climate modelling since the first IPCC report of 1990 (IPCC, 1990).

While climate models have consistently shown likely future decreases in mid-latitude rainfall, they have also consistently predicted that rainfall intensity – the amount of rainfall received on short timescales (less than a day) – will likely increase due to global warming in many regions (Min et al., 2011), including Australia. Hence future rainfall will likely be heavier, when it does fall, over regions experiencing rainfall decline.

Based on data available from the Bureau of Meteorology (Bureau of Meteorology, 2013), there has been a decreasing trend from 1900–2011 in the area of Australia with less than 10 per cent of annual average rainfall (defined as serious rainfall deficiency). This decrease is apparent in all States and Territories, except Victoria and south-west Western Australia where there has been little change and an increase respectively.

However, trends in the area with serious annual rainfall deficiency do not provide information about whether recent multi-year rainfall deficiencies were exceptional for particular regions. For the 13-year period 1997 to 2009, rainfall over continental south-eastern Australia (south of 33.5°S and east of 135.5 °E) was 11.4 per cent below the long-term average, making it the driest 13-year period on record by a large margin; the previous record was 7.8 per cent below average for the 13-year period 1933–45 (Timbal and Drosdowsky, 2012). Both the duration and intensity of the 1997–2009 rainfall deficit is without historical precedent in the instrumental record starting from 1900 (Timbal and Drosdowsky, 2012). For the 14-year period October 1996 to September 2010, around half of Victoria and half of Tasmania recorded lowest-on-record rainfall, and in south-west Western Australia areas of lowest-on-record rainfall covered western coastal areas between Cape Leeuwin and Kalbarri, and extending inland into the southern wheat belt (Bureau of Meteorology, 2010).

Drought conditions across large parts of the eastern half of the continent were dramatically broken by the La Niña event that began in the spring of 2010 (Braganza et al., 2011; Bureau of Meteorology, 2011). La Niña events are associated with warmer-than-average sea surface temperatures in tropical waters surrounding Australia and related changes in atmospheric circulation and typically cause high rainfall in Australia. Due to background warming of the oceans, the probability of La Niña events being associated with record temperatures is increasing.

During the 2010 and 2011 monsoonal period, a record La Niña event, record spring and summer rainfall over much of the Australian continent (Figure 3.7) and record high sea-surface temperatures were registered in the Australian region (Figure 3.8). The rainfall resulted in repeated severe flooding, in Queensland and Victoria in particular. In February 2011, tropical cyclones Carlos and Yasi brought extremely heavy rainfall around Darwin and the north Queensland coast respectively. The heavy rainfall of 2010 and 2011 ranks alongside previous strong La Niña events in the first half of the 1970s, the 1950s and around 1917. However, the record monsoonal rainfall in the northern tropics was consistent with a general trend of increased monsoonal rainfall across northern Australia in recent decades.

Over Australia, trends in heavy rainfall depend on the period of analysis and the metric of interest. For example, the annual number of days with more than 30mm of rain from 1950–2012 has decreased in much of southern and eastern Australia, but increased in the north (similar to the trend in average rainfall: Bureau of Meteorology, 2013). Similar results have been found for other metrics (Gallant et al., 2007).

Tropical cyclones

For the 1981–2 to 2006–7 cyclone seasons, no significant trends in the total numbers of cyclones or in the proportion of the most intense cyclones have been found in the Australian region, South Indian Ocean or South Pacific Ocean (Figure 3.9: Kuleshov et al., 2010). Only limited conclusions can be drawn regarding tropical cyclone intensity and numbers in the Australian region as a whole prior to 1981, due to a lack of consistent data prior to the start of the modern satellite period and the related issue of a small sample size of events from which to analyze changes over time. For the Queensland coast from Cairns southwards, there has been a decline in the frequency of severe land-falling tropical cyclones over the last century (Callaghan and Power, 2011). Studies using more data in the Northern Hemisphere show increased Atlantic hurricane activity over the past century consistent with increasing sea surface temperatures; however, definitive attribution of changes to increasing greenhouse gases remains premature (Vecchi and Knutson, 2007).

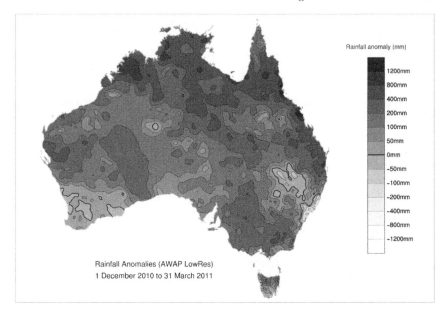

Rainfall anomaly (mm)

1200mm
800mm
400mm
200mm
100mm
50mm
0mm
-50mm
-100mm
-200mm
-400mm
-800mm
-1200mm

Rainfall Anomalies (AWAP LowRes)
1 December 2010 to 31 March 2011

Figure 3.7 Rainfall anomalies (departure from 1961–1990 average rainfall) in mm for
December 2010 to February 2011

Source: Bureau of Meteorology (Australia)

Noteworth extreme rainfall

Extreme rainfall was observed over the Kimberley region of Western Australia
and adjacent parts of the Northern Territory during the first half of March 2011.
Over 300mm of rain fell between 1 and 16 March across central and eastern
regions of the Kimberley with more than 700 mm falling over the Kimberley
Plateau, setting new rainfall records for the region.

In early March 2011 a tropical low pressure system caused falls of over 200mm
in the southern Gulf coast of Queensland on 2 March before moving southward
through the state producing more heavy falls. Notable daily falls from this system
included 477mm at Mornington Island on 1 March and 319mm at Bedourie on
6 March.

Exceptionally heavy rainfall occurred in northeast Tasmania on 23 and 24
March 2011 as a complex area of low pressure moved near the state. Gray
(Dalmayne Road) recorded 327.2mm in 24 hours, making it Tasmania's third-
highest daily rainfall total on record. The two-day totals were also extreme, with
Gray's total of 452.4mm having only been exceeded once before, on 4–5 April
1929.

Heavy rainfall and flash flooding persisted between 9 and 15 January 2011,
resulting in rainfall totals of 100–300mm across two-thirds of the state and consequently major and moderate flooding spanning north, west and central Victoria.

Riverine flooding began on Wednesday 12 on some rivers and continued until the end of the month on several northern rivers.

Darwin Airport recorded its highest 24-hour rainfall of 367.6mm of rain in the 24-hour period to 9am on 16 February. Darwin Airport three-day total (15–17 February 2011) was 684.8mm, breaking the previous three-day record.

Tropical moisture interacted with a cold front, triggering extreme rainfall across the Melbourne Metropolitan area, the North Mallee district and much of eastern Victoria between 4 and 6 February 2011. Daily rainfall totals between 100–200mm were widespread in the eastern and south-eastern suburbs of Melbourne and were the equivalent of what most stations would usually observe in an entire summer season. The exceptionally high daily rainfall totals resulted in severe flash flooding in numerous locations, with the south-eastern suburbs of Melbourne and the regional town of Mildura amongst the most severely affected.

A trough of low pressure brought very moist air across Tasmania and produced exceptionally heavy rainfall in the north between 12 and 14 January 2011. A new state record January daily rainfall of 282mm was set at Falmouth on the northern East Coast. In the northwest, Yolla exceeded its previous January daily rainfall record on both 13 and 14 January. Some sites had their highest January total rainfall, with a few receiving more than eight times the long-term monthly January average over the four-day spell.

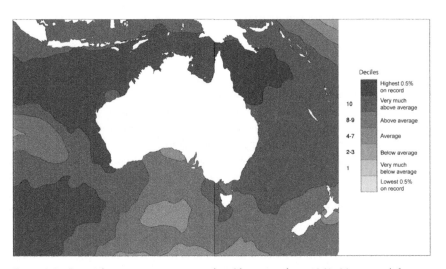

Figure 3.8 Sea surface temperature anomalies (departure from 1961–90 average) for September through to December 2010

Source: Bureau of Meteorology (Australia)

Note
a Highest on record sea surface temperature anomalies occurred in regions that studies have demonstrated have a high association with Australian rainfall. Sea surface temperatures in the Australian region have warmed by just less than 1°C since 1900.

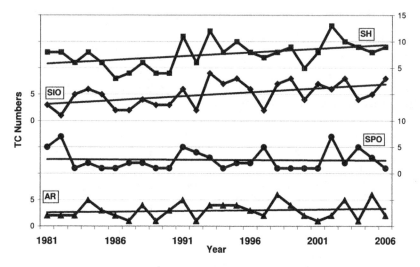

Figure 3.9   Annual numbers of major tropical cyclones for the 1981–2 to 2006–7
cyclone seasons, with linear trends

Source: Kuleshov et al., 2010

Notes
a Tropical cyclones (TC)
b Southern Hemisphere (SH) (squares, right axis),
c South Indian Ocean (SIO) (diamonds, left axis),
d South Pacific Ocean (SPO) (circles, right axis), and
e Australian Region (AR) (triangles, left axis), for the 1981–2 to 2006–7 cyclone
   seasons, with linear trends.

Extreme sea level

Observations from tide gauges indicate that the global average sea level rose by
around 1.7mm per year over the 20th century. Since 1993, this rate has increased
to around 2.8–3.2mm per year based on tide gauges and satellite altimetry
(Church and White, 2011). Extreme sea level events can be due to high tides,
local storm surges due to low pressure systems such as cyclones, distant storms
that generate high waves, and a rise in average sea level. Worldwide, there has
also been an increase in extreme sea levels, for example those that occur when
high tides and storm surges coincide, since 1970 (Menendez and Woodworth,
2010). Increases in extreme sea level events around Australia have been
significant at most sites. The average sea level rise, rather than changes in storm
surges, is the major reason for the rise in extreme sea level. El Niño is one of the
most important factors responsible for the interannual variability of extreme sea
levels (Bureau of Meteorology and CSIRO, 2011), and this will have played a
role in the extreme sea level trends. Tidal contributions to extreme sea levels are
especially significant along the Australian coast (Menendez and Woodworth,
2010).

A global perspective on projected changes

Projected changes in greenhouse gas and aerosol emissions during the 21st century are expected to cause further changes in global average temperature, sea-level and regional climate, including extreme events. The timing of a 4°C global warming depends on the emissions scenarios and the response simulated by a range of different climate models (see Chapter 2, this volume – Karoly et al., 2013).

The IPCC (2012) report concluded that it is virtually certain that increases in the frequency and magnitude of warm daily temperature extremes and decreases in cold extremes will occur at the global scale in the twenty-first century. It is very likely that the length, frequency and/or intensity of warm spells or heat waves will increase over most land areas.

Based on medium and high emissions scenarios (A1B and A2), a 1-in-20-year hottest day is likely to become a 1-in-2 year event by the end of the twenty-firstcentury in most regions. Under a low emissions scenario (B1), a 1-in-20-year event would likely become a 1-in-5-year event.

The IPCC (2012) also found that it is likely that the frequency of heavy precipitation or the proportion of total rainfall from heavy falls will increase in the twenty-first century over many areas of the globe. Based on a range of IPCC emissions scenarios (B1, A1B, A2), a 1-in-20-year maximum daily rainfall event is likely to become a 1-in-5- to 1-in-15-year event by the end of the twenty-first century in many regions.

There is medium confidence that droughts will intensify in the twenty-first century in some seasons and areas due to reduced precipitation and/or increased evapotranspiration (IPCC, 2012).

Average tropical cyclone maximum wind speed is likely to increase, although increases may not occur in all ocean basins. It is likely that the global frequency of tropical cyclones will either decrease or remain essentially unchanged (IPCC, 2012).

There is low confidence in projections of small spatial-scale phenomena such as tornadoes and hail because competing physical processes may affect future trends and because current climate models do not simulate such phenomena (IPCC, 2012).

It is very likely that mean sea level rise will contribute to upward trends in extreme coastal high water levels in the future (IPCC, 2012).

There is low confidence in projections of changes in some intrinsic patterns of natural climate variability, such as the El Niño–Southern Oscillation (IPCC, 2012).

Extreme events will have greater impacts on sectors with close links to climate, such as water, agriculture and food security, forestry, health and tourism. To respond to these challenges, the IPCC (2012) noted that measures that provide benefits under current climate and a range of future climate change scenarios, called low-regrets measures, are available starting points for addressing projected trends in exposure, vulnerability and climate extremes. They have the potential to offer benefits now and lay the foundation for addressing projected changes. Actions that range from incremental steps to transformational changes are essential for reducing risk from climate extremes.

Projected changes in Australian extreme weather

Projected changes in extreme events at the regional scale are inherently difficult to simulate in global climate models. Finer resolution regional climate models with a better representation of climate processes are usually required to improve the reliability of such projections.

There is limited information about projected changes in extreme weather over Australia for a Four Degree World. Most information is available for changes associated with less than 4°C global warming because (a) projections tend to be based on simulations for low to medium and high emission scenarios (A2, A1B and B1), rather than very high emissions (A1FI), and (b) many projections were focussed on the period 2030 to 2070, rather than 2090 and beyond. In the following discussion, the emission scenarios and years are noted, along with the approximate magnitude of global warming.

Extreme temperatures

Changes in the number of days over 35°C have been estimated for 15 sites for 2030 and 2070 (CSIRO and BoM, 2007). The warmest scenario considered was for A1FI emissions in 2070, which has a global warming range of 1.74 to 4.64°C. The upper end of this global warming range gives an annual mean warming of 4–5°C over most of Australia, reaching 5–6°C in central Australia (CSIRO and BoM, 2007, Appendix A). Under these conditions, the present (1971–2000) average annual number of days over 35°C increases substantially by 2070, e.g. Sydney increases from 3.5 days at present to 12, Canberra from 5 to 26 days, Melbourne from 9 to 26 days, Adelaide from 17 to 47 days, Perth from 28 to 67 days and Brisbane from 1 to 21 days (Table 3.1). Large decreases in extremely cold days are also simulated (CSIRO and BoM, 2007).

Pitman and Perkins (2008) assessed projected changes in the annual average intensity and frequency of the 99th percentile of maximum temperature (the hottest 1 per cent of events, hereafter referred to as $Tmax^{99}$) over Australia, based on 16 climate models. At each grid-cell, only climate models that simulated twentieth century climate variability with relative accuracy were considered. Projections included the high (A2) emission scenario in 2100, which has a corresponding global warming of 2.0–5.4°C (IPCC, 2007).

The intensity of $Tmax^{99}$ increases by 3–4°C over most of northern Australia, 4–5°C over most of southern Australia and more than 5.0°C along the south coast and southeast coast. The average frequency of $Tmax^{99}$ increases from 4 times per year at present to 5–10 times over most of southern and eastern Australia, and 10-30 times over most of northern and western Australia.

Table 3.1   Average number of days per year above 35°C at selected sites for the current
climate (average for 1971–2000) and for 2070

Site	Current	2070
Adelaide	17	47
Alice Springs	90	182
Brisbane	1	21
Broome	54	281
Cairns	3.8	96
Canberra	5	26
Darwin	11	308
Dubbo	25	87
Hobart	1.4	3.4
Melbourne	9	26
Mildura	32	76
Perth	28	67
St George	47	135
Sydney	3.5	12
Wilcannia	63	129

Source: CSIRO

Note

a Based on the A1FI emissions scenario, and the 90th percentile (warmest 10 per cent)
of 23 climate models (CSIRO and BoM, 2007).

Extreme rainfall

Changes in extreme daily rainfall, with return periods of 10–50 years, have been
estimated by Rafter and Abbs (2009) for 11 Australian regions for 2050 and
2090, based on 12 climate models driven by the high (A2) emissions scenario.
The global warming by 2090 in these models ranges from 2.5–3.7°C. By 2090
(Table 3.2), most models simulate increases in the intensity of the 1-in-20-year
event in most regions.

Drought

There is medium confidence that, globally, droughts will intensify in the twenty-
first century in some seasons and areas, due to reduced precipitation and/or
increased evapotranspiration (IPCC, 2012). Drought-affected areas also will
likely increase in extent (IPCC, 2007).

Drought occurrence is projected to increase over most of Australia, but particularly in south-western Australia (Hennessy et al., 2008; Kirono et al., 2011).

Table 3.2 Percentage change in the intensity of 1-day rainfall totals with a 20-year return period for the 2090 climate relative to that of 1980

Region	Model	CNRM CM3	CSIRO Mk3.0	CSIRO Mk3.5	GFDL CM2.0	GFDL CM2.1	MIROC 3.2 (medres)	MIUB ECHO-G	MPI ECHAM 5	MRI CGCM 2.3.2A	NCAR CCSM 3.0 (1)	NCAR CCSM 3.0 (3)	UKMO HadCM3
North West	mean	29.0	17.7	66.5	363.4	388.6	9.0	16.3	3.7	7.7	3.5	4.3	21.9
	median	25.6	16.7	44.2	68.6	222.4	10.4	13.0	0.4	-1.8	3.5	3.9	17.2
Central QLD	mean	37.7	9.4	29.3	82.9	185.2	20.4	20.5	9.7	-8.2	0.3	-4.0	35.9
	median	40.7	12.1	28.5	64.0	101.1	21.2	20.4	10.7	-12.3	-0.8	-6.8	35.3
North QLD	mean	37.8	12.5	34.9	2644.7	367.4	7.7	17.5	-8.9	-4.7	6.6	19.2	23.3
	median	34.3	7.2	40.7	176.0	145.2	11.8	19.5	-8.9	-4.3	0.9	17.1	18.2
QLD East Coast	mean	38.9	28.3	24.9	74.0	90.7	18.9	14.6	-1.0	-1.5	-21.8	-8.3	24.1
	median	58.1	27.6	30.6	64.0	74.7	21.2	18.8	3.0	-19.1	-23.8	-10.2	25.4
South East QLD	mean	66.8	26.6	21.0	35.2	43.6	26.4	8.0	18.6	4.7	-28.8	-11.2	13.3
	median	59.6	24.8	18.4	30.3	38.6	22.3	2.2	18.6	9.2	-26.0	-10.6	12.0
Eastern NSW	mean	51.2	16.2	16.1	19.0	21.5	26.4	20.5	22.8	20.5	-9.1	14.7	10.6
	median	45.1	11.1	14.0	13.0	21.7	24.1	20.3	19.0	13.5	-13.9	14.2	-1.2
Western NSW	mean	34.9	14.6	54.0	51.8	25.0	31.8	21.2	26.1	17.6	-1.9	3.9	22.7
	median	28.9	9.7	35.5	40.8	21.9	32.1	23.1	21.2	7.6	-3.9	-0.5	28.0
Victoria	mean	30.2	28.4	3.3	25.1	25.9	26.2	31.6	19.3	26.0	29.6	6.2	-1.4
	median	28.9	20.3	2.1	32.1	24.5	27.5	26.8	17.5	23.1	24.2	1.8	-4.1
Tasmania	mean	13.7	24.2	-6.6	30.3	25.5	37.8	30.9	18.0	35.4	37.7	11.1	7.2
	median	15.0	29.4	-7.5	28.7	26.9	35.5	30.7	19.7	43.4	36.7	0.4	7.2
South West	mean	27.0	23.9	23.1	31.8	48.1	23.8	22.4	29.6	16.3	-4.6	3.7	22.2
	median	20.0	22.5	14.5	24.9	38.2	23.2	16.7	26.0	5.6	-7.0	3.4	17.5
South West WA	mean	3.5	44.5	14.5	26.4	72.7	3.3	3.7	36.8	34.7	13.1	6.5	28.0
	median	-2.9	46.8	25.4	11.0	54.9	6.0	3.4	41.5	23.1	7.0	0.2	22.6

Source: CSIRO

Note

a Based on 12 climate models driven by the high (A2) emissions scenario. Decreases are shown in bold text. From Rafter and Abbs (2009). The large increases (exceeding 100 per cent) simulated by the GFDL model in the northern regions are likely due to a poor fit of the rainfall data to the generalized extreme value model in late twenty-first century, which was also found by Kharin et al. (2007).

By 2030, it is likely (greater than 66 per cent probability) that a 1-in-20-year drought during the 20th Century will become a 1-in-10-year drought over south-west Western Australia.

By 2050, this will include the Murray–Darling Basin, South Australia and Victoria, and by 2070 this will extend to eastern New South Wales and Tasmania. No significant increases in drought frequency are projected for north-west Western Australia or northern and central Queensland.

Hail

Projections of change in hail risk for the end of the century (CSIRO and BoM, 2007), based on the CSIRO Mark 3.5 model and a high (A2) emissions scenario, show an increase along the south-eastern coastline by the year 2070 (Figure 3.10). The results also show a decrease in hail risk along the south coast of Australia. However, since these results are based on only one climate model, confidence in the patterns of change is low.

The University of Oklahoma climate model was run at 1km resolution over the Sydney region to estimate changes in hail risk for 20012050 under a medium

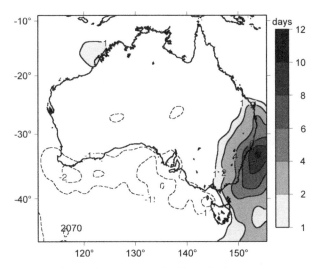

Figure 3.10 Projected changes for 2070 in risk of large hail

Source: Bureau of Meteorology (Australia)

Notes
a Risk = days per year with large hail.
b Large hail = hail of 2cm diameter.
c Shaded contours show increases in frequency, while dashed contours show decreases in frequency.
d From the CSIRO Mk3.5 model for the A2 emission scenario.

(A1B) emission scenario (Leslie et al., 2008). The central year is close to 2030, which corresponds to a global warming of 0.54–1.44°C (CSIRO and BoM, 2007). The average return periods for large and giant hail decrease by almost 50 per cent, i.e. the frequency almost doubles. For example, hail greater than 6cm in diameter that currently occurs once in eight years occurs once in five years during 1991–2050, and hail greater than 10cm that currently occurs once in fifty-one years occurs once in 28 years during 1991–2050.

Extreme wind

Projected changes in extreme daily wind-speeds (defined as the highest 1 per cent) from 19 climate models were analyzed by McInnes et al. (2011) for the medium (A1B) emissions scenario for 2081–2100 relative to 1981–2000. The associated global warming in this scenario (Table 3.3), is slightly less than 1.7–4.4°C (the IPCC [2007] range of warming for A1B emissions in 2090–99 relative to 1980–1999).

Over northern and central Australia, at least two-thirds of the models agree on small changes within ±2 per cent. Over southern and eastern Australia, there is a tendency for weaker extreme wind speeds, which is most pronounced in June to August.

Extreme fire weather

Over southern and eastern Australia, warmer and drier conditions are expected in future (CSIRO and BoM, 2007). Consequently, an increase in fire weather risk is likely, with more days of extreme risk and a longer fire season.

The annual average number of extreme fire weather days at 26 climate stations in south-eastern Australia was estimated by Lucas et al. (2007) for the current climate (1973–2007), using the Forest Fire Danger index (FFDI). Projected changes in daily temperature, humidity, wind and rainfall were generated from two climate simulations named CCAM (Mark 2) and CCAM (Mark 3) for the years 2020 and 2050, relative to 1990, for low (B1) and very high (A1FI) emission scenarios. These changes were applied to observed daily data at each climate station, and FFDI values were re-calculated. The number of extreme fire danger days generally increases 100–300 per cent by 2050 for the very high emissions scenario (Table 3.3). The global warming in 2050 for the very high scenario is 2.9°C (CSIRO and BoM, 2007).

Output from the CSIRO Mark 2 climate model was also downscaled at 56km resolution over Australia (using the Regional Atmospheric Modelling System: RAMS) for low (B2) and high (A2) emissions scenarios in 2050 and 2100 (Pitman et al., 2007). Under the high (A2) scenario in 2100, there is a 50 per cent increase in the January mean forest fire danger index (FFDI) over most of the continent.

It should be noted that projected changes to fire weather cannot be directly translated to changes in actual bushfires. The change in future fire activity is

Table 3.3   Average number of extreme fire weather days per year for 26 sites in south-eastern Australia

Values for "present" are averaged over 1973-2007. Projections for 2050 are for the very high (A1FI) emission scenario, from two climate simulations named CCAM (Mark2) and CCAM (Mark3)

Site	Present	2050 (CCAM Mark2)	2050 (CCAM Mark3)
Adelaide	1.2	2.3	3.8
Amberley	1.2	3.0	2.8
Bendigo	1.2	2.8	4.0
Bourke	4.8	14.6	13.9
Brisbane Airport	0.5	1.0	0.9
Canberra	1.6	3.7	5.1
Ceduna	11.8	17.3	18.5
Charleville	6.8	27.5	20.9
Cobar	4.8	14.4	14.1
Coffs Harbour	0.2	0.3	0.4
Dubbo	1.7	6.3	6.7
Hobart	0.1	0.1	0.2
Launceston AP	--	0.0	0.1
Laverton	1.9	3.5	4.6
Melbourne Airport	2.5	4.5	5.8
Mildura	7.3	12.8	15.9
Mt Gambier	1.4	2.2	2.9
Moree	2.2	8.5	8.0
Nowra	1.1	1.9	4.0
Richmond (NSW)	1.5	2.7	4.0
Rockhampton	0.6	1.2	1.5
Sale	0.6	1.1	1.9
Sydney AP	1.2	1.8	3.5
Wagga	4.2	9.9	11.1
Williamtown	1.4	2.4	4.1
Woomera	19.6	29.3	34.7

Source: Lucas et al., 2007

Note

a Values for 'present' are averaged over 1973–2007. Projections for 2050 are for the very high (A1FI) emission scenario, from two climate simulations named CCAM (Mark 2) and CCAM (Mark 3).

more difficult to determine because fire behaviour depends also on fuel type and accumulation, which may change in the future due to changes in rainfall, fire frequency and other factors (Williams et al., 2009).

Tropical cyclones

For the Australian region, the CCAM model has produced downscaled climate simulations on a 65km grid for a high (A2) emissions scenario for a period centred on 2070, when the global warming is 1.35–3.60°C (CSIRO and BoM, 2007). The CCAM projections show a strong tendency for a decrease in the frequency of cyclones in the Australian region (Abbs, 2010). On average, for the period 2051–90 relative to 1971–2000, the simulations show an approximately 50 per cent decrease in frequency, a small decrease (0.3 days) in the duration of a given cyclone and a southward movement of 100km in the genesis and decay regions (Table 3.4). On average, the southward movement in the decay region (the region into which weakened tropical cyclones migrate) is greater off the Queensland coast than off the coast of Western Australia.

The Regional Atmospheric Modelling System (RAMS) was used to further downscale to a grid-spacing of 15km for 40-year time slices centred on 1980, 2030 and 2070 (Abbs, 2010). For each time slice, 100 cyclone events were modelled. These simulations show a distinct shift towards stronger cyclones, with a larger percentage of cyclones producing high wind speeds (exceeding 25 m/s) in the 2070 climate.

Extreme sea levels

IPCC (2007) estimates of future sea level rise are 18–79cm by 2090–2099 relative to 1980–1999, based on climate modelling and allowing an extra 10 to 20cm for a possible rapid dynamic response of the Greenland and West Antarctic ice sheets (Meehl et al., 2007). Higher estimates have been suggested using statistical methods that relate sea level changes to temperature changes, but there has been debate about the validity of these approaches (Lowe and Gregory, 2010).

As stated above, extreme sea level events can be due to high tides, local storm surges due to low pressure systems such as cyclones, distant storms that generate high waves, and a rise in average sea level. Projected changes in extreme sea level events around southern Australia are likely to be dominated by the average sea level rise, rather than changes in storm surges (Colberg and McInnes, 2012). For the high (A2) emission scenario, the range of mean sea-level rise by 2090–2100 is 23–51cm, which corresponds to a global warming of 2.0–5.4°C.

Figure 3.11 shows the estimated increase in the frequency of extreme sea-level events caused by a 50cm mean sea-level rise for 29 Australian locations where good tidal records longer than 30 years exist (DCC, 2009). Extreme events that now happen every 10 years, on average, would happen about every 10 days in 2100, and become even more frequent around Sydney, with smaller increases around Adelaide and along parts of the Western Australian coast (DCC, 2009).

Table 3.4   Projected changes in total tropical cyclone numbers, cyclone days, duration of a given cyclone, genesis latitude and decay latitude for seven simulations, downscaled using CCAM to 65 km grid spacing, for the period 2051–90, relative to 1971–2000

	Number	Days	Duration (days)	Genesis (degrees latitude)	Decay (degrees latitude)
ECHAM5	−58%	−59%	−0.4	−1.1	−1.3
GFDL CM2.0	−53%	−55%	−0.3	−0.8	−1.1
GFDL CM2.1	−40%	−52%	−1.0	−1.4	−1.2
MIROC3.2 (medres)	−68%	−73%	−0.8	−1.1	−2.0
CSIRO Mk3.5	−39%	−44%	−0.2	−0.5	−0.2
UK HADCM3	−50%	−47%	+0.2	−0.7	−1.7
CSIRO Mk3.0	−28%	−23%	+0.2	−0.8	−1.9
Average	−48%	−50%	−0.3	−0.9	−1.3

Source: Abbs, 2010

Note
a Bold values indicate changes in cyclone numbers that are statistically significant at the 99 per cent level.

Conclusions

Australia's vulnerability to extreme weather events is evident in recent disasters. Changes in such weather events, and changes in exposure and vulnerability, can alter the impact of disasters.

Observational evidence of changes in extreme weather events over recent decades has been found globally and in Australia. From 1910–2011 the frequency of extreme high temperatures in Australia increased while the frequency of extreme low temperatures decreased. Increases in fire weather from 1973–2010 are significant at 16 of 38 Australian sites, mainly in the south east, with a lengthened fire season. A decrease in late autumn and winter rainfall across southern Australia in recent decades has likely been associated with an exacerbation of hydrological drought conditions during that time. There has been a slight increase in heavy precipitation days across eastern Australia. An increase in extreme sea levels has occurred since 1970. Since 1981, no significant trends in the total numbers of cyclones, or in the proportion of the most intense cyclones, have been found in the Australian region.

In a Four Degree World, Australia is expected to experience a large increase in extremely high temperatures, extreme fire weather, extreme rainfall events, tropical cyclone intensity, extreme sea levels, droughts in southern areas and hail along the east coast. A decrease in the frequency of extremely cold temperatures is expected, along with fewer tropical cyclones and a reduction in extreme winds and hail in southern Australia.

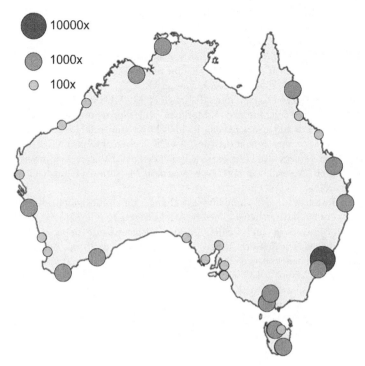

Figure 3.11 Estimated increases in the frequency of extreme sea-level caused by a mean
          sea-level rise of 50cm

Source: DCC, 2009

Note
a Risk circles indicate percentage increase in risk.

These changes will pose significant challenges for disaster risk management,
water and food security, ecosystems, forestry, infrastructure such as transport and
energy, as well as health and tourism. Risk is the combination of impact and
likelihood. Climate-related policy and planning needs to include consideration
of the risk of high-impact events that now may have low likelihood. Actions
that range from incremental steps to transformational changes are essential for
managing risks from climate extremes.

References

Abbs, D. 2010. *The Impact of Climate Change on the Climatology of Tropical Cyclones in
   the Australian Region.* CSIRO Climate Adaptation Flagship Working Paper 11, 24 pp.
ACE CRC. 2008. *Position Analysis. Climate Change, Sea-Level Rise and Extreme Events: Impacts
   and Adaptation Issues.* ACE CRC. http://www.cmar.csiro.au/sealevel/downloads/SLR_PA.pdf
   [accessed 26 July 2013], http://www.sealevelrise.info/access/repository/resource/c9b4b
   f42-acdd-102c-bf59-005056996a56/PA01_SLR_FIN_090616.pdf [accessed 26 July 2013].

Alexander, L., X. L. Wang, H. Wan and B. Trewin. 2011. Significant decline in storminess over southeast Australia since the late 19th century. *Australian Meteorological and Oceanographic Journal* 61: 23–30.

Alexander, L. V. and J. M. Arblaster. 2009. Assessing trends in observed and modelled climate extremes over Australia in relation to future projections. *International Journal of Climatology* 29: 417–35. doi:10.1002/joc.1730.

Braganza, K., S. B. Power, D. A. Jones, B. Trewin, J. M. Arblaster, B. Timbal, N. Plummer, P. K. Hope, J. S. Frederiksen and J. McBride. 2011. Update on the state of the climate, long-term trends and associated causes. In T. D. Keenan and H. Cleugh (eds), *Climate Science update for the Garnaut Review*. CAWCR Technical Report No. 036.

Bureau of Meteorology. 2011. An extremely wet end to 2010 leads to widespread flooding across eastern Australia. *Special Climate Statement* 24. National Climate Centre, Bureau of meteorology, 15 pp.

—2013. Australian climate variability and change: time series graphs. http://www.bom. gov.au/cgi-bin/climate/change/timeseries.cgi [accessed 26 July 2013].

Bureau of Meteorology and CSIRO. 2011. *Climate Change in the Pacific: Scientific Assessment and New Research. Volume 1: Regional Overview*, 257pp. Accessible via www. pacificclimatechangescience.org/publications/reports/ [accessed 20 July 2013].

Cai, W. and T. Cowan. 2012. Southeast Australia autumn rainfall reduction: A climate-change induced poleward shift of ocean-atmosphere circulation. *Journal of Climate.* http://journals. ametsoc. org/doi/abs/10.1175/JCLI-D-12-00035.1.

Church, J. A. and N. J. White. 2011. Sea-level rise from the late 19th to the early 21st century. *Surveys in Geophysics* 32: 585–602, doi:10.1007/s10712-011-9119-1.

Colberg, F. and K. McInnes. 2012. The impact of future changes in weather patterns on extreme sea levels over southern Australia. *Journal of Geophysical Research* 117, C08001, doi:10.1029/2012JC007919.

CSIRO and BoM. 2007. *Climate change in Australia*. CSIRO and Australian Bureau of Meteorology, 147 pp., http://www.climatechangeinaustralia.gov.au/technical_report. php [accessed 26 July 2013].

DCC. 2009. *Climate Change Risks to Australia's Coast: A First Pass National Assessment*. Department of Climate Change, 172 pp. http://www.climatechange.gov.au/publications/ coastline/climate-change-risks-to-australias-coasts.aspx

Della-Marta, P. M., D. A. Collins and K. Braganza. 2004. Updating Australia's high-quality annual temperature dataset. *Australian Meteorological Magazine* 53: 75–93.

Donat, M. G., L. V. Alexander, H. Yang, I. Durre, R. Vose, R. J. H. Dunn, K. M. Willett, E. Aguilar, M. Brunet, J. Caesar, B. Hewitson, C. Jack, A. M. G. Klein Tank, A. C. Kruger, J. Marengo, T. C. Peterson, M. Renom, C. Oria Rojas, M. Rusticucci, J. Salinger, A. S. Elrayah, S. S. Sekele, A. K. Srivastava, B. Trewin, C. Villarroel, L. A. Vincent, P. Zhai, X. Zhang and S. Kitching. 2013. Updated analyses of temperature and precipitation extreme indices since the beginning of the twentieth century: The HadEX2 dataset. *Journal of Geophysical Research*, doi:10.1029/2012JD018606.

Dunlop M., D. W. Hilbert, M. Stafford Smith, R. Davies, C. D. James, S. Ferrier, A. House, A. Liedloff, S. M. Prober, A. Smyth, T. G. Martin, T. Harwood, K. J. Williams, C. Fletcher and H. Murphy. 2012. *Implications for Policymakers: Climate Change, Biodiversity Conservation and the National Reserve System*. CSIRO Climate Adaptation Flagship, Canberra, 12 pp., http://www.csiro.au/nationalreservesystem [accessed 26 July 2013].

Fawcett, R. J. B., B. C. Trewin, K. Braganza, R. J. Smalley, B. Jovanovic and D. A. Jones. 2012. On the sensitivity of Australian temperature trends and variability to analysis methods and observation networks. *CAWCR Technical Report* 50, Centre for Australian Weather and Climate Research: Melbourne.

Frederiksen, J. S., C. S. Frederiksen, S. L. Osbrough and J. M. Sisson. 2010. Causes of changing southern hemisphere weather systems. In I. Jupp, P. Holper and W. Cai (eds), *Managing Climate Change: Papers from the Greenhouse 2009 Conference*. CSIRO Publishing, 278 pp.

Gallant, A. J. E., K. J. Hennessy and J. S. Risbey. 2007. Trends in rainfall indices for six Australian regions: 1910–2005. *Australian Meteorological Magazine* 56: 223–39.

Hennessy K., R. Fawcett, D. Kirono, F. Mpelasoka, J. Bathols, P. Whetton, M. Stafford-Smith, M. Howden, C. Mitchell and N. Plummer. 2008. An assessment of the impact of climate change on the nature and frequency of exceptional climatic events. CSIRO and Bureau of Meteorology, 33 pp., http://www.daff.gov.au/agriculture-food/drought/drought-program-reform/national_review_of_drought_policy/climatic_assessment [accessed 26 July 2013].

Hope, P. K., W. Drosdowsky and N. Nicholls. 2006. Shifts in the synoptic systems influencing southwest Western Australia. *Climate Dynamics* 26: 751–64.

Hunter, J. R. 2010. Estimating sea-level extremes under conditions of uncertain sea-level rise. *Climatic Change* 99: 331–50. doi:10.1007/s10584-009-9671-6.

Insurance Council of Australia. 2010. *Historical disaster statistics*. http://www.insurancecouncil.com.au/IndustryStatisticsData/CatastropheDisasterStatistics/tabid/1572/Default.aspx [accessed 22 April 2010].

IPCC. 1990. *Climate Change: The IPCC Scientific Assessment*. Report prepared for Intergovernmental Panel on Climate Change by Working Group I. J. T. Houghton, G. J. Jenkins and J. J. Ephraums (eds). Cambridge University Press: Cambridge New York and Melbourne, Australia, 410 pp.

—2007. *Climate Change 2007: The Physical Science Basis. Contribution of Working Group I to the Fourth Assessment Report of the Intergovernmental Panel on Climate Change*. Solomon, S., D. Qin, M. Manning, Z. Chen, M. Marquis, K. B. Averyt, M. Tignor and H. L. Miller (eds). Cambridge University Press: Cambridge and New York. http://www.ipcc.ch/publications_and_data/ar4/wg1/en/contents.html [accessed 26 July 2013].

—2012. Summary for Policymakers. In C. B. Field, V. Barros, T. F. Stocker, D. Qin, D. J. Dokken, K. L. Ebi, M. D. Mastrandrea, K. J. Mach, G. -K. Plattner, S. K. Allen, M. Tignor and P. M. Midgley (eds), Managing the Risks of Extreme Events and Disasters to Advance Climate Change Adaptation : A Special Report of Working Groups I and II of the Intergovernmental Panel on Climate Change. Cambridge University Press: Cambridge and New York, pp. 1–19.

Jones, D. A. and B. C. Trewin. 2002. On the adequacy of historical Australian daily temperature data for climate monitoring. *Australian Meteorological Magazine* 51: 237–50.

Jones, D., G. Wang and R. Fawcett. 2009. High-quality spatial climate data-sets for Australia. *Australian Meteorological and Oceanographic Journal* 58: 233–48.

Kharin, V. V., F. W. Zwiers et al. 2007. Changes in temperature and precipitation extremes in the IPCC ensemble of global coupled model simulations. *Journal of Climate* 20 (8): 1419–44.

Kirono, D. G. C., D. M. Kent, K. J. Hennessy and F. Mpelasoka. 2011. Characteristics of Australian droughts under enhanced greenhouse conditions: Results from 14 global climate models. *The Journal of Arid Environments* 75: 566–75.

Kuleshov, Y., R. Fawcett, L. Qi, B. Trewin, D. Jones, J. McBride and H. Ramsay. 2010. Trends in tropical cyclones in the South Indian Ocean and the South Pacific Ocean. *Journal of Geophysical Research* 115. D01101, doi:10.1029/2009JD012372.

Lavery, B., G. Joung and N. Nicholls. 1997. An extended high-quality historical rainfall dataset for Australia. *Australian Meteorological* Magazine 46: 27–38.

Lavery, B., A. Kariko and N. Nicholls. 1992. A historical rainfall data set for Australia. *Australian Meteorological Magazine* 40: 33–9.

Leblanc, M. J., S. O. Tweed, A. I. J. M. Van Dijk and B. Timbal. 2012. A review of historic and future hydrological changes in the Murray-Darling Basin. *Global and Planetary Change.* doi:10.1016/j.gloplacha.2011.10.012.

Leslie, L. M., M. Leplastrier and B. W. Buckley. 2008. Estimating future trends in severe hailstorms over the Sydney Basin: A climate modelling study. *Atmospheric Research* 87: 37–51.

Lewis, S. C. and D. J. Karoly. 2013. Anthropogenic contributions to Australia's record summer temperatures of 2013. *Geophysical Research Letters.* Online, http://onlinelibrary. wiley.com/doi/10.1002/grl.50673/abstract [accessed 26 July 2013].

Lowe. J. and J. Gregory. 2010. A sea of uncertainty. *Nature Climate Change.* doi:10.1038/ climate.2010.30.

Lucas, C., K. J. Hennessy and J. M. Bathols. 2007. Bushfire weather in Southeast Australia recent trends and projected climate change impacts. Bureau of Meteorology, CSIRO and Bushfire CRC, 84pp., http://www.royalcommission.vic.gov.au/getdoc/c71b6858-c387-41c0-8a89-b351460eba68/TEN.056.001.0001.pdf [accessed 26 July 2013].

Luke, R. H. and A. G. McArthur. 1978. *Bushfires in Australia.* Australian Government Publishing Service: Canberra, 359 pp.

McInnes, K., T. Erwin and J. Bathols. 2011. Global Climate Model projected changes in 10m wind speed and direction due to anthropogenic climate change. *Atmospheric Science Letters.* doi:10.1002/asl.341.

Meehl, G. A., T. F. Stocker, W. D. Collins, P. Friedlingstein, A. T. Gaye, J. M. Gregory, A. Kitoh, R. Knutti, J. M. Murphy, A. Noda, S. C. B. Raper, I. G. Watterson, A. J. Weaver and Z. -C. Zhao. 2007. Global Climate Projections. In S. Solomon, D. Qin, M. Manning, Z. Chen, M. Marquis, K. B. Averyt, M. Tignor and H. L. Miller (eds), *Climate Change 2007: The Physical Science Basis. Contribution of Working Group I to the Fourth Assessment Report of the Intergovernmental Panel on Climate Change.* Cambridge University Press: Cambridge and New York.

Menéndez, M. and P. L. Woodworth. 2010. Changes in extreme high water levels based on a quasi-global tide-gauge 58 data set. *Journal of Geophysical Research* 115: C10011. doi:10.1029/2009JC005997.

Min, S. K., X. Zhang, F. W. Zwiers and G. C. Hegerl. 2011. Human contribution to more-intense precipitation extremes. *Nature* 470: 378–81. doi:10.1038/nature09763.

Otto, F. E. L., N. Massey, G. J. van Oldenborgh, R. G. Jones and M. R. Allen. 2010. Reconciling two approaches to attribution of the 2010 Russian heat wave. *Geophysical Research Letters* 39 (4): L04702. doi:10.1029/2011GL050422.

Pitman A. J., G. T. Narisma and J. McAneney. 2007. The impact of climate change on the risk of forest and grassland fires in Australia. *Climatic Change* 84: 383–401. doi10.1007/ s10584-007-9243-6.

Pitman, A. J. and S. Perkins. 2008. Regional Projections of Future Seasonal and Annual Changes in Rainfall and Temperature over Australia Based on Skill-Selected AR4 Models. *Earth Interactions* 12 (12): 1–50.

Potter, N., C. Petheram and L. Zhang. 2011. *Sensitivity of Streamflow to Rainfall and Temperature in South-Eastern Australia during the Recent Drought.* MODSIM 12–16 December, Perth.

Power, S., F. Tseitkin, V. Mehta, S. Torok and B. Lavery. 1999. Decadal climate variability in Australia during the 20th century. *International Journal of Climatology* 19: 169–84.

Power, S., F. Tseitkin, S. Torok, B. Lavery and B. McAvaney. 1998. Australian temperature, Australian rainfall, and the Southern Oscillation, 1910–1996: Coherent variability and recent changes. *Australian Meteorological Magazine* 47: 85–101.

Queensland Floods Commission of Inquiry. 2011. Interim Report, 262 pp. http://flood-commission.qld.gov.au/publications/interim-report [accessed 26 July 2013].

Rafter, T. and Abbs, D. 2009. An analysis of future changes in extreme rainfall over Australian regions based on GCM simulations and Extreme Value Analysis. http://www.cawcr.gov.au/publications/researchletters/CAWCR_Research_Letters_3.pdf [accessed 26 July 2013]. Scroll to page 44 to find this paper.

Rahmstorf, S. and D. Coumou. 2011. *Increase of Extreme Events in a Warming World.* Proceedings of the National Academy of Science of the USA, 5 pp. doi:10.1073/pnas.1101766108.

Stott, P. A., D. A. Stone and M. R. Allen. 2004. Human contribution to the European heatwave of 2003. *Nature* 432: 610–14.

Timbal, B., J. Arblaster, K. Braganza, E. Fernandez, H. Hendon, B. Murphy, M. Raupach, C. Rakich, I. Smith, K. Whan and M. Wheeler. 2010. Understanding the anthropogenic nature of the observed rainfall decline across South Eastern Australia. *CAWCR Technical Report* 026.

Timbal, B. and W. Drosdowsky. 2012. The relationship between the decline of South Eastern Australia rainfall and the strengthening of the sub-tropical ridge. *International Journal of Climatology.* doi:10.1002/joc.3492.

Trewin, B. C. 2001. *Extreme Temperature Events in Australia.* PhD thesis, School of Earth Sciences, University of Melbourne.

Trewin, B. C. 2012. A daily homogenized temperature data set for Australia. *International Journal of Climatology*, published online 13 June 2012.

Trewin, B. and R. Smalley. 2013. Changes in extreme temperatures in Australia, 1910 to 2011. *Australian Meteorological and Oceanographic Journal*, submitted.

Vecchi, G. A. and T. R. Knutson. 2008. On Estimates of Historical North Atlantic Tropical Cyclone Activity. *Journal of Climate* 21: 3580–600.

Vic DHS. 2009. *January 2009 Heatwave in Victoria: an Assessment of Health Impacts.* Victorian Department of Health Services. http://docs.health.vic.gov.au/docs/doc/F7EEA405981101ACA257AD80074AE8B/$FILE/heat_health_impact_rpt_Vic2009.pdf [accessed 26 July 2013].

Victorian Bushfires Royal Commission. 2010. *Final Report, Volume 1.* Government Printer for the State of Victoria, Melbourne, 361 pp., http://royalcommission.vic.gov.au/Commission-Reports [accessed 26 July 2013].

Whetton, P. L., D. Karoly, I. Watterson, L. Webb, F. Drost, D. Kirono and K. McInnes. 2013. Australia's Climate in a Four Degree World. In P. Christoff (ed.), *Four Degrees of Climate Change: Australia in a Hot World.* Earthscan: London, ch. 2.

Williams, R. J., R. A. Bradstock, G. J. Cary, N. J. Enright, A. M. Gill, A. C. Leidloff, C. Lucas, R. J. Whelan, A. N. Andersen, D. J. M. S. Bowman, P. J. Clarke, G. D. Cook, K. J. Hennessy and A. York. 2009. *Interactions between Climate Change, Fire Regimes and Biodiversity in Australia: A Preliminary Assessment.* http://www.climatechange.gov.au/sites/climatechange/files/documents/04_2013/20100630-climate-fire-biodiversity-PDF.pdf [accessed 26 July 2013].

Part II
Ecological impacts

4 Changes to Australian terrestrial biodiversity

Lesley Hughes

Introduction

Australia is considered one of the most megadiverse countries in the world, being home to 7–10 per cent of the world's species (Mittermeier, Gil and Mittermeier, 2007). The continent's biodiversity is already subject to multiple threats, and rapid anthropogenic climate change will add to and interact with these existing stresses. The challenges for predicting the future of Australia's terrestrial plants and animals are immense. We have a far-from-adequate understanding of the multiple factors determining the distribution and dynamics of even single populations or species, let alone whole communities and ecosystems. Further, biological systems tend to respond to environmental drivers in a non-linear fashion, and the likelihood of sudden ecological surprises and rapid transformations will increase.

But despite the challenges, we must use whatever means we have to assess future risks, to provide a basis for adaptation planning. In this chapter I first discuss how the environmental and biogeographic context under which Australia's flora and fauna evolved offers us general guidance for predicting its future vulnerability and its potential to adapt. I then explore the likely consequences for species and ecosystems of future rapid climatic change, the potential for our biodiversity to adapt and the ultimate consequences of future loss.

Environmental and biogeographic context

Australia's rich terrestrial biodiversity has been shaped by the unique combination of its highly variable climate, its long period of isolation from other continents, its highly weathered and infertile soils, its flat topography and by the long history of human occupation (Orians and Milewski, 2007). These factors also offer general clues to the likely responses of species to current and future climatic change, by affecting species' exposure to stress and by determining their capacity to adapt.

Australia broke free from the super-continent of Gondwana approximately 45 million years ago. Its current biota is a combination of relict Gondwanan elements shared with South America and Africa, combined with later arrivals from Asia and New Guinea and with many endemic species that have evolved *in situ*. Endemicity is especially high in groups such as terrestrial mammals (87 per cent), flowering plants (92 per cent), fish (90 per cent), reptiles (93 per cent), frogs (94 per cent) and birds (45 per cent) (Steffen et al., 2009). Many of these species have narrow geographic and climatic ranges. Over 50 per cent of eucalypt species, for example, have climatic ranges that span less than 3°C of mean annual temperature, and approximately 25 per cent span less than 1°C (Hughes, Cawsey and Westoby, 1996). While factors other than climate are likely to play a role in limiting the ranges of most species, restricted distribution is a key factor predisposing species to increased vulnerability from rapid environmental change.

The risk of negative impacts on species from rapid future change may, in some regions, be somewhat mitigated by the species' pre-adaptation to the episodic nature of the Australian climate. Rapid climatic swings – from cyclonic or monsoonal depressions causing flooding to prolonged drought, especially across the arid and semi-arid regions – have acted as strong selective pressures on species to evolve opportunistic life styles and other features that confer resilience to extreme conditions (Steffen et al., 2009). Overall, it is generally considered that the dynamics of many Australian ecosystems are more driven by these episodic, extreme events and disturbances than are ecosystems in many other regions of the world (Orians and Milewski, 2007).

Australia's unique dominance of infertile soils will also influence future climate impacts. The combination of deep weathering during the Late Cretaceous and Tertiary periods, the long period of relative geological stability and the limited extent of recent (Quaternary) glacial activity has produced soils largely depleted of phosphorus and nitrogen (Attiwill and Leeper, 1987). Low levels of phosphorus and nitrogen, in particular, are associated with an evergreen, sclero-phyllous flora, characterized by hardened, long-lived leaves (Specht and Specht, 1999), and are important factors also controlling growth rates in animals (Orians and Milewski, 2007).

Low soil fertility has two important consequences for understanding future climate change impacts. Firstly, low nutrients are likely to limit the fertilization effect of rising atmospheric CO_2 although the lack of experimental data on the responses of Australian vegetation growing in native soils to elevated CO_2 limits quantification of this effect (see Hovenden and Williams, 2009). Secondly, vegetation growing on low nutrient soils tends to have higher flammability, via a complex set of interacting feedbacks, and the interaction of fire and soil fertility acts to maintain distinct vegetation boundaries in many environments (Lehmann and Hughes, in review). Australia is characterized by high fire frequency, with some regions burning annually. The expected increase in fire danger weather, especially in the south east, is expected to be one of the most significant drivers of future ecological change (Williams et al., 2009a).

The topography of the Australian continent also has important consequences for the distribution of species and their future adaptive capacity. Australia is the flattest of all continents, with 99 per cent of the landmass less than 1,000 metres above sea level, and with few summits exceeding 2,000 metres. This topography has important feedback effects on climate: for instance, the uplands are too low to generate significant orographic rainfall, contributing to the aridity of the inland (Orians and Milewski, 2007). The lack of topographic relief has meant the terrestrial biota has had few geographic barriers – such as mountain ranges – to limit past dispersal. In the future, however, this feature will also limit the ability of species to cope with increasing temperatures by shifting to higher elevation refuges. Consequently, keeping pace with shifting climate zones will require many terrestrial species to move overland by many tens or hundreds of kilometres by the end of the century (Hughes, 2003; Loarie et al., 2009; Leadley et al., 2010b;).

Finally, Australian ecosystems have been modified by human occupation for at least 40–65,000 years. The use of fire and hunting by Aboriginal peoples substantially modified the landscape (Bowman, 2003). Far greater impacts, however, have resulted from European settlement over the past 200 years, with large areas of the continent cleared or highly modified for agricultural and urban development (Cocklin and Dibden, 2009). Less than 10 per cent of pre-1750 vegetation remains in the intensive use zones of south-east and south-west Australia (SoE, 2011) and native vegetation loss continues at nearly one million ha annually with much of the remaining natural habitat now highly fragmented (SoE, 2011).

Australia has one of the worst records of species extinctions of any continent. Nearly 50 per cent of the world's known mammal extinctions have occurred in Australia in the last 200 years (Johnson, 2006). Over 50 extinctions of plants, birds and frogs have also been documented (Lindenmayer, 2007). Declines in distribution and abundance of many other species means they are likely to have little functional role in ecological communities. The current rate of species extinction (globally and in Australia) is estimated to be 100–1,000 times higher than background rates estimated from the fossil record (MEA, 2005). Over 1,700 species and ecological communities are known to be threatened and at risk of extinction (SoE, 2011) with the actual number at risk very likely to be considerably higher. Australia's Biodiversity Conservation Strategy (2010–30) listed: habitat loss, degradation and fragmentation; invasive species; unsustainable use of natural resources, changes to aquatic environments and flows; changing fire regimes; and climate change as major stresses on biodiversity. Climate change represents an additional stress, one that will add to, and interact with, existing pressures.

Australian landscapes at 4°C

Global meta-analyses of the potential impacts of future warming project large-scale shifts in biomes (Scholze et al., 2006; Gonzalez et al., 2010) and the functional collapse of many ecosystems at more than 3–4°C above pre-industrial levels (e.g. Warren et al., 2011). The main uncertainty is not *whether* such changes will occur, but their rate and extent (Leadley et al., 2010a).[1]

Some ecosystems – such as in the polar regions – are at risk because climate change will be large in an absolute sense. Others – such as tropical ecosystems at low latitudes – are vulnerable because the projected change is relatively large compared to their current range of inter-annual variability (Beaumont et al., 2011). Within the next 60 years, Beaumont et al. (2011) project that almost all of the Global 200 ecoregions (238 regions considered to support exceptional biodiversity [Olson and Dinerstein, 2002]) will face climatic conditions considered extreme compared to the baseline conditions of the 1961–90 period (based on the SRES A2 scenario, 4°C by 2100). The entire range of 89 ecoregions is projected to experience extreme monthly temperatures even with global warming of less than 2°C.

So what could we see happen between now and the possible arrival of a Four Degree World in the second half of this century? Impacts are likely to accrue in two non-mutually exclusive ways. Some change may be incremental. For example, gradual increases in mean temperatures or rainfall could result in gradual changes in ecotonal boundaries between ecosystems, such as those observed between rainforests and savannahs over the past few decades in northern Australia, thought to be mediated via changes in rainfall and fire (for instance, Fensham et al., 2003). But other changes could be abrupt and transformative. There is increasing evidence that complex systems such as ecosystems have critical thresholds – so-called tipping points – when a rapid transition occurs between one state and another (Scheffer and Carpenter, 2003; Scheffer et al., 2009; Laurance et al., 2011), and that these could be reached at or below 2°C global warming (Leadley et al., 2010a).

There is now some theoretical and empirical evidence that as different systems approach such tipping points, they exhibit some common early warning signals (Scheffer et al., 2009), including slower recovery from small perturbations. Empirical research on identifying early warning signals in ecosystems such as freshwater lakes and rangelands is emerging, but little has been done in Australia. Identification of early warning signals will be an important tool for predicting critical transitions, but for most terrestrial systems we do not have sufficient understanding of the underlying physiological and ecological processes and feedbacks, and in practice such signals may not be detectable against background noise and uncertainty until it is too late.

A further complication for predicting exactly when and where such critical thresholds could be reached is that few of the projections of ecosystem change consider concurrent changes such as the direct effect of rising atmospheric CO_2 which may differentially affect woody and herbaceous species (Warren et al., 2011). Increasing water use efficiency (WUE) over time by many plant species may also mean that some negative impacts projected by large-scale models may be over-estimated (Loehle, 2011). Other indirect impacts of climate change, such as changes in fire regimes, are likely to be key to transformational change in many regions. Fire frequency and intensity is driven largely by weather and fuel loads. Increasing severity of fire weather is virtually certain in many regions, in turn increasing the probability of ignition (Williams et al., 2009b). Rising atmospheric CO_2 may result in greater fuel loads in regions where water availability is not limiting (Williams et al., 2009b). Climate change will also affect the distributions and abundance of invasive species, with flow on effects to native communities (O'Donnell et al., 2012).

Just as some climates will disappear entirely and new climates without analogue will appear (Williams and Jackson, 2007), so too will some ecological assemblages disappear, to be replaced by new ones. The potential for ecological transformation can be illustrated, in a simplistic way, by considering the results of climate modelling described by Whetton et al. (2013, Chapter 2, this volume), who modelled analogous climates in a Four Degree World for a number of major centres in Australia. A comparison of the vegetation typical of those locations, with that currently supported in the regions with analogous climates, provides a crude assessment of the potential scope of future transformation. Consider for example, the rich tropical rainforest of the Cairns region, one of the most biodiverse areas in the continent. Under a mid-range rainfall scenario in a Four Degree World, the closest climate analogue to Cairns is Weipa, Queensland. Under the hottest and driest scenario, the closest analogue is Jabiru in the Northern Territory, while there were no Australian analogues found under the least hot, wettest scenario (see Whetton et al., 2013, Chapter 2, this volume). The Weipa district typically supports open forest dominated by stringybark eucalypts, while the vegetation of Jabiru is classified as savannah woodland. While these two regions certainly support extensive biodiversity, their level of species richness and endemism is considerably less than that supported by tropical rainforest.

An Australia-wide analysis of potential changes in vegetation classes and plant community composition using mid- (A1B) and high-range (A1FI) emissions scenarios for 2050 and 2070 predicts dramatic changes in the structure and composition of vegetation communities with a general decline in environments favouring trees and an increase in open woodlands, chenopod shrublands and grasslands (Dunlop et al., 2012). It is worth noting, however, that this analysis used only a single Global Circulation Model (CSIRO Mk3.5), and did not include potentially critical factors such as rising atmospheric CO_2, altered disturbance regimes and hydrology.

A number of reviews have identified those regions in Australia likely to be most vulnerable to loss of species and ecosystem function from climate change impacts and potentially to regime shifts (Table 4.1). Features that may confer increased susceptibility of these ecosystems include restriction of distribution of either the ecosystem in general, or of a high proportion of species, high exposure to factors such as increased sea level and changed fire regimes, those geographically limited in their capacity to shift, and those already under the most threat from fragmentation, reduction in environmental flows and invasive species. Key drivers of transformation will be changes in fire regimes, intensification of extreme events such as droughts, heat waves and tropical cyclones, and changes in hydrology (see Braganza et al., 2013, Chapter 3, this volume). Confidence in these projections is stronger for those ecosystems in coastal regions (where sea level rise is relatively well modelled) and in the south east and south west of Australia, where rainfall projections from climate models are more consistent.

Table 4.1   Regions in Australia considered most vulnerable to transformational change and biodiversity loss

Region/ecosystem	Projected impacts
Alpine & sub-alpine zones	True alpine habitat occupies only 0.15% of the Australian land surface and has limited high altitude refuge. Warming in the Australian Alps has occurred at about 0.2°C per decade (Hennessy et al. 2008) and substantial declines in spring snow depth have occurred since the 1960s (Nicholls 2005). A "worst case scenario" modeled for 2050 (+2.9°C, -24% precipitation) projects substantial declines in snow cover (e.g. areas with more than 60 days per year of snow decline by 95%) (Hennessy et al. 2008). Disappearing snow cover will have dramatic effects on many species already considered rare and threatened, especially those mammals dependent on snow cover to protect them from predation (Pickering, Good and Green 2004). Other potential impacts include expansion of woody species to higher elevations at the expense of herbaceous plants, increased competition from lower elevation species (both native and exotic), increased fire, and increasing mismatches in the timing of life cycles, especially between key resources such as bogong moths and the species that depend on them. The brutal reality is that the alpine zone as we know it today, is unlikely to exist at all in a Four Degree World.
Non-alpine montane areas	Higher elevation peaks in areas such as the Wet Tropics of North Queensland, are biodiversity hotspots with extremely high species richness and endemism. Warming and the lifting of the cloud base will increase extinction risks of sensitive species. An increase of 3.5°C has been projected to result in complete loss of the bioclimate of 30 of the 65 vertebrate species and the remaining species to retain, on average, only 11% of current climatic habitat (Williams et al. 2003). Another study projects 74% of rainforest bird species will become threatened as a result of projected mid-range warming (Shoo, Williams and Hero 2005). Major impacts on the endemic invertebrate fauna are also projected (Wilson et al. 2007, Yeates, Bouchard and Monteith 2002). Any decline in rainfall will increase the risk of fires penetrating into rainforests. Physical damage from increases in tropical cyclone intensity will also affect recruitment and successional dynamics within the forests (Shoo et al. 2011, Stork et al. 2007).
Freshwater wetlands	Many freshwater species in Australia have evolved under conditions of high inter-annual and seasonal variability but continuing reductions in the quantity and quality of river flows in regions such as the Murray Darling Basin will have severe impacts, especially on breeding habitat for birds (e.g. Pittock and Finlayson 2011). Ongoing competition for water from agriculture and urban areas will exacerbate the threats.

Region/ecosystem	Projected impacts
Coastal fringe habitats	In Northern Australia, estuarine mangrove habitats have extended inland into low-lying areas, at the expense of freshwater swamps (Mulrennan and Woodroffe 1998) and ongoing rises in sea level will exacerbate this trend. In other regions, landward extension of mangrove, saltmarsh and rocky shore habitats are likely to be restricted by coastal development and topography. Physical damage from increased storm surges will also affect beaches, rocky shores, mangroves and saltmarsh. Changes in upstream river flows will alter the quality and quantity of detritus flowing into estuaries and near-shore communities, disrupting detritus-based food webs.
Mediterranean woodlands, shrublands & heathlands	Myers et al. (2000) identified the Mediterranean shrublands and woodlands of south west WA as one of 25 global biodiversity "hotspots". Many species are threatened, narrow-ranged endemics (e.g. 20% of woody plants, (Hopper and Gioia 2004) and exist close to thresholds of temperature and rainfall (Abbott and Le Maitre 2010). Sharp declines in winter rainfall since the 1970s have resulted in deterioration of water quantity and quality with impacts exacerbated by extensive clearing for agriculture and dryland salinity (Yates *et al.* 2010a, Yates *et al.* 2010b). Future interactions of climate change with the root fungus *Phytophthora* spp., which affects many southwest plant communities, remain unknown (Pritchard 2011).
Tropical savannas	The fire prone savanna-woodlands of Northern Australia are experiencing severe impacts from invasive weeds and feral animals. Widespread declines of the small mammal fauna (Woinarski *et al.* 2011) are evident. This ecosystem will be increasingly vulnerable from any ongoing intensification of fire cycles (Laurance *et al.* 2011).
Offshore islands	Australia's offshore islands, numbering over 8000, and ranging in size from less than 1 ha to over 500,000 ha are home to many restricted endemics, and already highly vulnerable from exotic species and are particularly vulnerable to loss of habitat from future sea level rise (Laurance *et al.* 2011).

Note
a Sources such as Hughes 2003, Hennessy et al., 2007, Steffen et al., 2009 Hughes 2011, Laurance et al., 2011 and Murphy et al., 2012 provide additional detail.

Impacts on ecosystems in the northern regions, however, are far more speculative because of the lack of agreement amongst climate models as to the direction and magnitude of rainfall change (CSIRO and BoM, 2007).

Can Australian species adapt?

The three main options available to species in the face of a rapidly changing environment are (i) to shift their distribution, and thus evade the change by moving elsewhere to more suitable conditions, (ii) to undergo genetic change, and (iii) to stay put and adapt *in situ* (Hughes, 2012). These three options are not mutually exclusive. Globally, many species are already responding to recent climate change, and these responses provide some clues as to future adaptive capacity (see Table 4.2; end of this chapter). Unfortunately the general lack of long-term datasets in Australia limits our understanding of autonomous adaptation by Australian species, but some general conclusions can be drawn.

Shifting ranges

As climate zones continue to shift across the landscape, a significant determinant of species' ability to cope will be the rate at which their distributions can 'keep up'. Velocities of climate change over the past 60 years calculated for the geographic ranges of Australian birds vary from 1–76km per decade, with mean rates of 7.7 and 7.6km per decade for temperature and rainfall respectively (Van Der Wal et al., 2012). These rates are commensurate with those observed for range shifts in some species in recent decades. A global meta-analysis by Parmesan and Yohe (2003), for example, found that terrestrial species had moved poleward by an average of 6.1km per decade. More recent estimates, however, found rates of range shift two to three times higher (16.9km per decade) (Chen et al., 2011), suggesting that species shifts may be accelerating. These two compilations, however, are overwhelmingly dominated by species from the Northern Hemisphere and it remains to be seen if Australian species are able to disperse as rapidly. Further, most of the species shifts reported are for mobile animals such as birds, butterflies and pelagic marine species, with few for mammals and reptiles, and even fewer for plants. As indicated above, the low topographic relief and arid interior of the continent will present formidable barriers to dispersal, as will the highly fragmented nature of the landscape. Hard limits to range shifts will also be particularly acute for species on mountaintops, small islands, or those whose ranges abut southern coastlines (Hughes, 2012).

Genetic change

Increased thermal stress and drought are likely to impose strong selective pressure on species. Species with short generation times, high reproductive output and substantial genetic variability within populations will have the greatest potential to adapt via natural selection. Some species have undergone changes in genetic composition consistent with responding to recent warming (Umina et al., 2005), but very few species have been studied in this respect (Hoffmann and Sgro, 2011). But simply assuming that short-lived species will be able to adapt quickly enough is simplistic. A recent study of 94 species of *Drosophila*, the poster species of rapid evolution research, found that climate adaptation by the fruit fly was slower than expected. It is also likely that many species with narrow geographic limits will have tightly constrained evolutionary limits of thermal tolerance (Kellermann et al., 2012).

Phenotypic plasticity

Changes in behaviour, especially in relation to the timing of life cycles, have been the most commonly observed responses to climatic change thus far. Compilations of hundreds of datasets for Northern Hemisphere species show consistent advances in the seasonal timing of biological events in all major taxonomic groups studied. Thackeray et al. (2010), for example, show that the timing of life cycles of UK species has, on average, advanced 0.39 days per year, over a period of warming of 0.04–0.05°C per year. While linear extrapolations from these trends are probably simplistic for most species, they do indicate that phenological advances in the order of a month or more for a 4°C warming are possible. Given that phenological responses are already known to be highly variable even among groups of closely related species, the potential for increasingly decoupled interactions between species (such as between plants and pollinators) is likely to be an important driver of community-level change. Observed changes consistent with having a climate change 'signal' are relatively few in Australia – once again presumably due to the paucity of data rather than because Australian species are responding differently from those elsewhere. Those that have been recorded, such as the earlier arrival and later departure of migratory birds (Beaumont, McAllan and Hughes, 2006), and earlier emergence of butterflies (Kearney et al., 2010a), are generally consistent in magnitude and direction with those elsewhere.

Conclusions: What could we lose?

Current global species extinction rates already exceed the highest rates seen in the fossil record (Barnosky et al., 2011). These extinctions are mostly attributed to habitat loss, invasive species and direct exploitation. However, recent climate change has already been linked to population-level extinctions and declines in terrestrial mammals, birds, lizards, butterflies and some plants (e.g. McLaughlin et al., 2002; Sinervo et al., 2010) and has likely contributed to the extinctions of about 80 tropical amphibians in Central and South America (Pounds et al., 2006; McMenamin and Hannah, 2012).

Loss of only those species already considered threatened would constitute a mass extinction event of a similar magnitude to the five previous extinction episodes in the earth's history (Barnosky et al., 2011). Most global estimates of future extinction rates are based on combining the projections of species distribution models using either species-area relationships (e.g. Thomas et al., 2004b), or endemic-area relationships (Malcolm et al., 2006). While there has been much debate over the validity of different methods, virtually all published estimates of future risk project far higher rates than those observed in the second half of the 20th century, which are already approximately two orders of magnitude higher than in the Cenozoic fossil record (Leadley et al., 2010a). For example, 20–30 per cent of plant and animal species assessed by the Fourth Assessment Report of the IPCC (Fischlin et al., 2007) were considered to be at increased risk of extinction if global temperature increases exceed 2–3°C. There remains a high level of uncertainty as to how these predictions could translate into realized rates of species loss, and at what rate this could occur (Leadley et al., 2010a). It is possible that the rates could be overestimates if species are able to find climatic refuge in spatially heterogenous environments or be underestimates because they do not take into account dispersal limitations, species interactions and the potential for tipping points in ecosystems to be exceeded. It is also important to note that the majority of most commonly reported estimates, such as that of Thomas et al. (2004), who projected 18–34 per cent of species to be at increased risk of extinction by 2050, used only mid-range climate scenarios that project up to 3°C warming, but not beyond to 4°C degrees or more.

Few Australian species have been studied in enough detail for credible projections to be made as to their future fate. Indeed the only generalization that can be made with a high degree of confidence is that every species will be affected differently. However, some broad ecological principles can be applied to help understand patterns of vulnerability. Species with low reproductive rates, poor dispersal ability, narrow geographic and/or climatic ranges, restricted genetic variation, specialized to a particular habitat or food source, reliant on a narrow range of other species and those otherwise rare or threatened by other stressors are likely to be the most vulnerable (Steffen et al., 2009).

Projections from species distribution models (see Table 4.2; end of this chapter) offer a fairly gloomy outlook for most species, consistently projecting future declines in species' ranges and increased risk of extinction, even when optimistic rates of dispersal are assumed: for instance, for West Australian banksias (Fitzpatrick et al., 2008), koalas (Adams-Hosking et al., 2011), northern macropods (Ritchie and Bolitho, 2008), native rats (Green, Stein and Driessen, 2008), the greater glider (Kearney, Wintle and Porter, 2010b), quokkas (Gibson et al., 2010) and platypus (Klamt, Thompson and Davis, 2011). For some species, the models indicate that loss of range may be driven primarily by rainfall rather than temperature.

Relatively few Australian studies of impacts on species specifically incorporate projections of 4°C warming or above. Williams, Bolitho and Fox (2003) modelled the impacts of temperature increases up to 7°C for endemic vertebrates in north Queensland, finding that at 3.5°C, 38–67 per cent of frogs, 48–80 per cent of mammals, 43–64 per cent of reptiles and 49–72 per cent of birds would be 'committed to extinction', with 85–90 per cent of their suitable habitat lost.

At 5°C, 57 endemic frogs and mammals were projected to lose their climatic habitat altogether, with a further 8 species endangered, and at 7°C, all endemic vertebrates in the region would lose their climatic habitat. Fitzpatrick et al. (2008) modeled 100 species of West Australian banksias and found that with warming of 4.2°C, 91–97 per cent (depending on assumptions about dispersal ability) would experience climatic range contractions, and 17–24 per cent would lose their climatic habitat completely.

Ecosystems do not exist in isolation from human systems and the fate of our biodiversity will also depend on social, demographic, economic and political factors over the next few decades. Australian population growth is one of the highest in the developed world (about 1.2 per cent per year), and Australia's population is projected to grow to 31–43 million by 2056 and to 34–62 million by 2100, depending on assumptions about fertility, lifespans and net immigration (ABS, 2008). Increasing demand for food, water and other resources will continue to pressure Australian biodiversity (SoE, 2011), as will other drivers of biodiversity loss, such as invasive species. New stresses flowing from climate change adaptation measures in other sectors, such as shifting agricultural patterns, changed hazard reduction policies and reallocation of river flows to promote water security for urban settlements, also have the potential to have negative impacts on ecosystems.

Global average warming of 4°C will make the earth's climate hotter than it has been during the period over which most present day species evolved. The prospect that stabilization of greenhouse gases will occur within a time frame to 'allow ecosystems to adapt naturally to climate change' (UNFCCC, Article 2) appears increasingly unlikely. Australia's rich biodiversity is already subject to multiple threats from human activities, and these threats are highly likely to intensify, leading to transformed landscapes, many of which will be biologically impoverished compared to present. This prospect alone should be motivation enough to drive an urgent transition to a low carbon economy within the present decade.

Note

1   A variety of methods have been used to project the impact of future climate on biodiversity in Australia and elsewhere. These include extrapolation from the paleo-record (especially of the last 10,000 years), species distribution modeling, controlled experiments altering CO_2 and temperature, transplant experiments, observations of biological change over the past few decades correlated with changing climate, and risk assessments based on existing understanding of life history attributes that may affect vulnerability, in combination with estimates of exposure to future change and predicted adaptive capacity. These approaches differ markedly in both the scale of application, and the picture they provide of the future (see Table 4.2).

Table 4.2

Credible assessments of the risks posed by climate change for the Australian biota are key to devising effective strategies to increase resilience and ameliorate negative impacts. The methods to assess such risks are diverse, including extrapolation of known past changes, both in the paleorecord and over the past few decades; modeling of potential changes in species distributions and community structure based on current relationships between ranges and environmental parameters; experimental manipulations both in the field and laboratory; and examination of community composition along latitudinal and elevational gradients. The messages these tools deliver are similarly wide ranging, but most project profound changes to the structure and function of ecological communities in the future, with substantially increased risks of species loss and declining ecosystem function.

Table 4.2 Examples of methods used to project the impacts of future climate change on species and ecosystems, summarizing some of the advantages and disadvantages of each

Tool	How it works	What it tells us	Advantages & disadvantages
Paleoecology: clues from the past	Uses fossil data to reconstruct how species and ecosystems responded to past climate changes.	"Greenhouse climates" in the past were generally not favourable for the persistence of species (Mayhew 2012) and even relatively slow climate changes have been associated with surprisingly abrupt regional change. Past climate change has been associated with large-scale shifts in biomes, species extinctions, and re-assortment of species assemblages creating novel communities (Williams and Jackson 2007). Species responded individualistically to climate change, with some able to disperse rapidly over long distances, while others expanding from small populations in climatic refugia.	While some examples of rapid warming occurred on regional scales within just a few decades and thus provide useful comparisons, no past changes are exact analogues of the change projected for the next century. Past responses of biota to climate also occurred in intact, unfragmented landscapes without human impacts.
Comparative phylogeography	Past climatic changes have driven changes in species distributions and these changes have left 'genetic signatures' in present day species and populations.	Parallel evolutionary patterns in different groups of species indicate common responses to past climatic fluctuations. In areas of relatively high geographic relief, species were able to disperse in response to climatic change. In areas of low relief, however, species are most likely to have persisted in the landscape within patchy, localized refugia, rather than moving long distances (Byrne 2007).	Phylogeographic comparisons are a useful complement to paleoecological studies based on fossils, especially in areas where the fossil record is incomplete.
Extrapolation from recently observed changes	Long term datasets of species phenology (life cycles), distributions, morphology, and physiology provide information on the sensitivity of species to climate change, and their ability to adapt.	Climate change over recent decades has affected species and ecosystems in all regions (Chen et al. 2011), (Thackeray et al. 2010). Changes have been observed in life cycles, distributions, genetic composition, morphology, and productivity (see (Steffen et al. 2009).	Long term datasets in Australia are relatively rare compared to the Northern Hemisphere, limiting investigation of climate sensitivity. Uncertainty remains about the role of non-climatic drivers, such as changes in fire, grazing and land-use. Extrapolation to future warming is limited by lack of understanding of the linearity of responses, and the wide variability displayed even by closely related species.

Tool	How it works	What it tells us	Advantages & disadvantages
Species distribution models (SDMs) (also known as environmental niche models, bioclimatic envelope models)	Models quantify the relationship between the known distribution of a species and various environmental parameters (climate, soils, topography) to describe the species' environmental "envelope" or niche. This relationship is then used to project potential species distributions in the future, given a specific climate projection.	SDMs have been the principal tool to predict future changes in species distributions. Most modeling outputs suggest substantial declines in ranges may occur, even under optimistic assumptions about the capacity of species to disperse. Estimates of extinction risk based on model output for multiple species, indicate substantial increases in the number of species at risk over next few decades (e.g. (Thomas et al. 2004a), (Warren et al. 2011).	SDMs have many well-discussed limitations (reviewed in Elith and Leathwick 2009), including the assumption that species and climate are in equilibrium, and that other factors, such as species interactions, are relatively unimportant in setting distributional boundaries. Despite these limitations, SDMs have successfully been used to simulate observed range shifts of some species (Pearman et al. 2008) and are considered a useful "first cut" tool within species risk assessments. SDMs are also increasingly being coupled with other models based on more detailed understanding of the demography or physiology of particular species (where data are available).
Process-based models	Include key demographic (such as growth, birth, death, dispersal) or physiological (such as diapause, germination) processes to simulate either community or population change.	The most widely applied models in the context of climate change are forest gap models that simulate long term dynamics of forest structure, biomass and composition in response to climate and other drivers (Bugmann 2001). Species-specific mechanistic models seek to describe the fundamental niche of a species (e.g. Kearney and Porter 2004).	Process-based models can provide credible projections of responses of vegetation stands or individual species but few have been applied to large numbers of species because they require either long-term data (in the case of plant populations) or detailed physiological and ecological understanding of the species of interest (Lavergne et al. 2010).
Dynamic Global Vegetation Models (DGVMs)	Simulate changes in vegetation and its associated hydrological and biogeochemical cycles as a response to changes in climate (Prentice, Harrison and Bartlein 2011).	Models project large-scale changes in biomes (broad vegetation types) in the future.	DGVMs are a powerful method to investigate the relationship between biome-level change and ecosystem services. Their limitations include poor representation of functional diversity *within* communities, lack of simulation of changes in land use or disturbances (except fire), and lack of information at species level. Inclusion of CO_2 effects can reverse the direction of the predictions generated (Loehle 2011) and differences between outputs of different models also contribute to uncertainties in their utility for planning.

Tool	How it works	What it tells us	Advantages & disadvantages
Experiments	Manipulations of temperature, water & CO_2 in laboratory and field conditions investigate potential impacts and their physiological basis. Free Air Carbon Dioxide Enrichment (FACE) experiments in which natural communities are treated with elevated CO_2 concentrations have been set up in many different vegetation types globally (although only in northern savanna and temperate grasslands in Australia).	Increased atmospheric CO_2 has a fertilizer effect on many plants, increasing photosynthetic rate and growth, provided that nutrients, water and light are not limiting. Many plants have greater water use efficiency (WUE) at high CO_2 although this varies between plants with different photosynthetic pathways. Reductions in nitrogen content relative to carbon in plants tissues affect nutritional and defensive qualities of plant tissues, with flow on impacts to herbivores. Plants grown under continuously elevated CO_2 may eventually acclimate, with a leveling off of growth rate. Increased WUE may mitigate drought stress up to a point. Differences in CO_2 responsiveness between species will alter both inter- and intra-specific competition, changing both the structure and function of plant communities. Warming of plant and soil communities under field conditions alters many aspects of their structure, composition, phenology, and function.	Elevated CO_2 experiments have increased our understanding of how climate change could affect many physiological and ecological processes. However, most experiments have been performed on small scales, on relatively young plants, over short time periods, with non-limiting nutrients, light and water, and in the absence of pathogens, herbivores and competitors (Hovenden and Williams 2009). Scaling up from these experiments to understand community and ecosystem-level effects remains a challenge. Impacts of elevated CO_2 have been investigated for relatively few native plant species in Australia (Hovenden & Williams 2009).
Gradient studies	Quantifying turnover of species distributions or community traits along naturally occurring environmental gradients, as a surrogate for future climatic change (space for time substitution).	Most ecological communities exhibit substantial species turnover along ecological gradients, indicating that climate change could result in rapid changes in the community composition (Andrew and Hughes 2007).	Interpretation of species turnover along temperature gradients can be confounded by other latitude-related changes, such as photoperiod, and seasonality, or elevation-related changes such as UV-radiation.

References

Abbott, I. and D. Le Maitre. 2010. Monitoring the impact of climate change on biodiversity: The challenge of megadiverse Mediterranean climate ecosystems. *Austral Ecology* 35: 406–22.

ABS. 2008. Regional Population Growth Australia. Catalogue No. 3218. 0. Canberra, Australian Bureau of Statistics.

Adams-Hosking, C., H. S. Grantham, J. R. Rhodes, C. McAlpine and P. T. Moss. 2011. Modelling climate-change-induced shifts in the distribution of the koala. *Wildlife Research* 38: 122–30.

Andrew, N. R. and L. Hughes. 2007. Potential host colonization by insect herbivores in a warmer climate: a transplant experiment. *Global Change Biology* 13: 1539–49.

Attiwill, P. and G. Leeper. 1987. *Forest soils and nutrient cycles.* Carlton, Melbourne University Press.

Barnosky, A. D., N. Matzke, S. Tomiya, G. O. U. Wogan, B. Swartz, T. B. Quental, C. Marshall, J. L. McGuire, E. L. Lindsey, K. C. Maguire, B. Mersey and E. A. Ferrer. 2011. Has the earth's sixth mass extinction already arrived? *Nature* 471: 51–7.

Beaumont, L. J., I. A. W. McAllan and L. Hughes. 2006. A matter of timing: changes in the first date of arrival and last date of departure of Australian migratory birds. *Global Change Biology* 12: 1339–54.

Beaumont, L. J., A. Pitman, S. Perkins, N. E. Zimmermann, N. G. Yoccoz and W. Thuiller. 2011. Impacts of climate change on the world's most exceptional ecoregions. *Proceedings of the National Academy of Sciences of the United States of America* 108: 2306–11.

Bowman, D. M. J. S. 2003. Bushfires: a Darwinian perspective. In G. Cary, D. B. Lindenmayer and S. Dovers (eds), *Australia Burning: Fire Ecology, Policy and Management Issues.* CSIRO Publishing: Melbourne.

Bugmann, H. 2001. A review of forest gap models. *Climatic Change* 51: 259–305.

Byrne, M. 2007. Phylogeography provides an evolutionary context for the conservation of a diverse and ancient flora. *Australian Journal of Botany* 55: 316–25.

Chen, I. C., J. K. Hill, R. Ohlemuller, D. B. Roy and C. D. Thomas. 2011. Rapid Range Shifts of Species Associated with High Levels of Climate Warming. *Science* 333: 1024–6.

CSIRO and BoM. 2007. Climate change in Australia. 140. CSIRO Bureau of Meteorology: Melbourne.

Dunlop, M., D. W. Hilbert, S. Ferrier, A. House, A. Liedloff, S. M. Prober, A. Smyth, T. G. Martin, T. Harwood, K. J. Williams, C. Fletcher and H. Murphy. 2012. *The Implications of Climate Change for Biodiversity Conservation and the National Reserve System: Final Synthesis.* A report prepared for the Department of Sustainability, Environment, Water, Population and Communities, and the Department of Climate Change and Energy Efficiency. CSIRO Climate Adaptation Flagship: Canberra.

Elith, J. and J. R. Leathwick. 2009. Species Distribution Models: Ecological Explanation and Prediction Across Space and Time. *Annual Review of Ecology Evolution and Systematics* 40: 677–97.

Fensham, R. J., R. J. Fairfax, D. W. Butler and D. Bowman. 2003. Effects of fire and drought in a tropical eucalypt savanna colonized by rain forest. *Journal of Biogeography* 30: 1405–14.

Fischlin, A., G. F. Midgley, J. T. Price, R. Leemans, B. Gopal, C. Turley, M. D. A. Rounsevell, O. P. Dube, J. Tarazona and A. A. Velichko. 2007. Ecosystems, their properties, goods, and services. In M. L. Parry, O. F. Canziani, J. P. Palutikof, P. J. van der Linden and C. E. Hanson (eds), *Climate Change 2007: Impacts, Adaptation and Vulnerability. Contribution of Working Group II to the Fourth Assessment Report of the Intergovernmental Panel on Climate Change*. Cambridge University Press: Cambridge, pp. 211–72.

Fitzpatrick, M. C., A. D. Gove, N. J. Sanders and R. R. Dunn. 2008. Climate change, plant migration, and range collapse in a global biodiversity hotspot: the *Banksia* (Proteaceae) of Western Australia. *Global Change Biology* 14: 1337–52.

Gibson, L., A. McNeill, P. de Tores, A. Wayne and C. Yates. 2010. Will future climate change threaten a range restricted endemic species, the quokka (*Setonix brachyurus*), in south west Australia? *Biological Conservation* 143: 2453–61.

Gonzalez, P., R. P. Neilson, J. M. Lenihan and R. J. Drapek. 2010. Global patterns in the vulnerability of ecosystems to vegetation shifts due to climate change. *Global Ecology and Biogeography* 19: 755–68.

Green, K., J. A. Stein and M. M. Driessen. 2008. The projected distributions of *Mastacomys fuscus* and *Rattus lutreolus* in south-eastern Australia under a scenario of climate change: potential for increased competition? *Wildlife Research* 35: 113–19.

Hennessy, K., B. Fitzharris, B. Bates, N. Harvey, M. Howden, L. Hughes, J. Salinger and R. Warrick. 2007. Australia and New Zealand. In M. Parry, O. Canziani, J. Palutikof, P. van der Linden and C. Hanson (eds), *Climate Change 2007: Impacts, Adaptation and Vulnerability. Contribution of Working Group II to the Fourth Assessment Report of the Intergovernmental Panel on Climate Change* Cambridge University Press: Cambridge, pp. 507–40.

Hennessy, K. J., P. H. Whetton, K. Walsh, I. N. Smith, J. M. Bathols, M. Hutchinson and J. Sharples. 2008. Climate change effects on snow conditions in mainland Australia and adaptation at ski resorts through snowmaking. *Climate Research* 35: 255–70.

Hoffmann, A. A. and C. M. Sgro. 2011. Climate change and evolutionary adaptation. *Nature* 470: 479–85.

Hopper, S. D. and P. Gioia. 2004. The Southwest Australian floristic region: evolution and conservation of a global hot spot of biodiversity. *Annual Review of Ecology and Systematics* 35: 623–50.

Hovenden, M. J. and A. L. Williams. 2009. The impacts of rising CO_2 concentrations on Australian terrestrial species and ecosystems. *Austral Ecology* 35: 665–84.

Hughes, L. 2003. Climate change and Australia: trends, projections and impacts. *Austral Ecology* 28: 423–43.

Hughes, L. 2011. Climate change and Australia: key vulnerable regions. *Regional Environmental Change* 11: S189–95.

Hughes, L. 2012. Can Australian biodiversity adapt to climat change? In D. Lunney and P. Hutchings (eds), *Wildlife and climate change: towards robust strategies for Australian fauna*. Royal Zoological Society of Australia: Mosman, pp. 8–10.

Hughes, L., E. M. Cawsey and M. Westoby. 1996. Climatic range sizes of eucalyptus species in relation to future climate change. *Global Ecology and Biogeography Letters* 5: 23–9.

Johnson, C. 2006. *Australia's mammal extinctions*. Cambridge University Press: Cambridge.

Kearney, M. and W. P. Porter. 2004. Mapping the fundamental niche: physiology, climate, and the distribution of a nocturnal lizard. *Ecology* 85: 3119–31.

Kearney, M. R., N. J. Briscoe, D. J. Karoly, W. P. Porter, M. Norgate and P. Sunnucks. 2010a. Early emergence in a butterfly causally linked to anthropogenic warming. *Biology Letters* 6: 674–7.

Kearney, M. R., B. A. Wintle and W. P. Porter. 2010b. Correlative and mechanistic models of species distribution provide congruent forecasts under climate change. *Conservation Letters* 3: 203–13.

Kellermann, V., J. Overgaard, A. A. Hoffmann, C. Flojgaard, J. C. Svenning and V. Loeschcke. 2012. Upper thermal limits of *Drosophila* are linked to species distributions and strongly constrained phylogenetically. *Proceedings of the National Academy of Sciences of the United States of America* 109: 16228–33.

Klamt, M., R. Thompson and J. Davis. 2011. Early response of the platypus to climate warming. *Global Change Biology* 17: 3011–18.

Laurance, W. F., B. Dell, S. M. Turton, M. J. Lawes, L. B. Hutley, H. McCallum, P. Dale, M. Bird, G. Hardy, G. Prideaux, B. Gawne, C. R. McMahon, R. Yu, J. M. Hero, L. Schwarzkop, A. Krockenberger, M. Douglas, E. Silvester, M. Mahony, K. Vella, U. Saikia, C. H. Wahren, Z. H. Xu, B. Smith and C. Cocklin. 2011. The 10 Australian ecosystems most vulnerable to tipping points. *Biological Conservation* 144: 1472–80.

Lavergne, S., N. Mouquet, W. Thuiller and O. Ronce. 2010. Biodiversity and Climate Change: Integrating Evolutionary and Ecological Responses of Species and Communities. *Annual Review of Ecology, Evolution, and Systematics* 41: 321–50.

Leadley, P., H. N. Pereira, R. Alkemade, J. F. Fernandez-Manjarres, V. Proenca, J. P. W. Scharlemann and M. J. Walpole. 2010a. Biodiversity scenarios: projections of 21st century change in biodiversity and associated ecosystem services. Montreal, Technical Series 50.

Leadley, P., H. N. Periera, R. Alkemade, J. F. Fernandez-Manjarres, V. Proenca, J. P. W. Scharlemann and M. J. Walpole. 2010b. Biodiversity scenarios: projections of 21st century change in biodiversity and associated ecosystem services. Montreal, Technical Series 50.

Lehmann, C. E. R. and L. Hughes. In review. Soil fertility influences the flammability of vegetation through multiple and mutually reinforcing routes. PLoS One.

Lindenmayer, D. B. 2007. *On Borrowed Time: Australia's Environmental Crisis and What We Must Do About It.* Penguin: Melbourne.

Loarie, S. R., P. B. Duffy, H. Hamilton, G. P. Asner, C. B. Field and D. D. Ackerly. 2009. The velocity of climate change. *Nature* 462: 1052–U111.

Loehle, C. 2011. Criteria for assessing climate change impacts on ecosystems. *Ecology and Evolution.* doi:10.1002/ece3.7.

Malcolm, J. R., C. R. Liu, R. P. Neilson, L. Hansen and L. Hannah. 2006. Global warming and extinctions of endemic species from biodiversity hotspots. *Conservation Biology* 20: 538–48.

Mayhew, P. J. 2012. Extinctions in deep time. In L. Hannah (ed.), *Saving a Million Species: Extinction Risk from Climate Change.* Island Press: Washington, DC, pp. 141–56.

McLaughlin, J. F., J. J. Hellmann, C. L. Boggs and P. R. Ehrlich. 2002. Climate change hastens population extinctions. *Proceedings of the National Academy of Sciences of the United States of America* 99: 6070–74.

McMenamin, S. K. and L. Hannah. 2012. First extinctions on land. In L. Hannah (ed.), *Saving a million species: extinction risk from climate change.* Island Press: Washington, DC, pp. 89–102.

MEA. 2005. *Millenium Ecosystem Assessment: Ecosystems and Human Well-Being: Synthesis.* Island Press: Washington, DC.

Mittermeier, R., P. Gil and C. Mittermeier. 2007. *Megadiversity: Earth's Biologically Wealthiest Nations.* Conservation International, Cemex.

Mulrennan, M. E. and C. D. Woodroffe. 1998. Saltwater intrusion into the coastal plains of the Lower Mary River, Northern Territory, Australia. *Journal of Environmental Management* 54: 169–88.

Murphy, H., A. Liedloff, R. J. Williams, K. J. Williams and M. Dunlop. 2012. Queensland's biodiversity under climate change: terrestrial ecosystems. In *CSIRO Climate Adaptation Flagship Working Paper 12C.*

Myers, N., R. A. Mittermeier, C. G. Mittermeier, G. A. B. da Fonseca and J. Kent. 2000. Biodiversity hotspots for conservation priorities. *Nature* 403: 853–8.

Nicholls, N. 2005. Climate variability, climate change and the Australian snow season. *Australian Meteorological Magazine* 54: 177–85.

O'Donnell, J., R. V. Gallagher, P. D. Wilson, P. O. Downey, L. Hughes and M. R. Leishman. 2012. Invasion hotspots for non-native plants in Australia under current and future climates. *Global Change Biology* 18: 617–29.

Olson, D. M. and E. Dinerstein. 2002. The global 200: Priority ecoregions for global conservation. *Annals of the Missouri Botanical Garden* 89: 199–224.

Orians, G. H. and A. V. Milewski. 2007. Ecology of Australia: the effects of nutrient-poor soils and intense fires. *Biological Reviews* 82: 393–423.

Pearman, P. B., C. F. Randin, O. Broennimann, P. Vittoz, W. O. van der Knaap, R. Engler, G. Le Lay, N. E. Zimmermann and A. Guisan. 2008. Prediction of plant species distributions across six millennia. *Ecology Letters* 11: 357–69.

Pickering, C., R. Good and K. Green. 2004. Potential effects of global warming on the biota of the Australian Alps. Australian Greenhouse Office: Canberra.

Pittock, J. and C. M. Finlayson. 2011. Australia's Murray–Darling Basin: freshwater ecosystem conservation options in an era of climate change. *Marine and Freshwater Research* 62: 232–43.

Pounds, J. A., M. R. Bustamante, L. A. Coloma, J. A. Consuegra, M. P. L. Fogden, P. N. Foster, E. La Marca, K. L. Masters, A. Merino-Viteri, R. Puschendorf, S. R. Ron, G. A. Sanchez-Azofeifa, C. J. Still and B. E. Young. 2006. Widespread amphibian extinctions from epidemic disease driven by global warming. *Nature* 439: 161–7.

Prentice, I. C., S. P. Harrison and P. J. Bartlein. 2011. Global vegetation and terrestrial carbon cycle changes after the last ice age. *New Phytologist* 189: 988–98.

Pritchard, S. G. 2011. Soil organisms and global climate change. *Plant Pathology* 60: 82–99.

Ritchie, E. G. and E. E. Bolitho. 2008. Australia's savanna herbivores: bioclimatic distributions and an assessment of the potential impact of regional climate change. *Physiological and Biochemical Zoology* 81: 88090.

Scheffer, M., J. Bascompte, W. A. Brock, V. Brovkin, S. R. Carpenter, V. Dakos, H. Held, E. H. van Nes, M. Rietkerk and G. Sugihara. 2009. Early-warning signals for critical transitions. *Nature* 461: 53–9.

Scheffer, M. and S. R. Carpenter. 2003. Catastrophic regime shifts in ecosystems: linking theory to observation. *Trends in Ecology & Evolution* 18: 648–56.

Scholze, M., W. Knorr, N. W. Arnell and I. C. Prentice. 2006. A climate-change risk analysis for world ecosystems. *Proceedings of the National Academy of Sciences of the United States of America* 103: 13116–20.

Shoo, L. P., C. Storlie, J. Vanderwal, J. Little and S. E. Williams. 2011. Targeted protection and restoration to conserve tropical biodiversity in a warming world. *Global Change Biology* 17: 186–93.

Shoo, L. P., S. E. Williams and J. M. Hero. 2005. Climate warming and the rainforest birds of the Australian wet tropics: using abundance data as a sensitive predictor of change in total population size. *Biological Conservation* 125: 335–3.

Sinervo, B., F. Mendez-de-la-Cruz, D. B. Miles, B. Heulin, E. Bastiaans, M. V. S. Cruz, R. Lara-Resendiz, N. Martinez-Mendez, M. L. Calderon-Espinosa, R. N. Meza-Lazaro, H. Gadsden, L. J. Avila, M. Morando, I. J. De la Riva, P. V. Sepulveda, C. F. D.

Rocha, N. Ibarguengoytia, C. A. Puntriano, M. Massot, V. Lepetz, T. A. Oksanen, D. G. Chapple, A. M. Bauer, W. R. Branch, J. Clobert and J. W. Sites. 2010. Erosion of lizard diversity by climate change and altered thermal niches. *Science* 328: 894–9.

SoE. 2011. State of the Environment 2011. Independent report to the Australian Government Minister for Sustainability, Environment, Water, Population and Communities. Australian State of the Environment Committee: Canberra.

Specht, R. L. and A. Specht. 1999. Nutrient deficiencies. In *Australian Plant Communities: Dynamics of Structure, Growth and Biodiversity*. Oxford University Press: Oxford, pp. 277–301.

Steffen, W., A. Burbidge, L. Hughes, R. Kitching, D. Lindenmayer, W. Musgrave, M. Stafford Smith and P. Werner. 2009. *Australia's biodiversity and climate change*. CSIRO: Collingwood.

Stork, N. E., J. Balston, G. D. Farquhar, P. J. Franks, J. A. M. Holtum and M. J. Liddell. 2007. Tropical rainforest canopies and climate change. *Austral Ecology* 32: 105–12.

Thackeray, S. J., T. H. Sparks, M. Frederiksen, S. Burthe, P. J. Bacon, J. R. Bell, M. S. Botham, T. M. Brereton, P. W. Bright, L. Carvalho, T. Clutton-Brock, A. Dawson, M. Edwards, J. M. Elliott, R. Harrington, D. Johns, I. D. Jones, J. T. Jones, D. I. Leech, D. B. Roy, W. A. Scott, M. Smith, R. J. Smithers, I. J. Winfield and S. Wanless. 2010. Trophic level asynchrony in rates of phenological change for marine, freshwater and terrestrial environments. *Global Change Biology* 16: 3304–13.

Thomas, C. D., A. Cameron, R. E. Green, M. Bakkenes, L. J. Beaumont, Y. C. Collingham, B. F. N. Erasmus, M. F. de Siqueira, A. Grainger, L. Hannah, L. Hughes, B. Huntley, A. S. van Jaarsveld, G. F. Midgley, L. Miles, M. A. Ortega-Huerta, A. T. Peterson, O. L. Phillips and S. E. Williams. 2004a. Extinction risk from climate change. *Nature* 427: 145–8.

Thomas, C. D., S. E. Williams, A. Cameron, R. E. Green, M. Bakkenes, L. J. Beaumont, Y. C. Collingham, B. F. N. Erasmus, M. F. de Siqueira, A. Grainger, L. Hannah, L. Hughes, B. Huntley, A. S. van Jaarsveld, G. F. Midgley, L. Miles, M. A. Ortega-Huerta, A. T. Peterson and O. L. Phillips. 2004b. Biodiversity conservation – uncertainty in predictions of extinction risk – effects of changes in climate and land use – climate change and extinction risk – reply. *Nature* 430.

Umina, P. A., A. R. Weeks, M. R. Kearney, S. W. McKechnie and A. A. Hoffmann. 2005. A rapid shift in a classic clinal pattern in *Drosophila* reflecting climate change. *Science* 308: 691–3.

Warren, R., J. Price, A. Fischlin, S. D. Santos and G. Midgley. 2011. Increasing impacts of climate change upon ecosystems with increasing global mean temperature rise. *Climatic Change* 106: 141–77.

Whetton, P. L., D. Karoly, I. Watterson, L. Webb, F. Drost, D. Kirono and K. McInnes, 2013. Australia's climate in a Four Degree World. In P. Christoff (ed.), *Four Degrees of Climate Change: Australia in a Hot World*. Earthscan: London, ch. 2.

Williams, J. W. and S. T. Jackson. 2007. Novel climates, no-analog communities, and ecological surprises. *Frontiers in Ecology and the Environment* 5: 475–82.

Williams, R., R. Bradstock, G. Cary, N. Enright, A. Gill, A. Leidloff, C. Lucas, R. Whelan, A. Andersen, D. Bowman, P. Clarke, G. Cook, K. Hennessy and A. York. 2009a. Interactions between fire and climate change, fire regimes and biodiversity in Australia – a preliminary assessment. Canberra.

Williams, R. J., R. A. Bradstock, G. J. Cary, N. J. Enright, A. Gill, M,, A. C. Leidloff, C. Lucas, R. Whelan, A. N. Andersen, D. M. J. S. Bowman, P. J. Clarke, G. D. Cook, K. Hennessy and A. York. 2009b. Interactions between climate change, fire regimes and biodiversity in Australia: a preliminary assessment. Canberra, Report to the Department of Climate Change and Department of the Environment, Heritage and Arts.

Williams, S. E., E. E. Bolitho and S. Fox. 2003. Climate change in Australian tropical rainforests: an impending environmental catastrophe. *Proceedings of the Royal Society of London Series B – Biological Sciences* 270: 1887–92.

Wilson, R., J. Trueman, S. Williams and D. Yeates. 2007. Altitudinally restricted communities of Schizophoran flies in Queensland's wet tropics: vulnerability to climate change. *Biodiversity and Conservation* 16: 3163–77.

Woinarski, J. C. Z., S. Legge, J. A. Fitzsimons, B. J. Traill, A. A. Burbidge, A. Fisher, R. S. C. Firth, I. J. Gordon, A. D. Griffiths, C. N. Johnson, N. L. McKenzie, C. Palmer, I. Radford, B. Rankmore, E. G. Ritchie, S. Ward and M. Ziembicki. 2011. The disappearing mammal fauna of northern Australia: context, cause, and response. *Conservation Letters* 4: 192–201.

Yates, C. J., J. Elith, A. M. Latimer, D. Le Maitre, G. F. Midgley, F. M. Schurr and A. G. West. 2010a. Projecting climate change impacts on species distributions in megadiverse South African Cape and Southwest Australian Floristic Regions: opportunities and challenges. *Austral Ecology* 35: 374–91.

Yates, C. J., A. McNeill, J. Elith and G. F. Midgley. 2010b. Assessing the impacts of climate change and land transformation on *Banksia* in the South West Australian Floristic Region. *Diversity and Distributions* 16: 187–201.

Yeates, D. K., P. Bouchard and G. B. Monteith. 2002. Patterns and levels of endemism in the Australian Wet Tropics rainforest: evidence from flightless insects. *Invertebrate Systematics* 16: 605–19.

5 Australia's marine resources in a warm, acid ocean

Ove Hoegh-Guldberg, Elvira Poloczanska and Anthony Richardson

Introduction

One of the distinguishing features of our planet is the presence of an ocean that covers 71 per cent of its surface. This vast ocean nurtured life's beginnings and continues to support the biosphere and ultimately humanity. Approximately a quarter of the world's population lives along coastlines where people extract food, building materials, energy, cultural significance and income (Seto and Shepherd, 2009). Oceans are also important in connecting and transporting people and materials over great distances through coastal and ocean-going shipping. In the current period of rapid global change, oceans play a critical role by absorbing around 30 per cent of the carbon dioxide from anthropogenic sources and over 90 per cent of the heat generated by the associated enhanced greenhouse effect (IPCC, 2007). Without the ocean, climate change would be far more severe than it is today.

Australia is a maritime country with sovereign rights over an ocean territory that covers 16 million km^2 – almost twice the size of its land area. This ocean area supports industries which are extremely valuable to Australia and yield economic wealth estimated as $A42 billion per annum while the ecosystem services provided by Australia's oceans may yield a further $25 billion per annum (AIMS, 2012). Recreational fishing (supported by over $A3.3 billion in boat purchases alone), surfing (for instance, worth $A126–233 million per annum merely along Queensland's Gold Coast) and Great Barrier Reef tourism (which generates over $A6 billion per annum) are a few examples of the direct benefits that marine resources provide to the Australian economy (Poloczanska et al., 2007). In addition to the direct financial benefits to the Australian economy, our marine ecosystems also provide a wide array of other values, including social and lifestyle benefits, and indirect yet critically important services such as coastal protection, shoreline stabilization, greenhouse gas regulation, nutrient recycling and the maintenance of water quality (Poloczanska et al., 2007, Martinez et al., 2007).

Marine resources play an important role regionally. Many countries in the Asia and the Indo-Pacific region have large populations that reside along their coasts (Martinez et al., 2007). For instance, over 60 per cent of Indonesia's population lives along its 95,181 km of coastline (Hoegh-Guldberg et al., 2009), a proportion which increases to around 95 per cent for the island countries of the Indo-Pacific (CIA, 2010). Marine resources, consequently, are central to the well-being and food security of people throughout South-East Asia and the Indo-Pacific region. Risks posed by climate change to the economies, livelihoods and security of the region will impact Australia, given Australia's economic and development role in the South Pacific region.

Human impacts on marine environments and ecosystems

Despite the overriding importance of oceans and coasts to people, the world's coastal areas are rapidly degrading as result of human activities (Boesch et al., 2001; Boesch, 2002; Kremer et al., 2005). Human settlement, deforestation and agriculture along coastal areas have resulted in greater amounts of sediment, nutrients, pesticides and herbicides entering coastal waters. These additions to the coastal systems have consequently modified coastal marine ecosystems and contributed to algal blooms and the problematic outbreak of organisms such as the Crown of Thorns Starfish (Brodie et al., 2005; 2012). An increase in the movement of solid waste, plastics and toxins into coastal waters has further added to the degradation of coastal marine ecosystems (Shannon et al., 2011).

Expanding coastal populations have increased the extraction of fish and other organisms in many parts of the world to unsustainable levels (Pauly et al., 1998; Jackson et al., 2001; Pauly et al., 2003; Jackson, 2010,). As a result, fisheries have subsequently experienced dramatic decreases in abundance, with many fisheries collapsing. While these impacts have had serious implications for livelihoods and industry, the loss of ecologically important species such as herbivorous fish has also resulted in large-scale changes in the ecological structure and function of coral reefs (Hughes, 1994; Jackson et al., 2001). When combined with pollution and deteriorating water quality, these changes have transformed coastlines and subsequently reduced the well-being of coastal people. While Australia is in a good position to reduce and possibly reverse many of these human related impacts on its coastal regions, many countries, particularly many in SE Asia and the Indo-Pacific, have far less capacity to do so (Hoegh-Guldberg et al., 2009).

The impacts on marine ecosystems of pollution, unsustainable coastal development and overexploitation of fisheries are occurring under large-scale and fundamental changes to the physical and chemical properties of the ocean. The impacts and ramifications of these changes, however, are poorly understood or described. Particularly important is the likelihood that many of the changes arising from anthropogenic climate change will interact synergistically (Crain et al., 2008; Griffith et al., 2012) and amplify the sole influence of variables such as declining water quality, degrading coastal areas and overexploitation of marine organisms and ecosystems.

The impact of warming and acidifying ocean waters

Rising atmospheric CO_2 levels have resulted in a steady increase in the heat content of the upper 700m of the ocean, with a resulting 0.5°C increase in the average surface temperature of the ocean during the 20th century (IPCC, 2007; Levitus et al., 2012). Uptake of anthropogenic CO_2 has also resulted in the ocean becoming more acidic (as measured by decreasing pH), which has reduced the concentration of carbonate ions. Carbonate ions are part of the raw material that is used to make the calcium carbonate skeletons of many marine organisms including corals, molluscs and a range of marine plants. There is growing evidence that relatively minor perturbations in ocean carbonate chemistry could lead to profound changes in the carbon cycle, marine food webs and nutrient cycles with potential impacts on economically important fisheries (Doney et al., 2009).

Since the Industrial Revolution, the pH of the world's ocean waters has decreased by 0.1 pH units, which has caused a 30 per cent decrease in the concentration of carbonate ions (Caldeira and Wickett, 2003). These changes are rapidly approaching conditions that are unprecedented in the last million years at least (Raven et al., 2005, Pelejero et al., 2010). Changes to ocean heat content are also increasing sea levels, intensifying storm systems, changing ocean mixing and ventilation, wind patterns and currents, melting sea ice and the distribution of clouds and solar radiation (IPCC, 2007; Hoegh-Guldberg and Bruno, 2010).

Conditions are also changing rapidly within Australian waters. Sea surface temperatures (from the upper layers of the ocean) have increased by approximately 1°C since 1900, with some of the warmest temperatures being seen along half of Australia's coastline in 2010 (Braganza et al, 2013, Chapter 2, this volume). Monitoring of ocean alkalinity within Australia's tropical waters has revealed a downward trend in pH and carbonate ion concentrations similar to that seen globally (Tilbrook et al., 2011). Atmospheric warming has led to changes to ocean currents, such as the strengthening of the East Australian Current, which corresponds to a southward shift in sea surface climatology in south-eastern waters of around 3 degrees latitude or 350km over 1944–2002 (Ridgway et al., 2008). Sea levels around Australia have risen as the volume of the ocean has expanded as a result of heating and the increased addition of glacial water. As result, the risk of coastal inundation has increased, particularly in combination with extreme storm events (Church and White, 2006). The range of conditions that will influence marine environments around Australia are summarized in Figure 5.1.

Biological responses to recent climate change

Changes in the physical and chemical nature of the world's oceans are driving fundamental changes to marine ecosystems (Hoegh-Guldberg and Bruno, 2010). While oceans and marine ecosystems have not received the attention

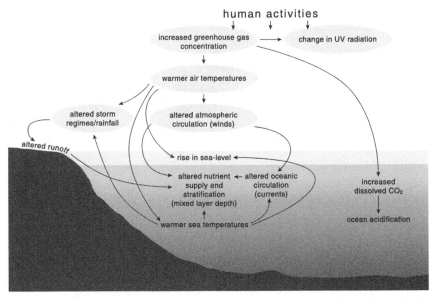

Figure 5.1   Key chemical and physical changes in the atmosphere and oceans as a result
      of climate change

Source: Poloczanska et al., 2007

afforded land-based ecosystems (Richardson and Poloczanska, 2008), there is now a growing literature describing changes in the distribution and abundance of marine species and communities, the loss of habitat forming species such as coral reefs and mangroves, and changes to marine ecosystem structures and processes (Hoegh-Guldberg and Bruno, 2010). These changes are largely consistent with the expected direction and intensity of climate change (Figure 5.2). Impacts relating to climate change have been observed via the responses of hundreds of different species and numerous fundamental ecosystem processes, such as primary productivity and the flow of energy and nutrients through trophic levels. Organisms as different as phytoplankton, zooplankton, fish and seabirds have shifted their distributions polewards and advances in reproductive timing during spring have been observed in many systems (Poloczanska et al., 2007). Warming of the upper ocean layers has also led to an increase in stratification (with a corresponding reduction in nutrient availability), which has further reduced the primary productivity of the least productive areas of the ocean. As a result, oligotrophic (low nutrient) gyres in the Pacific and Indian Ocean have increased by 6.6 million km^2 or 15 per cent over the period 1998 to 2006 (Polovina et al., 2008). The changes that are being seen throughout out the world's oceans are extensive and fundamental (Figure 5.2).

Australian marine ecosystems are revealing an increasing number of biological responses to changes in ocean temperature and ocean chemistry (for details

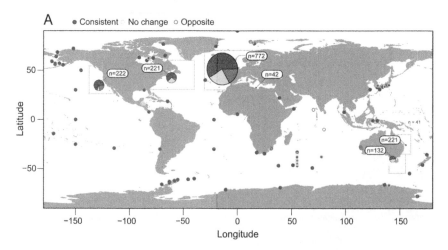

Figure 5.2 Locations where marine climate change impacts have been observed

Source: Poloczanska et al., 2013

Note

a Derived from 208 studies of 857 species of assemblages containing 1,735 individual
   observations. Pie charts used in regions bounded by dotted lines.

see Report Cards of Marine Climate Change in Australia, www.oceanclimate
change.org.au). For example, temperate macroalgae (seaweed) are retreating
from warmer waters on both the east and west coastlines (Wernberg et al., 2011)
and increases of warm-water fish species in south-east waters indicate the distribution of these organisms is shifting (Last et al., 2010). Extreme temperatures are
driving die-backs of coastal marine plants and animals as extremely warm days
affect intertidal and shallow water organisms and communities (Poloczanska et
al., 2007). Similarly, anomalously warm sea temperatures driven by high levels
of insolation during still conditions can have a big impact on organisms such as
coral reefs (Hoegh-Guldberg, 1999). For example, small increases in sea temperature (1–3°C) above the long-term summer maxima for even a few weeks can
cause mass coral bleaching. Coral bleaching is the breakdown of the symbiosis
between corals and dinoflagellates (*Symbiodinium*), the latter of which are critically important for trapping solar energy and providing energy and nutrients to
the coral host.

Mass coral bleaching across hundreds and sometimes thousands of km[2] has
been seen regularly on the Great Barrier Reef since the early 1980s, with no
reports of mass coral bleaching appearing in the scientific literature (or elsewhere
globally) prior to this time. The two most widespread events (triggered by seas
being 1–3°C above the long-term maxima for over a month) affected 50 per cent
of reefs within the Great Barrier Reef in 1998 and 2002 Berkelmans et al. 2004).
The relationship between mass coral bleaching and elevated sea temperature has
been extensively verified in laboratory and field studies, and is so reliable that

satellites flown by NASA and NOAA can reliably predict when and where mass coral bleaching is likely to occur by tracking sea surface temperature anomalies (Strong et al., 1997; Eakin et al., 2010; Strong et al., 2011). While the amount of mortality following mass bleaching events on the Great Barrier Reef has been relatively low (<10 per cent per event), observations from other Australian reefs (e.g. Scott Reef, Hoegh-Guldberg, 1999) and internationally (Wilkinson and Hodgson, 1999) reveal that coral reefs that experience elevated temperatures for longer (e.g. 1–3°C for a month or more) tend to have mortalities that may exceed 90 per cent of the corals on the reef. Heat stress events have also been accompanied by changes in ocean pH and carbonate ion concentrations (ocean acidification). While it is not possible to precisely identify the environmental factor responsible, the observation of declining coral calcification since 1990 (unprecedented in 400 years of coral core record examined) suggests that changing ocean conditions are beginning to impact on central processes such as calcification (De'ath et al., 2009). Recently, observations of slowing coral growth have been joined by rigorous long-term observations that show that the Great Barrier Reef has lost approximately 50 per cent of its coral populations since the early 1980s (De'ath et al., 2012). This is an extraordinary situation given that the Great Barrier Reef is one of the most pristine and best-managed coral reefs in the world.

Other factors, for example the changing characteristics of currents such as the East Australian Current (EAC), are being identified with an increasing number of changes within marine ecosystems such as the appearance and increased abundance of warm-water zooplankton, fish and benthic invertebrate species off eastern Tasmania (Pitt et al., 2010; Last et al., 2010; Johnson et al., 2011). One of the most striking examples is the southward movement of the sea urchin *Centrostephanus rodgersii* into Tasmanian coastal waters over the past several decades. Populations have expanded along the Tasmanian coast as a result of the transportation of larvae across the Bass Strait due to the strengthening of the EAC over the past several decades and rapid warming of coastal waters in northern Tasmania (Johnson et al., 2005). *C. rodgersii* is a voracious herbivore which has begun to change the structure of Tasmanian kelp communities, with negative ramifications for coastal biodiversity, and industries such as abalone and lobster fisheries (Ling, 2008). The scientific literature reveals that Australian marine organisms and ecosystems are changing extensively, rapidly and fundamentally in response to climate change (see Poloczanska et al., 2007 and Johnson et al., 2011, for more detailed information).

How can we know the future and what will the ocean be like in a Four Degree World?

The observation of extensive, rapid and fundamental changes to Australian marine ecosystems after a 0.7°C increase in the average global temperature raises concern about what will happen if average global temperatures rise to 4°C and beyond. Before answering this question, it is instructive to review how ecologists interested in climate change construct scenarios of the future and identify the nature of the uncertainties involved. As part of this exploration, the Great Barrier Reef will be used as an example of the types of impacts and scenarios that are likely if we continue along the pathway to a Four Degree World. This type of approach has also been extended to coral reefs in the South East Asian and Indo-Pacific regions (e.g. Hoegh-Guldberg, 2000; Hoegh-Guldberg et al., 2009).

Three types of information are used to construct ecosystem scenarios. The first involves an in-depth understanding of the physiological tolerance of marine organisms to key variables (e.g. sea temperature, alkalinity) that are changing as the climate changes. This field of science is often referred to as 'stress biology' and has a long history, stretching back to the beginnings of research fields such as physiological ecology. The central paradigm of these fields is that organisms are adapted to perform optimally within specific environments. Understanding limits to their ability to tolerate environmental variability is extremely important. Generally, organisms adjust their physiological behaviour to optimise their operation within a 'coping range', which is defined by upper and lower thresholds, beyond which organisms experience reduced performance and ultimately increased mortality. For example, reef-building corals undergo coral bleaching in laboratory experiments when they are exposed to temperatures 1–3°C above regional summer temperatures (Hoegh-Guldberg and Smith, 1989; Glynn and D'croz, 1990). This allows important insights into what might happen if seas surrounding reef-building corals increase another 1°C or more beyond today.

The output of these experimental studies links directly to the observations of how organisms and ecosystems respond to environmental change under field conditions. Typically, this second type of information provides a more subtle insight into the complex changes that are likely under changes to environmental conditions. Going back to the example of coral reefs, the laboratory-based conclusion that reef-building corals are sensitive to small temperature excursions (1– 3°C) above the average summer maxima has been verified through field observations that show that mass coral bleaching events occur under similar levels of heat stress in the field (Strong et al., 1997; Hoegh-Guldberg, 1999 ; Wilkinson and Hodgson, 1999). In addition to these types of observations, there is also value in looking at the current distribution of coral reefs relative to environmental factors (Kleypas et al., 1999). In this case, field evidence also identifies potential combinations of environmental factors which limit the distribution of a particular type of organism or community.

The last type of information that is used to construct scenarios involves projections of how environmental conditions are likely to change. In this respect, outputs of the community of General Circulation Models (GCMs) are invaluable for constructing perspectives on how key environmental variables within the environments are likely to change and a range of possible futures can be explored (IPCC, 2007). This is especially powerful if multiple models are used (e.g. CMIP5 models, Taylor et al., 2012). Combining this type of information has led to the conclusion that coral reefs such as the Great Barrier

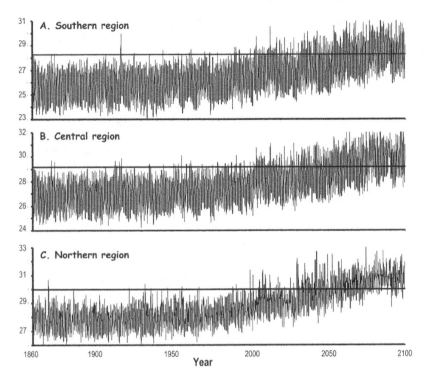

Figure 5.3 Sea temperature data on coral reefs at the northern end of the Great Barrier Reef from 1860 and projected to 2100

Source: Hoegh-Guldberg, 1999

Notes
a The northern end of the Great Barrier Reef = 11°S,143°E.
b Data generated by a GCM model (ECHAM4/OPYC3).
c Temperatures were generated for each month from 1860 to 2100, and were forced by a doubling of CO_2 in the atmosphere (~560 ppm). The horizontal line is the average threshold for bleaching at northern sites of the Great Barrier Reef.
d Full details to be found at Hoegh-Guldberg (1999).

Reef are in serious risk of losing their abundant reef-building coral communities (Figure 5.3), if society continues to pollute the atmosphere with carbon dioxide and other greenhouse gases (Hoegh-Guldberg, 1999; Done et al., 2003; Donner et al., 2005). These perspectives gain further credibility when new field observations (e.g. 40–50 per cent decline in coral cover on the Great Barrier Reef since 1980 – Bruno and Selig, 2007; Hughes et al., 2011; De'ath et al., 2012) are highly consistent with model projections.

The most recent studies (Frieler et al., 2012), based on the latest ensembles of climate models (Taylor et al., 2012), are very consistent with the conclusion of earlier studies (Hoegh-Guldberg, 1999; Done et al., 2003; Donner et al.,

2005) that the majority of existing coral reef ecosystems are likely to disappear in average global temperature rises much above 1.5°C above the preindustrial values. These studies are also complemented by similar conclusions for the Indian Ocean (Sheppard, 2003), Pacific Ocean (Hoegh-Guldberg, 2000) and the Coral Triangle (Hoegh-Guldberg et al., 2009).

Australian marine resources in 2°C and 4°C worlds

Using this information, it is possible to construct credible scenarios of what might happen to Australian marine resources under conditions associated with average global temperature increases of 2°C and 4°C above the pre-industrial period. As noted earlier, based on observations of more than 40 years, marine organisms are moving polewards and are changing their seasonal behaviour (e.g. reproduction, migratory timing). The fact that this has occurred with an increase in average global temperature of 0.7°C (IPCC, 2007) should give us extreme concern over increases in average global temperature that may involve 4°C or more of warming above the pre-industrial period. Ongoing, these changes are likely to drive us into a world that will be unrecognizable in terms of the organisms and ecosystems that will be present. Unfortunately, those ecosystems that will be winners in this world will not be spectacular like the coral reefs and kelp forests of our current world. Will tourists want to see the Great *Cyanobacterial* Reef of Australia?

Shifts in distributions (and aspects such as behavioural timing or phenology) of species could result in major rearrangement of marine ecosystems. One of the key challenges that marine organisms will face is that the new environments are likely to have different characteristics (e.g. light, pH, available habitat) and may be suboptimal. For example, reproduction for many marine species is linked to the appearance of phytoplankton within the water column at specific times of the year (Cushing, 1989). The appearance of phytoplankton is matched to high levels of solar radiation and the seasonal appearance of nutrients within the water column. If spawning times shift toward earlier times in the year, they are likely to occur when food (i.e. phytoplankton) is not yet available and conse-quently emerging organisms will potentially starve. Given that over 90 per cent of marine organisms depend on pelagic resources such as phytoplankton, the impacts of this simple, rapid shift in timing is likely to have widespread conse-quences for benthic as well as pelagic marine organisms, and would play havoc with marine resources that are currently providing important fisheries income for Australia.

Similar issues surround the potential for movement of organisms to higher latitudes. There has been speculation that the Great Barrier Reef will simply shift polewards (Hughes et al., 2012). The speed at which this would have to occur can be calculated as follows. Most corals at the northern end of the Great Barrier Reef are adapted to sea temperatures some 2°C warmer than at its southern end, some 2,000 km away. If the Great Barrier Reef were to keep pace with a 2°C rise in sea temperature over the next 100 years, it would have to shift its ecosystems by 2,000 km over 100 years. This would require migration of this complex marine ecosystem at the rate of 2,000km per 100 years or 20km per year. A similar calculation for a 4°C rise in sea temperature would require a speed of movement of the Great Barrier Reef (GBR) ecosystem of around 40 km per year. Given that the ability for coral species to disperse significantly over one generation is probably <10 km (Hoegh-Guldberg, 2009), and that many of them organisms and ecosystem processes would have to move and become established at sites 20–40 km away each generation, it is unlikely that the GBR ecosystem will migrate at the necessary speeds to keep up with climate change. The other issue associated with the migration of marine ecosystems such as the GBR is the lack of suitable conditions at higher latitudes. Coral reefs require high light levels and carbonate ion levels of >200 μmol kg^{-1} (water), both of which decrease significantly as one moves to higher latitudes (i.e. toward the poles). It is likely to be the combination of the three factors (i.e. light, chemistry and temperature) that controls the distribution of coral reefs worldwide (Kleypas et al., 1999). Consequently, the arrival of a few isolated coral species at higher latitudes is not proof that highly productive carbonate coral reef ecosystems will also migrate at rates that will match the speed required by rapid anthropogenic climate change.

Given these fundamental obstacles, the prospect for many marine ecosystems is not particularly good if average global temperature exceeds 2°C or progresses to 4°C and above over the next 100 years. Again, these issues have been explored extensively for coral reef ecosystems, which serve as an illustration of the likely changes to marine ecosystems at average global temperatures of 2°C or 4°C above those seen in the preindustrial period.

Figure 5.4 provides an illustration of how the Great Barrier Reef is likely to change over the coming decades and century. A fuller explanation of these scenarios and the supporting assumptions and evidence is presented and discussed by Hoegh-Guldberg et al. (2007). A situation similar to today in which regular bleaching events have an impact on reefs, but reefs mostly recover is represented in Panel A. Panel B illustrates the impact of high temperatures (+2°C) and reduced carbonate ion concentrations (~200 mmol kg^{-1} water). At this point, coral communities have lost the more sensitive species and are composed of tougher, less 'charismatic' massive corals that are in low abundance relative to a range of other more competitive organisms such as seaweeds, sponges and soft corals. Pushing sea temperatures beyond 3°C for more, and driving carbonate ion concentrations well below 200 μmol kg^{-1} (water), results in the almost total loss of reef building corals. Under these conditions, community calcification almost certainly rates fail to keep up with physical and biological erosion, resulting in a decrease in habitat complexity as the carbonate structures of coral reefs begin to break down. While the latter may take significant amounts of time to occur, the eventual loss of reef structure removes habitat for thousands of species, many of which are important to fisheries and tourism. The reduced carbon framework of coral reefs also eventually decreases their ability to protect coastlines from wave action, triggering a range of other impacts on associated marine habitats such as mangroves, beaches and seagrass beds.

Figure 5.4   Analogues from extent reefs on the Great Barrier Reef of the state of coral reefs under ocean warming and acidification in the future

Source: Based on Hoegh-Guldberg et al., 2007

Notes
a Scenarios CRS-A, CRS-B, and CRS-C are outlined in the accompanying table. The $[CO_2]_{atm}$ and temperature increases shown are those for the scenarios and do not refer to the locations photographed.
b (A) Reef slope communities at Heron Island.
c (B) Mixed algal and coral communities associated with inshore reefs around St. Bees Island near Mackay.
c (C) Inshore reef slope near the Low Isles, North Queensland.

At a more general level, much of Australia's marine resources, and those of its regional neighbours, will degrade significantly as we approach sea temperatures of 2°C above preindustrial period, which is widely seen as the 'guardrail target' sought by current international climate negotiations (Richardson et al., 2009a; Richardson et al., 2009b; 2011). These changes will require more substantial and innovative approaches to the management of marine resources. For example, the projected increase in the overlap of yellowfin and southern bluefin tuna habitat on the east coast of Australia indicate that the problems faced by management today, as a result of two species with different stock status sharing similar habitat, are likely to increase in the future (Hartog et al., 2011). In the wider South Pacific region, changes in the distributions of tuna and billfish stocks will have potentially serious implications for some small island nations who depend on tuna for food security and their economies and implications for fisheries governance such as licensing of foreign fishing vessels (McIlgorm, 2010; McIlgorm et al., 2010). Impacts such as reduced water quality along coastlines, the overexploitation of key functional groups of species and other effects arising from local stresses will need to be further reduced as Australia's marine ecosystems are pushed close to their physiological and ecological limits. It is very clear, however, that pushing ecosystems into a Four Degree World will result in their rapid loss, with a serious reduction or elimination of the services that marine ecosystems provide to the GDP and people of Australia and its regional neighbours.

What will this mean for Australia and its regional neighbours?

Marine resources that Australia and its regional neighbours enjoy will not be viable in a world that has an average global temperature of 4°C or more. In this world, coral reefs such as the Great Barrier Reef are likely not be dominated by corals and will have little resemblance to coral reefs. Regional fisheries will have collapsed as habitat degrades and ocean fisheries are transformed (Bell et al., 2011). There is a significant risk that the carbonate scaffolding and architecture of coral reefs, critically important to biodiversity, fish stocks and coastal protection, will begin to erode as calcification and the ability of coral reefs to maintain themselves against physical and biological erosion is vastly reduced. This will have potentially serious effects on the valuable resources represented by GBR fisheries and tourism (Hoegh-Guldberg and Hoegh-Guldberg, 2008). Erosion and inundation of coastal areas will put increasing pressure on coastal ecosystems such as mangroves, seagrass and salt marsh. Many of these systems represent important fisheries habitat and their reduction is likely to have significant impacts on the viability of key fisheries. A similar conclusion can be reached for Australia's regional neighbours if marine resources and services are similarly impacted by climate change and ocean acidification (Hoegh-Guldberg, 2000; Burke et al. 2002; Hoegh-Guldberg et al., 2009; McLeod et al., 2010; Bell et al., 2013).

Similarly, the migration of fish stocks away from where they are found today presents major challenges for future fishing efforts. Changes to reproductive timing and the potential mismatch between food resources in the larval stages of many marine organisms could have profound effects on the energy flow through marine ecosystems, resonating to higher trophic levels in Australia's marine ecosystems. At the same time, the migration of organisms to higher latitudes will potentially increase the risk of encounters with new diseases and novel predators or prey species. The widespread ecosystem changes being inflicted on Tasmanian coastal kelp forests by the invasive species, *Centrostephanus rodgersii* (described above) illustrate how just one change can have such major impacts on entire ecosystems and industries. A startling insight into a Four Degree World was given by the 2010/2011 marine 'heat wave' along 2,000km of the Western Australian coast, when water temperatures reached 4°C above normal for over 10 weeks (Wernberg et al., 2011). Widespread die-offs of fish, seaweeds and invertebrates (e.g. abalone) occurred and many tropical species were reported off the southern west coast and eastwards towards the Great Australian Bight, including whale sharks and manta rays that were sighted off Albany. Several fisheries and livelihoods were negatively impacted and adaptation responses were put in place to maximize recovery, e.g. the abalone fishery in the northern region was shut and abalone where bought in from unaffected areas to aid stock recovery.

Overall, the rapid rate of marine environmental change, combined with our limited comprehension of responses and interactions, means that our understanding and ability to respond to the large-scale changes that face Australia and its regional marine resources are insufficient to devise future management strategies. As we move towards a Four Degree World, there is now sufficient evidence to conclude that there will be very different marine communities forming along the Australian coastline. These communities will involve very different competitive and predator–prey interactions and are likely to be temporary in themselves given that global climate in a Four Degree World will be far from stability and will continue to change dramatically. As discussed above, these ecosystems and communities are unlikely to have the same charismatic appeal or the same potential to provide the same level of ecological goods and services that ecosystems such as coral reefs and kelp forests do today.

Conclusion

This analysis could be interpreted as being unduly pessimistic and alarmist. However, the extensive changes that have been observed and our deep understanding of many of the organisms involved (e.g. reef building corals) draw us to conclusions that are in the main very negative. There is little evidence to suggest that marine resources are robust enough to resist current and projected climate-change driven environmental changes, many of which are unprecedented in at least the last several hundred thousand years. The rapid decline of reef-building corals within the Great Barrier Reef emphasizes its sensitivity of marine ecosystems to both direct and global human pressure. Taking into account the known tolerance to change of marine organism and ecosystem processes, it becomes clear that Australian society faces major perturbations to its marine resources if sea temperatures rise to 2°C above preindustrial temperatures. Rapid increases to 4°C or above are almost unimaginable in terms of the ecological, social and economic impacts that are likely to eventuate. Effective adaptation to these challenges is likely to be impossible given how extensive, and how expensive, the required interventions would most likely have to be.

References

AIMS. 2012. The AIMS index of marine industry 2012. Australian Institute of Marine Science, 12pp. www.aims.gov.au [accessed 31 July 2013].

Bell, J., J. Johnson and A. Hobday. 2011. Vulnerability of tropical Pacific fisheries and aquaculture to climate change: cover and forward text. In J. D. Bell et al., *Vulnerability of Tropical Pacific Fisheries and Aquaculture to Climate Change: Summary for Pacific Island Countries and Territories*. Secretariat of the Pacific Community, Noumea: New Caledonia.

Bell J. D., C. Reid, M. J. Batty, P. Lehodey, L. Rodwell, A. J. Hobday et al. 2013. Effects of climate change on oceanic fisheries in the tropical Pacific: implications for economic development and food security. *Nature Climatic Change* 2013: 1–14.

Berkelmans R, G. De'ath, S. Kininmonth and W. J. Skirving. 2004. A comparison of the 1998 and 2002 coral bleaching events on the Great Barrier Reef: spatial correlation, patterns, and predictions. *Coral Reefs* 23 (1): 74–83.

Boesch, D., Burreson, E., Dennison, W., Houde, E., Kemp, M., Kennedy, V., Newell, R., Paynter, K., Orth, R. and Ulanowicz, R. 2001. Factors in the Decline of Coastal Ecosystems. *Science* 293: 1589–91.

Boesch, D. F. 2002. Challenges and opportunities for science in reducing nutrient over-enrichment of coastal ecosystems. *Estuaries* 25: 886–900.

Braganza, K., K. Hennessy, L. Alexander and B. Trewin. 2013. Changes in extreme weather. In P. Christoff (ed.), *Four Degrees of Climate Change: Australia in a Hot World*. Earthscan: London, ch. 3.

Brodie, J., K. Fabricius, G. De'ath and K. Okaji. 2005. Are increased nutrient inputs responsible for more outbreaks of crown-of-thorns starfish? An appraisal of the evidence. *Marine Pollution Bulletin* 51: 266–78.

Brodie, J. E., F. J. Kroon, B. Schaffelke, E. C. Wolanski, S. E. Lewis, M. J. Devlin, I. C. Bohnet, Z. T. Bainbridge, J. Waterhouse and A. M. Davis. 2012. Terrestrial pollutant runoff to the Great Barrier Reef: an update of issues, priorities and management responses. *Marine Pollution Bulletin* 65: 4-9.

Bruno, J. F. and E. R. Selig. 2007. Regional decline of coral cover in the Indo-Pacific: timing, extent, and subregional comparisons. *PLoS ONE* 2: e711.

Burke L, L. Selig and M. Spalding. 2002. *Reefs at Risk in Southeast Asia*. World Resources Institute, Washington, DC.

Caldeira, K. and M. E. Wickett. 2003. Oceanography: anthropogenic carbon and ocean pH. *Nature* 425: 365.

Church, J. and N. White. 2006. A 20th century acceleration in global sea-level rise. *Geophysical Research Letters* 33: L01602. doi:10.1029/2005GL024826.

Cia, U. 2010. The world factbook. Retrieved 20 August 2010.

Crain, C. M., K. Kroeker and B. S. Halpern. 2008. Interactive and cumulative effects of multiple human stressors in marine systems. *Ecology Letters* 11: 1304–15.

Cushing, D. H. 1989. A difference in structure between ecosystems in strongly stratified waters and in those that are only weakly stratified. *Journal of Plankton Research* 11: 1–13.

De'ath, G., J. M. Lough and K. E. Fabricius. 2009. Declining coral calcification on the Great Barrier Reef. *Science* 323: 116–19.

De'ath, G., K. Fabricius, H. Sweatman and M. Puotinen. 2012. The 27-year decline of coral cover on the Great Barrier Reef and its causes. *Proceedings of the National Academy of Science*, 109: 17995–9.

Done, T., P. Whetton, R. Jones, R. Berkelmans, J. Lough, W. Skirving and S. Wooldridge. 2003. Global climate change and coral bleaching on the Great Barrier Reef. In Department of Natural Resources, Q. G. (ed.) *Final Report to the State of Queensland Greenhouse Taskforce through the Department of Natural Resources and Minings, QDNRM, Brisbane*. http://www.nrm.qld.gov.au/science/pdf/barrier_reef_report_1.pdf and http://www.nrm.qld.gov.au/science/pdf/barrier_reef_report_2.pdf

Doney, S. C., V. J. Fabry, R. A. Feely and J. A. Kleypas. 2009. Ocean acidification: the other CO_2 problem. *Annual Review of Marine Science* 1: 169–92.

Donner, S. D., W. J. Skirving, C. M. Little, M. Oppenheimer and O. Hoegh-Guldberg. 2005. Global assessment of coral bleaching and required rates of adaptation under climate change. *Global Change Biology* 11: 2251–65.

Eakin, C. M., J. A. Morgan, S. F. Heron, T. B. Smith, G. Liu, L. Alvarez-Filip, B. Baca, E. Bartels, C. Bastidas and C. Bouchon. 2010. Caribbean corals in crisis: record thermal stress, bleaching, and mortality in 2005. *PLoS ONE* 5: e13969.

Frieler, K., M. Meinshausen, A. Golly, M. Mengel, K. Lebek, S. Donner and O. Hoegh-Guldberg. 2012. Limiting global warming to 2°C is unlikely to save most coral reefs. *Nature Climate Change*.

Glynn, P. and L. D'croz. 1990. Experimental evidence for high temperature stress as the cause of El Niño-coincident coral mortality. *Coral Reefs* 8: 181–91.

Griffith, G., B. Fulton, B. Gorton and A. J. Richardson. 2012. Predicting interactions among fishing, ocean warming, and ocean acidification in a marine system with whole-ecosystem models. *Conservation Biology* 26: 1145–52.

Hartog, J. R., A. J. Hobday, R. Matear and M. Feng. 2011. Habitat overlap between southern bluefin tuna and yellowfin tuna in the east coast longline fishery: implications for present and future spatial management. *Deep-Sea Research II* 58: 746–52.

Hobday, A. J., E. S. Poloczanska and R. J. Matear (eds). 2007. Climate impacts on Australian fisheries and aquaculture: implications for the effects of climate change. Report to the Australian Greenhouse Office, Canberra, Australia. October.

Hoegh-Guldberg, O. 1999. Climate change, coral bleaching and the future of the world's coral reefs. *Marine and Freshwater Research* 50: 839–66.

—2000. *Pacific in Peril: Biological, Economic and Social Impacts of Climate Change on Pacific Coral Reefs*. Greenpeace.

—2009. Climate change and coral reefs: Trojan horse or false prophecy? *Coral Reefs* 28: 709–13.

Hoegh-Guldberg, O. and J. Bruno. 2010. The impact of climate change on the world's marine ecosystems. *Science* 328: 1523–8.

Hoegh-Guldberg, O. and H. Hoegh-Guldberg. 2008. The impact of climate change and ocean acidification on the Great Barrier Reef and its tourist industry. Report to the Garnaut Climate Change Review, Canberra.

Hoegh-Guldberg, O., H. Hoegh-Guldberg, J. Veron, A. Green, E. D. Gomez, A. Ambariyanto and L. Hansen. 2009. The coral triangle and climate change: ecosystems, people and societies at risk. WWF Australia, Brisbane, p. 276.

Hoegh-Guldberg, O., P. Mumby, A. Hooten, R. Steneck, P. Greenfield, E. Gomez, C. Harvell, P. Sale, A. Edwards and K. Caldeira. 2007. Coral reefs under rapid climate change and ocean acidification. *Science* 318: 1737–42.

Hoegh-Guldberg, O. and G. J. Smith. 1989. The effect of sudden changes in temperature, light and salinity on the population density and export of zooxanthellae from the reef corals *Stylophora pistillata* and *Seriatopra hystrix*. *Journal of Experimental Marine Biology and Ecology* 129: 279–303.

Hughes, T., D. Bellwood, A. Baird, J. Brodie, J. Bruno and J. Pandolfi. 2011. Shifting base-lines, declining coral cover, and the erosion of reef resilience: comment on Sweatman et al. (2011). *Coral Reefs* 1–8.

Hughes, T. P. 1994. Catastrophes, phase shifts, and large-scale degradation of a Caribbean coral reef. *Science* 265: 1547.

Hughes, T. P., A. H. Baird, E. A. Dinsdale, N. A. Moltschaniwskyj, M. S. Pratchett, J. E. Tanner and B. L. Willis. 2012. Assembly rules of reef corals are flexible along a steep climatic gradient. *Current Biology* 22: 736–41.

IPCC. 2007. Climate Change 2007: The Physical Science Basis. Contribution of Working Group I to the Fourth Assessment Report of the Intergovernmental Panel on Climate Change. S. Solomon, D. Qin, M. Manning, Z. Chen, M. Marquis, K. B. Averyt, M. Tignor and H. L. Miller (eds). Cambridge University Press: Cambridge and New York, 996 pp.

Jackson, J. B. C. 2010. The future of the oceans past. *Philosophical Transactions of the Royal Society B: Biological Sciences* 365: 3765–78.

Jackson, J. B., M. X. Kirby, W. H. Berger, K. A. Bjorndal, L. W. Botsford, B. J. Bourque, R. H. Bradbury, R. Cooke, J. Erlandson, J. A. Estes, T. P. Hughes, S. Kidwell, C. B. Lange, H. S. Lenihan, J. M. Pandolfi, C. H. Peterson, R. S. Steneck, M. J. Tegner and R. R. Warner. 2001. Historical overfishing and the recent collapse of coastal ecosystems. *Science* 293: 629–37.

Johnson, C., S. Ling, J. Ross, S. Shepherd and K. Miller. 2005. Establishment of the long-spined sea urchin (*Centrostephanus rodgersii*) in Tasmania: first assessment of potential threats to fisheries. Tasmanian Aquaculture and Fisheries Institute, Australia.

Johnson, C. R., S. C. Banks, N. S. Barrett, F. Cazassus, P. K. Dunstan, G. L. Edgar, S. D. Frusher, C. Gardner, M. Haddon, F. Helidoniotis, K. L. Hill, N. J. Holbrook, G. W. Hosie, P. R. Last,, S. D. Ling, J. Melbourne-Thomas, K. Miller, G. T. Pecl, A. J. Richardson, K. R. Ridgway, S. R. Rintoul, D. A. Ritz, J. Ross, C. Sanderson, S. A. Shepherd, A. Slotwinski, K. M. Swadling and N. Taw. 2011. Climate change cascades: shifts in oceanography, species' ranges and subtidal marine community dynamics in eastern Tasmania. *Journal of Experimental Marine Biology and Ecology* 400: 17–32.

Kleypas, J. A., J. W. McManus and L. A. B. Menez. 1999. Environmental limits to coral reef development: where do we draw the line? *American Zoologist* 39: 146–59.

Kremer, H. H., M. Le-Tissier, P. Burbridge, L. Talaue-Mcmanus, N. Rabalais, J. Parslow, C. Crossland and B. Young. 2005. Land–ocean interactions in the coastal zone. *Science Plan and Implementation Strategy, Land-Ocean Interactions in the Coastal Zone.*

Last, P. R., W. T. White, D. C. Gledhill, A. J. Hobday, R. Brown, G. J. Edgar and G. T. Pecl. 2010. Long-term shifts in abundance and distribution of a temperate fish fauna: a response to climate change and fishing practices. *Global Ecology and Biogeography* 20: 58–72.

Levitus, S., J. Antonov, B. Boyer, O. Baranova, H. Garcia, R. Locarnini, A. Mishonov, J. Reagan, D. Seidov and E. Yarosh. 2012. World ocean heat content and thermosteric sea level change (0–2000 m), 1955–2010. *Geophysical Research Letters* 39: L10603.

Ling, S. D. 2008. Range expansion of a habitat-modifying species leads to loss of taxonomic diversity: a new and impoverished reef state. *Oecologia* 156: 883–94.

Martinez, M. L., A. Intralawan, G. Vazquez, O. Perez-Maqueo, P. Sutton and R. Landgrave. 2007. The coasts of our world: ecological, economic and social importance. *Ecological Economics* 63: 18.

McLeod E., R. Moffitt, A. Timmermann, R. Salm, L. Menviel, M. J. Palmer et al. 2010. Warming seas in the coral triangle: coral reef vulnerability and management implications. *Coastal Management* 38 (5): 518–39.

McIlgorm, A. 2010. Economic impacts of climate change on sustainable tuna and billfish management: insights from the Western Pacific. *Progress in Oceanography* 86: 187–91, Sp Iss SI.

McIlgorm, A., S. Hanna, G. Knapp, P. Le Floc'H, F. Millerd and M. Pan. 2010. How will climate change alter fishery governance? Insights from seven international case studies. *Marine Policy* 34: 170–77.

Pauly, D., J. Alder, E. Bennett, V. Christensen, P. Tyedmers and R. Watson. 2003. The future for fisheries. *Science* 302: 1359.

Pauly, D., V. Christensen, J. Dalsgaard, R. Froese and F. Torres. 1998. Fishing down marine food webs. *Science* 279: 860.

Pelejero, C., E. Calvo and O. Hoegh-Guldberg. 2010. Paleo-perspectives on ocean acidification. *Trends in Ecology & Evolution* 25: 332–44.

Pitt, N. R., E. S. Poloczanska and A. J. Hobday. 2010. Climate-driven range changes in Tasmanian intertidal fauna. *Marine and Freshwater Research* 61: 963–70.

Poloczanska, E., R. Babcock, A. Butler, A. Hobday, O. Hoegh-Guldberg, T. Kunz, R. Matear, D. Milton, T. Okey and A. Richardson. 2007. Climate change and Australian marine life. *Oceanography and Marine Biology: An Annual Review* 45: 407–78.

Poloczanska, E. S., C. J. Brown, W. J. Sydeman, W. Kiessling, D. S. Schoeman, P. J. Moore, K. Brander, J. F. Bruno, L. Buckley, M. T. Burrows, C. M. Duarte, B. S. Halpern, J. Holding, C. V. Kappel, M. I. O'Connor, J. M. Pandolfi, C. Parmesan, F. Schwing, S.-A. Thompson and A. J. Richardson. 2013. Global imprint of climate change on marine life. *Nature Climate Change*, published online 4 August 2013, doi:10.1038/NCLIMATE1958.

Polovina, J. J., E. A. Howell and M. Abecassis. 2008. Ocean's least productive waters are expanding. *Geophysical Research Letters* 35: L03618.

Raven, J., K. Caldeira, H. Elderfield, O. Hoegh-Guldberg, P. Liss, U. Riebesell, J. Shepherd, C. Turley and A. Watson. 2005. Ocean acidification due to increasing atmospheric carbon dioxide. Royal Society Special report, London.

Richardson, A. J. and E. S. Poloczanska. 2008. Ocean science: under-resourced, under threat. *Science* 320: 1294–5.

Richardson, K., J. Rockström, W. Steffen, K. Noone, Å. Persson, F. Chapin, E. Lambin, T. Lenton, M. Scheffner and C. Folke. 2009a. Planetary boundaries: exploring the safe operating space for humanity. *Ecology and Society* 14: 1–33.

Richardson, K., W. Steffen, H. J. Schellnhuber, J. Alcamo, T. Barker, D. M. Kammen, R. Leemans, D. Liverman, M. Munasinghe, B. Osman-Elasha, N. Stern and O. Wæver. 2009b. Synthesis report, Climate change: global risks, challenges and decisions. Copenhagen, 10–12 March 2009 (www.climatecongress.ku.dk).

Richardson, K., W. Steffen and D. Liverman. 2011. *Climate Change: Global Risks, Challenges and Decisions.* Cambridge University Press: Cambridge.

Ridgway, K., R. Coleman, R. Bailey and P. Sutton. 2008. Decadal variability of East Australian Current transport inferred from repeated high-density XBT transects, a CTD survey and satellite altimetry. *Journal of Geophysical Research* 113: C08039.

Seto, K. C. and J. M. Shepherd. 2009. Global urban land-use trends and climate impacts. *Current Opinion in Environmental Sustainability* 1: 89–95.

Shannon, K. L., R. S. Lawrence, M. D. Mcdonald and J. Selendy. 2011. Anthropogenic sources of water pollution: parts 1 and 2. *Water and Sanitation Related Diseases and the Environment: Challenges, Interventions and Preventive Measures,* p. 289.

Sheppard, C. R. C. 2003. Predicted recurrences of mass coral mortality in the Indian Ocean. *Nature* 425: 294–7.

Strong, A. E., C. S. Barrientos, C. Duda and J. Sapper. 1997. Improved satellite technique for monitoring coral reef bleaching. Proceedings of the Eighth International Coral Reef Symposium, Panama, June, pp. 1495–7.

Strong, A. E., G. Liu, W. Skirving and C. M. Eakin. 2011. NOAA's Coral Reef Watch program from satellite observations. *Annals of GIS* 17: 83–92.

Taylor K. E., R. J. Stouffer and G. A. Meehl. 2012. An overview of CMIP5 and the experiment design. *Bulletin of the American Meteorological Society* 93 (4): 485–98.

Wernberg, T., B. D. Russell, M. S. Thomsen, C. F. D. Gurgel, C. J. A. Bradshaw, E. S. Poloczanska and S. D. Connell. 2011. Seaweeds in retreat from ocean warming. *Current Biology* 21: 1828–32.

Wernberg, T., D. A. Smale, F. Tuya, M. S. Thomsen, T. J. Langlois, T. de Bettignies, S. Bennett and C. S. Rousseaux. 2011. An extreme climate event alters marine ecosystem structure in a global biodiversity hotspot. *Nature Climate Change* 3: 78–82.

Wilkinson, C. and G. Hodgson. 1999. Coral reefs and the 1997–1998 mass bleaching and mortality. *Nature Resources* 35: 16–25.

6 Agriculture in an even more sunburnt country

Mark Howden, Serena Schroeter and Steven Crimp

Introduction

Over more than two centuries, Australian agriculture has evolved to cope with the droughts and flooding rains of our sunburnt country. It has been shaped by such influences as climatic zones ranging from the seasonally wet and dry, hot monsoonal north to some of the most arid deserts in the world to the temperate cool and wet of parts of southern Australia. Climate has impacted on the choice of farming systems and management, productivity, product quality and costs and prices, amongst others. In addition to shaping production, climate also affects natural resource management, particularly with regard to degradation events, restoration opportunities and the longer-term effectiveness of interventions. Given the response of Australian agriculture to historical climate variations has been significant, it follows that the extensive climate changes involved in a Four Degree World (hitherto unseen in instrumental records) would have substantial effects on Australian agriculture and its natural resource base.

Australia has long benefited from its ability to produce more food than its population requires. This has occurred in part through the adept management of climate variability by the farming community and agribusiness supported by world-class research. At present, on average, about two-thirds of gross farm production of the major grain (wheat) and meat (beef) products are exported (ABARES, 2012). Consequently, Australia and other countries producing similar food surpluses compared with domestic consumption play an important role contributing towards global food security (Gregory and Ingram, 2008).

The export value of Australian agricultural products is also an important economic activity for Australia. For the year 2011–12, the total value of Australian grains and oilseeds export was $11,135 million; the total export value of meat and livestock products was $14,735 million; the total export value of horticulture was $1,732 million; and the total export value of wine was $1,859 million (ABARES, 2012). Wheat exports alone during 2011–12 were valued at $6,381 million. However, the impending impacts of climate change, in conjunction with other forces operating on agriculture, raise questions about the future of Australia's grain and livestock production rates and its capacity to be a consistent and substantial exporter of some agricultural commodities.

Food security exists when people have physical, social and economic access to sufficient, safe and nutritious food to meet their dietary needs and food preferences for an active and healthy life (FAO, 2002). Food security is generally considered to have four dimensions: availability, accessibility, utilization and stability. While food security currently is not critical for most Australians (Friel, 2010), it is of concern globally and it affects future national prospects for agriculture, so some broadscale global trends in food security are addressed here, focusing on crops, as these are critical components of both the national and international food systems. For example, in a recent report produced by the United Nations Economic and Social Commission for Asia and the Pacific (UNESCAP, 2009) it was identified that

> climate change holds the potential to radically alter agro-ecosystems in the coming decades and there is already evidence of devastating crop failures. Predictions concerning food production vary. However, even if overall production were to remain high, declines in certain parts of the Asia-Pacific region may be expected. Over the long term, adapting and mitigating impacts from climate change will have to be a top priority for all countries in the region.
>
> (UNESCAP, 2009: 11)

The gains in food security made during the Green Revolution arose largely from the global annual rate of growth in crop production exceeding the global annual rate of population growth: for example, in the 1960s and 1970s, year-on-year crop production increases of around 3 per cent exceeded population growth (2 per cent). But over the past decade this situation has changed, with crop production growth falling to about the same level or below global population growth: 1.2 per cent (**Figure 6.1**). This is short of the 1.7 per cent needed to meet expected future growth in food demand (Beddington et al., 2012).

Over a longer period, this supply–demand imbalance will have a significant impact on the availability and accessibility of crop-based foods particularly for poorer people. Consequently, a major effort is needed to increase crop production growth (IAASTD, 2010). However, in spite of the declining trend in productivity, there has been little if no increase in support of farming systems research. In the 1970s the total global agricultural research and development (R&D) as a proportion of total global R&D was approximately 6.8 per cent. In the last decade this has declined to approximately 1.8 per cent of total global R&D. Whilst increased investment will not guarantee an arrest in productivity declines, it is an important step to ensuring that agricultural systems science continues to improve and be applied to ensure resilient future farming.

Another warning sign for global food security is arising through changes in the variability of crop production: this relates to the stability dimension of food security. There has been a steady and substantial reduction over time in the variability of crop production with the coefficient of variation – in other words, the measure of fluctuations in crop output – decreasing to less than a third of its

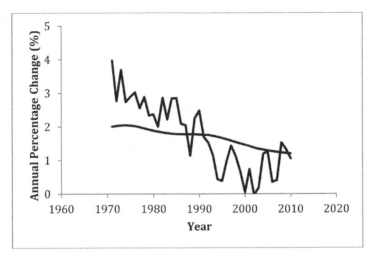

Figure 6.1 Global annual population growth and growth in global cereal crop
          production from 1961–2010 shown as 10-year running means

Source: FAO, 2012

Note
a Note that the representation of crop production here and in subsequent figures has
  data for maize removed due to the substantial recent non-food uses of maize arising
  from biofuel production policies.

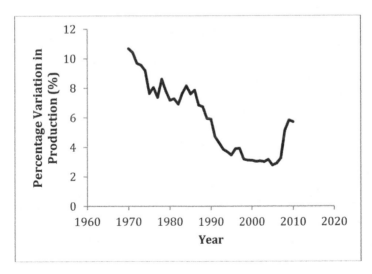

Figure 6.2 Coefficient of variation (%) of annual global cereal crop production
          1961–2010 shown as a 10-year running average

Source: FAO, 2012

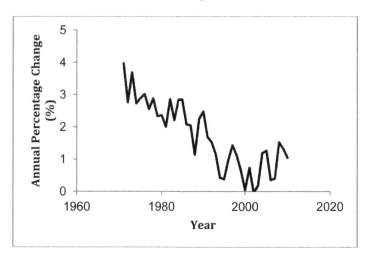

Figure 6.3   Growth in annual wheat yield (%) with 1961–2010 shown as a 10-year
running average

Source: FAO, 2012

previous values by the early 2000s (Figure 6.2). This very positive outcome has
arisen through the introduction of improved crop varieties and through improved
overall management that has reduced production risk and price fluctuations.

However, over the past few years there has been a noticeable upswing in
the variability of crop production with this returning to levels experienced 20
years ago (Figure 6.2). This deterioration in the stability of crop production is
a response to several climate extremes – including droughts and heatwaves in
Australia, Russia, Europe and the USA – and it may well have impacted on the
recent food price spikes and food shortages in some parts of the world (FAO,
WFP and IFAD, 2011). These recent events mar what has otherwise been a
remarkable outcome from investment in enhanced crop genetics and agronomy,
leading to a multi-decadal period when both average production increased and
the variability of production decreased.

The area planted to crops across the globe showed steady increases through to
the mid 1980s when 725Mha were grown annually with this dropping to about
670Mha by year 2003 and then again increasing to about 700Mha currently
(FAO, 2012). In contrast, crop yields – the other key component of production
– have shown strong trends with year-on-year yield growth dropping from around
3 per cent in the 1960s to about 1.2 per cent now (Figure 6.3). Again, this is less
than the 1.7 per cent needed to meet expected future growth in food demand
(Beddington et al., 2012).

These simple global analyses demonstrate that there are already substantial
existing challenges to the capacity of cropping systems to meet food security
demands in terms of production, yields and their variability. Similar issues arise
for the livestock sector. Projected climate changes arising from greenhouse gas

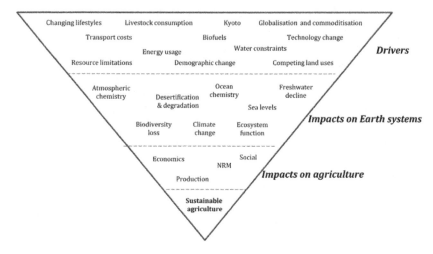

Figure 6.4 Global drivers of change, their impacts on earth systems and sustainable
agriculture

Source: Adapted from Howden et al., 2010

emissions seem likely to emphasize these existing challenges, through impacts on rainfall, temperatures and climate extremes (Easterling et al., 2007). The resulting global changes in agricultural trade and prices will impact on Australian agriculture, interacting with domestic changes and with climate variability. For example, estimates by Childs (2008) suggest that the projected impact of climate change-related food price increases will reduce the GDP of most Asian and African countries between 0.6 and 1.6 per cent, impacting on food trade. Importantly, climate change impacts will likely be co-occurring with a large range of other changes (Figure 6.4), introducing considerable uncertainty and complexity into longer-term decision-making. The impacts of climate change, in conjunction with these other supply-and-demand forces operating on agriculture, raise questions as to the sustainability of Australia's current grain and livestock production rates and our capacity to be a consistent and large exporter of some agricultural commodities. This chapter addresses briefly some of these issues following a summary of anticipated climate changes.

Australia's future climate and its impact

Uncertainties

Projections of climate changes are made using a suite of Global Circulation Models (GCMs). These model energy and mass transfers, biogeochemistry and atmospheric chemistry and other processes in and on the oceans, land and atmosphere. The GCMs are in turn driven by a range of scenarios of human development, technology and environmental governance that lead to different greenhouse gas emissions and changes in the radiative balance of the atmosphere (IPCC, 2007a). There is substantial variation between these GCMs in their capacity to represent past climate and in their response to future emissions scenarios (e.g. Deser et al., 2012), leading to uncertainty as to when specific changes such as 4°C increase may occur and consequently the rate of climate change (IPCC, 2007a). There are also differences between climate variables and scales, with more reliable projections of temperature than rainfall and more reliability at global scales than regional or local scales (Giorgi, 2005). Changes in average climate will be superimposed on large daily, seasonal and yearly variability, leading to possible significant changes in extreme events, particularly with 4°C or more warming, but these changes vary significantly between GCMs and downscaling methods (Solomon et al., 2007). Therefore, there is substantial and irreducible uncertainty as to the actual changes in climatic factors relevant to Australian agriculture. This is added to by uncertainty as to the impacts of such changes on agricultural systems and the effectiveness of adaptations to those impacts.

It is anticipated that global warming of 4°C or more will increase climate variability (Braganza et al., 2013, this volume). Australian agriculture is impacted heavily by climate variability. For example, national wheat production has varied by as much as 60 per cent from year to year as a result of low rainfall conditions, halving exports in some years (Howden et al., 2010), the El Niño–Southern Oscillation, Indian Ocean temperature gradients, atmospheric circulation over the Southern Ocean and the latitude and strength of the sub-tropical ridge being particularly important drivers of variability. Over the past decades, improved knowledge of these drivers of variability has been integrated with decision-making across the agricultural value chain, reducing risk and enhancing sustainability of the industries. Unfortunately, recent and future changes in these key climate drivers are not well simulated in GCMs (Christensen et al., 2007; Hegerl et al., 2007; Kent et al., 2011; Durack et al., 2012; Guilyardi et al., 2012). This contributes significantly to the uncertainty of future projections (Hallegatte, 2009; Wilby et al., 2009) with little likelihood of resolution in the near term (Hallegate, 2008; 2009). This uncertainty and potential increased variability will, by themselves as a function of sensible risk management, tend to lead to more conservative farming practices such as reductions in inputs (e.g. fertilizer) that will reduce yields.

A Four Degree World will likely be associated with production declines and associated negative impacts, in most of Southern Australia (e.g. Howden, 2002; Easterling et al., 2007). Even with atmospheric CO_2 concentrations of 600ppm or higher, the associated temperature increase and rainfall declines in excess of 20 per cent across much of this region will exceed any benefits arising through enhanced efficiency with which plants use water, radiation and nutrients (i.e. CO_2 fertilization effect).

Temperature

Australian agricultural systems are strongly influenced by average temperatures, which affect the choice of production system, and by high and low temperature extremes, which can cause severe impacts through, for example, heat stress damage and frost damage. Most of the major crops have strong physiological responses to temperature, with this driving their growth and reproductive stages (phenology). For instance, temperature increases across the season will shorten the duration of cereal crops (i.e. the time from germination to harvest), reducing the time to accumulate solar radiation and hence biomass and grain yield will decline. McKeon et al. (1988) suggest that a 2°C increase in temperature in Queensland would reduce wheat yields by 6 per cent while Wang et al. (1992) suggest that a 3°C increase in temperature could reduce mean yields in Wagga Wagga and Mildura by up to 50 per cent and in Horsham by 25 to 60 per cent, depending on cultivar.

Increased temperature will tend to increase evapotranspiration and vapour pressure deficit (the difference between how much moisture the air is holding and how much it can hold; e.g. Monteith, 1965), resulting in more rapid depletion of soil moisture in spring when the grain is filling and ripening. This will tend to reduce grain number, reduce harvest index, and in conditions of high soil nitrogen may result in 'haying off' and subsequent major reductions in effective yield (van Herwaarden, et al., 1998). A key adaptation to temperature increase involves selecting varieties with greater thermal time requirements and integrating this with changed planting dates and methods such as dry sowing, which allows earlier sowing than traditional methods (Chapman et al., 2012). In horticultural crops, higher temperatures would affect attributes such as sugar content and flavour as well as market synchronization (Webb and Whetton, 2010).

Extreme temperatures are also important. The climate projections derived from the GCMs and emissions scenarios suggest that well before 4°C is reached almost every region in Australia each year will be experiencing what were historically exceptionally hot conditions (Hennessy et al., 2008) with much higher frequencies of extreme temperatures than were historically recorded. In particular, high temperatures during flowering (anthesis) of crops can result in difficulties with pollination and other problems, dramatically lowering potential yield and also decreasing grain quality (e.g. Howden, 2002). High temperatures are increasingly being recognized as having a major impact on global food production (Lobell et al., 2010).

Rainfall

Rainfall is a critical factor in Australian agriculture. It affects what crop varieties are used, where and how crops are grown, as well as having an impact on annual production, product quality and soil degradation, amongst many other elements. Climate projections for 4°C or more indicate substantial rainfall reductions in southern Australia (often 25 per cent or higher) and about an even chance for either a decrease or increase in the northern parts of Australia (see Whetton et al., 2013, Chapter 2, this volume; Hennessy et al., 2007). Projected rainfall changes in the main farming zones vary substantially between seasons, with decreases particularly likely in winter and spring and with a low likelihood of increases in rainfall in these seasons (CSIRO and BoM, 2007). While some of the rainfall decreases projected in the scenarios do not seem large (e.g. 25 per cent), in a grain-cropping location like Birchip in northern Victoria, such reductions would result in more than a doubling of the frequency of 'exceptional' droughts, a reduction by 90 per cent of the frequency of high rainfall years, and the rainfall historically experienced in half of all years would be experienced in only 19 per cent of years.

Wheat crops during the last decade have experienced significant declines during extended dry periods (ABARES, 2012), reducing the amount available for export. The prospect of increased frequency and severity of droughts (see Whetton et al., 2013; Braganza et al., 2013 [Chapters 2 and 3, this volume]; and Hennessy et al., 2008) is likely to exacerbate this situation. The sensitivity of future crop yield to rainfall changes was assessed by Howden (2002) and Luo et al. (2005), who found that in most sites there was high sensitivity to reductions in mean rainfall; however, yield was less sensitive to increases in mean rainfall. This is consistent with observations of yield across years and regions, with yields in high rainfall years demonstrating various impacts from diseases, pests, water-logging and nutrient leaching (e.g. Stephens and Lyons, 1998).

Rainfall has also historically been associated with determining land-use in Australia, Goyders Line in South Australia being perhaps the most well-known example (Nidumolu et al., 2012). Reductions in rainfall and increases in potential evaporation rates appear likely to reduce the area cropped in Australia, with the inland margins of the cropping belt moving towards the coast and only small compensatory increases in cropping on the coastal margin occurring due to other land use pressures (Nidumolu et al., 2012). Thus reductions in rainfall of the scale indicated above would not only reduce site-based yield, but they would also reduce the area cropped.

Reductions in rainfall are also likely to favour light-textured, sandy soils rather than heavy soils with high clay content (van Ittersum et al., 2003; Ludwig and Asseng, 2006), as in sandy soils, small rainfall events contribute to soil water in the plant available range, whereas this moisture maybe unavailable to plants in heavier clay soils (Lawes et al., 2009). Sea level rises may similarly reduce areas suitable for cropping – particularly with regard to sugarcane – due to salinity intrusion and flooding (Murphy and Sorensen, 2001).

The regional and industry impacts of the above changes could be marked. Gunasekera et al. (2008) estimated that with levels of global warming considerably less than the +4°C assumed for this book (0.8–2.8°C), Australia would see a decline in wheat production of up to 13 per cent and beef production of 19 per cent by 2050. Indicative decreases in production per unit area of core agricultural commodities are up to 40 per cent under the more extreme scenarios of mean rainfall decline, notwithstanding the positive impacts of elevated CO_2 on yield (Howden, 2002).

Increases in extreme daily rainfall seem likely (Braganza et al., 2013, this volume). For example, the intensity of the 1-in-20-year daily rainfall event is likely to increase by 5 to 70 per cent by the year 2050 in Victoria, up to 25 per cent in northern Queensland by 2050 and up to 30 per cent by the year 2040 in south-east Queensland (Hennessy et al., 2007). Intense rainfall is particularly relevant to soil erosional processes and climate change could increase already problematic rates of soil erosion leading to longer-term yield decline (McKeon et al., 1988; 2004; Littleboy et al., 1992).

Agriculture is also significantly affected by soil degradation processes such as dryland salinization. This could potentially reduce under a scenario with less rainfall due to a reduction in groundwater recharge (van Ittersum, et al., 2003). However, John et al. (2005) project that if summer rainfall increases to offset less winter rainfall, salinity will remain the same, or might even increase under climate change. Other soil degradation processes such as wind erosion are likely to increase due particularly to expected reductions in ground cover arising from longer dry spells (Crimp et al., 2010).

Evaporation

Evaporation is a key factor for both dryland and irrigated agriculture as it strongly influences yields in many situations and is the primary determinant of water demand. Evaporation (or evaporative demand) is likely to increase with climate change (CSIRO and BoM, 2007; Whetton et al., 2013, this volume) and this, combined with anticipated reductions in rainfall, suggests a significant increase in drought risk over most of Australia (Hennessy et al., 2008). There has been some debate over how evaporation may change in the future and the methods appropriate to evaluating this (Gifford et al., 2005). To examine this issue we briefly explore potential changes in evaporation, calculated using the well-established Penman–Monteith equation (Allen et al., 1998), for three sites across the cropping zones: Emerald (Queensland), Birchip (Victoria) and Kellerberrin (WA).[1] The increase in potential evaporation was calculated to be consistently higher (30 to 50 per cent) using the GCM output (Table 6.1). The increase in potential evaporation was caused by not just a change in the mean temperature in the GCM output but a change in the temperature distribution (increased variance) with the increasing frequency of very hot days disproportionately increasing potential evaporation. This effect has also been found in assessments of urban water demand under climate change (Howden and Crimp, 2008). Consequently, global warming is likely to significantly increase potential evaporation increasing water demands by agriculture but the estimated degree of change is critically dependent on the method used: another source of uncertainty in future projections.

Table 6.1   Increases (%) in mean annual potential evaporation (Penman-Monteith; Allen 1998) for Emerald (Qld), Birchip (Vic.) and Kellerberrin (WA) for 2030 and 2050 calculated from GCM output (CSIRO Mk 3.5) or from perturbing the historical climate records by the same mean change in maximum and minimum temperatures as found in the GCM output

	2030		2050	
	GCM *output*	Modified historical	GCM *output*	Modified historical
Emerald	7.8	5.2	9.5	7.2
Birchip	8.6	5.7	10.3	7.3
Kellerberrin	7.9	6.0	9.4	7.4

Table 6.2.   Catchments in the Murray–Darling Basin and the prospective changes in water availability under 'dry', median and 'wet' scenarios for 2030[2]

	Climate change (dry)	Climate change (median)	Climate change (wet)
Condamine-Ballonne	−26	−8	+19
Lachlan	−30	−11	+6
Goulburn-Broken	−45	−14	−3
Murray	−41	−14	+7

Water availability and quality

The surface and groundwater resources that supply water used in irrigated agriculture in Australia are likely to be substantially affected by lower average rainfall and higher evaporation in a 4°C-plus Australia. For example, annual water availability in the Murray–Darling Basin could change significantly by 2030, with possible substantial decreases of 26 to 45 per cent in some catchments, through to possible increases of up to 19 per cent in one (Table 6.2). The median scenarios, however, all indicate reductions in average annual flow although increased annual variability in rainfall may increase the size of flood events.

Reductions in water availability will likely worsen as one moves from north to south in the Murray–Darling Basin. In the case of southern catchments like the Goulburn Broken (in Victoria), there has already been a 15 per cent reduction in rainfall and a 45 per cent reduction in water availability over the drought-affected decade up to 2010 (CSIRO, 2008). There may also be reductions in water quality, for instance, as salt concentrations increase (Beare and Heaney, 2002).

Projected average declines in river flows and higher flow variability in southern Australia are expected to reduce irrigation water availability (Quiggin et al., 2010; Jones and Page, 2001; Sanders et al., 2010). This will further reduce the production levels and alter commodities grown in these regions, with the impacts of climate change expected to interact with ongoing changes in institutional arrangements. Increasing water scarcity in key irrigation areas such as the Murray–Darling Basin region is predicted to significantly reduce production rates by 2030 (Sanders et al., 2010) well before a 4°C temperature increase occurs.

Pests, diseases and weeds

Climate change is likely to alter the range, severity and species of pests, diseases and weeds. However, the specific changes that might occur are uncertain, and few studies have extrapolated existing knowledge to changes associated with a 4°C world. There may be a range of possible outcomes (Chakraborty et al., 1998). For example, with the wheat disease stripe rust (*Puccinia striiformis*), a temperature rise may increase the amount of this rust but not necessarily mean additional yield losses with the changes in impact of this rust varying regionally, with management and with cultivar. The fungal disease Take-all (*Gaeumannomyces graminis*) can cause major crop losses when there are extended periods of high soil moisture. Its severity may be reduced if there is an increase in rainfall variability and drier winters as suggested by the climate scenarios covered here. Septoria blotch (*Septoria tritici*) incidence is affected by sowing time and rainfall at heading. The current scenarios of reduced rainfall over southern Australia (less severe infection) but increased temperature (more severe infection) result in an uncertain outcome. Viral diseases such as Barley Yellow Dwarf, which rely on transfer by aphids, may increase with warmer winter temperatures with potential additional risks via the positive effects of CO_2 concentration on aphid populations (e.g. Newman et al., 2003). Climate change may also affect the balance between soil-based pathogens like *Fusarium graminearum* and their antagonists such as *Trichoderma*, but again, outcomes are uncertain. In some instances, changes in farm management to reduce evaporative losses (e.g. zero tillage) may also interact with disease risk. In recent years the increase in the prevalence of *Rhizoctonia* has anecdotally been linked to wetter than normal conditions combined with zero tillage practices.

The impact of insects on Australian crops in a 4°C world is currently uncertain. Some experiments indicate that climate change and increases in atmospheric CO_2 may increase insect damage. This can occur as a result of compensatory feeding when elevated CO_2 reduces leaf nitrogen concentrations (i.e. the insect has to eat more to maintain nitrogen intake; Lincoln et al., 1986). In other cases, increased CO_2 results in increased concentrations of plant defensive compounds such as condensed tannins, and this plus lowered nitrogen concentrations with elevated CO_2 can reduce insect herbivore weight gains, increase mortality and lower fecundity (e.g. Gao et al., 2008).

There are also concerns that a range of weed species (especially summer-growing C_4 weeds) will increase their competitive advantage under elevated CO_2 and higher temperatures (e.g. IPCC, 2007b). This may become even more problematic with emerging evidence that the widely used herbicide glyphosate could become less effective under elevated CO_2 (Ziska et al., 1999) and the possibility that the number of days suitable for spraying operations could reduce significantly (Figure 6.5, Howden et al., 2007a).

Food consumption and its implications

In addition to the threats to food production arising from climate change, there are likely to be significant upward pressures on food consumption arising from population growth and, especially in Asia, the increased consumption of protein derived from grain-fed livestock, linked to food preference changes and net income. Australia's population is increasing rapidly, with recent years experiencing record population growth resulting from increased net immigration and a policy-driven reversal of the decline in its birth rate (ABS, 2008; 2012). The net effect of climate change on food supply, coupled with increased aggregate demand, is that Australia's food surpluses will likely shrink and potentially become negative in some years under certain climate change and population scenarios: especially scenarios involving warming of 4°C or more.

These projections are not inconsistent with, and seem to exacerbate, existing trends. For example, over 30 years, Australia's average annual wheat export has dropped from 80 per cent to 65 per cent of production due largely to increased domestic demand (ABARES, 2012). However, individual years can vary dramatically from the long-term trends, particularly during years with above-average production – for example, during 2011–12, wheat exports rose to 82 per cent of gross production as a result of above-average production and stable domestic consumption rates, leading to a significant increase in product available for export in that year. The long-term trend, however, shows there are likely to be significant periods with more restricted crop exports, and this may give rise

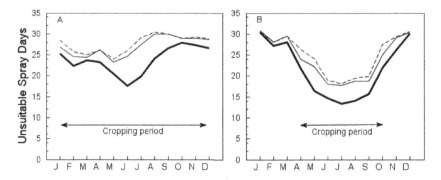

Figure 6.5 Frequency of days per month unsuitable for spraying for Emerald (Queensland) and Kellerberrin (Western Australia) for the historical baseline, 2030 and for 2070

Source: Howden et al., 2007

to global implications such as those demonstrated recently, where climatic and other disruptions in key grain exporting nations generated major price spikes, leading to social disruption and increased malnourishment in developing nations (Gregory and Ingram, 2008).

Adaptation and mitigation

There is a range of adaptations that can and will be employed to counter some of the negative effects detailed above (e.g. Table 6.3). Many of these will be extensions of existing approaches to manage climate risk and enhance production but some will need proactive investment such as development of climate change-ready crop varieties (Stokes and Howden, 2010). In conjunction with this will be the need to increase the adaptive capacity of agricultural sector decision-makers (Nelson et al., 2008; Crimp et al., 2010).

The prospect of global warming of 4°C or more is likely to instigate major efforts to reduce net greenhouse gas emissions and this effort may restrict the application of some greenhouse gas emission-intensive adaptations, such as increased nitrogenous fertilizer applications to counter reductions in grain protein (Howden et al., 2010). There may also be pressure to reduce demand for products that have high levels of embedded greenhouse gas emissions, such as red meat. Similarly, agricultural lands can be seen as an option for 'emergency drawdown' of atmospheric CO_2 concentrations or for production of biofuels, and these influences could have substantial impacts on Australian food production.

Conclusion

Average global warming of 4°C or more will likely have profound impacts on Australian agriculture. Changes in average temperature in conjunction with associated changes in temperature extremes, rainfall, evaporation and floods and drought will likely reduce production of the major commodity groups, increase the variability of production and impact on product quality. In addition, such climate changes will likely change the location of agriculture, particularly at the dry and wet margins of existing activities, as well as increase risks of some forms of natural resource degradation such as soil erosion. Changes in other factors such as crop diseases are more ambiguous whilst some issues such as dryland salinity may benefit from such climate change. These climate change impacts will interact with other change drivers, making long-term predictions of the future state of agriculture highly uncertain. Effective adaptations to these climate changes will involve a range of technical, managerial, community and institutional responses, including building the capacity to access, implement and evaluate the effectiveness of adaptations.

There is a general view that farmers and farming systems in Australia are highly adaptive, developing management, technologies and other responses to a range of challenges and opportunities. Often, these adaptations have been in the face of fairly well-defined, single factors, such as changes in relative price of inputs or

Table 6.3   A subset of the adaptation options available to adapt farming systems to climate change

Altering inputs such as varieties/species to those with more appropriate thermal time and vernalization requirements and/or with increased resistance to heat shock and drought, increased responsiveness to CO_2, altering fertilizer rates to maintain grain quality consistent with the prevailing climate, altering amounts and timing of irrigation and other water management
Wider use of technologies to 'harvest' water, conserve soil moisture (e.g. crop residue retention) and to use and transport water more effectively where rainfall decreases
Water management to prevent water logging, erosion and nutrient leaching where rainfall increases
Altering the timing or location of cropping activities
Diversifying income through altering the integration with other farming activities such as livestock raising
Improving the effectiveness of pest, disease and weed management practices through wider use of integrated pest and pathogen management, development and use of varieties and species resistant to pests and diseases and maintaining or improving quarantine capabilities and monitoring programs
Developing improved climate forecasting and its use to reduce production risk

Source: Stokes and Howden, 2010

outputs, or to market access or changes in consumer preferences. By contrast, this chapter suggests, climate change has multiple, related dimensions, and many of the possible adaptations include high degrees of uncertainty in the nature, degree and timing of the change involved. The changes that may be needed are not only directly associated with climate changes (and hence productivity) at local, regional and global scales, but also occurring through the emerging low-carbon economy and its associated shifts in input prices and potential new products such as carbon storage, and additionally through its impacts on global food security (Keating and Carberry, 2008). How will Australian farmers, farming systems, cropping industries and governments adapt in the face of such uncertainty?

For the most part, adaptation research and action has been more in keeping with the exploration of incremental options or 'adjustments' to existing farming systems (Rickards and Howden, 2012). However, the effectiveness of such tactical adaptation options is limited when modest changes in temperature and rainfall are exceeded. Under a 4°C change in global temperatures, the effectiveness of tactical adaptation options will likely be severely limited and will likely require the examination of adaptation that also encompasses more radical change: 'longer-term, deeper transformations'. This pursuit of transformation will both be increasingly likely and desired in a Four Degree World.

A few examples of transformational adaptation in Australian agriculture are already available for investigation. These examples illustrate that such change can involve serious challenges, risks and benefits. They also reinforce that climate change and adaptation are not happening in isolation; there is already a complex collection of change processes in play. Consequently, research and policy attention needs to be paid to transformational adaptation – not to promote it, but rather to establish a decision-environment that supports it and reduces risk.

Finally, it should be recognized that 'adaptation' is an ongoing process that is part of good risk management, whereby drivers of risk are identified and their likely impacts on systems under alternative management are assessed and acted upon (Howden et al., 2007b). In this respect, adaptation to climate change is similar to adaptation to climate variability, changes in market forces (cost/price ratios, consumer demands etc.), institutional or other factors. Isolating climate change from other drivers of risk may be helpful during the initial stages of assessment when awareness of the relative importance of this risk factor is still low. Operationally, however, translating adaptation options into adaptation actions requires consideration of a more comprehensive risk management framework (Meinke et al., 2006). This would allow exploration of quantified scenarios dealing with the key sources of risk, providing more effective decision-making and learning for farmers, policymakers and researchers: an increase in the 'climate knowledge' (Howden et al., 2007b). There are consequently substantial research and policy challenges in ensuring that Australia remains a sustainable cornerstone of domestic and global food security in a changing Four Degree World.

Notes

1   The equation is applied to either daily GCM (CSIRO Mk3.5) output for each site or to historical climate where the minimum and maximum temperature are increased by the same amount as the changes in the GCM runs following the method of Reyenga et al. (2000).
2   The scenarios considered for 2030 were based on future global climate models from the Intergovernmental Panel on Climate Change 4th Assessment Report simulating low (temperature increase of 0.45°C), medium (temperature increase of 1.03°C) and high (temperature increase of 1.6°C) levels of global warming, following the method of IPCC (2007a). The 'dry extreme' scenario was based on the second driest result from the 'high global warming' model; the 'median' scenario was based on the median result from the 'medium global warming' model; and the 'wet extreme' scenario was based on the second wettest result from the 'high global warming' model (Chiew et al. 2008).

References

ABARES. 2012. Agricultural commodity statistics 2012. Australian Bureau of Agricultural and Resource Economics, Canberra. Available online at www.daff.gov.au/abares/publications [accessed 25 July 2013].

ABS. 2008. Population Projections: Australia 2006–2101. http://www.abs.gov.au/Ausstats/abs@.nsf/mf/3222.0 [accessed February 2013].

ABS. 2012. Australian Demographic Statistics, June 2012. http:// http://www.abs.gov.au/ ausstats/abs@.nsf/mf/3101.0 [accessed February 2013].

Allen, R. G., L. S. Pereira, D. Raes and M. Smith. 1998. Crop evapotranspiration: guidelines for computing crop water requirements – FAO irrigation and drainage paper 56. *Food and Agriculture Organization of the United Nations*. Rome, 300: 6541.

Beare, S. and A. Heaney. 2002. Climate change and water resources in the Murray–Darling Basin, Australia: impacts and possible adaptation. *2002 World Congress of Environmental and Resource Economists*, 24–27 June 2002. Monterey, CA, USA.

Beddington, J. R., M. Asaduzzaman, M. E. Clark, A. Fernandez Bremauntz, M. D. Guillou, D. J. B. Howlett, M. M. Jahn, E. Lin, T. Mamo, C. Negra, C. A. Nobre, R. J. Scholes, N. Van Bo and J. Wakhungu. 2012. What next for agriculture after Durban? *Science* 335 (6066): 289–90.

Braganza, K., K. Hennessy, L. Alexander and B. Trewin, B. 2013. Changes in extreme weather. In Christoff, P. (ed.) *Four Degrees of Climate Change: Australia in a Hot World*. Earthscan: London, ch. 3.

Bunce, J. A. 2012. Responses of cotton and wheat photosynthesis and growth to cyclic variation in carbon dioxide concentration. *Photosynthetica* 50 (3): 395–400.

Chakraborty, S., G. M. Murray, P. A. Magarey, T. Yonow, R. G. O'Brien, B. J. Croft, M. J. Barbetti, K. Sivasithamparam, K. M. Old, M. J. Dudzinski, R. J. Sutherst, L. J. Penrose, C. Archer and R. W. Emmett. 1998. Potential impacts of climate change on plant diseases of economic significance to Australia. *Australasian Plant Pathology* 27: 15–35.

Chapman, S. C., S. Chakraborty, M. F. Dreccer and S. M. Howden. 2012. Plant adaptation to climate change: opportunities and priorities in breeding. *Crop and Pasture Science* 63: 251–68.

Chiew, F. J. S., J. Teng, D. Kirono, A. J. Frost, J. M. Bathols, J. Vaze, N. R. Viney, W. J. Young, K. J. Hennessy and W. J. Cai. 2008. Climate data for hydrologic scenario modelling across the Murray–Darling Basin: a report to the Australian Government from the CSIRO Murray–Darling Basin Sustainable Yields Project. CSIRO: Australia. 42 pp.

Childs, N. and K. James. 2009. *Factors Behind the Rise in Global Rice Prices in 2008*. USDA, Economic Research Service, Outlook Report No. RCS-09D-01. Available at: www.ers. usda.gov/publications/rcs-rice-outlook/rcs09d01 [accessed 25 July 2013].

Christensen, J. H., B. Hewitson, A. Busuioc et al. 2007. Regional climate projections. In S. Solomon, D. Qin, M. Manning, Z. Chen, M. Marquis, K. B. Averyt, M. Tignore and H. L. Miller (eds), Climate change 2007: the physical science basis. *Contribution of Working Group I to the Fourth Assessment Report of the Intergovernmental Panel on Climate Change*. Cambridge University Press: Cambridge.

Crimp, S. J., C. J. Stokes, S. M. Howden, A. D. Moore, B. Jacobs, P. R. Brown, A. J. Ash, P. Kokic and P. Leith. 2010. Managing Murray–Darling Basin livestock systems in a variable and changing climate: challenges and opportunities. *The Rangeland Journal* 32: 293–304.

CSIRO. 2008. Water availability in the Murray-Darling Basin. A report to the Australian Government from the CSIRO Murray-Darling Basin Sustainable Yields Project. CSIRO, Australia. 67pp.

CSIRO and BoM. 2007. Climate change in Australia. Technical Report. www. climatechangeinaustralia.gov.au.

Deser, C., R. Knutti, S. Solomon and A. S. Phillips. 2012. Communication of the role of natural variability in future North American climate. *Nature Climate Change* 2: 775–9.

Durack, P. J., S. E. Wijffels and R. J. Matear. 2012. Ocean salinities reveal strong global water cycle intensification during 1950 to 2000. *Science* 336: 455–8.

Easterling, W., P. Aggarwal, P. Batima, K. Brander, L. Erda, M. Howden, A. Kirilenko, J. Morton, J. F. Soussana, J. Schmidhuber and F. Tubiello. 2007. In M. L. Parry, O. F. Canziani, J. P. Palutikof, P. J. van der Linden and C. E. Hanson (eds), Climate Change 2007: Impacts, Adaptation and Vulnerability. *Contribution of Working Group II to the Fourth Assessment Report of the Intergovernmental Panel on Climate Change.* Cambridge University Press: Cambridge, pp. 273–313.

FAO (Food and Agriculture Organization of the United Nations). 2002. The State of Food Insecurity in the World 2001. Rome: FAO.

—2012. FAOSTAT. http://faostat3.fao.org/home/index.html [accessed 25 July 2013].

FAO, WFP and IFAD. 2011. The State of Food Insecurity in the World 2011. Economic growth is necessary but not sufficient to accelerate reduction of hunger and malnutrition. Rome: FAO.

Friel, S. 2010. Climate change, food insecurity and chronic diseases: sustainable and healthy policy opportunities for Australia. *NSW Public Health Bulletin* 21 (5–6): 129–33.

Gao, F., S. R. Zhu, Y. C. Sun, L. Du, M. Parajulee, L. Kang and F. Ge. 2008. Interactive effects of elevated CO_2 and cotton cultivar on tri-trophic interaction of *Gossypium hirsutum*, *Aphis gossyppii*, and *Propylaea japonica*. *Environmental Entomology* 37: 29–37.

Gifford, R. M., G. D. Farquhar, M. L. Roderick and N. Nicholls. 2005. Pan evaporation: an example of the detection and attribution of trends in climate variables. http://www.science.org.au/natcoms/nc-ess/documents/nc-ess-pan.evap.pdf [accessed 25 July 2013].

Giorgi, F. 2005. Interdecadal variability of regional climate change: implications for the development of regional climate change scenarios. *Meteorology and Atmospheric Physics* 89: 1–15.

Gregory, P. J. and J. S. I. Ingram. 2008. Climate change and the current 'food crisis'. CAB Reviews: Perspectives in Agriculture, Veterinary Science, Nutrition and Natural Resources 33 (099): 1–10.

Guilyardi, E., H. Bellenger, M. Collins, S. Ferrett, W. Cai and A. Wittenberg. 2012. A first look at ENSO in CMIP5. *Clivar Exchanges* 58: 29–32.

Gunasekera, D., C. Tulloh, M. Ford and E. Heyhoe. 2008. Climate change: opportunities and challenges in Australian agriculture. *Proceedings of Faculty of Agriculture, Food and Natural Resources Annual Symposium 2008*, University of Sydney.

Hallegatte, S. 2008. Adaptation to climate change: do not count on climate scientists to do your work. *Regulation2point0*, Working paper 458.

—2009. Strategies to adapt to an uncertain climate change. *Global Environmental Change-Human and Policy Dimensions* 19 (2): 240–47.

Hegerl, G., F. Zwiers, P. Braconnot, N. Gillett, Y. Luo, J. A. Marengo, N. Nicholls, J. Penner and P. Stott. 2007. Understanding and attributing climate change. In S. Solomon, D. Qin, M. Manning, Z. Chen, M. Marquis, K. B. Averyt, M. Tignore and H. L. Miller (eds), Climate change 2007: the physical science basis. *Contribution of Working Group I to the Fourth Assessment Report of the Intergovernmental Panel on Climate Change.* Cambridge University Press: Cambridge.

Hennessy, K., B. Fitzharris, B. C. Bates, N. Harvey, S. M. Howden, L. Hughes, J. Salinger and R. Warrick. 2007. Australia and New Zealand. In M. L. Parry, O. F. Canziani, J. P. Palutikof, P. J. van der Linden and C. E. Hanson (eds), Climate change 2007: impacts, adaptation and vulnerability. *Contribution of Working Group II to the*

Fourth Assessment Report of the Intergovernmental Panel on Climate Change. Cambridge University Press: Cambridge, pp. 507–40.

Hennessy, K. J., R. Fawcett, D. Kirono, F. Mpelasoka, D. Jones, J. Bathols, P. Whetton, M. Stafford Smith, M. Howden, C. Mitchell and N. Plummer. 2008. An assessment of the impact of climate change on the nature and frequency of exceptional climatic events. CSIRO and BoM: Melbourne, 31 pp. http://www.bom.gov.au/climate/droughtec/ [accessed 25 July 2013].

Herwaarden, A. F. van, G. D. Farquer, J. F. Angus, R. A. Richards and G. N. Howe. 1998. 'Haying-off', the negative grain yield response of dryland wheat to nitrogen fertiliser: I. Biomass, grain yield, and water use. *Australian Journal of Agricultural Research* 49 (7): 1067–81.

Howden, S. M. 2002. Potential global change impacts on Australia's wheat cropping systems. In O. C. Doering, J. C. Randolph, J. Southworth and R. A. Pfeifer (eds), *Effects of Climate Change and Variability on Agricultural Production Systems*. Kluwer Academic Publications: Dordrecht, pp. 219–47.

Howden, S. M. and S. J. Crimp. 2008. Drought and high temperature extremes: effects on water demand and electricity demands. In P. W. Newton (ed.), *Transitions: Pathways Towards Sustainable Urban Development in Australia*. CSIRO Publishing: Collingwood, Vic., pp. 227–44.

Howden, S. M., S. J. Crimp and C. Sayer. 2007a. The effect of climate change and spraying opportunities: a risk assessment and options for adaptation. In M. Donatelli, J. Hatfield and A. Rizzoli (eds), Farming systems design. *Proceedings of the International Symposium on methodologies for integrated assessment of farm production systems*. European Society of Agronomy: pp. 197–8.

Howden, S. M., J. F. Soussana, F. N. Tubiello, N. Chhetri, M. Dunlop and H. M. Meinke. 2007b. Adapting agriculture to climate change. *Proceedings of the National Academy of Sciences* 104: 19691–6.

Howden, S. M., H. Meinke and R. M. Gifford. 2010. Grains. In C. J. Stokes and S. M. Howden (eds), *Adapting Australian Agriculture to Climate Change*. CSIRO Publishing: Collingwood, pp. 21–48.

IAASTD. 2009. Agriculture at a crossroads: global report. International Assessment of Agricultural Knowledge, Science and Technology for Development. Island Press: Washington DC.

IPCC. 2007a. Climate change 2007: the physical science basis. In S. Solomon, D. Qin, M. Manning, Z. Chen, M. Marquis, K. B. Averyt, M. Tignor and H. L. Miller (eds), *Contribution of Working Group I to the Fourth Assessment Report of the Intergovernmental Panel on Climate Change*. Cambridge University Press: Cambridge.

—2007b. Climate change 2007: impacts, adaptation and vulnerability. In M. L. Parry, O. F. Canziani, J. P. Palutikof, P. J. van der Linden and C. E. Hanson (eds), *Contribution of Working Group II to the Fourth Assessment Report of the Intergovernmental Panel on Climate Change*. Cambridge University Press: Cambridge.

John, M., D. Pannell and R. Kingwell. 2005. Climate change and the economics of farm management in the face of land degradation: dryland salinity in Western Australia. *Canadian Journal of Agricultural Economics* 53 (4): 443–59.

Jones, R. N. and C. M. Page. 2001. Assessing the risk of climate change on the water resources of the Macquarie river catchment. In P. Ghassemi, P. Whetton, R. Little and M. Littleboy (eds), *Integrating Models for Natural Resources Management Across Disciplines, Issues and Scales*. Modelling and Simulation Society of Australia and New Zealand, Canberra.

Keating, B. A. and P. S. Carberry. 2008. Emerging opportunities for Australian agriculture? In *Proceedings of the 14th Australian Society of Agronomy Conference*, September 2008, Adelaide, SA.

Kent, D. M., D. G. C. Kirono, B. Timbal and F. S. Chiew. 2011. Representation of the Australian sub-tropical ridge in the CMIP3 models. *International Journal of Climatology*: 1–10.

Lawes, R. A., Y. M. Oliver and M. J. Robertson. 2009. Integrating the effects of climate and plant available soil water holding capacity on wheat yield. *Field Crops Research* 113 (3): 297–305.

Lincoln, D. E., D. Couvet and N. Sionit. 1986. Response of an insect herbivore to host plants grown in carbon dioxide enriched atmospheres. *Oecologia* 69: 556–60.

Littleboy, M., D. M. Freebairn G. L. Hammer and D. M. Silburn. 1992. Impact of soil erosion on production in cropping systems. II Simulation of production and erosion risks for a wheat cropping system. *Australian Journal of Soil Research* 30: 775–88.

Lobell, D. B., M. Burke and M. P. Reynolds. 2010. Economic impacts of climate change on agriculture to 2030. *Climate Change and Crop Production* 1: 38–49.

Luo, Q. Y., W. Bellotti, M. Williams and B. Bryan. 2005. Potential impact of climate change on wheat yield in South Australia. *Agricultural and Forest Meteorology* 132 (3–4): 273–85.

McKeon, G., W. Hall, B. Henry, G. Stone and I. Watson. 2004. *Pasture Degradation and Recovery in Australia's Rangelands: Learning from History*. Queensland Department of Natural Resources, Mines and Energy: Brisbane.

McKeon, G. M., S. M. Howden, D. M. Silburn, J. O. Carter, J. F. Clewett, G. L. Hammer, P. W. Johnston, P. L. Lloyd, J. J. Mott, B. Walker, E. J. Weston and J. R. Wilcocks. 1988. The effect of climate change on crop and pastoral production in Queensland. In G. I. Pearman (ed.), *Greenhouse: Planning for Climate Cchange*. CSIRO: Melbourne, pp. 546–63.

Meinke, H., R. Nelson, P. Kokic, R. Stone, R. Selvaraju and W. Baethgen. 2006. Actionable climate knowledge: from analysis to synthesis. *Climate Research* 33: 101–10.

Monteith, J. L. 1965. Evaporation and environment. Symposia of the Society for Experimental Biology 19: 205–34.

Murphy, S. F. and R. C. Sorenson. 2001. Saltwater intrusion in the Mackay coastal plains aquifer. *Proceedings of the Australian Society of Sugar Cane Technologists* 23: 70–76.

Nelson, R., S. M. Howden and M. Stafford Smith. 2008. Using adaptive governance to rethink the way science supports Australian drought policy. *Environmental Science and Policy* 11: 588–601.

Newman, J. A., D. J. Gibson, A. J. Parsons and J. H. M Thornley. 2003. How predictable are aphid population responses to elevated CO_2? *Journal of Animal Ecology* 72: 556–66.

Nidumolu, U. B., P. Hayman, S. M. Howden and B. Alexander. 2012. Re-evaluating the margin of the South Australian grain belt in a changing climate. *Climate Research* 51: 249–60.

Quiggin, J., D. Adamson, S. Chambers and P. Schrobback. 2010. climate change, uncertainty, and adaptation: the case of irrigated agriculture in the Murray–Darling Basin in Australia. *Canadian Journal of Agricultural Economics* 58 (4): 531–54.

Reyenga, P. J., S. M. Howden, H. Meinke and G. M. McKeon. 2000. Modelling global change impacts on wheat cropping in south-east Queensland, Australia. *Environmental Modelling and Software* 14: 297–306.

Sanders, O., T. Goesch and N. Hughes. 2010. Adapting to water scarcity. Canberra: Australian Bureau of Agricultural and Resource Economics, *Issues and Insights* 10.5.

Stephens, D. J. and T. J. Lyons. 1998. Rainfall-yield relationships across the Australian wheatbelt. *Australian Journal of Agricultural Research* 49: 211–23.

Stokes, C. and S. M. Howden (eds). 2010. *Adapting Agriculture to Climate Change: Preparing Australian Agriculture, Forestry and Fisheries for the Future.* CSIRO Publishing: Collingwood, 296 pp.

Tubiello, F. N., J. Amthor, K. Boote, M. Donatelli,W. Easterling, G. Fischer, R. Gifford, S. M. Howden, J. Reilly and C. Rosenzweig. 2007. Crop response to elevated CO_2 and world food supply. *European Journal of Agronomy* 26: 215–33.

UNESCAP. 2009. State of the Environment in Asia and the Pacific 2009. United Nations Economic and Social Commission for Asia and the Pacific. Available online at: http://www.unescap.org/65/documents/Theme-Study/st-escap-2535.pdf [accessed 25 July 2013].

Van Ittersum, M. K., S. M. Howden and S. Asseng. 2003. Sensitivity of productivity and deep drainage of wheat cropping systems in a Mediterranean environment to changes in CO_2, temperature and precipitation. *Agriculture, Ecosystems and Environment* 97: 255–73.

Wang, Y. P., J. R. Handoko and G. M. Rimmington. 1992. Sensitivity of wheat growth to increased air temperature for different scenarios of ambient CO_2 concentration and rainfall in Victoria, Australia: a simulation study. *Climate Research* 2: 131–49.

Webb, L. and P. H. Whetton. 2010. Horticulture. In C. J. Stokes and S. M. Howden (eds), *Adapting Australian agriculture to climate change.* CSIRO Publishing: Collingwood, pp. 119–36.

Whetton, P., D. Karoly, I. Watterson, L. Webb, F. Drost, D. Kirono and K. McInnes. 2013. Australia's Climate in a Four Degree World. In P. Christoff (ed.), *Four Degrees of Climate Change: Australia in a Hot World,* Earthscan: London, ch. 2.

Wilby, R. L., J. Troni, Y. Biot, L. Tedd, B. C. Hewitson, D. M. Smith and R. T. Sutton. 2009. A review of climate risk information for adaptation and development planning. *International Journal of Climatology* 29: 1193–215.

Ziska, L. H., J. R. Teasdale and J. A. Bunce. 1999. Future atmospheric carbon dioxide may increase tolerance to glyphosate. *Weed Science,* 608–15.

7 Compounding crises

Climate change in a complex world

Will Steffen and David Griggs

A Four Degree World is daunting enough when considering climate on its own, but when considered in the context of other changes that are occurring at the global level – relating to population growth and other changes in demographics, resource availability, global geopolitics, trade, biodiversity loss and ecosystem degradation, equity issues and many more factors – the probability of interacting or compounding crises is likely to be very high. The increasingly tight connectivity of globalized society increases the risk of such crises, as a shock in one part of the global system can be propagated rapidly around the planet.

Such complex shocks are already occurring. Consider, for example, the global financial crisis and the food price spikes of 2008 and 2011, with the latter possibly contributing to the recent unrest in the Middle East, the so-called 'Arab Spring'. In so far as climate change is a contributing factor, such shocks and crises will only become more probable and more severe, especially if the temperature rise reaches 4°C or more above pre-industrial levels.

Complexity and the human enterprise: the view from the past

Contemporary society is not the first in the history of humans on earth to have faced compounding shocks or pressures. Earlier complex societies in the Holocene also faced these – albeit not at the global level – and many of them collapsed as a result. In many of the most well-studied cases, regional climatic shifts due to natural variability were often a contributing factor (Costanza et al., 2006). Examination of these societal collapses can offer insights into the risks that contemporary society faces from climate change, particularly those associated with a Four Degree World.

Two of the best known examples of collapses – those of the Mayan Empire in meso-America and of the Akkadian Empire in present-day Syria – were linked to unusually dry climatic periods that overwhelmed the resilience of these societies (Cullen et al., 2000). The decline of the Roman Empire coincided with the transition of the climate from the 'Roman Climate Optimum', a somewhat warmer, drier and more stable climatic period at the height of the empire (300 BC to AD 300), to one less hospitable and more variable (Gunn et al., 2004). Perhaps the classic example of a climate-induced collapse was the disappearance of the

Greenland Norse community at the end of the Medieval Climate Anomaly, an approximately 400-year warm period centred around the North Atlantic region that allowed the settlement of southern Greenland by people of European lifestyles just before AD 1000. About 400 years later, the Norse quickly and somewhat mysteriously disappeared (Diamond, 2005).

In all of these cases, though, the collapse was not driven directly or exclusively by climatic shifts in a simple cause–effect relationship. Features of the institutional organization, value systems and socio-economic dynamics of the civilizations themselves played at least as strong a role in their demise, as did climate, strongly hinting of multiple, compounding stresses and interacting impacts (Costanza et al., 2006).

Some important lessons can be learned from these earlier societies. Although there is no consensus on the precise explanatory factors that describe their collapses, several generic hypotheses have been put forward to explain why some societies collapsed in the face of external pressures while others transformed, survived and even thrived. Two of these explanations have particularly direct relevance for twenty-first-century society. Joseph Tainter proposes that as societies evolve they generally solve problems by becoming more complex and more highly organized. This is an effective response to problems to a point, but as the societies become ever more complex, they erode resilience and are less adaptive, thus becoming more vulnerable to collapse in the future (Tainter, 1988). Jared Diamond proposes that if societies cling to core values that have become dysfunctional as the world changes around them, they become increasingly vulnerable to challenges and shocks and thus prone to collapse (Diamond, 2005).

Whatever the complex causes of the collapse of these earlier civilizations, their populations had the opportunity to disperse and move to new lands that were either unpopulated or lightly populated. That option does not exist for contemporary populations. In fact, the world of today is vastly different from anything that has come before it in terms of human experience, complexity and connectedness. Although many contemporary societies have achieved unprecedented wealth (albeit very unevenly distributed), sophisticated technologies, ever-increasing economic efficiency and global-level connectivity, these developments may have eroded resilience compared to that of the simpler, less integrated, less interconnected and less economically efficient (but with more in-built redundancies) societies of the past.

The Anthropocene: a planet under pressure

Not only are the contemporary, globalized societies of today vastly different from any that have preceded them, but the environmental changes that they are facing – and indeed, to a large extent, causing – are also unprecedented. The consequences of a Four Degree World, then, would be played out in the context of very dynamic, rapidly changing contemporary, globalized societies, already under considerable stress from other environmental and socio-economic pressures.

The fact that human activities have caused most of the observed warming of the climate system over the past half-century, primarily through the emission of greenhouse gases, is now beyond reasonable doubt (IPCC, 2007). However, climate change is only one of many changes to the global environment over the past century or so that have been driven by the burgeoning human enterprise (Steffen et al., 2004).

First, the current rate of extinction of biological species is 100 to 1,000 times greater than the background rate (MA, 2005), suggesting that the earth may be entering the sixth great extinction event in its history, but the first to be driven by a biological species (*Homo sapiens*).

Moreover, human activities are now responsibility for 'fixing' more nitrogen (converting unreactive to reactive forms) than all natural N-fixing processes in the terrestrial biosphere combined (Galloway and Cowling, 2002). This additional reactive nitrogen pollutes local lakes and rivers, reduces biodiversity by fertilizing fast-growing species at the expense of rarer species that occupy nutrient-poor niches and contributes the powerful greenhouse gas nitrous oxide to the atmosphere. These and many other global-level changes to the environment are shown in Figure 7.1 (Steffen et al., 2004, and references therein).

Accompanying these global environmental changes, and interacting with them, is an equally far-reaching set of changes to the socio-economic fabric of the human enterprise (Figure 7.2, Steffen et al., 2004, and references therein). Changes include a rapid rise in human population, an even more dramatic rise in economic activity, much greater exploitation – by rate, volume and extent – of natural resources, and dramatic increases in transportation, trade and communication. Perhaps the most striking feature of Figure 7.2 is the remarkable change in rate of all 12 indicators around 1950, after the end of the Second World War. This phenomenon has been called The Great Acceleration (Hibbard et al., 2006) and marks a fundamental change in the human–environment relationship.

Taken together, the interacting socio-economic and environmental changes at the planetary level depicted in Figures 7.1 and 7.2 are often referred to as *global change*. Perhaps an appropriate geological term – and concept – to define the period of this profound shift is the *Anthropocene*.

The term Anthropocene was first proposed in 2000 by Nobel Laureate Paul Crutzen (Crutzen and Stoermer, 2000; Crutzen, 2002). It is based on scientific perceptions of the nature and impacts of recent global change and refers to the fact that humans have now become so large in numbers and pervasive in activity that they rival some of the great forces of Nature in their influence on the functioning of the Earth System.

The influence of humans on the climate system is now well known, but human activities are influencing the Earth System in many other ways. For example, the acidity of the ocean is rising rapidly (Royal Society, 2005), over 50 per cent of land ecosystems are now human dominated (Ellis et al., 2010), about a third of

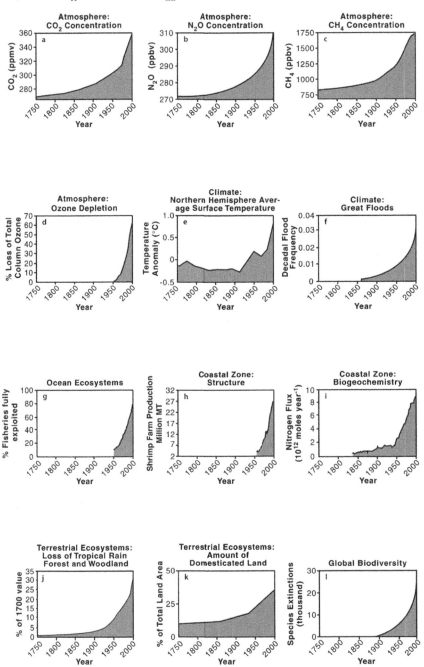

Figure 7.1 Changes in the global environment, 1750–2000

Source: Steffen et al., 2004

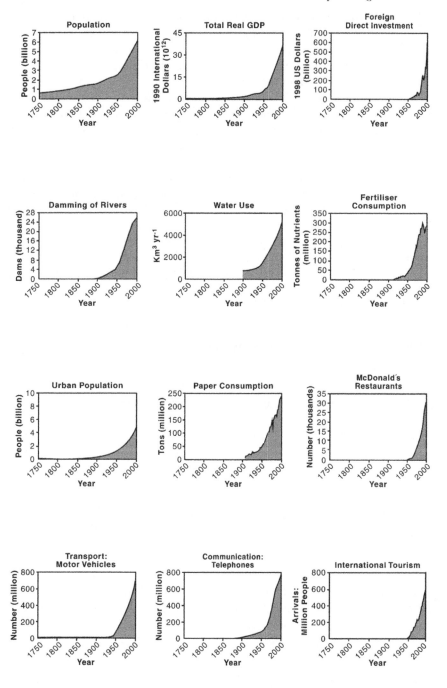

Figure 7.2 Changes in the human enterprise, 1750–2000
Source: Steffen et al., 2004

all accessible freshwater is appropriated for human purposes (Postel, 1998; Oki and Kanae, 2006), and the loss of biological diversity is now at least two orders of magnitude greater than the background extinction rate (MA, 2005).

The human enterprise itself is also under considerable pressure in the 21st century. Resource constraints are beginning to have a demonstrable effect on global change. The oil price spikes of 2007–8 and 2011 are examples of how even a small imbalance in the supply–demand relationship of a finite resource can propagate rapidly through the global economic system. Less is known about the potential for 'peak phosphorus' to occur this century (e.g. Cordell et al., 2009), but its implications in terms of our capability to feed a still-rising human population are significant. Communication and transportation are changing at astounding rates, leading to a state of hyperconnectivity that can transmit information – and misinformation – at phenomenal rates around the globe. Per capita incomes and rates of consumption in the industrialized world have increased at a rapid rate since the Second World War, and several large developing countries, such as China, Brazil, India and South Africa, are now integral parts of this world. Yet equity issues remain stubbornly difficult to solve and are driving deleterious social outcomes across the global, even in wealthy countries (Wilkinson and Pickett, 2009).

Tipping elements in the Earth System

The rapidly changing human enterprise, itself now in a novel situation never before experienced by humanity, is, in addition, facing a global environmental context that is also unique. The advent of the Anthropocene implies that the earth is leaving the current epoch, the Holocene. This exit is no mere fact of scientific curiosity or quirk of labeling.

The Holocene, the recent 10,000–11,000-year period of relative climate stability, is the only state of the Earth System that we know for certain is capable of supporting complex human civilizations (Steffen et al., 2011). It may be possible that complex societies can continue to prosper and thrive through the period of rapid changes in the Anthropocene, but that assertion is based on a rather optimistic leap of faith rather than on a careful, evidence-based analysis.

One of the most prominent causes for concern in the Anthropocene is that the very severe forcing of the climate system implied by a Four Degree World would lead to highly nonlinear, abrupt and often irreversible changes to which contemporary society would find it difficult or impossible to adapt. The notion of *tipping elements* in the Earth System (Lenton et al., 2008; Richardson et al., 2011) is central to the risk of abrupt and irreversible change.

The concept of tipping elements is based on complex system science (e.g. Scheffer, 2009) and refers to the observation that systems, and in this case sub-systems of the Earth System, can have multiple states with abrupt transitions between them. This behaviour is counterintuitive compared to the much better known logic of cause–effect, in which the response of a system is proportional to the amount of forcing it experiences. Systems with tipping points (thresholds) may be generally unresponsive to changes in a forcing factor for a long time, until the tipping point is approached. An analogy is the continuous addition of weight to a bridge. For a while the bridge appears unresponsive and handles the additional weight without problems. Then, with a small amount of additional weight, a critical threshold (tipping point) is transgressed, the bridge can no longer bear the weight, and it suddenly and spectacularly collapses. The general principle is simple: as the tipping point is crossed, small changes in the forcing factor lead to rapid and surprisingly large changes in the system.

Figure 7.3 is a global map showing the location of various tipping elements in the Earth System (Richardson et al., 2011). The existence of such tipping elements is not based only on theoretical considerations or on model simulations, but rather each of them has been observed in records of earth's history. They are real phenomena with identifiable risks for human wellbeing should tipping points be transgressed in a Four Degree World. As shown in Figure 7.3, the tipping elements can be classified into: (i) those based on the melting of ice or frozen soil or sediments; (ii) those based on rapid changes to atmospheric or oceanic circulation; and (iii) those based on changes to major biomes or marine ecosystems.

Table 7.1 provides more details on many of the tipping elements shown in the figure, including the transition time for the shift from one state to another of the system, the impacts for humanity that crossing the tipping point would produce, and the temperature range within which the threshold is likely to lie. For all but one of the tipping elements shown in the table, temperature is the

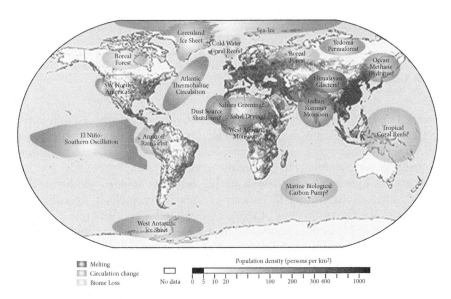

Figure 7.3: Tipping elements in the Earth System, overlaid on the human population density on Earth

Source: Richardson et al., 2011

Table 7.1   Vulnerability of tipping elements to a 4°C global warming

Tipping element	Level of global warming	Transition timescale	Key impacts
Arctic sea ice	0.5–2°C	~10 yr (rapid)	Amplified warming, ecosystem change
Greenland ice sheet	1–2°C	>300 yr (slow)	Sea level, +2–7 m
West Antarctic ice sheet	3–5°C	>300 yr (slow)	Sea level, +5 m
Atlantic thermohaline circulation	3–5°C	~100 yr (gradual)	Regional cooling, ITCZ shift, regional sea level
El Nino-Southern Oscillation (ENSO)	3–6°C	~100 yr (gradual)	Drought in SE Asia and elsewhere
Indian summer monsoon	N/A	~1 yr (rapid)	Drought, decreased carrying capacity
Sahara/Sahel and West African monsoon	3–5°C	~10 yr (rapid)	Wetting or drying of the Sahel
Amazon rainforest	3–4°C	~50 yr (gradual)	Biodiversity loss, decreased rainfall, biome switch to grassland or savanna
Boreal forest	3–5°C	~50 yr (gradual)	Dieback and biome switch to grassland or woodland
Yedoma permafrost	4–6°C	~100 yr (gradual)	CH_4 and CO_2 release

Source: Estimates are based on Lenton et al., 2008 and have been updated by T. Lenton in Richardson et al., 2011

major, or one of the most important, forcing factors that could drive a shift in the system. The exception is the Indian summer monsoon, where the forcing factor is aerosol loading over the subcontinent, which affects the land–sea temperature differential and thus the behaviour of the monsoon.

The transition times for a system to shift from one state to another once a threshold is crossed vary greatly between systems. For example, it is possible that the thresholds for loss of most of the Greenland and West Antarctic ice sheets could be crossed later this century, but the time needed for that volume of ice to be lost would be centuries or millennia. By contrast, it is likely that the tipping point for the Arctic sea ice has already been crossed and that within a few decades the Arctic Sea will be ice free during the northern hemisphere summer months.

All of the tipping elements shown in Table 7.1 have estimated thresholds that could be crossed in a Four Degree World. For several of them – Arctic sea ice, the Greenland ice sheet, and conversion of the Amazon rainforest to a savannah or woodland – crossing the threshold is more likely than not to occur this century. Others become more likely if the temperature continues to rise beyond 4°C.

The consequences for human society of crossing these tipping elements are particularly serious in three major areas. First, loss of large amounts of ice from the polar ice sheets would contribute to sea-level rise that would continue for centuries and would ultimately be measured in metres. Second, changes in oceanic and atmospheric circulation would change regional precipitation patterns, further affecting agriculture and urban water supplies. Third, rapid changes in the composition, structure and functioning of large ecosystems on land and in the ocean would result in significant losses of biodiversity, undermining the capability of these ecosystems to provide services that benefit humanity. Adapting to shifts in these tipping elements would undoubtedly present formidable challenges to contemporary society in their own right, but such changes will not occur in isolation from other changes occurring in the socio-economic sphere and in the environment at local levels.

Compounding global crises

As noted earlier in the discussion about the changing human–environment relationship in the past and in contemporary society in the Anthropocene, environmental pressures, such as changes in climate, do not act in isolation in a simple cause–impact relationship. Rather, they are invariably intertwined with other changes in the environment as well as changes in the human enterprise, ranging from alterations of economic policy to changes in demographic patterns and shifts in underlying core values of society. Until the recent past, most of these interacting stresses have acted upon societies at local and regional levels, in contrast to the novel situation of a globalized contemporary society in which our own planetary-level life support system is in question.

Recent analyses of the challenges facing humanity in the 21st century have highlighted the risks associated with compounding global crises resulting from these complex interactions between society and environment (e.g. Walker et al., 2009; Biggs et al., 2011; Folke et al., 2011). Figure 7.4, adapted from Walker et al. (2009), is an elegant visual representation of the nature of these compounding crises. In addition to the multiple, interacting drivers of change, two other features of these crises stand out in the figure. First, many of the unwanted outcomes are the result of feedbacks in the system (the broken arrows in the figure) rather than the initial impacts of the global drivers on the system. Second, the major sectors – climate, ecosystems, human health and economy – cannot be treated in isolation from one another. In short, simple cause–effect logic will fail in understanding these global crises; they lie squarely in the realm of complex system science.

Some progress has been made in understanding the nature of these compounding global crises despite their complexity. For example, many crises are typified by largely independent stressors acting on interconnected systems, thus generating feedbacks and often surprising outcomes that are difficult to predict and manage. A good example is the global food crisis of 2008.

Global drivers   **Unwanted outcomes**

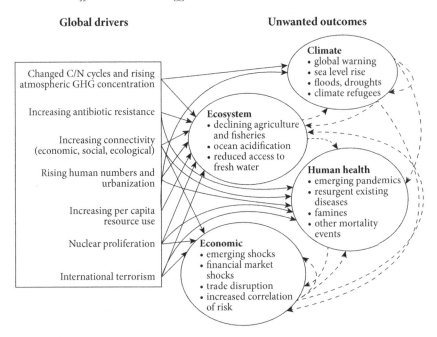

Figure 7.4   Unwanted social outcomes resulting from the interactive effects of both biophysical and social drivers in the Earth System

Source: Folke, 2011

A recent analysis of this food crisis has explored how the types of factors shown Figure 7.4 operated in that crisis (Biggs et al., 2011). The oil price spike of 2007–08 acted as a strong, underlying global driver and trigger, as oil-based fuels underpin much of the global food system from production to packaging, transport and marketing. However, other drivers and initial responses to the rising prices compounded the crisis. Climate change-related drivers played an important role in two ways. First, the drought in Australia reduced food exports, and in a future global food system on the edge of undersupply, a small drop in Australian output could have global implications. Second, a significant switch away from food and towards biofuel production in the American agricultural sector also likely contributed to the rapid rise in food prices. Responses to the price rises in some countries, such as the grains export ban in Russia, may have also exacerbated the situation.

An Australian example of the interacting stressors syndrome is the Great Barrier Reef (GBR) (see also Hoegh-Guldberg et al., 2013, Chapter 5 in this volume). The GBR is subject to a wide range of local and regional pressures, ranging from the proximate (direct) pressures of fishing and tourism to the regional-level pressure of sediment and nutrient runoff into the coastal seas from the adjacent agricultural areas of North Queensland and the passage of large merchant ships through the GBR (Great Barrier Reef Marine Park Authority,

2009). Compounding these pressures are a number of climate-related stressors of a global nature. These include the two well-known stressors of rising surface water temperature, which leads to coral bleaching events, and the increasing acidity of the ocean owing to the rising atmospheric concentration of CO_2, a significant fraction of which dissolves in the ocean (Hoegh-Guldberg et al., 2007). On top of this, climate change also affects the GBR through sea-level rise, which can inundate sea turtle nesting sites, and through the impacts of tropical cyclones, which can cause significant structural damage to the reef as they cross it, with the amount of damage dependent on the path and severity of the cyclone (Great Barrier Reef Marine Park Authority 2011).

Effective management responses at the local and regional levels can reduce those stressors and increase the resilience of the GBR towards the global-level stressors. For example, careful management of the tourism industry and the creation of large 'no-take' zones to reduce fishing pressure have significantly increased the resilience of the GBR. However, despite these advances in reducing local and regional stressors, the impacts of the global-level stressors are now apparent. Since 1979 there have been eight mass bleaching events on the GBR with none reported before that date (Done et al., 2003). Over the last two decades, there has been a significant reduction across the GBR in coral calcification rate, linear extension and coral density, all indicators of coral growth (De'ath et al., 2009). The interacting impacts of all of these stressors taken together are serious; over the past 27 years there has been a 50 per cent reduction in the coral cover of the GBR (De'ath et al., 2012).

Another feature of many compounding global crises is the 'cascade effect', in which an initial impact is transmitted and amplified by a number of feedbacks in the global human–environment system. The cascade effect is greatly facilitated by the rapidly increasing connectivity in the global economic system, which means that shocks in one location can propagate rapidly around the globe. The Global Financial Crisis is a good example of a cascading crisis in the socio-economic sphere, but not without links to the climate system. Although climate change did not play a role in triggering this cascade, the mitigation of climate change figured prominently in the response, with a few countries pouring their stimulus funding into clean energy systems while many others squandered theirs on stimulating short-term consumption.

Finally, climate change presents a type of complexity new to global crises. Within the climate system itself, there are very long lag times between the drivers of change and their consequences. This feature is typified by its global scale, the fact that the consequences are often known but will occur far in the future, and the risk of irreversible changes. These long lag times characteristic of the climate system greatly complicate the public discourse on the issue, as is obvious in the quality of much of the debate on climate change in Australia over the past few years, and also highlight the lack of adequate regulatory or management institutions that can cope with such long timescales.

Perhaps the best example of this feature of climate change is the slow response of sea-level rise to the emissions of greenhouse gases and the consequent warming. This is particularly so for the contribution of the polar ice sheets to sea-level rise, as noted in Table 7.1, where the threshold for a major loss ice from Greenland could well be transgressed within the next couple of decades but the transition time (before the consequences are fully felt) is many centuries. The consequences of a 5m sea-level rise, for example, would be enormous if societies did not proactively plan for it, and loss of ice from the polar ice sheets is essentially irreversible in any timeframe meaningful for human societies.

Even more subtle is the potential for emissions of carbon dioxide and methane from organic material stored in the frozen soil of the northern high latitudes. Again, the transition time is potentially long – in the order of a century or two – but the consequences could be very large. The most recent analysis of permafrost carbon (Schuur et al., 2011) found that for a high-emissions/high-warming scenario – the type of emission trajectory that would lead to a Four Degree World later this century – emissions of carbon (almost entirely carbon dioxide) from this frozen source would be 30–63 billion tonnes by 2040 but could reach 232 to 380 billion tonnes by 2100 and 549–864 billion tonnes by 2300, showing the long lag times involved. By comparison, current total emissions per year of carbon from fossil fuel combustion are approaching 10 billion tonnes. These projections reflect a strong feedback loop in which emissions of carbon from permafrost drive more warming, which in turn drives more emissions of carbon from permafrost, and so on.

Returning to Figure 7.4, at present the feedbacks from climate change to the other sectors are sometimes significant, but many of the other drivers and feedbacks are of similar orders of magnitude. That would change dramatically in a Four Degree World, in which climate change would not only dominate most of the direct impacts on sectors, but would trigger many more feedback loops than are currently shown in Figure 7.4.

Attempting to predict the types compounding global crises that will emerge in a Four Degree World (and probably at lower levels of temperature increases) is virtually impossible, but it is reasonable to say that such crises will be common, profound and exceptionally difficult to cope with. Given the highly connected nature of the human enterprise in the twenty-first century, it is difficult to foresee situations in which a compounding crisis will affect Australia alone; rather, we will most likely be strongly linked into phenomena that are truly global in scale, especially those that are strongly manifest in the Asia-Pacific region.

The Earth System as a single, complex system: tipping towards an uninhabitable state?

The tipping elements shown in Figure 7.3 and Table 7.1 are sub-systems of the Earth System as a whole. What if the Earth System as a whole, including the climate system, itself has a tipping point? The notion is not as far-fetched as it may seem. Given the long lifetimes of significant fractions of the additional CO_2 in the atmosphere (Archer and Brovkin, 2008) and the amplifying feedback mechanisms in the carbon cycle (e.g. Krey et al., 2009; Schurr et al., 2011), it is likely that strong warming scenarios will result in a long-lasting high temperature world (e.g. Solomon et al., 2009).

There is considerable evidence from the past that the Earth System behaves as a single, interacting system (Scheffer, 2009). During the late Quaternary period in earth history, the period during which hominins and fully modern humans have evolved, the earth has existed in two states – the long glacial state (ice ages) and the much shorter warm intervals that punctuate the ice age world (e.g. Petit et al., 1999). Other features of Earth System behaviour are typical of a complex system: (i) the close correlation between climate (temperature) and greenhouse gas concentrations (feedback loops); (ii) the tight bounds on the variation of temperature and carbon dioxide and methane concentrations between ice ages and warm periods (limit cycles); and (iii) the c.100,000-year cycling between ice ages and warm periods, triggered by changes in earth's orbit around the sun but largely driven by the internal dynamics of the Earth System (phase locking).

The global mean temperature difference between an ice age and a warm period is approximately 5–6°C. A Four Degree World may mean that the Earth System has already crossed a global threshold on the way to a much warmer state, a 6–7°C world which would eventually become ice free and which could be stable for a very long period of time, as it has in the recent past in terms of earth history (Zalasiewicz et al., 2012). Such a state, however, would be much hotter than the earth that *Homo sapiens* has evolved in and much hotter than our physiology has ever experienced across much of our current geographic range. It is hard to image that contemporary human societies would be able to survive in a planet where much of its surface would be a hostile environment for our species.

Towards global sustainability

It is clear from this and other chapters in this volume that a Four Degree World will be very difficult to live, let alone prosper, in, and so effective approaches are needed to limit the magnitude of warming to significantly lower levels. However, as this chapter has demonstrated, climate change does not act in isolation from a large number of other global-level environmental and socio-economic changes.

One approach to dealing with the interacting environmental challenges is based on a small set of planetary boundaries (Rockström et al., 2009a; 2009b) that define the safe operating space for humanity. These planetary boundaries are based on hard-wired features of the Earth System and form the non-negotiable basis for securing a sustainable future for humanity on the planet. Transgressing one or more planetary boundaries may be deleterious or even catastrophic due to the risk of crossing thresholds that will trigger non-linear, abrupt environmental change within continental- to planetary-scale systems.

Climate change is one of the nine planetary boundaries, and Rockström et al. recommended a boundary value of 350 ppm CO_2 (or no more that $+1$ W m^{-2} in radiative forcing), which would limit global average warming to very much below 4°C (and even below 2°C). The complete set of planetary boundaries, with their control variables and suggested boundaries, are:

- climate change (CO_2 concentration in the atmosphere <350 ppm and/or a maximum change of $+1$ W m^{-2} in radiative forcing);

- ocean acidification (mean surface seawater saturation state with respect to aragonite ≥ 80 per cent of pre-industrial levels);
- stratospheric ozone (<5 per cent reduction in O_3 concentration from pre-industrial level of 290 Dobson Units);
- biogeochemical nitrogen (N) cycle (limit industrial and agricultural fixation of N_2 to 35 Tg N yr^{-1}) and phosphorus (P) cycle (annual P inflow to oceans not to exceed 10 times the natural background weathering of P);
- global freshwater use (<4000 km^3 yr^{-1} of consumptive use of runoff resources);
- land system change (<15 per cent of the ice-free land surface under cropland);
- rate at which biological diversity is lost (annual rate of <10 extinctions per million species);
- chemical pollution (not yet quantified);
- atmospheric aerosol loading (not yet quantified).

Figure 7.5 shows the current status of the control variables for the seven boundaries that have been quantified compared to the 'safe operating space', which is shown in the centre of the Figure as the lightly-shaded circle. It is estimated that humanity has already transgressed three planetary boundaries: those for climate change, rate of biodiversity loss, and changes to the global nitrogen cycle.

The important point is that climate change is affecting a planetary life support system that is already under other stresses, such an excess loading of nitrogen, and is suffering an erosion of resilience through the loss of biological diversity. In addition to these environmental stresses, however, it is important to remember that changes in the socio-economic sphere are just as important for the types of compounding global crises described in this chapter.

As indicated earlier there is increasing evidence that the natural Earth System behaves as a single interacting system. However, this is also increasingly the case for our modern society as a whole. Things that at first glance appear not to be connected, such as the economic system, population and ageing, ores and mineral production, conflict and terrorism, energy production and social systems, at closer inspection are all part of an intricate web where changes in one of these elements has knock-on effects on another element, which in turn impacts on yet another element, and so on. To add even further to the complexity, all of these are also connected to and interact with the natural system.

To give just one example, increases in the frequency and magnitude of extreme weather events, such as floods, droughts, wind storms, tropical cyclones etc., are expected as a result of climate change (IPCC, 2007a; 2012). The impacts of these extreme events will be most severely felt in developing countries (IPCC 2007b; 2012).

There are several reasons why this will be the case. For instance, impacts are worse – many developing countries are already more flood and drought prone and a large share of the economy is in climate sensitive sectors. Also, many developing countries have a high level of vulnerability and a weak ability to adapt to existing and emerging climate-related pressures because of their lack of financial, institutional and technological capacity and access to relevant knowledge.

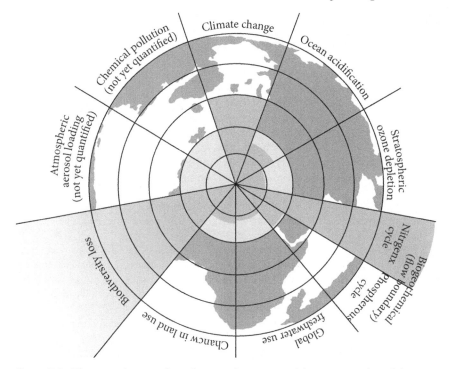

Figure 7.5 The nine planetary boundaries and estimates of the current value of the control variable compared to the boundary estimate

Source: Rockström et al., 2009

Hence, climate change is likely to impact disproportionately upon the poorest countries and the poorest persons within countries, exacerbating inequities in health status and access to adequate food, clean water and other resources. This in turn may lead to large numbers of environmental refugees, something that is already being seen in many places around the world from North Africa to Pakistan.

Again, just as there are tipping points in the natural system due to amplifying feedback mechanisms, it is likely, if our modern society also behaves as a single complex system, that elements within this system also have the potential for tipping points where small changes in driving conditions can lead to large consequences. It can be argued that the way the economic system behaved to create the global financial crisis is an example of such behaviour.

As indicated earlier, one approach to dealing with complex interacting environmental challenges is to define a safe operating space for humanity within the Earth System based on a small set of planetary boundaries. In the same way it may be possible to define a safe operating space for humanity within our modern society by defining a set of sustainability boundaries. To date, because of the complexity of the systems involved, this has not been attempted, but it may be necessary if we are to understand how best to respond effectively to the threats imposed by a Four Degree World.

References

Archer, D. and V. Brovkin. 2008. The millennial atmospheric lifetime of anthropogenic CO_2. *Climatic Change* 90: 283–97.

Biggs, D., R. Biggs, V. Dakos, R. J. Scholes and M. Schoon. 2011. Are we entering an era of concatenated global crises? *Ecology and Society* 16: 27.

Cordell, D., J. -O. Drangert and S. White. 2009. The story of phosphorus: global food security and food for thought. *Global Environmental Change* 19: 292–305.

Costanza, R., L. Graumlich and W. Steffen (eds). 2006. Integrated History and Future of People on Earth. Dahlem Workshop Report 96, 495 pp.

Crutzen, P. J. 2002. Geology of mankind: the Anthropocene. *Nature* 415: 23.

Crutzen, P. J. and E. F. Stoermer. 2000. The 'Anthropocene'. *Global Change Newsletter* 41: 17–18.

Cullen H. M., P. B. DeMenocal, S. Hemming, G. Hemming, F. H. Brown, T. Guilderson and F. Sirocko. 2000. Climate change and the collapse of the Akkadian empire: evidence from the deep sea. *Geology* 28: 379–82.

De'ath, G., K. E. Fabricus, H. Sweatman and M. Puotinen. 2012. The 27-year decline of coral cover on the Great Barrier Reef and its causes. *Proceedings of the National Academy of Sciences (USA)*. doi/10.1073/pnas.1208909109.

De'ath, G., J. M. Lough and K. E. Fabricius. 2009. Declining coral calcification on the Great Barrier Reef. *Science* 323: 116–19.

Diamond, J. 2005. *Collapse: How Societies Choose to Fail or Succeed*. Viking: New York, 592 pp.

Done, T. P., R. Whetton, R. Jones, R. Berkelmans, J. Lough, W. Skirving and S. Wooldridge. 2003. Global climate change and coral bleaching on the Great Barrier Reef. Australian Institute of Marine Science.

Ellis, E. C., K. Klein Goldewijk, S. Siebert, D. Lightman and N. Ramankutty. 2010. Anthropogenic transformation of the biomes, 1700 to 2000. *Global Ecology and Biogeography* 19: 589–606.

Folke, C., Å. Jansson, J. Rockström, P. Olsson, S. Carpenter, F. S. Chapin, A. -S. Crepin, G. Daily, K. Danell, J. Ebbesson, T. Elmqvist, V. Galaz, F. Moberg, M. Nilsson, H. Österblom, E. Orstrom, Å. Persson, G. Peterson, S. Polasky, W. Steffen, B. Walker and F. Westley. 2011. Reconnecting to the biosphere. *Ambio* 40: 719–38.

Galloway, J. N. and E. B. Cowling. 2002. Reactive nitrogen and the world: two hundred years of change. *Ambio* 31: 64–71.

Great Barrier Reef Marine Park Authority. 2009. Great Barrier Reef outlook report 2009. July 2009, GBRMPA, Townsville, Australia.

Great Barrier Reef Marine Park Authority. 2011. Impacts of tropical cyclone Yasi on the Great Barrier Reef: a report on the findings of a rapid ecological impact assessment. July 2011, GBRMPA, Townsville, Australia.

Gunn, J., C. L. Crumley, E. Jones and B. K. Young. 2004. A landscape analysis of Western Europe during the early Middle Ages. In C. L. Redman, S. R. James, P. R. Fish and J. D. Rogers (eds), *The Archaeology of Global Change: The Impact of Humans on their Environments*, Smithsonian Institution Press: Washington, DC, pp. 165–85.

Hibbard, K. A., P. J. Crutzen, E. F. Lambin, D. Liverman, N. J. Mantua, J. R. McNeill, B. Messerli and W. Steffen. 2006. Decadal interactions of humans and the environment. In R. Costanza, L. Graumlich and W. Steffen (eds), *Integrated History and Future of People on Earth*, Dahlem Workshop Report 96, MIT Press: Boston, MA, pp. 341–75.

Hoegh-Guldberg, O., P. J. Mumby, A. J. Hooten, R. S. Steneck, P. Greenfield, E. Gomez,

C. D. Harvell, P. F. Sale, A. J. Edwards, K. Caldeira, N. Knowlton, C. M. Eakin, R. Iglesias-Prieto, N. Muthiga, R. H. Bradbury, A. Dubi and M. E. Hatziolos. 2007. Coral reefs under rapid climate change and ocean acidification. *Science* 318: 1737–42.

Hoegh-Guldberg, O., E. Poloczanska and A. Richardson. 2013. Australia's marine resources in a warm, acid ocean. In P. Christoff (ed.), *Four Degrees of Climate Change: Australia in a Hot World*, Earthscan: London, ch. 5.

Intergovernmental Panel on Climate Change (IPCC). 2007. Climate Change 2007: The Physical Science Basis. Contribution of Working Group I to the Fourth Assessment Report of the Intergovernmental Panel on Climate Change, S. Solomon, D. Qin, M. Manning, Z. Chen, M. Marquis, K. Averyt, M. M. B. Tignor, H. L. Miller Jr and Z. Chen (eds) Cambridge University Press: Cambridge and New York, 996 pp.

IPCC. 2012. C. B. Field, V. Barros, T. F. Stocker, D. Qin, D. J. Dokken, K. L. Ebi, M. D. Mastrandrea, K. J. Mach, G. -K. Plattner, S. K. Allen, M. Tignor and P. M. Midgley (eds.), Cambridge University Press: Cambridge, 582 pp.

Lenton, T. M., H. Held, E. Kriegler, J. W. Hall, W. Lucht, S. Rahmstorf, H. J. Schellnhuber. 2008. Tipping elements in the earth's climate system. *Proceedings of the National Academy of Sciences (USA)* 105: 1786–93.

Krey, V., J. G. Canadell, N. Nakicenovic, N. Abe, H. Andruleit, D. Archer, A. Grubler N. T. M. Hamilton, A. Johnson, V. Kostov, J. Lamarque, N. Langhorne, E. G. Nisbet, B. O'Neill, K. Riahi, M. Riedel, W. Wang and V. Yakushev. 2009. Gas Hydrates: Entrance to a Methane Age or Climate Threat? *Environmental Research Letters* 4: 1–6. doi:10.1088/1748-9326/4/3/034007.

MA (Millennium Ecosystem Assessment). 2005. *Ecosystems and Human Well-being: Synthesis*. Island Press: Washington, DC.

Oki, T. and S. Kanae. 2006. Global hydrological cycles and world water resources. *Science* 31:, 1068–72.

Petit, J. R., J. Jouzel, D. Raynaud, N. I. Barkov, J.-M. Barnola, I. Basile, M. Bender, J. Chappellaz, M. Davis, G. Delaygue, M. Delmotte, V. M. Kotlyakov, M. Legrand, V. Y. Lipenkov, C. Lorius, L. Pépin, C. Ritz, E. Saltzman and M. Stievenard. 1999. Climate and atmospheric history of the past 420,000 years from the Vostok ice core, Antarctica. *Nature* 399: 429–36.

Postel, S. L. 1998. Water for food production: will there be enough in 2025? *BioScience* 48: 629–38.

Richardson, K., W. Steffen, D. Liverman, T. Barker, F. Jotzo, D. Kammen, R. Leemans, T. Lenton, M. Munasinghe, B. Osman-Elasha, J. Schellnhuber, N. Stern, C. Vogel and O. Waever. 2011. *Climate Change: Global Risks, Challenges and Decisions*. Cambridge University Press: Cambridge, 502 pp.

Rockström, J., W. Steffen, K. Noone, Å. Persson, F. S. Chapin, III, E. F. Lambin, T. M. Lenton, M. Scheffer, C. Folke, H. J. Schellnhuber, B. Nykvist, C. A. de Wit, T. Hughes, S. van der Leeuw, H. Rodhe, S. Sörlin, P. K. Snyder, R. Costanza, U. Svedin, M. Falkenmark, L. Karlberg, R. W. Corell, V. J. Fabry, J. Hansen, B. Walker, D. Liverman, K. Richardson, P. Crutzen and J. A. Foley. 2009a. A safe operating space for humanity. *Nature* 461: 472–5.

—2009b. Planetary boundaries: exploring the safe operating space for humanity. *Ecology and Society* 14: 32.

Royal Society. 2005. *Ocean acidification due to increasing atmospheric carbon dioxide*. June. The Royal Society: London.

Scheffer, M. 2009. *Critical Transitions in Nature and Society*. Princeton University Press: Princeton, NJ, 384 pp.

Schuur, E. A. G., B. Abbott and the Permafrost Carbon Network. 2011. High risk of permafrost thaw. *Nature* 480: 32–3.

Solomon, S., G. K. Plattner, R. Knutti and P. Friedlingstein. 2009. Irreversible climate change due to carbon dioxide emissions. *Proceedings of the National Academy of Sciences (USA)* 106: 1704–9.

Steffen, W., A. Sanderson, P. D. Tyson, J. Jäger, P. Matson, B. Moore III, F. Oldfield, K. Richardson, H. J. Schellnhuber, B. L. Turner and R. J. Wasson. 2004. *Global Change and the Earth System: A Planet Under Pressure*. The IGBP Global Change Series. Berlin, Springer-Verlag, Heidelberg: New York.

Steffen, W., Å. Persson, L. Deutsch, J. Zalasiewicz, M. Williams, K. Richardson, C. Crumley, P. Crutzen, C. Folke, L. Gordon, M. Molina, V. Ramanathan, J. Rockström, M. Scheffer, J. Schellnhuber and U. Svedin. 2011. The Anthropocene: from global change to planetary stewardship. *Ambio* 40: 739–61.

Tainter, J. A. 1988. *The Collapse of Complex Societies*. Cambridge University Press: Cambridge.

Walker, B. H., S. Barrett, S. Polasky, V. Galaz, C. Folke, G. Engström, F. Ackerman, K. Arrow, et al. 2009. Looming global-scale failures and missing institutions. *Science* 325: 1345–6.

Part III

Social and economic impacts

8 Compounding social and economic impacts

The limits to adaptation

Ross Garnaut

Introduction

The climate within which human civilization and Australian society will advance, stagnate or decline through the lives of our children and grandchildren and beyond will be determined by how we think about and respond to the risks of climate change
over the next decade.

A global average temperature rise of 4°C from pre-industrial levels (+4°C GW or 3.5°C above 1990 levels) is well outside the relatively stable temperatures of the last 12,000 years, which have provided the environmental context for the development of human civilization. This Four Degree World would be unknown territory for modern humans and probably for our species at any time in the past.

Even the best mitigation efforts will leave Australians dealing with difficult climate change and they and other members of humanity will have no choice but to try to adapt. But to what will they be adapting? And what will be their chances of sustaining and building upon the fabulous legacy of 12,000 years of human civilization and a quarter of a millennium of modern economic growth?

A false dichotomy is sometimes drawn between adaptation and mitigation, as if these were alternative responses to climate change. Mitigation is the first and most important element of an adaptation strategy. The cost of adaptation and whether a planned adaptive response has any chance of working depend on the effectiveness of mitigation and therefore the extent of climate change.

Adaptation is an inevitable accompaniment of mitigation. As earlier chapters suggest, we are already feeling large impacts of climate change with warming of less than 1°C since pre-industrial times. Some impacts are affecting Australia directly. Examples include the disruption of old patterns of agriculture with less rain in the growing season from April to October in southern Australia, and increased frequency and intensity of extreme weather events (Garnaut, 2008: 106–12; Howden et al., 2013 [Chapter 6, this volume]). Warming of less than 1°C has already forced major changes in food and insurance markets; in what, where and when we plant in Australian agriculture; in resources allocated to management of natural disasters; and in the costs of utilities supplying water and electricity.

Other impacts are being felt indirectly, for example through pressures on global food prices from the intensification of extreme weather events (Garnaut, 2011b: 132–3; Tolero, 2011). These have contributed to failures of state stability in and to displacement of people from some countries and regions, applying pressures on refugee and immigration policies in many countries.

The range of possible climate outcomes that flow from Australia's and other countries' mitigation efforts remains wide. There is still a chance that global mitigation efforts will hold the atmospheric concentration of greenhouse gases to 450 ppm of CO_2 equivalent, corresponding to a reasonable chance of holding global warming to something near 2°C.

The climate outcomes from processes initiated at the Copenhagen Climate Conference in 2009 and taken forward in Cancun in 2010 and Durban in 2011 cannot yet be defined even in broad brush because existing commitments and promises of future agreements say little about what happens after 2020. They have been interpreted to suggest that atmospheric concentrations of greenhouse gases of 550 or 650 ppm are possible – most likely leading eventually to global average temperature increases of 4°C or more. However, depending on what we all do next on mitigation, much better and much worse outcomes remain possible.

There is some uncertainty about the amount of warming associated with any given increase in greenhouse gas concentrations, and about some of the important impacts from any extent of warming. This means that Australians now and in the future face uncertainty about the level of their adaptation challenge.

But for all the uncertainty, when we compare the most likely physical and biophysical effects of 4°C warming as described elsewhere in this book – including shocks of magnitudes that have in the past turned out to be unmanageable for modern human social, economic and political systems – planning for adaptation to a Four Degree World within established state structures seems an indulgence of fantasy.

So, current adaptation policy is necessarily about preparation for the 2°C warming – or a bit more – that would be an inevitable accompaniment of successful global mitigation policies. The rest for now is for hopes and prayers, and not for policy planning. If our generation fails to mitigate emissions and bequeaths a temperature increase of 4°C or more to future generations, present discussions about how they should try to manage their circumstances are unlikely to be of much worth.

The difference in impact between 2°C and 3°C was examined in detail in the 2008 Garnaut Climate Change Review (Garnaut, 2008: Chapters 4, 5, 6 and 11). It is large enough for it to be in Australia's interests to make the extra effort required, as its fair share of a global mitigation effort, to hold or to bring back greenhouse gas concentrations to 450ppm (Garnaut 2008: Chapter 11).

Temperature increases beyond 3°C would be associated with increasing risks to the stability of state and society. But whatever happens to the state and ordered society, humans will continue to make their lives as best they can. The extent of climate change will shape their chances of salvaging more rather than less from their civilizational inheritance. There is no expected level of warming at which we can say that so much damage has been done by climate change that there is not much point in putting effort into stopping more.

Building blocks for adaptation

Beyond doing as much as we can on mitigation, there are two main building blocks for a productive response to the adaptation challenge (Garnaut, 2008, ch. 15; Garnaut 2011b, Chapter 8). The first is to make sure we have a strong, flexible economy, with smoothly functioning markets. The second is to make sure that governments, businesses and households have sound information about possible impacts of climate change on various regions and activities. These building blocks will assist the adaptation of future Australians up to the point where climate change overwhelms the state.

Climate change is bound to impose shocks and hard times on Australians and others now and in the future. Australians in future will do better if they are working with a productive economy that is in a strong fiscal position in preparation for a shock, and has the structural flexibility that comes from well-regulated markets.

Adaptation to climate change will be more effective, and lower in cost, the more individual Australians and enterprises as well as governments are involved in working through the choices, anticipating problems before they arrive and taking into account all of the risks in their investment decisions.

Soundly functioning markets assist households, communities and businesses to respond effectively to the impacts of climate change. Markets provide the most effective avenue for addressing many of the uncertainties posed by climate change. Australia's prime asset in responding to the adaptation and mitigation challenges that lie ahead is the prosperous, open and flexible market-oriented economy that has emerged from reform over the last quarter century.

Some domestic and international markets for particular goods and services will be especially important to Australia's adaptation response. These markets may require increased policy attention to remove barriers that limit their ability to contribute to efficient adaptation. Included in this category are markets for insurance and finance, water and food.

However, there are limits to the extent of climate change within which each of these markets is effective. Households and businesses are able to manage many risks effectively through the insurance and financial markets. As the frequency and intensity of severe weather events increase with climate change, demand will rise for related insurance and financial services.

The recent innovation and deepening in insurance markets shows their considerable potential to promote adaptation to climate change. By its nature, however, conventional insurance is of limited value when an adverse event is likely to have similar impacts over wide areas of the world. Nor is conventional property insurance of much help when the uncertainty mainly involves the timing rather than the extent of an impact.

An example is significant sea-level rise, which would make it inevitable that large numbers of coastal properties would be inundated or rendered vulnerable to extreme storm events. But uncertainty would remain about the timing of the loss. There might then be scope for developing new property insurance products that share characteristics with traditional life insurance. Life insurance covers the risk of timing of death, although the fact of eventual death is itself certain. The development of innovative products that matured on loss of property and that would provide the means of buying housing elsewhere if the insured event occurred could be developed by the commercial insurance sector. The commercial viability of such instruments would depend on insurance companies being able to develop a balanced portfolio of insurance and financial risks in a world of climate change.

But no portfolio would be resilient against the costs of meeting many large claims from a single source or correlated sources associated with the unhappier end of the range of possible climate change. This is one highly practical example of the limits of adaptation.

The challenges for rural and urban water supply result from the interaction of climate change with increased demand from growth in population and economic activity. The limited scope of markets has complicated the task of allocating water to its most valuable uses. Australia's rural water market is the result of many years of reform, but barriers to efficient operation remain. While extraction of in-stream flows has been regulated and subsequently subject to a price, access to groundwater and surface flow has often been left as a common property resource, with predictable consequences.

Barriers to efficient water management in a changing climate persist. For example, in water markets, regional restrictions on trading remain a significant barrier. Severe water shortages in urban centres have led to the development of a number of desalination plants in Australia over the past few years, at high cost. The Productivity Commission has questioned the cost-effectiveness of some of this expenditure (Productivity Commission, 2011). Wider market exchange of water, with bids based on supplies from desalination plants competing with bids embodying supplies from a range of sources, including-long distance storage, is likely to have produced a good result at lower cost.

But here with water, too, there are limits to the effectiveness of a market. A sound market will not be able to avoid highly disruptive outcomes if expected average precipitation falls sharply or if rainfall becomes much more variable or if run-off is greatly diminished by evaporation associated with increased temperatures.

In the absence of effective and ambitious global action, deep participation in international trade in food as an importer as well as in Australia's traditional role as an exporter is going to be important for Australian food security. This is going to require the easing of inhibitions about the import of food. This will be stressful for many Australians, but the alternatives will be worse.

Free trade in food is essential to food security in a world of moderate climate change (Garnaut, 2008, pp. 375–6; Garnaut 2011b, Chapter 10; Martin and

Anderson, 2012). But the controls introduced by many countries on exports of food through the food price spikes of 2008 and 2011 suggests that free trade in food is unlikely to survive the pressures from extreme global warming (Garnaut 2011a; 2011c; Tolero, 2011; Martin and Anderson, 2012).

The provision of the best possible information on the impacts of climate change to households, businesses and decision-makers in government is the second element of a sound foundation for effective adaptation to climate change. Sound information allows people and enterprises and governments at all levels to see problems in advance and to develop low-cost responses to them. In the absence of forward-looking information on climate change impacts, decisions will be made in response to crisis without the benefit of long reflection, consideration of alternatives and opportunities to adopt responses that require long preparation.

Here one can draw attention to a cost of denial of climate change science beyond its interference with the development of sound mitigation policies. If many Australians are persuaded that the mainstream science is wrong or unreliable then they are denied information that is essential to the exercise of sound judgements about decisions that affect the quality and cost of adaptation.

As the average rainfall declines sharply with each passing decade in the south west of Australia (Garnaut, 2008: 106–10; Howden et al., 2013; Karoly et al., 2013, this volume), a farmer who shares the scientific knowledge that is the common heritage of humanity will make different decisions about land use than one who thinks that a series of dry winters is a passing phase. The regulators of power transmission in a state that has just been devastated by a bushfire during what would once have been described as once-in-a-century conditions will make different decisions if they know from science that once-in-a-century events will now occur every few years (Braganza et al., 2013, Chapter 3 in this volume).

Improvement of applied climate science and dissemination of the outcomes will not assist adaptation decisions by those who have closed their minds to uncomfortable reality. Regrettably, resistance to uncomfortable realities identified by science is a common human response to unpleasant scientific knowledge (Doherty, 2009). As with immunization against communicable diseases, community responses to slow infection with HIV/AIDS and other applications of scientific knowledge to collective action against some threat to human wellbeing, some citizens' rejection of scientific reality about climate change can damage the adaptive response for others in the community.

Beyond the foundations of a flexible and productive economy and well-informed community, the government as owner of some types of infrastructure, as regulator of others and with responsibility for land-use planning, is necessarily at the centre of many adaptation decisions (Garnaut, 2011b, Chapter 8).

Sound regulatory decisions – for example in relation to zoning of residential land – can avoid much waste of resources. Intervention of this kind generates strong community resistance, as it affects individual lifestyle choices and property values. Mandatory exclusion of some activities because of likely climate change is unlikely to be successful in the absence of widely shared perspectives on impacts of climate change. At the same time, the failure to enforce regula-tions that embody knowledge from climate science is likely to be followed by demands for compensation by the wider community when the eventual impacts of climate change become apparent. Compliance with these demands is likely to be fiscally demanding and inequitable.

As Hughes (2013) and Hoegh-Guldberg et al. (2013) argue in Chapters 4 and 5 of this volume, climate change is a significant and additional pressure on ecosystems and biodiversity in Australia. This is one specific area in which delib-erate adaptive policy responses will be important to good outcomes (Garnaut, 2011, Chapter 8).

Climate change will affect ecosystems and biodiversity by shifting, reducing or eliminating natural habitats. In Australia, many species of flora and fauna are at risk from rapid climate change because of their restricted geographic and climatic range. Where ecosystems and species have low tolerance for change, altered climatic conditions can trigger irreversible outcomes such as species extinction.

Just as greenhouse gas emissions without a carbon price represent a market failure, the decline in Australia's biodiversity can be attributed at least in part to a failure to correct through public policy the market's failure to value the natural estate. This failure, combined with the vulnerability of Australian ecosystems to climate change, provides a strong argument for the establishment of market mechanisms to ensure the resilience of Australia's ecosystems. For example, the Henry Tax Review identified the important role government can have in protecting biodiversity and ecosystems through specified payments, for example, in management agreements with landholders (Australian Treasury, 2010).

There is increasing private philanthropic interest in maintaining biodiversity, but government is likely to remain the major source of funds for conservation. Separate but complementary incentives for carbon sequestration and other ecosystem services will allow the respective benefits to be sold in separate markets, with landowners selling into both and making decisions that maximize total incomes and benefits to themselves. Sound policies to preserve biodiversity in the light of climate change along these lines would be effective against moderate climate change. Above some limit, however, diverse ecosystems would be overwhelmed by increases in temperature and other manifestations of climate change.

Things fall apart

The 2008 Garnaut Review concluded by noting that when human society receives a large shock to its established patterns of life the outcome is unpre-dictable in detail but generally problematic (Garnaut, 2008: 591–2). When human institutions are subject to stress that exceeds their capacity to absorb change we can expect fractures to institutions that are essential to the effective functioning of state and markets alike. Things fall apart.

The Review noted that the initial financial shocks that hit Australia in the 1890s, central Europe in the 1930s or Indonesia in the 1990s were substantial but turned out to be small in comparison to the chain of events that followed. In themselves, these shocks could have been expected to cause a pause in growth, but not one that would throw history from its course. But each shock was large enough to exceed some threshold of society's capacity to cope with change. In each case, what might have been a recession of substantial but ordinary magnitude became a great depression. The associated social convulsions changed political institutions fundamentally and as permanently as human institutions can be changed. They shifted the whole trajectory of political stability and economic growth.

The 2008 Review was written before the critical phase of the Great Crash of 2008 was precipitated by the collapse of Lehman Brothers in September 2008. The timely, powerful and concerted fiscal and monetary expansion in the substantial economies in late 2008 and through 2009 prevented the worst possibilities from that immense financial shock (Garnaut with Llewellyn-Smith, 2009). Nevertheless, the shock of the Great Crash to European and United States financial and political life has left a long-term legacy of economic under-performance that has led to loss of incomes that greatly exceeds the scale of the original shock, and which may yet prove too large for stability in globally important national and international institutions.

Unmitigated climate change, or mitigation too weak to avoid dangerous climate change, could give human society a shock larger than any imposed by 1890s, 1930s, late 1990s or 2000s fractures in the global financial system.

Every degree of warming above 2°C increases risks and costs by large amounts. Warming of 4°C and more would precipitate such large change in global economic and political conditions as to force the reshaping of national boundaries. It may lead to a small number of more effective states combating anarchy by absorbing others. It may lead to extended anarchy. The survival of states with anything like current boundaries and roles would be one of the less likely eventualities.

The case for strong mitigation is a conservative one. With the advent of a Four Degree World, we can be sure that the challenges to critical institutions would be considerable … and that some would fail.

Here we are talking about failure with global consequences. A shock from weakly mitigated climate change could unhinge Australian political and economic stability. But even if there were no such direct effect, there would be no islands of stability in Melbourne or Mildura if sea level rise displaces from their homes a substantial proportion of the people of Bangladesh and West Bengal, and many in the great littoral cities of Dhaka, Kolkata, Shanghai, Guangzhou, Ningbo, Bangkok, Jakarta, Manila, Ho Chi Minh, Yangon, Karachi and Mumbai. If changes in monsoon patterns and to the flows of the great rivers from the Tibetan plateau disrupt agriculture among the immense concentrations of people that have grown around the reliability of water flows from this area since the beginning of human civilization, it will not just be a problem for the people of India, Bangladesh, Pakistan, Vietnam, Myanmar and China.

The problems of unmitigated or weakly mitigated climate change will be for all humanity.

The threats to the stability of the institutions that underpin modern civilization will be the more difficult to manage because many of the shocks from climate change will come in sudden large events or series of events. The risks of sea level rise may suddenly be realized in an extreme climatic event – for example, a storm surge from a cyclone in the sea of Bengal or across South-East Asia. The risks to agriculture may be manifest sharply in the effects of drought or flood in a number of major food-producing countries, causing global food prices suddenly to rise way beyond anything in earlier experience. Such shocks would pose special challenges to institutional stability.

Avoiding Four Degrees

The Australian Parliament in mid-2011 legislated a set of policies that extended considerably the Australian contribution to the global mitigation effort. That legislation embodies arrangements for increasing Australian mitigation ambition over time in line with increasing global action. The set of Australian mitigation policies introduced in recent years, including energy efficiency measures and the Renewable Energy Target as well as carbon pricing, have slowed and could end what had been a rapid increase in Australian emissions over a long period of time. But the larger importance of the new Australian policies is the support that they give to Australia in contributing its fair share in a global effort that increases in ambition and effect over time.

Over two decades, the international community has groped its way towards an international system for climate change mitigation that introduces a possibility of holding temperature increases to around 2°C. However, global aggregate emissions continue to rise. We no longer have time for such slow progress: the concentrations of greenhouse gases are already approaching levels that are likely over time to generate a 2°C increase in average temperatures. Emissions have grown more rapidly since the turn of the century than the most widely used scenarios developed in the 1990s had suggested, largely because growth was stronger and more energy intensive and energy more emissions intensive than had been anticipated (Garnaut et al., 2009). If temperature increases are going to be kept to 2°C, there must be an early and large reduction in global emissions trajectories.

In contrast to the world up to the 1992 Rio Earth Summit, emissions growth in the 21st century was overwhelmingly concentrated in developing countries. My own calculations on 'business as usual' emissions for the Climate Change Review Update (Garnaut, 2011c; 2011b) suggested that in the absence of new policy action to change established trends, developing countries would account for the whole of the increase in global emissions from 2005 to 2030; developed country emissions as a whole were expected to remain steady between 2005 and 2030. In the absence of policy action, China would account for 41 per cent of global emissions in 2030 and developing countries 70 per cent. Whatever weight is given to the requirements of historical responsibility and justice, effective global mitigation now requires major and early reductions from business as usual emissions in China and other developing countries.

The 1997 Kyoto Protocol was an attempt to develop a comprehensive 'top-down' agreement in which responsibility for constraining emissions was allocated across developed countries and enforced internationally. The international community has learned slowly and painfully that such an agreement with parameters suitable for major progress on mitigation is not within reach for the foreseeable future. It is not possible because the major powers, the United States but also China, are unwilling to bind themselves to strong international mitigation agreements. It is also not possible because there are no effective sanctions against breaches of commitments, as demonstrated by Canada walking away without penalty from its Kyoto Protocol pledges.

Subsequent developments raise a question about whether a comprehensive 'top-down' agreement is even desirable. In anticipation of a legally binding agreement, governments settle into negotiating mode and seek to minimize commitments. By contrast, when considering a domestic commitment, governments are prepared to look more openly at the boundaries of realistic commitments and to go further in defining mitigation targets.

A different approach to setting national targets began to emerge at Copenhagen, took firm shape at Cancun and was elaborated in subsequent UNFCCC meetings in Durban and Doha.

The new approach carries some important features over from the early international discussions. The scientific co-operation remains centrally important to the collective effort. The two-degree objective, mechanisms for measurement and verification of emissions, and instruments for international trade in entitlements have been developed or strengthened. Ideas about mechanisms for transferring resources for mitigation and adaptation from developed to developing countries have been given substantive shape (although still little money).

The big departure from the old regime is in the setting of country targets for constraining emissions. It has been accepted that substantial developing countries will make commitments to constrain emissions, in the form of reductions in emissions intensity or 'business-as-usual' emissions. (Intensity targets are strongly preferred to business as usual, as they are capable of objective and unambiguous calculation.) It is accepted if only by default that these and developed country commitments to absolute reductions in emissions are voluntary and represent serious domestic undertakings and are not binding under international law. The voluntary targets are set domestically rather than within a comprehensive international agreement. The pressures to make them ambitious come from domestic politics and review and commentary from other countries – a process that is known as 'pledge and review'. The new process can be described as 'concerted unilateral mitigation'.

For concerted unilateral mitigation to be effective, one major gap in the international regime needs to be filled. The regime needs some framework for guiding assessments of the level of mitigation in each country that amounts to a fair share of an international effort to achieve the agreed global effort. It would be useful and probably necessary for heads of governments committed to strong global mitigation outcomes to appoint an expert group to develop such a framework for allocating the global effort among countries. Within the context of concerted unilateral mitigation, each country would be free to accept or reject guidance provided by such a framework. The framework would become a focus of international review of each country's effort and evolve over time in response to discussion and experience.

To conclude the discussion of the evolution of the global climate change regime, international trade in emissions entitlements has struck some large practical problems. Within the European emissions trading system, the many regulatory and fiscal interventions are forcing much larger reductions in emissions than carbon pricing. These together with slow growth in economic activity and the realization of unexpected opportunities for low-cost abatement have caused emissions permit prices to fall to levels that are well below the economic cost of emissions and the value of abatement. The low prices raise questions about the effectiveness of the scheme. Although controlled in quantum, use of offsets at very low prices from the Clean Development Mechanism (CDM) has pushed prices even lower. In the absence of quantitative controls, access to the CDM has pushed New Zealand permit prices down to negligible levels. Low European prices would, if uncorrected, introduce low prices into other emissions trading systems with which Europe is linked, notably Australia from 2015.

It is understood by economists that broadly based carbon pricing achieves more carbon emissions reduction at similar cost, or similar abatement at lower cost, than large numbers of separate regulatory and fiscal interventions. Considerable emissions reductions have been achieved in recent years in many countries through regulatory and fiscal interventions. However, the cost advantages of general carbon pricing become more important as mitigation targets become more ambitious, and are likely to be essential to achieving the deep reductions in emissions that will be necessary to achieve the agreed global objective. The contemporary problems of uneconomically low prices in domestic and international trading schemes can therefore be seen as a threat to achievement of long-term global mitigation goals. A tightening of emissions reduction targets is necessary to restore prices that relate appropriately to the cost and value of abatement in a world that is meeting its emissions reduction targets.

The CDM has emerged as the most important locus for international trade in carbon units and for a number of years contributed substantially to incentives for investment in emissions reduction in developing countries.

As analyzed in the recent report of an independent review panel, the CDM is experiencing chronic oversupply of abatement units (CDM, 2012). Prices have fallen to levels that barely cover transaction costs. With recent and prospective reforms, the CDM is a legitimate offset mechanism with a potentially valuable place in a global system of climate change mitigation (CDM, 2012). The review panel concluded that a major tightening of emissions reduction targets and widening of access on the demand side would be necessary to correct the chronic oversupply.

I would suggest as well a tightening of access on the abatement supply side, with only least-developed countries having unconditional access. Within this proposal of mine, other developing countries would have access as suppliers to the CDM if they chose to do so if they accepted domestically binding emissions constraints and were living within those constraints without double counting of abatement for which CDM credits had been awarded. If this approach were adopted by the international community, international mechanisms would need to be developed – perhaps through the established arrangements for Joint Implementation – to monitor double counting of emissions.

There is good and bad news in the story of humanity's struggle to find a basis for effective collective action on climate mitigation. The early news was never going to be all good on an issue as complex, difficult and new to the international community as this one.

The best news is of immense importance: emissions generally seem to be on paths to meet or exceed the Cancun targets. They are on track to meet or exceed the pledges even in the cases of China and the United States – the world's biggest emitters of greenhouse gases, the largest and most influential economies, and countries whose pledges represent dramatic reductions in established trajectories. Moreover, the achievement of current pledges is being achieved at less cost than was anticipated by most analysts. Early and widely based progress at surprisingly low cost establishes sound foundations for a large and early increase in national mitigation ambition.

Far from reaching a peak in emissions in 2025, as President Bush foreshadowed in 2007, it now seems that United States emissions reached their highest level in the year in which the President was speaking and have been declining since then. It is not a decline in economic activity that dragged emissions down: United States output last year is now significantly higher than in 2007. The United States appears to be near a path to meeting its Cancun targets on emissions reductions (National Resource Defence Council, 2012; Resources for the Future, 2012).

The European Union is on track to achieve its unconditional target to reduce emissions by 20 per cent on 1990 levels by 2020 (European Environmental Agency, 2012). Slow economic growth has subdued demand for emissions-intensive goods and services, but the extent of reduction and the low price of abatement in the emissions trading scheme suggest that emissions reductions have been achieved at lower cost than had been anticipated.

In Australia, too, emissions growth has been well below anticipated levels over recent years, tending around zero, despite the continuation of robust expansion of population, output and emissions-intensive resource investment for export. In the electricity sector, stagnant or declining demand has intersected with increased renewable energy production forced by the renewable energy target to cause faster decarbonization than had been suggested in early estimates.

China's 12th Five Year Plan 2011–15 embodies far-reaching measures to constrain emissions within the intensity targets that the Chinese government has communicated to the international community (NDRC, 2012). In 2011, the first year of the new Plan, emissions continued to grow strongly. This was deeply discouraging for the international mitigation effort. However, policies to give effect to the new Plan began to bite in 2012 and, together with economically driven structural change, changed the emissions trajectory in 2012 to an extent that over-performance against the pledge now seems possible (Garnaut, 2013).

Influential Chinese policies include a range of regulatory and fiscal measures to promote energy efficiency (Xinhua, 2013); direct regulatory action to close plants with emissions intensity above some threshold defined to be acceptable (Mai and Feng, 2013); subsidies to research, development and application of renewable energy production and other low-emissions activities; and public funding for transformation of the electricity grid to reduce transmission losses and to facilitate integration of intermittent supplies of renewable energy into the national market (NDRC, 2012).

Emissions reductions in China are coming from many sources. In the electricity sector, for example, the replacement of small and high emissions coal-based generators by ultra-supercritical plants reduced emissions per unit of electricity by 2.5 per cent per annum from 2007 to 2011, and is expected to continue to reduce them by an average of 1.7 per cent for each of the next several years simply by closure of environmentally inefficient plants that have been identified (Mai and Feng, 2013). It is estimated that thermal power production increased only by 0.6 per cent in 2012 after many years of increasing at near-double digit rates. Within this low thermal power number, the proportion of gas rose rapidly from a low base. All substantial low-emissions sources of power increased rapidly: hydroelectric power by 20 per cent; nuclear by 17 per cent; and wind by 36 per cent (Garnaut, 2013). It now seems possible that Chinese coal consumption may reach a peak within the current Five-Year Plan 2011–15 – an outcome that would represent a radical change from earlier experience and expectations and contribute to building foundations for strengthening of global mitigation efforts (Garnaut, 2013).

Conclusion

Australians in future will have to manage the world as they find it. We are likely to be leaving them with a difficult task. We should seek to avoid leaving them with an impossible one. A realistic examination of the limits of adaptation drives us back to taking every chance to contain global warming within low limits, and if possible within the agreed international objective of limiting global warming to 2°C.

To take the chance that has been created by the emergence of a viable international regime built on concerted unilateral mitigation, and by the success so far of substantial countries in meeting pledges within that regime, we promptly need to do three things.

First, leaders who are committed to avoidance of extreme global warming need to establish a group of experts to define an allocation of emissions reduction responses that adds up to a global mitigation solution, and which is widely accepted as distributing responsibilities equitably across countries. Within the framework of concerted unilateral mitigation, the resulting framework would guide voluntary national decisions.

Second, all substantial countries, developed and developing, would need to build on unexpectedly rapid and economically low-cost reductions in emissions so far by tightening 2020 targets. Countries and regions which have stronger conditional alongside their unconditional targets, like the European Union and Australia, would activate conditional targets. Others would review targets in the light of stronger international action.

Third, all substantial countries would prepare for the Paris Conference of the Parties to the UNFCCC, in 2015, with a mind to committing to post-2020 reductions in emissions entitlements that add up to the 2°C objective. That would require acceptance in all substantial countries of reductions in emissions entitlements towards average per capita levels less than half the average for the world as a whole today.

This seems difficult because it *is* difficult. But the new framework of concerted unilateral mitigation and the marked changes in emissions trajectories so far within that framework suggest that it is possible. Hard as it may be, effective mitigation to avoid extreme climate change will be less difficult and more feasible than attempts to plan for adaptation to a Four Degree World.

References

Australian Treasury. 2010. *Australia's Future Tax System: Final Report*. Canberra.

Braganza, K., K. Hennessy, L. Alexander and B. Trewin. 2013. Changes in extreme weather. In P. Christoff (ed.), *Four Degrees of Climate Change: Australia in a Hot World*. Earthscan: London, Chapter 3.

CDM. 2012. Climate change, carbon markets and the CDM: a call to action. Report of the High Level Panel on the CDM Policy Dialogue, Bonn.

Doherty, P. 2009. Climate change/culture change. Keynote address for the Inaugural Festival of Ideas at the University of Melbourne.

Garnaut, R. 2008. The Garnaut climate change review. Cambridge University Press: Melbourne.

—2011a. Garnaut climate change review update paper 3, Global emissions trends. www.garnautreview.org.com.au [accessed 10 February 2013].

—2011b. Garnaut climate change review update paper 4, Transforming rural land use. www.garnautreview.org.au [accessed 10 February 2013].

—2013. National contributions to the global mitigation effort: issues for Australia and China, unpublished paper presented to NDRC-SIC Carbon Market Internal Workshop on the Design and Development of Cost-Effective Market Mechanisms for Carbon Emissions Reductions in China, 31 January, Beijing. Published as: China's Climate Change Mitigation in International Context, in R. Garnaut, Cai Fang and Ligang Song (eds), China: A New Model for Growth and Development, Australian National

University E-press and Social Sciences Academic Press China: Canberra and Beijing, pp. 281–300.

Garnaut, R., S. Howes, F. Jotzo and P. Sheehan. 2009. The implications of rapid development for emissions and climate change mitigation. In D. Helm and C. Hepburn (eds), *The Economics and Policy of Climate Change*. Oxford University Press: Oxford, pp. 81–106.

Garnaut, R. with D. Llewellyn-Smith. 2009. *The Great Crash of 2008*. Melbourne University Publishing: Melbourne.

Hoegh-Guldberg, O., E. Poloczanska and A. Richardson. 2013. Australia's marine resources in a warm, acid ocean. In P. Christoff (ed.), *Four Degrees of Climate Change: Australia in a Hot World*: Earthscan: London, Chapter 5.

Howden, M., Schroeter, S. and Crimp, S. 2013. Agriculture in an even more sunburnt country. In Christoff, P. (ed.), *Four Degrees of Climate Change: Australia in a Hot World*. Earthscan: London, ch. 6.

Hughes, L. 2013. Changes to Australian terrestrial biodiversity. In P. Christoff (ed.), *Four Degrees of Climate Change: Australia in a Hot World*. Earthscan: London, ch. 4.

Mai, Y. and S. Feng. 2013. Increasing China's coal-fired power generation efficiency. Unpublished paper presented to NDRC-SIC Carbon Market Internal Workshop on the Design and Development of Cost-Effective Market Mechanisms for Carbon Emissions Reductions in China, 31 January, Beijing.

Martin, W. and K. Anderson. 2012. Export restrictions and price insulation during commodity price booms. *American Journal of Agricultural Economics*. 94 (2): 422–7.

Productivity Commission. 2011. *Australia's Urban Water Supply*. Melbourne and Canberra, April.

National Development and Reform Commission (NDRC). 2012. China's policies and actions for addressing climate change. Beijing, November. http://qhs. ndrc. gov. cn/zcfg/ WO201211225885 3945 9161.pdf

National Resource Defence Council. 2012. Closer than you think: latest CO_2 pollution data and forecasts show target within reach. New York, July 2012. http://www.nrdc.org/ globalwarming/closer-than-you-think-ib.asp [accessed 10 February 2013].

Resources for the Future. 2012. U. S. may come close to 2020 greenhouse gas emissions target, summarized in *Scientific American*. http://www.scientificamerican.com/article. cfm?id=U.S.-may-come-close-to-2020-greenhouse-gas-emissions-target [accessed 10 February 2013].

Tolero, M. 2011. *Food Prices: Riding the Rollercoaster*. International Food Policy Research Institute: Washington, DC.

Xinhua. 2013. China sets slower energy consumption targets. 25 January. http://news. xinhua.net.com/english/China/2013-01-24/c_132125842.htm [accessed 10 February 2013].

9 Health impacts in Australia in a Four Degree World

Anthony J. McMichael

Introduction

Two plus two equals four, though not when considering impacts in a warming world. Much of the recent modelling of the impacts (physical, ecological and biological) of human-induced warming has assumed global temperature increases this century of the order of 2°C. But what of the impacts at around 4°C? The magnitude of risks to human health in a world that is an average of 4°C warmer than in pre-industrial times (circa AD 1750) will not be simply twice the risks due to 2°C warming. Biological organisms and ecological systems are not simple mechanistic Newtonian devices. When living entities are exposed to increasing external stressors, the increase in impact is generally not linear – indeed, a different type of impact can emerge once a critical threshold of stress is passed.

As the average temperature rises in Australia, there will be a similar upward-turning escalation of climatic impact on many aspects of human health and wellbeing. Assorted disorders, diseases, distress and deaths will occur at much higher rates. The non-linear risk increase, the likely exceeding of some thresholds and uncertainty about future configurations of other social and environmental influences on health outcomes preclude a comprehensive projection of climatic impacts on health and survival in an Australia where the global average temperature has risen by 4°C or more (a Four Degree World). Guesses and highly qualified speculations are possible, but we must recognize that we are moving even further 'into the unknown' when contemplating a future Four Degree World and the resultant, potentially very damaging, changes in environmental and social conditions.

To start at the simpler end of the health-impact spectrum, we can be confident that the projected increase by one or more orders-of-magnitude in the frequency of very hot episodes in a +4°C Australia (see Braganza et al., 2013, Chapter 3 in this volume) will have serious health consequences – especially in a population that may already be carrying into late adulthood the detrimental health-eroding legacy of having been overweight and obese in childhood more than a half-century earlier. Similarly, +4°C warming will greatly increase the other great weather extremes for which the young and homesick Dorothea Mackellar pined in her iconic poem 'My Country', written in London a century ago. Deaths, injuries, poverty and mental trauma will, as ever, result from various disasters of flood, drought and fire.

Projection of other future health risks in a +4°C climate then gets tougher. A Four Degree World could seriously erode the essential foundations of human population health – food yields, water supplies and the constraints on infectious disease rates, population displacement, conflict and warfare. But will various infectious diseases, especially those spread by 'vector' mosquitoes, become resurgent and extend their geographic range in Australia? (Or might some part of Australia become too hot and perhaps too dry to support such vectors and the lifecycle of particular infectious agents?) An even more complex question is: if climatic extremes coincide with very great increases in numbers of displaced persons from the adjoining Asian and Pacific region, perhaps unavoidably housed in emergency, poorly resourced settlements, might Australia be faced with unusual epidemics of cholera and rampant childhood diarrhoeal diseases? Further, might our healthcare system and public health activity become overwhelmed and inadequate to the mounting task of risk reduction, damage repair and recovery? These are complex multi-faceted situations in which many concurrent influences other than altered climatic conditions affect human biology, psychology and health. Projecting the rate at which ice might melt at higher temperatures, or how coral reefs are likely to respond to steadily increasing temperatures, is an inherently simpler task than projecting human health outcomes within the 'noisy' setting of unknowable trends in other risk factors, including variegated cultural practices, consumer behaviours and other external exposures.

Clearly, this chapter cannot offer a fully itemised schedule of estimated future health impacts. The risks to human health and wellbeing from changes in climatic conditions are wide-ranging, diverse and differ greatly in character and complexity of causation. For most of those risks climate change will be a multiplier or amplifier of risk, not its initiator. Only some risks are amenable to formal modelling, particularly when considered within such a qualitatively different future Australia and future world. For small changes in climate, a simpler extrapolation of impact levels in recent past experience to the postulated future is reasonable. But for larger climatic changes and all that will flow from them, this conventional approach is not warranted.

We should instead pay more attention to the range of human impacts of a diverse but plausible range of future conditions and scenarios. Accordingly, we should be readier to make policy decisions on a precautionary basis that recognises the extremes of adverse human consequences that *could* result. A simple entry point for understanding these limitations to future high-exposure risk modelling is to review the experience of Europe in the hot summer of 2003.

Death in Paris: impacts beyond simplistic expectation

In Paris in August 2003 the great European heatwave of that summer caused a surge in the daily death rate during and in the several days following (van den Torren et al., 2004). Around 1,000 additional deaths occurred. A more typical heatwave had hit Paris a month earlier, when temperatures rose for five to six days, peaking at around 8°C above the July norm. During that earlier heatwave an excess of around 100 deaths occurred. In early August, in contrast, temperatures peaked for several days at around 12°C above the August norm, and the heatwave lasted longer, for nine to ten days. There were several other relevant non-meteorological differences between the two heatwaves. First, the August event entailed high levels of several health-damaging air pollutants, especially newly formed ozone, the increased level of which was probably largely due to the 'catalytic' effect of higher temperature. Second, more young families were out of town on summer holidays in August, leaving many older relatives with reduced advice and support. Even so, most of the tenfold difference in the death toll between the two heatwaves was due to the unusually great amount of thermal stress in the August event, occurring at a level greater than the physiological coping capacity of many of the more vulnerable citizens. They over-heated, became dehydrated, had serious failures of heart and lung functioning, and died.

In comparing those two heatwave impacts, a straight-line extrapolation of health risk from lower to much higher temperatures would obviously have seriously underestimated the actual impact of the hotter event. Simple linear arithmetic did not apply. Instead, within that Parisian population, some threshold of coping capacity had apparently been exceeded during the August event, and so the death rate jumped upwards.

Climatologists have estimated that the 2003 European heatwave, historically a once-in-several-centuries event, is on track to becoming just an average annual heatwave by mid-century – and perhaps an average summer day by later in this century (Stott et al., 2004). Note, however, that those estimates were based on climate change scenarios from around a decade ago, scenarios that entail warming of around 2–3°C by later this century. We are on notice that an increase of 4°C is now looking likely by 2100 (see Christoff, 2013a, Chapter 1 in this volume; World Bank, 2012).

Similar changes in the frequency of such extreme heat events are expected within Australia this century (see Chapter 2). In the absence of radically climate-proofed cities, towns and dwellings, and given that the human organism cannot evolve biologically within a non-Darwinian timespan of just decades, rates of serious health events and deaths due to heatwaves will almost certainly escalate, especially since an increase in weather variability is an expected and prominent feature of future warming. Hence there are similar projections, for Australia, of increased frequency and (or) severity of other extreme weather events that maim, kill and cause ensuing infections and post-traumatic stress disorders, including floods, bushfires, coastal surges, hailstorms (particularly in eastern Australia) and cyclones (likely to become more severe though not more frequent as offshore ocean surface waters become warmer) (see Braganza et al., 2013, Chapter 3, this volume). These projections have all been given greater plausibility by the recent systematic analyses of evidence that, worldwide, extreme weather events are indeed becoming more evident (Coumou and Rahmstorf, 2012).

Escalations in risks of disease, illness, injury and death due to 4°C warming would require commensurate increases in the capacity of the healthcare system to respond quickly and cope with the enormous demand, and to be able to do so in conditions of lost, destroyed or damaged power, communications and physical infrastructure. During the unusually severe heatwave of late January to early February 2009 in Melbourne and Adelaide, some aspects of public infrastructure and services failed under stress – power supplies, morgue capacity and transport systems. In Adelaide many dozens of rail services were cancelled because of heat-induced buckling of the railway lines and emergency commercial refrigeration vans were hired to provide extra storage space for dead bodies.

The impacts of temperature extremes on human biology and health provide an easy entry-point to this discussion. The full range of direct and indirect climatic influences on human population health is much more diverse in its content.

Types of climate-related health impacts

There are three categories of health impacts from climate change (Butler and Harley, 2010). Primary impacts result from communities and particular occupational groupings being directly exposed to extremes of weather: heat, rain (and flooding), hail, snowstorms, wind and bushfires. On a broader front, though one step removed, there are direct impacts on immediate post-event mental health, jobs, livelihoods, community morale and other aspects of human wellbeing.

Secondary health impacts arise from the environmental and ecological consequences of changes in climatic conditions. These include impairment of food yields and human nutrition, changes in the range and seasonality of various infectious diseases, and the generation and dispersal of various air pollutants (e.g. ozone) and aeroallergens from pollens and spores. If changes in climatic conditions reduce freshwater availability, this can compromise domestic hygiene, drinking water safety, local food yields and personal hydration. One interesting and unforeseen secondary health consequence in some other parts of the world reflects the increasing salinity of coastal groundwater (well water) due to sea level rise. Studies in low-lying coastal Bangladesh have revealed this as a likely cause of increased blood pressure – including an increase in late-pregnancy complications because of raised maternal blood pressure – due to the often-substantial increase in daily salt intake (Kahn and Vineis, 2012).

Tertiary health impacts have a more complex and protracted causal chain. They emerge more slowly and affect the fundamental supports of human wellbeing, health and survival. These are less easy to study in a specific and quantitative way (and are therefore of less interest to conventional epidemiological research). Examples include the physical and mental health consequences of impoverishment (especially in rural communities) due to downturns in family income and the loss of livelihoods; emotional anxieties and behavioural disturbances in young children becoming apprehensive or fearful about the future; the wide-ranging health consequences (both negative and positive) of displacement and relocation of communities and families due to mounting climatic and environmental adversity; and the more unsettling prospect of rising tensions and conflicts over dwindling natural resources, including arable land, freshwater supplies and (particularly for island coastal-dwelling communities) space for settlements and daily living.

As we move down that list of primary, secondary and tertiary impacts, the possibility of characterizing the type, timing and magnitude of future health impacts under +4°C conditions, let alone how those impacts would differ between different geographic regions and socio-economic groups, becomes increasingly difficult. Tertiary impacts can mostly only be described in words, not numbers, and in relation to each of a plausible future set of circumstances.

For health impacts higher up the list and able to be estimated in a +4°C future, we should note again the Paris heatwave example. There will be many such non-linear changes in future health impacts in Australia if 4°C of warming occurs. Indeed, there would probably be rather rapid upwards step-changes in the rates of occurrence of some health outcomes as critical thresholds or barriers are breached, such as sufficiently altered wind and humidity conditions enabling the southern movement of infected mosquitoes from Papua New Guinea across the Torres Straits.

Indeed, a hotter future would not only be one in which, in health impact terms, two plus two equals, say, ten, but one in which some *qualitative* changes in the types and patterns of health risks would also occur. For example, we have little capacity to foresee the range of physical and mental health disorders, along with the health consequences of tensions and conflicts, which may arise if the flow of asylum-seekers and climatic-environmental refugees from the Asian and Pacific regions becomes a torrent of displaced and desperate humanity. Nor can we know the full cascade of consequences likely to result from declines in the productivity of agriculture in those regions (and in parts of Australia). How will declining food yields combined with growing populations affect food prices, child nutrition and development, adult health and economic productivity, trading patterns, competition for arable land and regional geopolitical stability?

Plus 4°C: only a bit more warming than has been expected?

This first part of the chapter makes clear that it would be naïve to imagine we can produce confident quantitative estimates of changes in the rates (and geographic ranges) of many, perhaps most, of the adverse health impacts of a Four Degree World for Australia. But we can certainly alert ourselves to the most likely direction of those changes, and how the profile of disease, distress and deprivation across and within the population is likely to alter. Yet in addressing the likely impacts of such warming we have no choice but to start with a knowledge base derived from a world that we know, and to use it to project forward to one that may actually not be a simple variation on a familiar theme. Indeed, it may be a very unfamiliar world.

That point is easily underscored. In palaeo-climatic terms a Four Degree World would equate to the Miocene world of 10–15 million years ago (Hansen and Sato, 2008). There were no recognisable pre-humans then, let alone any members of the actual *Homo* genus. Indeed, in those mid-Miocene times the great ape lineage was still emerging from smaller and more primitive primates. It is, in principle, possible that in a Four Degree World, if sustained over many centuries (and probably becoming still warmer as amplifying feedback processes kicked in), there would once again be few (if any) humans.

Globally, it is very likely that a Four Degree World would seriously erode the essential foundations, the underpinnings, of human population health discussed earlier – food yields, water supplies, natural constraints on infectious disease rates and ranges, the many 'providing and protecting' functions of ecosystems and the physical security of settlements. In rich countries these foundations can seem abstract and distant, and lacking apparent relevance to human health. Reinforced by the prevailing individualistic 'world-view' recently fortified by the ascendance of neoliberal values and assumptions, 'health' is widely viewed as the personal outcome of free-range consumer choices and behaviours, a few dodgy genes and a quota of day-to-day luck.

However, the profile and real significance of the risks to human population health in a Four Degree World can only be properly understood by recognizing that climate change and its environmental and social consequences are *systemic and ecological* in character. They are outside the conventional frame within which we think about 'environmental risks to health'. Climate-related risks generally impinge on whole communities, whole populations, and will typically act over long periods of time, often via complex multi-stage causal paths. That is, these climatic-environmental changes are *not* just another entry on the list of discrete environmental hazardous exposures (such as the many documented toxic workplace exposures, elevated lead concentrations in local air, water and soil, and locally generated air pollutants) that predominantly affect unlucky individuals, occupational groups or local communities (McMichael, 1999).

Current mainstream modelling studies (Braganza et al., 2013; Whetton et al., 2013 [Chapter 2 and 3, this volume]) suggest that the expected main features of Australia's climate in a Four Degree World include temperature increases of 3°C to 5°C in coastal areas and 4°C to 6°C in inland areas; a likely decline in rainfall in southern Australia (particularly in winter) of up to about 50 per cent and uncertain rainfall changes in other regions; sea level rise of up to about 1.1 metres in 2100, increasing to more than 7 metres during subsequent centuries, even with no further global warming; and increases in extremely high temperatures, extreme rainfall, extreme fire weather, large hail on the east coast, increased tropical cyclone intensity, and greater storm-related coastal flooding.

While the size of the temperature rise is of primary concern, the actual *duration* of over-heating at +4°C would be a very important determinant of the extent and chronology of adverse health impacts in Australia and elsewhere. For example, if +4°C conditions persisted for centuries, as is likely (Stager, 2011), and if the Himalayan glaciers disappeared, then life-supporting river flows in China, South Asia and South East Asia would dwindle markedly. This would include many of the great rivers of the region, including the Yangtze, Ganges, Brahmaputra, Meghna and Mekong. The ensuing cascade of adverse health consequences (e.g. reduced food yields and consequent increases in infant/child mortality) is easy to imagine. So too is the likely rise in trans-boundary conflicts and environmental refugee flows.

Various studies have concluded that in a Four Degree World the already-existing water scarcity would be greatly exacerbated, particularly in northern and eastern Africa, the Middle East and South Asia (World Bank, 2012). Likewise, a protracted +4°C world would see widespread loss of human habitat, including coastal farmland, as slowly expanding oceans rise by two (and probably more) metres over several centuries. If human population numbers had not already declined by then, this would surely engender a 'slow-burn' crisis of food shortages, poor health, starvation and conflict.

Can we learn from the distant past?

Before considering categories of health consequences of a +4°C Australia it is of interest to look at the health-and-survival impacts of three of the great −4°C cooling events in the long history and prehistory of human societies (McMichael, 2012). Three distinctive cooling episodes, the first two pre-historical and the third one historical, reflect the impacts on human health and survival of major volcanic eruptions, casting a veil of cooling ash, aerosols and debris around the world.

First, the Toba eruption occurred about 74,000 years ago, during which global average temperatures fell by 5–10°C for 5–10 years. This event presumably wiped out plant and animal food sources and contaminated fresh water, and caused an estimated 90 per cent mortality among early humans already in the South Asian region and a close call for dispersing (Out-of-Africa) groups of modern *Homo sapiens*.

Second, the Younger Dryas event, which occurred around 12,800–11,600 BP, saw a 5–10°C drop (for instance, in Europe) occur within around 250 years. The cooling lasted for 1,000 years, causing drying in Nile Valley and diminishing river flows, resource conflicts and the abandonment of settlements (evidenced by shattered skulls, spear heads), and the collapse of early Natufian proto-farming settlements in the (Turkish) Anatolian plateau (northern region of the 'Fertile Crescent').

Third, during the 'AD 536 Event', attributed to a volcanic eruption, average global temperature fell by 3–4°C and persisted for 5–10 years throughout Eurasia and beyond. This may have triggered the (bubonic) Plague of Justinian, imported from northern Africa, and breaking out in Constantinople and then throughout the Eastern Roman Empire (McMichael, 2012). This brief cooling may have facilitated the survival of infected fleas travelling north from Ethiopia (or other ancient Eastern African grain-export ports) to the Mediterranean coast with grain shipments and their stowaway rats, destined for Constantinople. It is also thought to be implicated in the collapse of the Moche civilization, in coastal northern Peru, beginning abruptly around 536 AD, and in the rapid demise of 'Early Iron Age' culture associated with acute harvest failure, dire weather and high mortality, including in central Sweden, beginning in 536 AD.

These are three very different examples, from hunter-gatherer times, pre-agrarian settlements and a period of well-developed agrarianism. All indicate the central importance to human wellbeing and health of food supplies and nutrition. When climates change, whether with significant warming *or* cooling, or with either substantial increases *or* decreases in rainfall, harvests and livestock are at risk. Nutrition, health and survival are then jeopardized and social disorder, tensions and conflicts frequently result.

Unfortunately, there are no documented +4°C warming periods during the Holocene from which we can draw further relevant insights. At the spatial level of hemisphere and major geographic region (Western Europe, China, Central America, etc.), temperatures did not vary up or down from the Holocene average by more than about 1.5°C, on decadal or centuries-long timescales (McMichael, 2012).

Health risks from +4°C warming in Australia: overview

Extremes of heat stress, in community and workplace

Higher average temperatures mean large increases in the frequency of extreme heat episodes. As Australia's temperature rose from 1960 to 2010 by 0.9°C the number of record hot days more than doubled (CSIRO and BoM, 2007). With a rise of 2°C, the annual number of very hot days (over 35°C) is estimated to increase by around fourfold in the majority of capital cities and by twentyfold to twenty-fivefold in Darwin and Brisbane. Across northern Australia the extreme daily temperature that currently occurs about once per 20 years is projected to occur every one to two years by later this century (IPCC, 2012). These increases will presumably be very much greater with twice that amount of warming.

For the Australian population in general, and especially the more vulnerable (low-income families, the elderly, those with underlying cardio-respiratory diseases, etc.) living in a Four Degree World, summer accompanied by more short-term heat extremes would be potentially lethal and widely damaging. If Australia's average temperature increased by around +4°C this century, the estimated total national number of yearly temperature-related deaths would increase from around 5,800 in 1990 to 6,400 in 2020, 7,900 in 2050 and 17,200 in 2100 (Bambrick et al., 2008), with estimates including adjustment for population growth and ageing. Meanwhile, adverse health effects from cold extremes would recede.

A particular and under-recognized health threat will impinge on segments of the workforce. Heat exposure is intrinsic to some jobs (outdoors, foundry-workers, unventilated factory settings, etc.). In a +4°C Australia there would be a substantial increase in the number of health-endangering episodes and situations in the workplace, affecting cardiovascular risks, severe dehydration and kidney damage/failure, impairments of judgement (leading to injuries), mood and behaviour (Kjellstrom et al., 2009). Economic productivity would also decline, and may do so precipitously at the higher temperatures not previously modelled.

There is one glint of silver lining to this cloud: there will be fewer skiing injuries – indeed by later in the century, there would be no such injuries on Australia's former natural ski slopes.

Other extreme weather events

Similar escalations in deaths, injuries and major health events would accompany the analogous increases in other extreme weather events that would be associated with background warming in Australia, and amplified by those warmer circumstances.

There would be major differences between geographic regions in frequency and severity of each type of event. Comparison of the projected numbers of people affected by flooding in Southern (Mediterranean) Europe versus the United Kingdom in a 4–5°C warmer world indicates – though not as a direct climate-zone analogue – the extent of the potential low-high latitude between major Australian regions in the probable impacts of flooding in a Four Degree World. Serious warming-related flooding in Southern Europe is progressively reduced to zero as the temperature rises, while it rises sevenfold in the northern UK (Ciscar et al., 2011). In Australia the most relevant focus of comparison may be between the north east (increasingly flood-prone) and the south and south west regions (increasingly drought-prone).

Infectious diseases

Many infectious disease agents, and the other animals or insects that respectively either host or transmit some of them, are sensitive to climatic conditions. It is common experience in Australia that salmonella food poisoning occurs much more often in the summer months. The risks of transmission of food-borne and water-borne infectious diseases will generally rise at higher temperatures – especially for infections caused by bacterial or protozoal (multicellular) organisms with metabolism and replication that are temperature-dependent.

The climatic and environmental influences on various of Australia's indigenous mosquito -borne viral diseases, such as Ross River fever and Murray Valley Encephalitis (diseases with natural animal hosts and complex ecology), are yet to be fully elucidated. For some other mosquito-borne infections, such as dengue fever (currently largely confined to north-east Queensland), we already know much. For dengue, the approximate estimation from modelling future changes associated with a business-as-usual global climate change scenario is that the geographic region suitable for transmission may extend southwards, thereby increasing the population at risk of exposure from around half a million to five to eight million Australians by the end of the twenty-first century (Bambrick et al., 2008) (see Table 9.1).

Table 9.1   Infectious diseases likely to be introduced or reintroduced to a +4°C warmer and institutionally stressed Australia, or have their current Australian rate and range extended

---

Newly introduced

- Japanese encephalitis
- Chikungunya (may already be present; occurs in some Pacific Islands and Southeast Asia)
- Cholera (?)

Re-introduced

- Tuberculosis (already present in some remote and disadvantaged Australian communities, although not yet in multi-drug resistant form as occurs in some neighbouring countries)
- Malaria (the anopheline mosquito vector species is present in northern Australia)
- Dengue (currently imported sporadically, but could become endemic)

Extension of, or change in, geographic range and seasonality

- Ross River virus
- Barmah Forest virus
- Murray Valley Encephalitis
- Gastroenteritis ('food/water poisoning'): salmonella, campylobacter, shigella dysentery, others
- Bat-borne viral diseases, such as Hendra virus (likely, but bat response to warming is uncertain)

Meanwhile, the small minority of infectious diseases that occur more often in the winter than the summer months (such as rotaviral gastroenteritis and respiratory syncytial disease) will presumably recede at these higher temperatures.

Food yields, nutrition, health and survival

> In different regions of the world, including the United States, Africa, India, and Europe, nonlinear temperature effects have been found on important crops, including maize, wheat, soya, and cassava ... Under the SRES A1FI scenario, which exceeds 4°C warming by 2100, yields are projected to decrease by 63 to 82 per cent. The potential for damages to crops because of pests and diseases plus nonlinear temperature effects is likely to grow as the world warms toward 2°C and above.
>
> (World Bank, 2012, ix)

In Australia and overseas, climate change will fundamentally affect food yields and quality, and where and how we produce food. Climatic conditions affect almost every aspect of food production: the plant and animal species or strains used, average and year-to-year yields, product quality, risks of infestations and infections, what soil types are preferred, the choice of management systems and technologies, and so on. In Australia, if rainfall continues to decline around the drier fringe of southern Australia, the viability of crop farming in that region will be further restricted (see Howden et al., 2013, Chapter 6, this volume). Horticultural crops that require winter chill, such as stone fruits, may become unproductive in hotter conditions. Irrigated agricultural production in the Murray–Darling Basin could decline by up to 92 per cent by 2100 if climate change brings a long-term drying trend to that region (Garnaut, 2008).

We have long assumed that Australia is secure and self-sufficient in food production. But the world is changing. Most modelled results indicate that Australia is the one high-income continent where downturns in food yields would be widespread at warmer temperatures. If the future, warmer, climate in the Murray Darling Basin deteriorates, with insufficient river water flows and with a decline in rainfall needed for winter wheat to germinate (Whetton et al., 2013, Chapter 2, this volume), then food self-sufficiency may decline markedly, even for staples (Howden et al., 2013, chapter 6, this volume).

There is no published research on how food yields under +4°C conditions would affect food prices, availability, consumption and hence human nutrition and health in Australia. As food prices rise, the first to suffer nutritionally are the low-income households and remote groups with limited food choices. Healthy child development would be compromised, along with all of the consequent (and often serious) lifelong impairments to health that modern epidemiological research has revealed over the past two decades. In remote indigenous communities, the residual hunting and gathering of native foods would be blighted by temperature extremes, enforcing greater reliance on imported refined energy-dense foods, the basis of the same sort of health-damaging diet that has been imposed on Native American populations in northern Canada as warming has adversely transformed the local landscape and biota.

We should note, too, that food crises and infectious diseases are not separate unrelated outcomes. Either can predispose to the other. Undernutrition increases biological susceptibility to infection, as do the increases in social dislocation and disorder due to hunger (Katona and Katona, 2008). There is plenty of contemporary evidence for this from refugee camps in poor countries. Meanwhile, the debilitation and death caused by many serious infectious disease epidemics can reduce farming activity and food production capacity. Higher-income populations in today's world should not imagine that the historical horrors of food crises and disease epidemics in past times, separately and together, are now consigned to the past. Substantial warming of 4°C at global level will be detrimental to agricultural yields nearly everywhere. We are not immune to a repeat of history under conditions of extreme climate change.

Over the centuries many episodes of serious under-nutrition and starvation, many associated with extreme droughts, drenching or periods of great cold, have been followed by outbreaks of infectious diseases (McMichael, 2012).

Lice-borne typhus caused most of the deaths during the 1840s Irish Great Famine. The climatic extremes and the resulting Great Famine in the early 14th-century Europe caused various disease epidemics, impoverishment and social disruption (Jordan, 1996; Behringer, 2010a), and may have rendered much of the population vulnerable to severe infections and death from the Black Death in the 1340s. Perhaps the greatest excesses of deaths from starvation and infectious diseases in Europe occurred during the seventeenth century temperature trough of the Little Ice Age, particularly in Central Europe (Behringer, 2010b). Although Europe's populations were increasing during the seventeenth and eighteenth centuries, nutrition and stature among the struggling rural population were declining and crowding in villages and towns made for more unhygienic conditions. After the climatically more congenial Middle Ages, average adult heights fell by six to seven centimetres during the seventeenth and eighteenth centuries (Steckel, 2004). Nutrition and stature in England, the frontrunner in the early industrial revolution, did not improve in the first half of the less-cold nineteenth century. The privation, crowding, hunger and factory working conditions that were emerging throughout industrializing Europe fostered intensified, often lethal, infectious diseases (including smallpox, measles, typhus, diarrhoeal diseases, cholera and tuberculosis: McMichael, 2009).

In modern Australia, and looking beyond food yields, prices and undernutrition in a much warmer world, there will be greatly heightened emotional and economic stresses in affected rural regions. These would greatly amplify the already-emerging and apparently climate-related upturn in various mental health problems and disorders, and in the loss of rural community morale, particularly in those with low resilience and inadequate social-capital resources (Berry et al., 2011a; 2011b; McMichael, 2010).

Other more diffuse risks to health

The preceding example leads us into this open-ended category of other more diffuse (tertiary) risks to health. One such example of likely great and increasing importance to Australia is that, in the Asian and Pacific regions in a +4°C world, the future flow of environmental migrants and refugees will inevitably increase, perhaps dramatically. In the words of the Asian Development Bank: 'Asia and the Pacific will be amongst the global regions most affected by the impacts of climate change ... As a result, it could experience population displacements of unprecedented scale in the coming decades' (Asian Development Bank, 2011: vi). This outflow of people will be driven by a mix of major stresses, including those due to population pressures, water shortage, climate change, soil exhaustion, food insecurity and loss of coastal habitat, especially in many of the low-lying small Pacific Island states (see Christoff and Eckersley, 2013, Chapter 11, this volume).

During the third to fifth centuries AD, the productive lands of the Western Roman Empire were a magnet for the crowded, land-starved and underfed Germanic tribes, massing on the north-eastern border as their regional climate became cooler and farming more difficult. Pushing from behind were the Hunnic tribes, heading west to leave the drought-stricken Central Asian steppes. Europe may again face similar pressures as climatic change in North Africa and the Middle East proceeds. For similar reasons, Australia is likely to remain, at least relatively, an attractive haven for populations afflicted by an even greater degree of environmental and socio-political stress.

Migration and displacement entail a wide and variable mix of risks to health – particularly for those that are moving, but also for those left behind and, often, for the receiving host communities. The possibilities include impoverishment and under-nutrition, exposures to infectious diseases, injuries and deaths (e.g. drowning), mental trauma and physical conflict situations (McMichael et al., 2012). Further, if public health surveillance and support programmes falter under the probable economically stressed conditions, various incoming groups may introduce serious infectious diseases such as multi-drug resistant tuberculosis. A Four Degree World would be very different from any in which environmental refugees have previously been studied, and hence the pattern and character of people movements is hard to foresee as are the likely numbers. There could also be much displacement from the Middle East and Sub-Saharan Africa.

Impacts on the health system

Australia's healthcare system will come under exponentially increasing pressure as temperatures rise. There is likely to be an initial shift in rates of some injuries, health disorders and heat-related deaths, subsequently merging into a transformation in the profile of types of disease and health disorders and in the sheer size, sometimes urgency, of an escalating climate-related demand. Intensified heatwaves in an overheating Australia (with an ageing population) will place increasing stresses on healthcare systems and on the vital penumbra of supportive infrastructure (power, transport, communications, etc.). Climate change – along with other environmental disruptions and social-demographic changes in and around Australia and the neighbouring Asian and Pacific region – will amplify the likelihood of new infectious diseases entering Australia or of existing ones flaring up and spreading. There would then be a manyfold increase in the population's infectious disease burden. In a Four Degree World, the map of infectious diseases in Australia would change radically, especially in segments of the population that by then would be underfed, weakened and susceptible to infection.

The potentially huge changes in the demands on, and the institutional and staffing profile of, the healthcare system would require a massive recurrent national expenditure. Health insurance policies may change for the worse if the climatic crisis precipitated a national (probably global) financial crisis, let alone economic collapse. The fact is that we cannot realistically imagine what changes a +4°C Australia would impose on environmental and ecological conditions, liveability of cities, rural livelihoods, social institutions, government-decision making processes and the profile of human health and survival. Nor can we guess the costs.

Future healthcare costs are merely hinted at in recent experiences of unusually extreme weather events in Australia. Extreme weather disasters today cause injuries, disease and death; they also cause social disruption and incur billions of dollars in damage costs. This is well illustrated by the December 2010 and January 2011 flooding in Queensland and the tropical cyclones Anthony and Yasi. Over 75 per cent of Queensland was declared a disaster zone; 35 people were killed by the floods; and overall about 2.5 million people were adversely affected (QFCI, 2011).

Those floods and cyclones were hugely disruptive to Queensland health services (Queensland Health, 2011). The heightened demands and stresses included:

- flooding and cyclones necessitated cancelling 1,396 booked elective surgeries because of the combination of increased demand on hospitals and staff unavailability;
- over 200 current patients in cyclone-stricken areas were transferred to Brisbane hospitals, hugely increasing 'long waits' for elective surgery;
- more than 17,000 tetanus/diphtheria vaccines were distributed in order to reduce the risk of infectious disease; and
- Queensland Health's phone service answered 54,881 calls from flood-affected areas.

The flooding also seriously damaged existing health infrastructure. The Queensland and Federal governments subsequently spent $18 million over two years to repair damage to health facilities (Queensland Health, 2011). To provide long-term mental health support following the floods and cyclones, $37.8 million was also provided for 2011–13 to fund the Queensland Mental Health Natural Disaster Recovery Plan. Serious enough today, these current weather disaster costs will look small in a +2°C Australia – and will look like petty cash in a +4°C Australia.

Concluding comment

This chapter has offered a very approximate estimation and/or description of the main types of adverse impacts of a Four Degree World on Australia's population health. The key point to recognize is that, in reality, we cannot confidently foresee the full range and magnitude of health threats that would then prevail. Would that extent of heating, amplified by another 2–3°C by the urban 'heat island' effect, cause big-city and suburb residents to relocate to the coasts, southern Tasmania or New Zealand? In fact, we will be mostly sailing blind into a future environment, landscape and set of social conditions and geopolitical relations that may be radically disrupted and different from today's. The changes due to a 2°C rise will not be a simple doubling of the changes at +1°C, and the changes and impacts at +4°C will not be twice those at 2°C.

That message, surely, conveys an important long-term perspective, warning of the inadequacy of relying on continued incremental attempts at technical and procedural adaptation. Future historians (if any) may look back and wonder why we acted in such myopic and reactive-only fashion, unable or unwilling to see the likely long-term consequences for life on earth if world temperatures continued to rise, initially by 4°C and then more.

The first readily observable impacts will be the continuing upturn in health damage due to escalating extremes of heat and more extreme and frequent weather disasters – especially floods, fires, storms and sea-surges. Their adverse impacts on physical safety, respiratory diseases, infectious diseases (direct unhygienic exposures and altered ecological conditions for mosquitoes etc.) and post-traumatic depression would all be much greater than those that have been more conventionally anticipated and modelled in relation to lesser scenarios of warming. Meanwhile, other less-obvious changes will be gathering momentum.

Despair and mental health disorders (including suicide rates) will rise in vulnerable farming communities as local conditions get warmer, evaporation accelerates, local rainfall systems weaken or shift, and extremes of weather and weather disasters impair or destroy agricultural output. Falling food yields will cause escalating prices and nutrition and health will suffer, particularly in low-income families and in poorer and remote communities. The patterns of infectious diseases and their underlying ecological and physical contexts will begin to change (including readier movements of infectious agents across national borders in the greater South East Asian region), and in disrupted and impoverished social and environmental circumstances epidemics will occur more readily.

The great threat to human health from a Four Degree World later this century underscores just how reliant is the biological wellbeing, health and survival of human populations on climatic and wider environmental conditions. From an *anthropocentric* perspective, our concern over the future health-and-survival impacts of climate change recognizes is well justified. However, for moral reasons alone, we must also recognise the serious risks posed by climate change to the non-human world (including biodiversity and the viability of ecosystems). Besides, these natural assets too have impacts on farm yields, water supplies and the quality of air, water and soil. These endangered natural systems are key parts of our health-and-life-support system. Earth's overall life-support system is already facing serious threats and stresses as the apparent safe limits, or 'planetary boundaries', of various component systems are reached and breached (Rockström et al., 2009). Inevitably, those various components will be much more threatened and disrupted in a Four Degree World (see Steffen and Griggs, 2013, Chapter 7, this volume).

The very great risks that a Four Degree World poses to human health in Australia and elsewhere, while somewhat unknowable in advance, surely provide a compelling reason for taking immediate and radical actions on behalf of long-term *primary prevention* and not just tinkering with electorally timid adaptive policies and actions. The two oncoming generations will live part of their lives in the late 21st century. Subsequent generations may find themselves in a radically self-rearranging natural world, increasingly unsuitable as a liveable habitat for humans.

References

Asian Development Bank. 2011. *Climate Change and Migration in Asia and the Pacific*. Manila, Philippines.

Bambrick, H., K. Dear, R. Woodruff et al. 2008. *The Impacts of Climate Change on Three Health Outcomes: Temperature-Related Mortality and Hospitalisations, Salmonellosis and Other Bacterial Gastroenteritis, and Population at Risk From Dengue*. Cambridge University Press: Cambridge.

Behringer, W. 2010a. *A Cultural History of Climate*. English edition, Polity Press: Cambridge, pp. 103–6.

Behringer, W. 2010b. *A Cultural History of Climate*. English edition, Polity Press: Cambridge, pp. 111–13.

Berry, H. L., A. Hogan, J. Owen, D. Rickwood and L. Fragar. 2011a. *Climate change and farmers' mental health: risks and responses*. Asia Pacific Journal of Public Health 23: 119S–132.

Berry, H. L., A. Hogan, S. Peng Ng and A. Parkinson. 2011b. *Farmer health and adaptive capacity in the face of climate change and variability. Part 1: health as a contributor to adaptive capacity and as an outcome from pressures coping with climate related adversities*. International Journal of Environmental Research and Public Health 8: 4039–54.

Butler, C. D and D. Harley. 2010. *Primary, secondary and tertiary effects of the eco-climate crisis: the medical response*. Postgraduate Medical Journal 86: 230–34.

Braganza, K., K. Hennessy, L. Alexander and B. Trewin. 2013. Changes in extreme weather. In P. Christoff (ed.), *Four Degrees of Climate Change: Australia in a Hot World*. Earthscan: London, ch. 3.

Christoff, P. 2013. Introduction: Australia in a four degree world. In P. Christoff (ed.), *Four Degrees of Climate Change: Australia in a Hot World*. Earthscan: London, ch. 1.

Christoff, P. and R. Eckersley. 2013. No island is an island: security in a Four Degree World. In P. Christoff (ed.), *Four Degrees of Climate Change: Australia in a Hot World*, Earthscan: London, ch. 11.

Ciscar, J., A. Iglesias, L. Feyen, L. Szabo et al. 2011. *Physical and economic consequences of climate change in Europe*. PNAS 108 (7): 2678–83.

Coumou, D. and S. Rahmstorf. 2012. A decade of weather extremes. *Nature Climate Change* 2: 491–6.

CSIRO and Bureau of Meteorology. 2007. *Climate Change in Australia*. CSIRO and Bureau of Meteorology, Melbourne.

Garnaut, R. 2008. *The Garnaut Climate Change Review: Final Report*. Cambridge University Press: Cambridge.

Hansen, J. and M. Sato. 2008. *Paleoclimate Implications for Human-Made Climate Change*. http://arxiv.org/ftp/arxiv/papers/1105/1105.0968.pdf [Last accessed 28 November 2012].

Howden, M., S. Schroeter and S. Crimp. 2013. Agriculture in an even more sunurnt country. In P. Christoff (ed.), *Four Degrees of Climate Change: Australia in a Hot World*. Earthscan: London, ch. 6.

IPCC. 2012. *Special report on extreme events (SREX): managing the risks of extreme events and disasters to advance climate change adaptation*. http://www.ipcc-wg2.gov/SREX/ [accessed 23 July 2013].

Jordan, W. C. 1996. *The Great Famine: Northern Europe in the Early Fourteenth Century*. Princeton University Press: Princeton, NJ.

Katona, P. and J. Katona. 2008. The interaction between nutrition and infection. *Clinical Infectious Diseases* 46: 1582–8.

Kjellstrom, T., I. Holmer and B. Lemke. 2009. *Workplace heat stress, health and productivity: an increasing challenge for low and middle-income countries during climate change. Global Health Action 2.* Published online 11 November 11 2009. doi: 10.3402/gha.v2i0.2047.

McMichael, A. J. 2009. Human population health: sentinel criterion of environmental sustainability. *Current Opinion in Environmental Sustainability* 1: 101–6.

—2011. *Drought, drying and mental health: lessons from recent experiences for future risk-lessening policies. Australian Journal of Rural Health* 19: 227–8.

—1999. *From hazard to habitat: rethinking environmental health. Epidemiology* 10: 460–63.

—2012. Insights from past millennia into climatic impacts on human health and survival. *Proceedings of the National Academy of Sciences* 109: 4730–37.

McMichael, C. E., J. Barnett and A. J. McMichael. 2012. *An ill wind? Climate change, migration and health. Environmental Health Perspectives* 120 (5): 646–54.

QFCI (Queensland Floods Commission of Inquiry). 2011. *Queensland Floods Commission of Inquiry: Interim Report. Brisbane.* http://www.floodcommission.qld.gov.au/publications/interim-report [accessed: 23 July 2013].

Queensland Health. 2011. *The Centre for Trauma, Loss and Disaster Recovery.* http://www.health.qld.gov/au/recovery_resources/html/the_centre.asp [accessed 23 July 2013].

Rockström, J., W. Steffen, K. Noone et al. 2009. *A safe operating space for humanity.* Nature 461: 472–5.

Stager, C. 2011. *Deep future: the next 100,000 years on earth.* Scribe/Thomas Dunne Books/St Martins Press: New York.

Steckel, R. H. 2004. New light on the 'dark ages': the remarkably tall stature of Northern European men during the medieval era. *Social Science History* 28 (2): 211–29. doi:10.1215/01455532-28-2-211.

Steffen, W. and D. Griggs. 2013. Compounding crises: climate change in a complex world. In P. Christoff (ed.), *Four Degrees of Climate Change: Australia in a Hot World.* Earthscan: London, ch. 7.

Stott, P. A., D. A. Stone and M. R. Allen. 2004. *Human contribution to the European heatwave of 2003. Nature 432 (7017): 610–14.*

UN Habitat. 2011. *Cities and Climate Change: Global Report on Human Settlements 2011.* UN Habitat: New York.

Van den Torren, S., F. Suzan, S. Medina et al. 2004. *Mortality in 13 French cities during the August 2003 heatwave.* American Journal of Public Health 94 (9): 1518–20.

Vineis, P. and A. Kahn. 2012. *Climate change-induced salinity threatens health.* Science 338: 1028–29.

Whetton, P., D. Karoly, I. Watterson, L. Webb, F. Drost, D. Kirono and K. McInnes. 2013. Australia's climate in a Four Degree World. In P. Christoff (ed.), *Four Degrees of Climate Change: Australia in a Hot World.* Earthscan: London, chapter 2.

World Bank. 2012. *Turn Down the Heat: Why a 4°C Warming World Must be Avoided. World Bank, Washington, DC.* http://climatechange.worldbank.org/content/climate-change-report-warns-dramatically-warmer-world-century

10 Hot in the city

Planning for climate change impacts in urban Australia

Jan McDonald

Introduction

Australia's climate is already changing as a result of human influence. Over the past 50 years, we have experienced increased average and maximum temperatures, decreases in daily minimum temperatures, a 10–40 per cent increase in fire weather, and drying trends across the south west and south east (Chapters 2 and 3, Hennessy et al., 2005; BoM and CSIRO 2007).

With four degrees of warming, the number of extreme heat days (days over 35°C) in Australian cities will increase dramatically, from 3.5 to 12 days in Sydney, 9 to 26 days in Melbourne, 28 to 67 days in Perth, 1 to 21 days in Brisbane and 11 to 308 days in Darwin (Braganza et al., 2013 [ch. 3, this volume]; CSIRO and BoM, 2007). Rainfall and severe hail events are expected to intensify (CSIRO and BoM 2007; Rafter and Abbs 2009) and the number of extreme fire danger days for a projected 2.9°C warming is expected to increase by between 100 and 300 per cent (CSIRO & BoM 2007; Braganza et al., 2013, ch. 3, this volume). The frequency of cyclone activity is projected to decrease, although the intensity of such events is likely to increase (Whetton et al., 201, ch. 2, this volume).

The IPCC projections of sea level rise for 2–5.4°C of global warming are conservatively in the range of 23–51cm by 2100 (IPCC, 2007). Even small rises in sea level will greatly shorten the average recurrence interval (ARI) for coastal inundation events (Australian Government, 2009). For example, a sea level rise of 20cm would reduce the ARI for what is currently a 1-in-100 year storm surge in south-east Queensland to 61 years. The interval drops to just 9 years with a rise of 1 metre (Wang et al., 2010).

It is trite but perhaps salutary to point out that, in Australia, these climate change impacts will take effect in conjunction with population growth and movement and other demographic change. A severe cyclone will cause less property damage in a sparsely developed area than in a densely populated city, although impacts on biodiversity and natural values or other economically valuable industries may be significant. The severity of impacts will also be mediated by what adaptation measures have been implemented: drought will be less disruptive to urban populations that have already reduced their water consumption or improved water storage and supply.

Over 90 per cent of Australia's population lives in a city or major regional centre. Nearly 70 per cent of Australians live in just six major cities and the population of these urban centres is increasing at a faster rate than the overall population (ABS, 2008). The preference for coastal living means that 83 per cent of the population lives within 50km of the coast and between 160,000 and 250,000 existing properties are at risk of coastal flooding with a sea level rise of 1.1m (Australian Government, 2009). With such high levels of urbanization and concentration of population into a handful of urban centres, the impacts of climate change on Australian cities is receiving closer attention.

The impacts on Australian cities will be both direct and indirect. As Chapter 9 has indicated, human health impacts from greater air pollution, heat stress, and an increase in heat-related violence will follow from heatwave events. There will also be major social and business disruption and economic loss as a result of the energy and transport infrastructure failures associated with extreme hot weather. Sea level rise will lead to an increase in the frequency of coastal erosion and inundation with attendant impacts on private and public infrastructure and assets. More intense rainfall and storm events will cause property damage from flooding, wind damage and hail, as well as risks to human life and health. Drying conditions will create profound water supply challenges for many urban centres, affecting the quality and quantity of water for domestic and industrial uses, as well as public sporting and recreational assets. These examples serve only to illustrate the numerous complex interactions between climate change effects and their manifestation in an urban context and to highlight the need for urban planners and managers to account for these events in their land use, building, public health, infrastructure and asset management and other strategies.

This chapter examines the way in which land use planning in Australia is accounting for the impacts of climate change and the implications of our urban populations, as at 2012. Section two examines the different planning responses to three types of climate change impact – sea level rise and coastal hazards, bushfire conditions and heatwave. It also discusses progress on adaptation planning in Australia's six largest cities. Section three recognizes the limitations of new planning measures for existing urban centres and the likelihood of future climate- or weather-related disasters. It outlines key features of recent responses to natural disasters. Section four considers some of the key barriers to enhanced adaptation planning in urban Australia and how they can be addressed.

Planning for impacts

The impacts of climate change in urban centres is a function of the physical effects of higher temperatures, rising sea levels and extreme weather; the location, design and construction of our cities and built environments; underlying population health; governance arrangements and social practices, norms, and attitudes. Land use planning is widely regarded as the critical mechanism by which to prevent exposure to climate change impacts in Australian cities and towns (COAG 2002; 2004; WHO 2009; Abel et al., 2011; Measham et al., 2011). In conjunction with building standards, public education, emergency management plans and hazard reduction initiatives, planning can ensure that new communities minimize exposure to climate change impacts and guide redevelopment and urban in-fill to reduce where possible the exposure of existing communities and infrastructure.

Not surprisingly, the incorporation of climate change impacts into land use planning frameworks is a very recent phenomenon. As the following discussion shows, there is also a wide variation in the extent and rigour of climate change adaptation planning for different risks – for coastal hazards, new planning measures are likely to cover the impacts associated with four degrees of warming, whereas bushfire planning deals poorly the exacerbation of risk from climate change. Projected increases in extreme heat events receive virtually no attention in planning frameworks for urban Australia.

Coastal hazards

The impacts of sea level rise on coastal communities continue to dominate adaptation planning activity (Parliament of Australia, 2009; Government of Australia, 2010). Management is split across land use planning, coastal management, climate change and emergency management sectors, as well as between local, state and Commonwealth government (Harvey and Woodroffe, 2008; Norman 2009).

Despite the governance challenges that this regulatory fragmentation creates, all Australian states have planning laws relating to coastal hazards generally. In the past five years, most have introduced new provisions that enhance, elucidate or partially replace existing provisions with measures aimed specifically at hazards exacerbated by climate change and sea level rise, although recently some states have begun to weaken or dismantle these measures. Most jurisdictions have now adopted a planning benchmark for sea level rise (SLR) that guides building heights and set-backs from erosion and inundation lines, and require decision-makers to consider the effects of king tides and storm surge on higher sea levels in calculating such set-backs. Areas calculated to be at high risk are typically reflected in strategic planning instruments such as overlays or hazard management plans and generally permit only very limited forms of development, such as re-locatable or temporary dwellings and infrastructure.

The actual SLR benchmark differs across the country, ranging from 1.0m above 1990 levels by 2100 in South Australia (State of SA, 1992), to 0.9m in Western Australia (State of WA, 2010), to 0.8m in Northern Territory, Tasmania and Victoria (State of Tasmania, 2012; State of Victoria 2008).[1] The NSW sea level rise planning benchmark of 0.9 has recently been repealed, leaving individual local councils with the ultimate discretion over what approach to take (State of NSW, 2010; State of NSW, 2012). The asset life of proposed developments is relevant in assessing the sea level rise benchmark that must be followed. Some frameworks recognize that certain types of development will have a shorter lifespan than others – building a carport will create a less enduring infrastructure legacy than siting a new coastal suburb – and therefore these frameworks set a lower benchmark for sea level rise by 2040 and 2050. The implications of these reforms are potentially significant. For example, the *State Planning Policy 3/11 : Coastal Protection* (Queensland) (suspended) mapped high and medium coastal hazard areas in a way that places about 10 per cent of all Queensland properties within those designations (Property Council of Australia, 2011) and therefore made these subject to restrictions on future development. Strong opposition from the property industry and the election of a new state government resulted in the suspension of the Coastal SPP after only eight months, and its replacement with the Draft Coastal Protection State Planning Regulatory Provision Protecting the Coastal Environment (State of Queensland, 2012), which contains no formal planning benchmark or mapping of coastal hazard areas.

While several instruments refer to the importance of retreat as an option and a few voluntary buyback schemes are emerging, there is little evidence of mandatory or unfunded retreat being adopted yet. The approach currently being advocated is to allow for longer-term staged retreat by prohibiting new development or intensification in high hazard areas or only allowing development with a limited life-span (State of Victoria, 2008; State of NSW, 2010 [repealed]; Abel et al., 2011; State of Queensland, 2011). The *Queensland Coastal Plan* required local authorities to prepare a coastal hazard adaptation strategy for urban areas that are projected to be located within a high hazard area by 2100 and incorporate the strategy into relevant local planning instruments. The strategy was required to indicate mitigation works or actions that would be undertaken, with costs, funding arrangements and timelines. In developing the strategy, the authority must assess the cost effectiveness of a range of options, including retreat, avoidance and defence (State of Queensland, 2011). These requirements are now under review following the suspension of the entire *Queensland Coastal Plan*.

Bushfire

The impacts of climate change on coastal hazards will be both chronic, in the form of gradual inundation through sea level rise, and acute, through exacerbation of storm surge, inundation and erosion events. By contrast, the likely impact of climate change on bushfire risks is an increase in the potential frequency and severity of individual bushfire events (see Chapter 3). This makes it harder to incorporate climate change impacts into bushfire planning.

All jurisdictions have general planning controls on development in bushfire-prone areas (State of Queensland, 2003; State of NSW 2006; State of WA 2006, 2010; ACT, 2008; State of SA 2009; State of Victoria, 2011; State of Tasmania, 2012;) and all require compliance with the Building Code of Australia and AS3959 – Construction of Buildings in Bushfire Prone Areas. Bushfire-prone areas are generally mapped spatially or defined in relation to the proximity of vegetation. In some states, mapping is left to local governments, while in others it is the responsibility of the state. Given substantial projected increases in fire weather, the accurate mapping of increased bushfire risk should not be left to individual local authorities whose budgets are subjected to numerous competing demands. Acting on a recommendation of the Victorian Bushfires Royal Commission (VBRC), the Victorian Department of Planning and Community Development has developed a statewide Bushfire Overlay, informed by hazard mapping from the Department of Sustainability and Environment and the Country Fire Authority, for introduction into all planning schemes (White, 2011).

Some planning instruments make general reference to the increase in bushfire risk posed by climate change (State of Queensland, 2003; State of WA, 2006), but provide no formal mechanism by which that risk is to be considered. Data on future climate should inform the mapping of bushfire areas, but it appears that the rigour with which that currently occurs depends on the resources of the agency responsible. In Queensland, State Planning Policy 1/03 'Mitigating the adverse impacts of flood, bushfire and landslide' requires the identification of hazard areas and consideration of a lot's suscep-tibility to these hazards but the Policy implementation guidelines currently provide that inclusion of climate change impacts in bushfire assessment is not considered feasible and is therefore not required (State of Queensland, 2003a; 2003b Schedule 3). In Victoria, mapping for the new Bushfire Management Overlay is based on vegetation classes. It takes into account fuel loads, patch sizes and buffers for dealing with areas that may be vulnerable to ember attack. The potential impacts of climate change on bushfire behaviour have been taken into account largely by favouring a more conservative approach to mapping the overlay (Macintosh et al., 2012).

The bushfire planning framework in most states and territories aims to avoid locating major new residential development and vulnerable uses in areas designated as highly bushfire prone, or to mitigate risks though development controls relating to mandatory access and egress require-ments, dedicated water supply, construction standards and defendable space prescriptions.

On 7 February 2009, Victoria had the worst bushfires in the nation's recorded history when, on 'Black Saturday' – a day of exceptionally high temperatures and winds – fire claimed 173 human lives and destroyed 2,029 homes. Since then, bushfire planning and protection in Victoria have undergone the most significant reforms. The Victorian Bushfires Royal Commission found that the State Protection from Wildfire Policy was completely inadequate (VBRC, 2010, ch. 6; White, 2011) because it afforded no guidance on how local councils should identify bushfire risk areas or exercise their discretion in relation to development approvals in bushfire prone areas, particularly in guiding how to balance bushfire risk reduction and biodiversity conservation (White, 2011). The new *State Planning Policy Framework* provisions prioritize the protection of human life over other policy considerations (State of Victoria, 2012), while the *Bushfire*

Management Overlay provides detailed guidance on the way in which bushfire risks should be considered in development assessment decisions.

However for existing communities in bushfire-prone areas, such planning reforms offer little comfort and there are limited options for risk mitigation. Retreat is widely discussed in the context of coastal development but receives far less attention in relation to bushfire-prone areas, despite a property acqui-sition scheme having operated in the 1970s following fires in the Dandenong ranges (VBRC, 2011, chapter 6; White, 2011). The VBRC criticized the public commitment of the State and Federal Governments to rebuild devastated communities in exactly the same locations and recommended that 'the State develop and implement a retreat and resettlement strategy for existing devel-opments in areas of unacceptably high bushfire risk, including a scheme for non-compulsory acquisition by the State of land in these areas' (VBRC, 2011, Recommendation 46). While a voluntary buy-back scheme has been introduced, and has had significant uptake, it has not formed part of a wider retreat and reset-tlement strategy as recommended by the VBRC.

Heatwaves

The impacts of higher temperatures will be exacerbated in Australian cities by the urban heat island (UHI) effect (Wang and McAllister, 2011). It can be up to 7°C warmer in Melbourne's CBD, for example, than in surrounding suburbs (City of Melbourne, 2009). The combined effect of more extreme hot weather days and the UHI effect is likely to cause major increases in mortality, morbidity and social disruption in Australia's urban population (see Chapter 9). Recent heat waves in south-eastern Australia have claimed hundreds of lives (State of Victoria, 2009) and caused massive business and social disruption through the failure of critical electricity and public transport infrastructure. The World Health Organization's guidance on planning for heatwaves lists long-term urban planning as a core element of any heatwave strategy (WHO, 2009), yet no Australian regime requires planners to address the impacts of hotter cities. Only Queensland, Victoria and South Australia have any form of heatwave management or response plan and these documents are all focused on preparation, warning and response to extreme heat events rather than prevention through better urban form or building design (Queensland, 2004; South Australia, undated; Victoria, 2011a).

Individual local authorities are examining the issue and identifying 'hotspots' within their cities that would benefit from tree planting and other cooling strat-egies and there are increasing requirements for better insulation in new buildings. Currently, however, there is no overarching policy guidance or planning instru-ments on how and when this should be done, although the Sydney Metropolitan Plan 2036 proposes a review of its building sustainability index, Basix, to address heat-sensitive building design (State of NSW, 2010c).

There may be a range of reasons for this difference between adaptation planning for increased coastal hazards, for bushfire hazards and for heatwaves.

Firstly, heatwave risks lack the visual power conveyed by images of houses falling into the sea, people kayaking down their flooded main street, or cars and houses ablaze. They do not excite the public imagination or sentiment in the same way as bushfires, floods or coastal erosion, and have not resulted in the same level of policy review and reform after the event. Secondly, heatwaves are still considered a public health issue, and this prompts a public health/emergency management response rather than a long-term planning response. Thirdly, there are many individual responses to heatwave that can be made simply and cheaply, such as choice of clothing, diet and work pattern (Wang and McAllister, 2011). Redesigning and retrofitting Australia's cities will be far costlier and more complicated. At four degrees of global warming, however, the efficacy of simpler and individuated strategies may become more limited – for instance, we have already seen power systems crash due to spiking demand caused by mass use of air conditioning – and the constraints of our existing built environment will become more apparent and harder to overcome. There is therefore a strong case for greater attention to the planning considerations in order to ensure that future urban spaces account for the possibility of much hotter conditions.

City-based adaptation planning initiatives

By far the most comprehensive Australian city adaptation plan, in terms of both content and plan methodology, is the City of Melbourne's *Climate Change Adaptation Strategy 2009* (City of Melbourne, 2009). The plan systematically identifies, assesses and ranks climate change risks and adaptation options. It includes a list of 'high value' adaptation options that will deliver benefits regardless of the future climate change experienced in the city. These include expanding storm water harvesting and re-use, developing and implementing a heatwave response action plan and alert system, reducing the urban heat island effect, limiting the effects of sea level rise through controls on development, enhancing communications and early warning systems, monitoring potential exposure to legal liability and ongoing monitoring of risks (City of Melbourne, 2009).

Coordinated city-wide adaptation planning is hindered by the division of most metropolitan centres into numerous local government units. The City of Melbourne's Adaptation Strategy applies only within the City of Melbourne, which encompasses the CBD and inner city suburbs with a total resident population of merely 80,000. This jurisdiction is small compared with Metropolitan Melbourne's resident population of 3.6 million, so its coverage is obviously limited. It nonetheless provides a valuable template for similar initiatives by neighbouring councils or, better still, state co-ordination of a Metro-Melbourne wide approach.

To overcome this fragmentation of local government jurisdictions in NSW, the State government is coordinating the Sydney Metropolitan Plan 2036, one objective of which is that Sydney should lead the Asia-Pacific Region in capital city adaptation to climate change (State of NSW, 2010c). Planning is now underway on the development of an adaptation strategy for Sydney in furtherance of that objective.

No other state capital has undertaken systematic adaptation planning. Brisbane City Council includes a range of adaptation actions in its Plan for Action on Climate Change and Energy 2007 (BCC, 2007), with particular focus on water security, public communication and education, flood and storm surge planning, and enhanced shade and weather protection in public spaces. The ACT's Climate Change Strategy (ACT, 2007a) lists adaptation as a core objective, with the Strategy's first Action Plan (ACT, 2007b) focusing on assessing the vulnerability of urban areas to climate impacts. Adelaide has no city-wide adaptation plan and the state adaptation framework proposes no substantive actions for infrastructure and urban areas (State of SA, 2010). The City of South Perth developed a Draft Climate Change Strategy in 2010, proposes a comprehensive vulnerability assessment by 2013 and an adaptation strategy by 2011. Preparation of the adaptation strategy is ongoing (City of South Perth, 2010, 2011).

This brief review highlights the limited extent of adaptation planning in Australian cities. Internationally, there have been numerous studies of urban vulnerability and adaptation, with a particular emphasis on developing country mega-cities (World Bank 2010; 2011; Feiden 2011; EEA, 2012). Several adaptation planning tools have been developed and there are a few prominent examples of city-based planning, including London, New York and Toronto (Ligeti et al., 2007; Toronto Environment Office, 2008; New York City Panel on Climate Change, 2010; Greater London Authority 2011; EEA, 2012). Aspects of New York's adaptation approach relating to the relocation of electrical equipment out of basements and more flood-resistance coastal design have already been credited with lessening the impact of Hurricane Sandy (Tollefson, 2012).

The experience of these cities highlights the importance of identifying climate risks then linking them to adaptation strategies and options, and the organizations, agencies or affected parties responsible for their delivery. They also point to the governance challenges involved in implementing strategies across agencies within local government and as between local-level government and state or national departments. Despite some strong examples, the potential for such city-based planning remains under-exploited both in the breadth and quality of coverage and implementation mechanisms (Preston et al., 2010). With Australia's highly urbanized population and associated exposure to climate change impacts, there is an urgent need to improve city-based adaptation planning whether that be through local-level initiatives or state-led processes.

The process by which these adaptation measures are developed and implemented will be as important as the measures themselves. Successful models in other global cities have emphasized the importance of public education and engagement, the need for downscaled projections of likely impacts, the formulation of options that include building on existing projects in the development and implementation of a municipal adaptation strategy (Ligeti et al., 2007). Public participation is also considered critical in the implementation of contentious decisions and plans, particularly in respect of iconic places such as beaches and coasts (Leitch and Robinson, 2011). Adaptation plans that apply broader principles of environmental decision-making or ecologically sustainable development and combine adaptation considerations with other policy goals will contribute to policy coherence and are more likely to win public acceptance.

Adaptation planning involves costly research and technical inputs. Most of the urban plans developed to date have received funding through Commonwealth adaptation grants programmes, and local council planning officers report that this external funding was critical (Macintosh et al., 2012). Even once adaptation plans for cities are developed, their implementation will entail even greater costs. About 80 per cent of the US$70–80 billion per annum that the World Bank estimates will be required for global adaptation between 2010 and 2015 are in sectors related to urban areas (World Bank, 2011). This estimate relates only to the costs of adaptation to new impacts and does not account for any existing 'adaptation deficit' in capacity to deal with current climate variability and extremes. Some of these costs will be incremental, and can be covered through local-level revenue raising, such as budgetary prioritization, special rates and charges, and bonds. Major engineered solutions and infrastructural adaptations will involve large one-off expenditures. Australian governments at all levels are yet to grapple with the challenge of financing these options.

The urban infrastructure legacy and disaster response

Given the substantial infrastructural legacy of past planning decisions in urban Australia and the possible increased frequency and intensity of climate-related extreme events in a Four Degree World (Chapter 3), it is highly likely that climate change related disasters will adversely affect our cities and towns in the future, regardless of what planning measures we put in place. The buildings and their occupants are already located in harm's way, so land use planning's principal strategy of locating development away from hazards cannot realized. Our recent experience of floods, cyclones, heatwaves and bushfire suggests that extreme events will inevitably result in property damage, business disruption, and in some cases personal injury or loss of life in existing urban areas, so other measures will be needed to prepare our cities for a Four Degree future. These are likely to be a combination of public information and education campaigns relating to changing attitudes and expectations about the limits of adaptation and emergency preparedness; enhanced emergency response plans and capabilities; and regulatory controls such as a requirement to retro-fit properties (pool fencing requirements being the obvious precedent).

From a policy-maker's perspective, the aftermath of a major disaster opens a critical window of opportunity in which to introduce adaptation measures and institutional arrangements, while public opinion favours strong action to prevent recurrence. Recent disasters have triggered formal inquiries and reviews with wide-ranging recommendations for legal, policy and operational reform. Commissions of Inquiry have become common vehicles for conducting disaster post mortems – and Queensland Floods Royal Commissions are the most notable recent examples. Implementation of inquiry findings and recommendations varies widely. The Victorian government has enacted special legislation giving effect to an election commitment to implement all of the 67 recommendations of the VBRC, but the results of earlier inquiries such as that following the 2003 Canberra bushfires have not enjoyed the same level of political take-up (Bonyhady, 2010). The insights gained from these inquiries are often not limited to the circumstances of a particular state and offer valuable lessons for other jurisdictions and other extreme events. Experience to date suggests that we do best at shutting the gate only after our own horses have bolted, but one hopes that we can improve our learning from the experience of others.

The handling of recovery operations is also likely to change if climate change brings about an intensification of weather-related extreme events. The Queensland government's response to the 2010–11 floods and Cyclone Yasi provides an interesting example of new approaches to recovery from major disasters. The Queensland Reconstruction Authority (QRA) was established by the QRA Act 2011 only one month following the Brisbane floods. The Act is expressed to apply to reconstruction activities relating to the floods and Cyclone Yasi, though there is scope for additional events to be added to assist in the protection, rebuilding and recovery of affected communities (QRA, 2001, s42). As a body aimed at recovery, the QRA is subject to a two-year sunset clause, after which time the Authority's remaining obligations default to the State Coordinator-General. The QRA is not responsible for analyzing the causes of the floods and associated losses or making recommendations for reform. The QRA has wide powers to undertake reconstruction and development works and to expedite regulatory decisions or approval processes. It can override local planning schemes and may acquire land to undertake works or to implement a development scheme.

A valuable feature of the Act with interesting implications for the future design of retreat strategies is the power of the QRA to designate land 'acquisition land' for reconstruction purposes (QRA, 2011, s44). The owner of 'acquisition land' is not obliged to surrender the land immediately, but may only ever dispose of it to the Authority or another approved entity, such as a local government. This allows residents to remain in property that is not considered suitable for long-term human occupation for as long as they wish. This ameliorates the harshness of compulsory acquisition, while still ensuring that land will be transferred to other uses in the longer term. In the meantime, however, residents who choose to remain on designated acquisition land continue to be exposed to the risk of a recurrence of the 'inland tsunami' that swept through the small farming town in 2011, which prompted the designation in the first place.

As part of the Grantham Development Plan, the Locker Valley Regional Council has offered a land swap for residents affected by the flood. The

Development Plan designates affected areas as a Limited Development (Constrained Land) Zone, in which new residential development is prohibited. Houses within this zone that have not participated in the council's land swap program will become acquisition lands, requiring owners to offer the land to council prior to any future transfer (QRA, 2011: 48; Lockyer Valley Regional Council 2011a, 2011b).

Improving adaptation in urban Australia: drivers and barriers

The bolting of adaptation components on to existing planning frameworks will be the dominant model for most sectors affected by climate change, at least while the impacts occur slowly enough to be addressed incrementally. The current range of planning responses to climate change are based on projected temperature increases of less than 4°C, partly because four degrees of warming is considered less probable than more conservative projections (IPCC, 2007), and partly because the increasing uncertainty associated with higher temperatures makes decision-making even harder. Incremental adjustments are far easier to make than radical transformations like the relocation or reconstruction of entire communities. Incremental approaches create links between future changes and current priorities and involve less disruption to existing rights and expectations. But incremental change is not appropriate for planning decisions with long lives, where the possibility of different future climates would necessitate different planning responses today (Stafford Smith et al., 2011).

A range of analyses are contributing to our understanding of how best to deal with these uncertainties. Approaches include the selection of 'no-regret' or 'high value' strategies that are beneficial regardless of climate change; reversible and flexible options; the incorporation of 'safety margins' in into new investments; the use of soft or behavioural adaptation strategies and mechanisms by which to reduce decision time horizons (Desai, 2009; Dobes, 2010; Staffordet al., 2011, citing Hallegatte, 2009).

The under-resourcing of agencies given the task of developing or implementing adaptation strategies remains a significant barrier to increasing climate resilience (Australian Government, 2010; Measham et al., 2011). There are significant gaps in knowledge about local impacts and the social and economic cost implications of different adaptation options (Australian Government, 2010). Planning instruments have to strike an appropriate balance between respecting local government autonomy and providing enough clarity that under-resourced councils can perform their obligations effectively. Councils with limited resources are simply overwhelmed by the cost and technical challenges of hazard mapping and associated planning responses. Recent research in Queensland suggests that the widely disparate implementation of SPP 1/03, the planning policy for non-coastal hazards, is due in part to the wide discretion that the policy gives local decision-makers (Bajracharya et al., 2011). Similarly, the Victoria Bushfires Royal Commission found that some local authorities with bushfire prone land had not prepared a bushfire-specific local planning policy or wildlife management overlay, or that the policy was so general as to be ineffectual, largely because they lacked the resources and capacity to undertake the task with so little guidance. The VBRC recommended that a model local planning policy be developed that could provide a basis for authorities with limited capacity to prepare their own instruments from scratch (BVRC, 2011). Similar problems have been encountered in relation to planning for coastal hazards in Victoria, with local government struggling to implement framework objectives in the absence of detailed guidance and direction (Macintosh, 2012). Despite the seemingly strong preference of local governments for strong state guidance on adaptation requirements, 2012 has seen the beginnings of a 'retreat from adaptation' as the state level in some states under new conservative governments, particularly in relation to coastal planning.

Governance arrangements are also problematic and demand further attention from researchers and policy makers. The statutory constraints on local government powers limit their capacity to implement adaptation measures single-handedly, hence the focus in this paper on state planning initiatives. The cost of some adaptations options will also mean a role for the Federal Government. Negotiation of roles and responsibilities across three tiers of government will complicate and slow progress on adaptation, but is critical for achieving effective governance arrangements in the long term.

Regardless of resourcing or statutory mandate, the quality and implementation of adaptation planning ultimately depends on the institutional culture (Measham et al., 2011) and commitment of the administering agency. Adaptation tends to be sidelined where a local authority conceptualizes adaptation as an 'environmental issue' rather than an issue concerning the whole of a local government's activities (Measham et al., 2011).

Fear of litigation and legal liability also appears to be a significant barrier to adaptation in an urban planning context. Local authorities face the invidious choice of exposing themselves to future claims in respect developments they approve in vulnerable locations, or risking appeals against the refusal of a development in a high-risk area. Legal challenges can be expected whenever commercial interests are affected by new requirements; any ambiguity or inadequacy in drafting or the exercise of discretion will be tested. The operation of legislative frameworks for coastal climate impacts has already been tested in four Australian states, with the results of litigation varying considerably based on the terms of the planning law and associated instruments and the tribunal considering the matter. Attempts to impose conditions on approval that serve to shorten planning horizons are also likely to face challenge if the statutory foundation for imposing them is in unclear in any way. For example, the now-repealed NSW Sea Level Rise Planning Guideline permitted authorities to grant planning approvals that ended or were reviewed either at a specified future date or on the occurrence of a specified event trigger (such as the inward migration of an erosion line) (State of NSW, 2010a). To date, there has been limited uptake of this more flexible approach to handling future uncertainty because of its political unpalatability and concerns about impacts on developers' ability to obtain finance for projects conditioned in this way.

Concerns about exposure to liability in respect of planning decisions with future climate change implications are also affecting the willingness of local governments to progress the adaptation agenda (McDonald 2007, 2010; City of Melbourne 2009; Parliament of Australia 2009; Australian Government 2010). When New South Wales introduced its Planning for Bush Fire Protection Guidelines and associated statutory provisions in 2006, it resulted in local authorities referring all development applications on bushfire-prone land to the Rural Fire Service because they did not want to be responsible for having approved a development that was ultimately affected by fire. The increased workload of the RFS was immense – for example, there were 4,500 referrals of new development applications just in the six months from July–December 2009. Legislative amendments have now clarified that local authorities, not the RFS, are principally responsible for undertaking development assessments in bushfire-prone areas. But in order to ensure the political acceptability of this return to local government responsibility, an exemption from legal liability was also enacted for acts and advice relating to bushfire-prone land done by planning authorities in good faith (Local Government Act, 1993 NSW, s733; State of NSW, 2010b). Judicial concern about the uncertainty of future impacts and potential intergenerational legal liability has been one of the key bases for the Victorian Civil and Administrative Tribunal overruling several coastal developments in recent years (VCAT, 2008; 2010).

Adaptation planning will involve trade-offs between interests: public values relating to amenity, recreation and environmental goods may be inconsistent with the protection of private property. Coastal planning authorities face choices between measures that protect beachfront properties and those that ensure the long term protection of the beach as a public recreational asset. Tensions between bushfire mitigation and native vegetation protection influenced planning decisions in areas affected by the 2009 Victorian bushfires. Differing perceptions of fairness about the protection of private property over public assets and the allocation of adaptation resources also hinder local planning responses (Leitch and Robinson, 2011). When loss of life and property have already occurred, these trade-offs seem far more obvious and straightforward than they are before the fact, but this highlights an underlying tension in effective and equitable adaptation: pressure decision-makers face enormous pressure to make anticipatory decisions that cause only minimal disruption to the status quo, but these 'softly-softly' decisions may deny communities the benefits of taking decisive action in response to past events.

Conclusions

Many of the impacts of climate change will be felt severely in Australia's cities and towns due to their high concentrations of people and complex, valuable infrastructure. Reforms to land use planning in Australia have so far concentrated on the impacts of climate change on coastal hazards. While planning regimes require consideration of bushfire-prone areas in development controls, implementation of associated regulations and planning is patchy and there is minimal evidence of climate change considerations informing the assessment of such risks. Land use planning to reduce urban heat island effects remains very limited. Individual cities are taking steps to enhance the appropriateness of urban form for hotter conditions, but like other climate change impacts, clearer state-level guidance is more likely to deliver consistent outcomes.

With over 70 per cent of Australia's population living in just six major cities, it should be easy to develop adaptation plans that can reduce climate risks for many millions of people and infrastructure and limit damage to assets worth billions of dollars. Yet progress on city-based adaptation planning has been slow. The City of Melbourne's Strategy provides an important exemplar for other municipalities, but co-ordinated initiatives are needed for entire metropolitan areas whose governance is fragmented across numerous local authorities. These planning activities will require both funding and institutional commitment.

Planning for climate change impacts in Australian cities faces numerous barriers but none of these is insurmountable. Strategies are emerging for dealing with the uncertainties inherent in future climate projections. Better resourcing and clearer statutory mandates will make the task of local planning easier and yield better quality outcomes. Clarification of liability issues and the enactment of statutory protections for local authorities will clear the path for more courageous adaptation initiatives. Greater public awareness of the need for adaptation should drive changes in organizational culture and the commitment of individual civic leaders.

Perhaps most important is the need to build on the experience of past events and ensure that measures are in place to prevent their recurrence. Major weather-related disasters provoke national awareness of climate change risks and the possibility that 'this could happen to us' creates brief opportunities for preventive action, even in places not directly affected by the event. Our record of learning from the mistakes of others has not been impressive in other spheres of resource and environmental management, yet in a Four Degree World, we can ill afford not to.

Notes

1   A planning code on sea level rise, storm surge and shoreline vulnerability is currently under development in Tasmania.

References

Abel N., R. Gorddard, B. Harman, A. Leitch, J. Landridge, A. Ryan and S. Heyenga. 2011. Sea level rise, coastal development and planned retreat: analytical framework, governance principles and an Australian case study. *Environmental Science & Policy* 14: 279–88.

Australian Bureau of Statistics. 2008. *Australian social trends: population distribution.* http://www.abs.gov.au/AUSSTATS/abs@.nsf/Lookup/4102.0Chapter3002008 [accessed 12 June 2013].

Australian Government, Department of Climate Change. 2009. *Climate change risks to Australia's coasts: a first pass national assessment.*

Australian Government, Department of Climate Change and Energy Efficiency. 2010. *Developing a National Coastal Adaptation Agenda: A report on the national climate change forum.* Canberra.

Australian Capital Territory (ACT). 2007a. *Weathering the change: ACT climate change strategy 2007–2025.*

—2007b. *Climate change action plan 1 2007–2011.*

—2008. Planning for rushfire risk mitigation general code.

Bajracharya, B., I. Childes and P. Hastings. 2011. Climate change adaptation through land use planning and disaster management: Local government perspectives from Queensland. 17th Pacific Rim Real Estate Society Conference, Climate change and property: its impact now and later, 16–19 January, Gold Coast, Australia.

Braganza, K., K. Hennessy, L. Alexander and B. Trewin. 2013. Changes in extreme weather. In P. Christoff (ed.), *Four Degrees of Climate Change: Australia in a Hot World.* Earthscan: London, ch. 3.

City of Melbourne. 2009. Climate change adaptation strategy.

City of South Perth. 2010. Climate change strategy 2010–2015.

COAG (Council of Australian Governments). 2002. *Natural disasters in Australia: reforming mitigation, relief and recovery arrangements.* Canberra.

—2004. *Report of the national inquiry on bushfire mitigation and management.* Canberra.

CSIRO and BoM. 2007. Climate change in Australia. CSIRO and Australian Bureau of Meteorology, 147 pp. www.climatechangeinaustralia.gov.au [accessed 12 June 2013].

EEA (European Environment Agency). 2012. *Urban adaptation to climate change in Europe.* Copenhagen.

Feiden, P. 2011. *Adapting to climate change: cities and the urban poor. International Housing Coalition*: Washington, DC, 27 pp.

Greater London Authority. 2011. *Managing risks and increasing resilience.* London.

Hallegatte, S. 2009. Strategies to adapt to an uncertain climate change. *Global Environmental Change Human and Policy Dimensions* 19: 240–47.

Hanson, S. et al. 2007. *A Global Ranking of Port Cities with High Exposure to Climate Extremes.* Paris: OECD.

Harvey, N. and C. Woodroffe. 2008. Australian approaches to coastal vulnerability assessment. *Sustainability Science* 3: 67–87.

Hennessy, K., C. Lucas, N. Nicholls, J. Bathols, R. Suppiah and J. Ricketts. 2005. *Climate change impacts on fire-weather in south-east Australia.* CSIRO Marine and Atmospheric Research, Aspendale, 34 pp.

Hennessy, K., B. Fitzharris, B. C. Bates, N. Harvey, S. M. Howden et al. 2007. Australia and New Zealand. In M. L. Parry, O. F. Canziani, J. P. Palutikof, P. J. van der Linden and C. E. Hanson (eds), *Climate Change 2007: Impacts, Adaptation and Vulnerability Contribution of Working Group II to the Fourth Assessment Report of the Intergovernmental Panel on Climate Change.* Cambridge University Press: Cambridge, pp. 507–40.

IPCC. 2007. *Climate Change 2007: The Physical Science Basis. Contribution of Working Group I to the Fourth Assessment Report of the Intergovernmental Panel on Climate Change Summary for Policymakers.* Cambridge University Press: Cambridge.

Leitch, A. and Robinson, C. 2012. *Shifting Sands: Uncertainty and a local community response to sea levels and policy in Australia.* In Measham, T. and Lockie, S. (eds) *Risk and Social Theory in Environmental Management.* CSIRO Publishing, Collingwood, VIC, Australia, pp. 117–31.

Lockyer Valley Regional Council. 2011a. *Locker Valley Community Recovery Plan.* http://www.lockyervalley.qld.gov.au/images/PDF/community%20recovery%20plan.pdf [accessed 12 June 2013].

—2011b. *Grantham Relocation Policy.* http://www.lockyervalley.qld.gov.au/images/PDF/grantham_relocation_policy_master_final_with%20map.pdf [accessed 12 June 2013].

Macintosh, A. 2012. Coastal climate hazards and urban planning: how planning responses can lead to maladaptation. *Mitigation & Adaptation Strategies for Global Change.* doi 10.1007/s11027-012-9406-2.

McDonald, J. 2007. A risky climate for decision-making: the liability of development authorities for climate change impacts. *Environmental and Planning Law Journal* 24: 405–17.

—2010. Paying the price of adaptation: compensation for climate change impacts. In T. Bonyhady, A. Macintosh and J. McDonald (eds), *Adapting to Climate Change in Australia: Law and Policy.* Federation Press: Annandale, NSW.

Measham, T., B. Preston, T. Smith, C. Brooke, R. Gorddard, G. Withycombe and C. Morrison. 2011. Adapting to climate change through local municipal planning: barriers and challenges. *Mitigation and Adaptation Strategies for Global Change* 16 (8): 889–909.

New York City Panel on Climate Change. 2010. *Climate change adaptation in New York city: building a risk management response.* New York Academy of Sciences, New York.

Norman, B. 2009. Principles for an intergovernmental agreement for coastal planning and climate change in Australia. *Habitat International* 33: 293–9.

Parliament of Australia, House of Representatives Standing Committee on Climate Change, Water, Environment, and the Arts. 2009. *Managing our coastal zone in a changing climate.* Canberra.

Preston, B., R. Westaway and E. Yuen. 2010. Climate adaptation planning in practice: an evaluation of adaptation plans from three developed nations. *Mitigation and Adaptation Strategies for Global Change.* doi 10.1007/s11027-010-9270-x.

Property Council of Australia. 2011. Queensland coastal plan eroding investor confidence, says property council. *International Business Times,* 7 April. http://au.ibtimes.com/articles/131589/20110407/queensland-coastal-plan-eroding-investor-confidence-says-property-council.htm [accessed 12 June 2013].

Rafter, T. and D. Abbs. 2009. An analysis of future changes in extreme rainfall over Australian regions based on GCM simulations and Extreme Value Analysis. http://www.cawcr.gov.au/publications/researchletters/CA WCR_Research_Letters_3.pdf [accessed 12 June 2013].

Stafford Smith, D. M., L. Horrocks, A. Harvey and C. Hamilton. 2011. Rethinking adaptation for a four degree world. *Philosophical Transactions of the Royal Society* A 369: 196–216.

State of New South Wales. 1979. *Environmental Planning and Assessment Act.*

—2006. *Planning for bushfire protection guidelines.*

—2009. *Policy statement on sea level rise.*

—2010a. *NSW coastal planning guideline: adapting to sea level rise 2010.*

—2010b. Department of Planning factsheet: Facilitating councils' assessing low risk and low impact development applications on bush fire prone land. s. 79BA of the Environmental Planning and Assessment Act 1979 (2010).

—2010c. Department of Planning and Infrastructure: *Metropolitan plan for Sydney 2036* (2010).

—2012. Department of Environment and Heritage, Repeal of sea level rise planning guidelines. http://www.environment.nsw.gov.au/climatechange/sealevel.htm [accessed 12 June 2013].

State of Queensland. 2009. *Sustainable Planning Act.*

—2011. *Queensland Coastal Plan.*

—2004. *Queensland Heatwave Response Plan.*

State of South Australia. 1992. Coastline: coastal erosion, flooding and sea level rise standards and protection policy, no. 26. January.

—Undated. State emergency service extreme heat plan.

—2009. Minister's code: undertaking development in bushfire protection areas.

—2010. Prospering in a changing climate: a draft climate change adaptation framework for South Australia.

State of Tasmania. 2005. *Tasmania Fire Service: guidelines for development in bushfire prone areas of Tasmania.*

—2011. Draft planning directive: bushfire prone areas code, 2011.

State of Victoria. 1987. *Planning and Environment Act.*

—2008. Ministerial direction no. 13 and general practice note 2008: managing coastal hazards and the coastal impacts of climate change. Coastal advisory note: how to consider sea level rise along the Victorian Coast. Department of Sustainability and Environment.

—2008. State planning policy framework, cl 15. 08 (managing coastal hazards and the coastal impacts of climate change) (incorporating the Victorian Coastal strategy).

—2009. Victorian DHS. January 2009 heatwave in Victoria: an assessment of health impacts. Victorian Department of Health Services. http://www.health.vic.gov.au/chiefhealthofficer/downloads/heat_impact_rpt.pdf [accessed 12 June 2013].

—2011. Heatwave plan for Victoria: protecting health and reducing harm from heatwaves.

State of Western Australia. 2010. State coastal planning Policy no. 2. 6 (as amended 2010).

—2010. WA planning for bushfire protection (ed.2). 2010 interim guidelines.

—2006. SPP 3. 4: Natural hazards and disasters, cl5.

Tollefson, J. 2012. Hurricane sweeps US into climate-adaptation debate. *Nature* 491: 167–8.

Toronto Environment Office. 2008. *Ahead of the storm: preparing Toronto for climate change.* Toronto City Council.

Victorian Bushfires Royal Commission. 2010. *Final report.*

Victorian Civil and Administrative Tribunal. 2010. Gippsland Coastal Board v South Gippsland Shire Council (No. 2) [2008] VCAT 1545.

—2010. East Gippsland Shire Council v Taip [2010] VCAT 1222. 28 July.

Wang, X., M. Stafford Smith, R. McAllister, A. Leitch, S. McFallan et al. 2010. *Coastal inundation under climate change: a case study in South East Queensland.* CSIRO Climate Adaptation Flagship Working Paper No. 6. CSIRO, Brisbane. http://www.csiro.au/resources/CAF-working-papers.html [accessed 12 June 2013].

Wang, X. and R. McAllister. 2011. Adapting to heatwaves and coastal flooding. In H. Cleugh, M. Stafford Smith, M. Battaglia and P. Graham (eds), *Climate Change: Science and Solutions for Australia.* CSIRO Publishing: Allandale.

Whetton, P. L., D. Karoly, I. Watterson, L Webb, F. Drost, D. Kirono and K. McInnes. 2013. Australia's climate in a Four Degree World. In P. Christoff (ed.), *Four Degrees of Climate Change: Australia in a Hot World.* Earthscan: London, ch. 2.

White, A. 2011. Black Saturday: planning for bushfires. QELA Annual Conference, Gold Coast, Australia, 25–27 May.

WHO (World Health Organization). 2009. *Improving public health responses to extreme weather/heat-waves-EuroHEAT: technical summary.* Copenhagen: WHO Regional Office for Europe.

World Bank. 2010. *Climate risk and adaptation in asian mega-cities: a synthesis report.*

—2011. *Guide to climate change adaptation in cities.*

11 No island is an island

Security in a Four Degree World

Peter Christoff and Robyn Eckersley

Introduction

As early as 1977, Lester Brown from the Worldwatch Institute wrote that 'threats to security may now arise less from the relationship of nation to nation and more from the relationship of [humanity] to nature' (Brown, 1977: 6). Today, climate change is widely acknowledged to pose the biggest environmental security threat of all, but there remains considerable debate and confusion over how best to characterize and respond to this threat. To the popular imagination, climate change evokes the threats and challenges posed by the transboundary movement of so-called 'climate refugees'. To traditional security analysts, climate change is typically characterized as a 'threat multiplier' to national security. Yet climate change also poses a fundamental challenge to the idea of territorial defence and invites a re-examination of the basic purpose of security, the meaning of national interest, conventional responses to insecurities and the conditions for long-term security.

This chapter briefly reviews projected climate change impacts in Australia's region and shows that projected changes caused by global average warming of 4°C or even less pose very serious threats. It then reviews efforts to address climate change from a national security standpoint and highlights some of the contradictions that arise from constructing climate change simply as an external threat to the nation-state. We show how national security can be reconceptualized and integrated into a broader, nested framework of human security in ways that avoid these contradictions. This framework also directs attention to the key dimensions of Australia's existing domestic policies (such as its growing investment in, and dependency on, resource industries and its growing trade in fossil fuels) that undermine both homeland/national security and human security in the region in the medium and long term. We conclude by pointing to some of the core domestic and foreign policy responses that flow from this nested framework, which would safeguard both Australia and the region from the risks of climate change.

Regional predictions of impacts of a Four Degree World

Recent estimates and projections for the impacts of global warming in the Asia Pacific region, including in reports by the IPCC, the Asian Development Bank (ADB) and individual country agencies, contain a common narrative. The region is highly vulnerable to climate change, with many 'climate hotspots', and many countries and communities already struggling to deal with the phenomena of 'natural disasters' caused by climatic variability, such as cyclones, droughts and extreme rainfall. The ADB report on climate and migration observes that Asia and the Pacific is one of the world's most natural disaster-prone regions. Eight of the fifteen countries at highest risk of experiencing three or more natural hazards annually are in Asia and the Pacific, while half of the top sixty at risk of experiencing two or more hazards are in the region. There is a strong correlation between areas most at risk from natural hazards and areas at greatest risk of being impacted by climate change (ADB, 2012).

Even well before we get to a Four Degree World, and certainly once we are there, the following impacts are expected within the Asia Pacific region:

- progressive inundation of low-lying states and deltaic regions caused by sea-level rise and storm surges, causing the decline or abandonment of coastal settlements and the displacement of coastal populations;
- an increase in the intensity and frequency of extreme events: storms, floods, droughts and forest fires;
- growing water shortages caused by the decline of glacial melt from the Himalayas, and changing rainfall patterns;
- a decrease in food security and the rise (or return) of regions of food shortages and mass starvation as crops fail and marine fisheries collapse;
- an increase in disease and associated mortality;
- an increase in economic hardship and growing problems for the stability of poorer states within the region;
- significant impacts on the already stressed ecosystems and biodiversity of the region, including elevated rates of extinction over the coming century in regional ecosystems.

These are, as Steffen and Griggs note in Chapter 7, compounding problems. The higher the increase in global and regional temperature, the greater the vulnerability of regional states and communities to these impacts, and the more likely that already low levels of capacity to deal with them will be overrun by circumstances and events. The situation will be particularly acute in China, South Asia, South-East Asia, Indonesia and, especially, the Pacific. For example, coastal flooding poses the greatest climate change-related induced risk in Asia, with around one-third of its population living in areas considered to be at risk. These populations are concentrated in large cities in low-lying coastal areas in Bangladesh, China, India, Indonesia, the Philippines and Vietnam (Brecht et al., 2012). The Mekong Delta will be particularly affected, as will coastal communities in Bangladesh and India, which will suffer from inundation and increasing frequency of storm-related intrusions.

Indonesia, with a population of 240 million and including territory spread across 17,000 islands, is especially vulnerable. Some 1.1 per cent of Indonesia's population lives in the one-metre low elevation zone, and 6.4 per cent in the three-metre zone prone to coastal flooding in a Four Degree World. This would imply the potential displacement of up to 15 million people in the latter instance. Malley (2011) suggests that rising sea levels will also severely affect coastal cities, where sea-level rise and subsidence caused by depletion of groundwater tables would combine to increase the vulnerability of the densely populated north coast of Java. Changes in marine conditions would pose a significant threat to coastal fisheries, a major source of food in Indonesia.

If temperatures rise rapidly, Indonesia will experience a decline in production of its staple food crop – rice. Java produces half of Indonesia's rice crop. It is likely to suffer longer, drier seasons, reducing the capacity for multiple harvests each year. These factors, among others, are likely to exacerbate already entrenched socio-economic divisions, increase pressure on government for ameliorative and adaptation support, and potentially lead to internal political destabilization. Malley (2011) suggests three responses are possible: persistence despite calamity; internal immigration – continuing and exacerbating a pattern that has been evident in Indonesia for many decades; and emigration to neighbouring countries (under peaceful circumstances, he assumes). He also suggests that state failure is unlikely 'in the next twenty years'.

The survival of certain Pacific countries is at extreme risk from sea-level rise. More than 50 per cent of the region's population lives within 1.5 km of the shoreline. Many islands are less than a few meters above sea level. Thus, an increase of as little as half a metre, along with increased storm surges, would completely inundate many critical areas and threaten their populations (IPCC, 2007). Global warming of 4°C could entail a sea-level rise of up to 1 metre by 2100 and much more over time. Even if warming were limited to 2°C, global average sea levels would continue to rise by up to 1.5 to 4 metres by 2300 (Schellnhuber et al., 2012: xv).

The risks and impacts of sea-level rise differ regionally and between low (e.g. atoll) and high (e.g. volcanic) islands. Low islands are much more vulnerable to saltwater contamination of both groundwater and soils. Seawater intrusion into underground water aquifers is already experienced by many coastal communities. Both low and high islands are equally vulnerable to sea-level rise, due to the concentration of human activity in coastal areas and the difficulty in relocating to the interior of high islands (Barnett and Campbell, 2010). These represent acute security threats to low-lying atoll Pacific nations. As the Vice-President of the Republic of Palau, Elias Camsek Chin, declared in his address to the UN General Assembly in 2008: 'Never before in all history has the disappearance of whole nations been such a real possibility … This is a security matter which has gone unaddressed.'

Implications: national versus human security?

Assessments of the security implications arising from both existing and projected impacts of climate change vary widely, depending on whether they are analyzed from the standpoint of national security, human security or ecological security.

National security analysts typically focus on external threats to the state's territorial integrity and strategic interests. From this conventional perspective, climate change is a 'threat multiplier'. Its direct and indirect impacts include the instability and possible violent conflict that may flow from the increasing incidence of extreme weather events, increasing resource scarcity (such as water, arable land and energy resources), the mass movement of so-called 'climate refugees', the spread of infectious diseases, instability arising from food shortages and rising food prices, damage to critical infrastructure, disputes arising from access to new shipping lanes, and sea level rise (which can also lead to loss of territory and disputes over maritime boundaries and access to offshore resources) (Busby, 2007; 2008; CNA, 2007; Paskal, 2007; Dupont, 2008a, b; Jasparro and Taylor, 2008; Briggs, 2012). Strategic analysts have also identified a range of direct and indirect 'threats' arising from climate change to the military itself, such as threats to the integrity of coastal bases and other assets through sea level rise and extreme weather (CNA, 2009).

In contrast, a human security perspective emphasizes the multiple and inter-secting ways in which climate change threatens the wellbeing of individuals and human communities, including physical and mental health, economic livelihood, community resilience and identity and belonging (UNDP, 1994; CHS, 2003; Matthews et al., 2010; Altman et al., 2012). Although there are broad and narrow approaches to understanding human security (the former emphasizing freedom from fear and freedom from want, as well as acute and chronic threats to human wellbeing; the latter focusing on acute threatens to physical and psychological safety), both take a people rather than state-centred perspective and focus on a wider variety of threats – traditional and non-traditional, external and internal (Owen, 2004).

Finally, environmental security extends this frame further by including ecosystem integrity and biodiversity protection as core security referents, not simply for their fundamental role in underpinning and safeguarding human security but also because nonhuman species are morally entitled to protection in their own right (Dalby, 2009).

Security is a primordial and deeply politicized concept (Booth; 2005: 23; McDonald, 2012a). It is something that everyone accepts as vital, but there is much dispute over the fundamental security referent, the response to insecurity and the conditions for producing lasting security. Traditional security analysts have resisted efforts to broaden the security referent, even though they increas-ingly acknowledge a growing range of 'non-traditional' sources of insecurity, including climate change. In contrast, as Ole Weaver points out, '[t]he discourse on "alternative security" makes meaningful statements not by drawing primarily on the register of everyday security but through its contrast with national security' (Weaver 1995: 49). These alternative and more critical discourses effectively seek to rework elements of the classical concept – threat, sovereignty – and show how they can take on new forms under new conditions, while maintaining the codes of urgency (1999: 51). They also question existing political priorities and trade-offs in asking, for example, why governments have adopted a highly risk-averse and precautionary posture towards some risks (e.g. terrorism) but not others (e.g. climate change), even though the consequences may be more catastrophic and more likely in the absence of anticipatory measures (Eckersley, 2009).

Our approach is to show how a human security framework can highlight the ways in which efforts to enhance national security in conventional terms can sometimes undermine human wellbeing and ecosystem integrity while also undermining national security in the longer term (Floyd, 2008; 2010; Dalby, 2009). We will show that Australia's 2009 Defence White Paper and its 2013 National Security Strategy are both vulnerable to this criticism, despite their brief inclusion of climate change in the list of new security 'threats'.

However, it does not necessarily follow that national security and human security must be understood as opposing and mutually exclusive ways of conceiving security, despite their different security referents. National security may be reframed in ways that also promote human and environmental security in both Australia and the region. This requires moving beyond a narrow, defence-focused national security frame that constructs climate change impacts as if they were external threats arising from outside the nation. This not only obscures the fundamental drivers of climate change but also leads to the misallocation of responsibility and to actions (or inactions) that may make matters worse. We know that the multiple risks of climate change, unlike military threats, are not deliberately intended (even if they are increasingly foreseeable), that they are the by-products of activities carried out by both 'us' and 'them' (but in our region mainly 'us'), and that their resolution usually carries common benefits (e.g. Deudney, 1990). In order to highlight the different policy implications that flow from a national *versus* human security frame, compared to a nested national *and* human security frame, we single out for special attention the two iconic issues in the debate about climate change and security: climate change-induced migration and climate change and conflict.

Climate change-induced migration

There are no reliable global or regional estimates of the number of people that might be forced to relocate due to climate change by the end of this century. According to the International Migration Organization, estimates of large-scale people displacement from climate change (both internally and internationally) range from 200 million to 1 billion by mid-twenty-first century (IOM, 2009: 43). In a Four Degree World, we can expect to see the biggest movement of people in human history. A significant portion of this movement will occur in Australia's region, given the vulnerability described above.

The bulk of forced migration due to climate change is expected to involve poor people who are most vulnerable to climate change impacts, and most resettlement is also expected to occur within poor countries. (Although these migrants often described as climate refugees, they are not strictly refugees within the meaning of the Geneva Convention since they are not seeking to escape direct or deliberate persecution.[1] 'Climate-related displaced persons' is therefore a more accurate descriptor.)

Landlessness, homelessness, socio-economic marginalization, food and health insecurity, and loss of belonging are some of the most important effects of displacement due to climatic changes. Climate-induced migration will increase pressure on infrastructure and services; enhance the risk of conflict; and lead to deterioration of social, health, and educational indicators for those who are forced to move. Forced migration in Australia's region will also impose an important potential brake on the region's recent rapid economic growth, with significant consequences for patterns of trade and general prosperity. Climate-induced migration is most likely to have destabilizing effects when it involves significant numbers and when the recipient country has limited or no capacity to accommodate displaced persons.

Against this background, it is a national self-deception to frame climate-induced migration as an external 'threat' to national security, as has been the habit in Australia with certain other border movements over the past decade. Such a response signals a return to paranoid nationalism, which views our island continent as a fortress to be defended through border patrols and fails to draw connections between Australia's fossil-fuelled affluence and the reasons why many in our neighbourhood may be uprooted.

Most people do not wish to move from their homes, neighbourhood and country – it is a choice forced upon them by circumstances over which they have no or very little control. Recent experience in the Asia Pacific region with communities devastated by extreme events (such as super typhoon Bopha, which struck the Philippines in early December 2012 and killed over 1,000 people) has indicated that severely impacted communities are – partly because of the nature of the impact inflicted upon them – unlikely to have the resources to migrate. From a national *and* human security frame, the best response to the growing prospect of climate-induced displacement and migration is not simply to provide emergency relief but also to assist vulnerable populations to adapt to climate change while simultaneously giving priority to mitigation, which will reduce the likelihood of migration and ensure that climate impacts remain within a range that can be managed by vulnerable communities.

However, since significant climate change-induced migration is still expected to occur in the region even at 2°C global average warming, then Australia, as a rich, developed country, should play a key role in developing an international and regional response to ensure a fair and orderly resettlement. This could possibly take the form of initiating and framing discussions about stand-alone agreements such as a regional agreement on climate-displaced peoples, and an

International Convention on Climate-Displaced Peoples (see also Biermann and Boas, 2008; Hodgkinson et al., 2010; McAdam, 2012).

Climate change and violent conflict

A narrow, defence-based understanding of national security tends to overplay the links between climate change and violent conflict (e.g. Kaplan, 1992; for a critique, see Adger and Barnett, 2007; Hartmann, 2009). To date, only a very weak direct causal connection between climate change and violence has been empirically demonstrated. Indeed, there is a general consensus that environmental problems are usually only one of many complex factors implicated in violent conflict; that conflicts are more likely to be intra-state rather than inter-state; and that state and society problem-solving capacity are central to explaining whether violent conflict will arise (Kaplan, 1992; Myers, 1993; Levy, 1995; can, 2007; Busby 2007; 2008; WGBU, 2007: 30, 39–40). Climate change is therefore best understood as exacerbating pre-existing conflicts but there is very little evidence to show that it is a unique cause of conflict.

Nonetheless, the increasing incidence of extreme climate change events that bring sudden shocks to livelihoods in already poor societies is likely to contribute to instability, violence and sometimes even revolution. For example, 'post-disaster instability' may lead to a growth in recruitment to armed gangs and militias while further reducing the capacity of already frail states to manage law and order (Barnett, 2009). It is also more likely in the context of significant poverty and inequality, slow economic growth or economic collapse and poor governance (Nel and Righarts, 2008). While at present, as Boston, Nel and Righarts (2009: 7) put it, there is no credible evidence [linking] global warming to conflicts over territorial integrity and national control over economic resources, there can be no doubt that this situation will change if sea levels rise considerably and as droughts lead to escalating food prices and mass starvation, as is expected under the 4°C (or less) scenario. For example, the 2010 Russian heatwave led to a dramatic drop in the export of grain from Russia to North Africa and the Middle East, and the ensuring spike in grain and bread prices has been identified as a contributing factor to the Arab Spring revolts in that region (Johnstone and Mazo, 2011).

The first best response from Australia to the increasing risk of instability and conflict in the region is the pursuit of a strong national mitigation target that is consistent with scientific recommendations, complemented by additional climate finance and development assistance for decarbonization and adaptation in the region, and pursuit of an international and regional co-operation as mentioned above. Greater investment in military preparedness for climate-related disaster assistance is also essential.

Australia's response

Official conceptualizations of national security, and of 'the national interest', by successive governments in Australia have struggled to comprehend and accommodate many of the complex interdependencies that now characterize our globalized world, of which climate change is Exhibit Number One.

Former Labor Prime Minister Kevin Rudd had sought to break with this tradition by framing climate change as a major security threat, but this appeared to gain very little traction (Rudd, 2008; 2009; McDonald, 2012b). The Rudd government's 2009 Australian Defence White Paper contained only a very brief discussion of climate change, singling out potential resource conflicts and mass migration flows (Department of Defence, 2009: 30–1). However, the White Paper concluded that 'large-scale strategic consequences of climate change are … not likely to be felt before 2030', which is the time horizon of the Paper (Department of Defence, 2009: 31). This may be contrasted with the UK Ministry of Defence's Strategic Defence Review, which placed the rise of the Asia Pacific region and climate change at the top of its list of 'the five major trends that will impact on the international context for defence in the coming decades' (UK Ministry of Defence, 2010: 13).

The Defence White Paper also maintained a very traditional understanding of Australia's national security as focused on

> ensuring Australia's freedom from attack or the threat of attack, maintaining our territorial integrity and promoting our political sovereignty, preserving our hard-won freedoms, and sustaining our fundamental capacity to advance economic prosperity for all Australians.
>
> (Department of Defence, 2009: 20)

In contrast, the Gillard Labor government more recently offered a much broader framework of 'sustainable security' to guide Australia's engagement with Asian region in its Australia in the Asian Century White Paper (Australian Government, 2012a). This more comprehensive framework encompassed national security as well as the collective economic and political security, food and energy security in the region, the human security of individuals in the region 'and the security of the natural system as the globe enters a period of rising temperatures and new environmental challenges' (Australian Government, 2012a: 224). The White Paper also gave considerable prominence to the Asian region's growing contribution to global greenhouse gas emissions and its growing vulnerability to climate change (69). In particular, it noted that 'In 2009, fossil fuels accounted for about 82 per cent of Asia's energy mix, with coal alone accounting for around 47 per cent' and that 'without a shift to low-carbon development, growth in emissions is projected to rise significantly' (69).

What the *Australia in the Asian Century* White Paper did not mention is that Australia is one of the world's largest exporters of fossil fuels, predominantly to Asian markets. Indeed, the Gillard government's Energy White Paper 2012, released in the very same month as the *Australia in the Asian Century* White Paper, envisaged Australia playing a continuing role as a major fossil fuel supplier to Asia and other 'growth markets', with continuing strong growth in coal and gas production (including onshore and offshore LNG projects and coal seam gas) (Australian Government, 2012b).

There is little point in offering a comprehensive framework of 'sustainable security' for the region if some of the core elements in the framework – such as Australia's economic, energy and trade policies – are pursued in ways that ignore or directly undermine other elements, such as food security, human security and the security of natural systems in Australia and the region. The primary virtue of adopting a broader security framework is to make connections between different security referents (individuals, states, regions, natural systems), to identify conflicts and synergies between different policy responses in support of each referent and to develop and pursue an integrated response that maximizes those synergies.

The failure to make these critical connections is perpetuated in the Gillard government's national security strategy – *Strong and Secure: A Strategy for Australia's National Security* – released shortly after the *Australia in the Asian Century* White Paper in January 2013 (Australian Government, 2013). The strategy draws a sharp distinction between human and national security, and returns to a narrow conceptualisation of national security as 'primarily concerned with the protection of Australia's sovereignty, population and assets, and shaping a favourable international environment' (Australian Government, 2013: 230).

The new strategy gives special prominence to cyber-security, terrorism, trans-national crime and corruption, and border security but relegates climate change in a shopping list of broader global challenges with national security implications (31). Yet it offers no specific details on how this particular 'broader challenge' might be addressed other than 'Partnering with developing States in our region to manage the implications of climate change'; 'Working with countries experiencing or emerging from natural disasters or conflict' (34); and 'Working with likeminded regional middle powers to manage proactively the strategic implications of shared global challenges, including climate change, and food and energy security' (39).

Even from a traditional national security perspective, both the Rudd government's 2009 White Paper and the Gillard government's national security strategy miss the mark by providing no assessment of the risks of climate change to the Australian Defence Forces' (ADF) capabilities. Climate change will compromise the ability of the ADF to discharge its traditional role in safeguarding Australia given the expected rising cost of transport fuels and the increasing risk of damage to critical infrastructure and other assets, including coastal and inland bases from rising seas, storm surges and forest fires. For example, the major forest fires that accompanied Russia's heatwave in July 2010 caused severe damage to a naval logistics base at Kolomna outside Moscow, destroying headquarters, warehouses containing aeronautical equipment and vehicles, and reportedly torching 200 aircraft (Agence France-Presse, 2010).

Assessments of the risks of climate change to the military are now routine in the United States, where strategic analysts have identified threats to critical infrastructure and other assets (particularly overseas military bases), key transportation corridors and sources of raw materials. The US Center for Naval Analysis also concluded that the US's excessive national dependence on oil burdens the military, undermines combat effectiveness, and exacts a huge price tag – in dollars and lives' (CNA, 2009: vii). The 2010 US Quadrennial Defense Review not only recognizes climate change as a 'threat multiplier' but identifies energy efficiency as 'force multiplier' and the US Department of Defense (DoD) has emerged as an aggressive energy innovator and has embarked upon a program of retrofitting its military installations with energy saving and renewable technologies to ensure its own energy security by reducing exposure to disruption of supply and also reduce running costs (DoDUS, 2010: 87).

While the ADF plays a different role from the US military, they can and should take steps to reduce their own contribution to climate change while minimizing their exposure to its threats. This would include reducing the ADF's overall carbon bootprint and increasing energy security by reducing its dependence on fossil fuels (Australia, like the US, is a net importer of oil).

The ADF also has an important role to play in remedial adaptation, both domestically and in the near Asia Pacific region, providing emergency relief and humanitarian assistance in response to extreme weather events and other sudden and severe climate impacts, as it did following the 2004 Boxing Day tsunami.

However, there are also limits to what the ADF can do. While it may have the capability to defend the nation from invading armies and to provide emergency relief in times of disaster, it is not equipped to handle encroaching oceans, deserts or diseases, or prevent the loss of biodiversity, fisheries, agricultural productivity and human livelihoods of Australian citizens. If the impacts of climate change are to be minimized, then it is necessary to look beyond defence policy and the role of the military to other policy domains.

National security in the service of human security

There are good reasons for the development of a 'whole-of-government' national security strategy in response to climate change (Camilleri, 2012). Neither the Australian Department of Defence nor any other single government department or agency (whether federal, State or local) is able to manage the complex security challenges raised by climate change, many of which offer a fundamental challenge to the idea of territorial defence. However, a 'whole-of-government' approach to national security is nonetheless needed, which transcends the idea of territorial defence from external attack, along with the Cold War mentality of 'us-versus-them', and recognizes the complex interdependencies that now characterize our globalized world.

We therefore offer the following reformulated definition:

> National security involves a set of conditions that enables a state to safeguard the physical and mental wellbeing and livelihoods of its citizens, and the integrity of its territory, including life support systems and ecosystems, from both direct and indirect threats and risks.

Unlike the 2009 Australian Defence White Paper and 2012 National Security Strategy, our definition does not assume that all threats and risks are necessarily 'external' to, or generated outside, the nation state.[2] It would therefore acknowledge Australia's complicity in the production of the risks associated with climate change that now threaten homeland security. Yet the formulation is still broad enough to encompass traditional security threats, such as armed attack and WMD proliferation, as well as more recent threats, such as terrorism. Putting the safety and wellbeing of Australian citizens, and the ecosystems upon which they depend, front and centre in a national security strategy should be the first duty of any state. Given the ample scientific evidence to indicate that, without urgent mitigation, climate change is very likely to compromise this safety and wellbeing catastrophically, then it follows that an aggressive emissions mitigation policy must be seen as a central component of Australia's national security response. The risks of 'weather of mass destruction' should be taken no less seriously than those posed by 'weapons of mass destruction'.

Second, focusing on the conditions that enable a state to safeguard the wellbeing of its citizens means that Australia must integrate and harmonize its domestic and foreign policy. Like Australia's now-abandoned 'Forward Defence Policy', one can consider national security, more broadly defined, to depend on regional stability across social, economic and ecological dimensions.

Third, such a formulation is also compatible with the human security framework endorsed by the United Nations, which includes both freedom from fear, freedom from want, and freedom to live in dignity (UNGA, 2010: 2). That is, if the broad formulation of national security suggested here is pursued with full sensitivity to the complex interdependencies between nation-states and communities in a globalized world, and with full acceptance of Australia's international obligations as a developed nation to take the lead in mitigating climate change, then Australia's national security strategy would also be compatible with human security in the broader region and beyond.

There would be strong public support for broadening Australia's national security framework to encompass human security. A recent study by Juliet Pietsch and Ian McAllister found 'that, in line with the United Nations' new security paradigm, the Australian public sees four clear aspects to its security – health, the environment, the economy and defence. Moreover, lifestyle issues concerning health and environmental security are more significant concerns than the traditional ones of defence and the economy. The human security paradigm is clearly understood by the public and has real and significant political and electoral consequences' (2010: 240).

Conclusion

The American political scientist Chalmers Johnston called 9/11 and the continuing War on Terror 'blowback', caused by United States' imperial foreign and defence policies from the 1950s to the start of this century. If we do realize a Four Degree World, with all its multiple insecurities, we will have cause to call the results for Australia 'climate' blowback or 'carbon' blowback, caused in part by our sooty amalgam of domestic economic, foreign, defence and trade policies.

By contrast, we need a new 'forward defence policy' that regards the frontline for countering threats – including those generated by climate change – to human and environmental security in Australia as existing in the near Asia Pacific region, where mitigation and reducing climate vulnerability should be a priority for Australian development and aid programmes. This 'forward defence policy' must be coupled with a 'homeland climate security policy' aimed at ending our reliance on fossil fuels for local energy, and on the export of fossil fuels as an economic staple.

Climate change is a clearly complex security challenge that requires breaking out of the constraining silo of defence-thinking and developing a whole-of-government response that integrates national security strategy with other domestic and foreign policies, and with human security in the region. Some of the key policy responses that would flow would include:

- rapid decarbonization of Australia's domestic economy, both in terms of its reliance on fossil fuels for local energy, and on the export of fossil fuels as an economic staple, and a comprehensive adaptation policy;
- an innovative ADF that seeks to reduce its carbon bootprint and enhance its preparedness for an increasing humanitarian assistance role in the region;
- a regional human security strategy that focuses on reducing vulnerability to the impacts of climate change using development and aid programs to increase adaptive resilience in the near Asia Pacific.

Of all the direct and indirect threats and risks facing people and states, it is climate change that most graphically demonstrates how much Australia's fate is ultimately linked to the fate of its neighbours. In this sense, it is clear that 'no island is an island' – not even one as big as ours.

Notes

1 See Article 1, The 1951 United Nations Convention relating to the Status of Refugees.
2 Michael Evans attempts a similar exercise but falls into the trap of assuming that only externally generated risks are relevant: According to Evans, 'National security entails the pursuit of psychological and physical safety, which is largely the responsibility of national governments, to prevent both direct and indirect threats and risks primarily from abroad from endangering the survival of these regimes, their citizenry, or their ways of life' (Evans, 2007: 123).

References

ADB (Asia Development Bank). 2012. *Addressing Climate Change and Migration in Asia and the Pacific: Final Report*. http://www.adb.org/sites/default/files/pub/2012/addressing-climate-change-migration.pdf [accessed 20 July 2013].

Adger, W. N. and J. Barnett. 2007. Climate change, human security and violent conflict. *Political Geography* 26: 639–55.

Agence France-Presse. 2010. Forest fires destroy Moscow military base. *Defence News* 3 August 2010. http://www.defensenews.com/article/20100803/DEFSECT02/8030306/Forest-Fires-Destroy-Moscow-Military-Base [accessed 20 July 2013].

Altman, D. J. Camilleri, R. Eckersley and G. Hoffstaedter (eds). 2012. *Why Human Security Matters: Rethinking Australian Foreign Policy*. Allen & Unwin: Sydney.

Australian Government. 2012a. Australia in the Asian Century White Paper. Department of the Prime Minister and Cabinet, Canberra, October.

—2012b. Energy White Paper 2012: Australia's Energy Transformation. Department of Energy, Resources and Tourism, Canberra, October.

—2013. Strong and Secure: A Strategy for Australia's National Security. Department of Prime Minister and Cabinet, Canberra, January.

Barnett, J. 2009. 'Climate Change and Human Security in the Pacific Islands'. In J. Boston, P. Nel and M. Righarts (eds), *Climate Change and Security: Planning for the Future*. Wellington: Institute of Policy Studies, 59–70.

Barnett, J. and J. Campbell. 2010. *Climate Change and Small Island States*. Earthscan: London.

Biermann, F. and I. Boas. 2008. 'Protecting climate refugees: the case for a global protocol'. *Environment*: (November–December). http://www.environmentmagazine.org/Archives/Back%20Issues/November-December%202008/Biermann-Boas-full.html [accessed 20 July 2013].

Booth, K. 2005. Critical explorations. In K. Booth (ed.), *Critical Security Studies and World Politics*. Lynne Reinner: Boulder, CO: 1–25.

Boston, J. P. Nel and M. Righarts (eds). 2009. *Climate Change and Security: Planning for the Future*. Institute of Policy Studies: Wellington.

Brecht, H., S. Dasgupta, B. Laplante, S. Murray and D. Wheeler. 2012. Sea-level rise and storm surges: high stakes for a small number of developing countries. *The Journal of Environment and Development* 21 (1): 120–38.

Briggs, C. M. 2012. Climate security, risk assessment and military planning. *International Affairs* 88 (5): 1049–64.

Brown, L. 1977. Redefining national security. Worldwatch paper 14, Worldwatch Institute: Washington.

Busby, J. 2007. *Climate Change and National Security: An Agenda for Action*. Council of Foreign Relations Report. http://www.cfr.org/publication/14862 [accessed 20 July 2013].

—2008. Who cares about the weather? Climate change and US national security. *Security Studies* 17 (3): 468–504.

Camilleri, J. 2012. Human security and national security: the Australian context. In D. Altman, J. Camilleri, R. Eckersley and G. Hoffstaedter (eds), *Why Human Security Matters: Rethinking Australian Foreign Policy*. Allen & Unwin: Sydney.

CNA Corporation. 2007. *National Security and the Threat of Climate Change*. The CNA Corporation, Alexandria, VA. http://securityandclimate. cna. org [accessed 19 April].

—2009. *Powering America's Defence: Energy and the Risks to National Security*. The CNA Corporation, Alexandria, VA. http://www.cna.org/documents/PoweringAmericasDefense.pdf. [accessed 22 December 2009].

Commission on Human Security (CHS). 2003. *Human Security Now: Report of the Commission on Human Security*. UN: New York.

Dalby, S. 2009. *Security and Environmental Change*. Polity Press: Cambridge.

Department of Defence. 2009. *Defending Australia in the Asian Pacific Century: Defence White Paper 2009*. Canberra: Australian Government.

Department of Defense (DoD US). 2010. *Quadrennial Defence Review Report*. February.

Deudney, D. 1990. The case against linking environmental degradation and national security. *Millennium* 19 (3): 461–76.

Dupont, A. 2008a. 'Climate change and security: managing the risks', commissioned for the Garnaut Climate Change Review. http://www.garnautreview.org.au/CA25734E0016A131/WebObj/05Security/$File/05%20Security.pdf [accessed 20 July 2013].

—2008b. The strategic implications of climate change. *Survival* 50 (3): 29–54.

Dyer, G. 2008. *Climate Wars*. Random House: New York.

Eckersley, R. 2009. Environmental security, climate change and globalising terrorism. In D. Grenfeld and P. James (eds), *Rethinking Insecurity, War and Violence: Beyond Savage Globalization?* Routledge: London, pp. 85–97.

Evans, M. 2007. Towards an Australian national security strategy: a conceptual analysis. *Security Challenges* 3 (4): 113–30.

Floyd, R. 2008. The environmental security debate and its significance for climate change. *The International Spectator* 43 (3): 51–65.

—2010. *Security and the Environment*. Cambridge University Press: Cambridge.

Hartmann, B. 2009. Lines in the shifting sand: the strategic politics of climate change, human security and national defence. Paper presented at Rethinking Security in a Changing Climate Conference, Oslo, 22–24 June.

Hodgkinson, D., T. Burton, H. Anderson and L. Young. 2010. The hour when the ship comes in: a convention for persons displaced by climate change. *Monash University Law Review* 36: 69–120. http://www.ccdpconvention.com [accessed 20 July 2013].

International Dialogue on Migration. 2012. *Climate Change, Environmental Degradation and Migration*. International Organization for Migration: Geneva.

IOM (International Organization for Migration). 2009. *Migration, Environment and Climate Change: Assessing the Evidence*. International Organization for Migration: Geneva.

IPCC. 2007. Fourth Assessment Report: Climate Change. Working group II: Impacts, Adaptation.

Jasparro, C. and J. Taylor. 2008. Climate change and regional vulnerability to transnational security threats. *Geopolitics* 13 (2): 232–56.

Johnstone, S. and J. Mazo. 2011. Global warming and the Arab Spring. *Survival* 53 (2): 11–17.

Kaplan, R. D. 1992. The coming anarchy. *The Atlantic Monthly*, February: 44–76.

Laczko, F. and C. Aghazarm. 2009. *Migration, Environment and Climate Change: Assessing the Evidence*. Geneva, International Organization for Migration.

Levy, M. A. 1995. Is the environment a national security issue? *International Security* 20 (2): 35–62.

McAdam, J. (ed.). 2012. *Climate Change and Displacement: Multidisciplinary Perspectives*. Hart Publishing: Oxford.

McDonald, M. 2012a. *Security, the Environment and Emancipation*. Routledge: Abingdon.

—2012b. The failed securitisation of climate change in Australia. *Australian Journal of Political Science* 47 (4): 579–92.

Maas, A. and Tänzler, D. 2009. Regional security implications of climate change: a synopsis. Paper for DG External Relations of the European Commission under a contract for the German Ministry for the Environment, Nature Protection and Nuclear Safety. January. Adelphi Consult.

Malley, M. S. 2011. Indonesia. In D. Moran (ed.), *Climate Change and National Security: A Country-Level Analysis*. Georgetown University Press: Washington, DC.

Matthew, R. A., J. Barnett, B. McDonald and K. L. O'Brien (eds). 2010. *Global Environmental Change and Human Security*. MIT Press: Cambridge, MA.

Myers, N. 1993. *Ultimate Security: The Environmental Basis of Politics Stability*. Norton: New York.

Owen, T. 2004. 'Challenges and opportunities for defining and measuring human security. *Disarmament Forum* 3: 15–24.

Paskal, C. 2007. How climate change is pushing the boundaries of security and foreign policy. http://www.chathamhouse.org.uk/files/9250_bp0607climatecp.pdf [accessed 20 July 2013].

Pietsch, J. and I. McAllister. 2010. 'Human security in Australia: public interest and political consequences'. *Australian Journal of International Affairs* 64 (2): 225–44.

Preston, B., R. Suppiah, I. Macadam and J. Bathols. 2006. *Climate Change in the Asia/Pacific Region: A Consultancy Report Prepared for the Climate Change and Development Roundtable*. CSIRO, Collingwood.

Nel, P. and M. Righarts. 2008. Natural disasters and the risk of violent civil conflict. *International Studies Quarterly*. 52 (1) March: 159–85.

Rudd, K. 2008. First national security statement to the Australian Parliament. 4 December. http://www.royalcommission.vic.gov.au/getdoc/596cc5ff-8a33-47eb-8d4a-9205131ebdd0/TEN.004.002.0437.pdf4 [accessed 20 July 2013].

—2009. The PM's address to the Lowy Institute. *The Australian*. 6 November. http://www.theaustralian.com.au/news/nation/the-pms-address-to-the-lowy-institute/storye6frg6nf-12257951415194. [accessed 10 September 2012].

Schellnhuber, H. J., W. Hare, O. Serdeczny, S. Adams, D. Coumou, K. Frieler, M. Martin, I. M. Otto, M. Perrette, A. Robinson, M. Rocha, M. Schaeffer, J. Schewe, X. Wang and L. Warszawski. 2012. *Turn Down the Heat: Why a 4°C Warmer World Must Be Avoided*. A Report for the World Bank by the Postdam Institute for Climate Impact Research and Climate Analytics. November 2012.

UK Ministry of Defence. 2010. Adaptability and partnership: issues for the strategic defence review. Cm 7749, February.

UNDP (United Nations Development Programme). 1994. *Human Development Report 1994: New Dimensions of Human Security*. United Nations Development Program: New York.

UNDR (United Nations Development Report). 2007–2008. Fighting climate change: human solidarity in a divided world.

UNGA (United Nations General Assembly). 2009. Climate change and its possible security implications: report of the Secretary-General. 11 September 2009. A/64/350. http://www.unhcr.org/refworld/docid/4ad5e6380.html [accessed 20 July 2013].

—2010. Human security report of the Secretary-General. 8 March. A/64/701.

US Department of Defense. 2010. Quadrennial Defense Review 2010. DoD: Washington, DC.

Weaver, O. 1995. Securitization and Desecuritization. In R. D. Lipschutz (ed.) *On Security*. Columbia University Press: New York.

Werz, M. and L. Conley. 2012. *Climate Change, Migration and Conflict: Addressing Complex Crisis Scenarios in the 21st Century*. Center for American Progress and Heinrich Böll Foundation Stiftung: Washington, January.

WGBU (German Advisory Council on Global Change). 2007. *World in Transition: Climate Change as a Security Risk*. Earthscan: London. http://www.wbgu.de/wbgu_jg2007_engl.pdf [accessed 20 July 2013].

Part IV
Adaptation

12 Challenges and opportunities for climate change adaptation in Australia's region

Andrew Hewett[1]

Introduction

It is becoming increasingly clear that humanity is failing to rise to the challenge of addressing climate change. Our emissions are rising faster than expected and we are neglecting the people most vulnerable to the impacts of climate change, both in our region and around the world. The United Nations Environmental Program's Executive Director, Achim Steiner, recently reflected on these trends and stated:

> I think that the historians will one day write off the decade of 2010–2020 as one of the tragic moments of indecision ... of an international community and a world economy that was perfectly capable of moving to another level of carbon emissions trajectories but didn't choose to do so for what will then seem perhaps, completely extraneous reasons.
>
> (Steiner, 2011)

There is no doubt we are headed in the wrong direction. Climate change is already negatively impacting the lives and livelihoods of poor women and men around the globe. In our region, the human security of millions is being threatened. For example, Oxfam's partners across the Pacific are experiencing increasing salt-water intrusion due to rising sea levels as well as more frequent and intense storm events. This salt water is killing off food crops and poisoning fresh water wells. Climate change is eroding these communities' access to basic needs such as food and water. There has never been a more important time to assist developing countries in coping with the impacts of climate change and to reduce our emissions, which are driving this deadly trend. Despite this urgency, effective adaptation to climate change for the most vulnerable countries remains elusive.

Building upon the broad definition of human security offered by Christoff and Eckersley (2013, Chapter 11, this volume), I will explore the context of vulnerability to climate change in Australia's regional neighbourhood, especially South-East Asia and the island states of the South Pacific Ocean, paying particular attention to food security challenges. This chapter will then move to consider the tripartite political challenge Australia faces in relation to effective adaptation to climate change in developing countries. The challenge is, first, that current financial pledges to enable adaptation are too low to protect adequately the lives and livelihoods of people in developing countries. Second, the region currently lacks suitable frameworks and mechanisms to effectively deliver adaptation support. Third, global efforts to reduce greenhouse gas emissions are grossly inadequate. Without much stronger mitigation action, the adaptation challenge will be exacerbated beyond Australia's – and perhaps planetary – response capacities. Together these issues produce a perfect storm that urgently requires addressing.

Hand in hand with enhanced efforts to reduce climate change pressures, there is a need to focus on the adaptation challenge, especially, but not only, in developing countries. A sharp ethical challenge is raised, for the reality is that those people and communities who are most affected by climate change are those who have been least responsible for the crisis and who have the fewest resources to cope and adapt.

Climate change impacts in the near Asia-Pacific region

Many of Oxfam's partners – local community organizations – are on the front line of climate change. For them climate change is not a possible risk, it is an increasingly harsh reality. Climate change is affecting communities' livelihoods, their susceptibility to humanitarian disasters and, as disease patterns change, their health. Their stories reveal the human face of the issue. For example, Niu Loane, a local farmer on the island nation of Tuvalu, reports that it is harder to grow traditional taro and pulaka because the soils are becoming saltier. Rising sea levels and more frequent tidal inundations are poisoning the land and fresh water wells (Oxfam, 2010c). Reverend Tafue Lusama reports that local fish stocks are rapidly declining due to the coral reefs being bleached from warmer oceans. He says that now 'It is cheaper for a person to … buy a tin of fish … which is processed thousands of miles away … than buying fish from local fishermen' (Crikey, 2011). These stories are just the tip of the iceberg when it comes to human security and climate change.

Oxfam's 2011 report 'Growing a better future' (Oxfam, 2011) reported that the price of staple foods such as maize, already at an all-time high, will more than double in the next 20 years. While there are other important factors underlying these increases – such as the lack of investment in agricultural development in developing countries and the distortions of the global trading system – up to half of these increases will be due to climate change.

Climate change's impact on food production and hence on prices will manifest in a number of ways. First, it will apply a further brake on growth in crop yields. It has been estimated that rice yields may decline by 10 per cent for each 1°C rise in dry growing season minimum temperatures. Sub-Saharan countries could experience catastrophic declines in yield of 20–30 per cent by 2080, rising as high as 50 per cent in Sudan and Senegal (Oxfam, 2011).

Second, the increasing frequency and severity of extreme weather events such as heatwaves, droughts, storms and floods can wipe out harvests at a stroke.

Already, creeping changes in the seasons, such as longer, hotter dry periods, shorter growing seasons and unpredictable rainfall patterns, are bewildering poor farmers in many developing countries, making it harder for them to know when best to sow, cultivate and harvest their crops. Poor farmers' coping mechanisms are being exhausted. Frequently, they are without reliable and sufficient incomes, savings or access to healthcare or social insurance, Shocks from climatic disasters or shifting seasons often force them to go without food, sell off assets critical to their livelihoods or take their own children out of school. Short-term coping strategies can have long-term consequences, causing a downward spiral of deeper poverty and greater vulnerability. These effects would wipe out any positive impacts from expected increases in household incomes, trapping generations in the invidious cycle of food insecurity.

Many developing countries need financial assistance to address the challenges of climate change. Our collective approach to climate change adaptation needs to be multifaceted. It should include actions such as building resilience at the community level, supporting disaster risk reduction, building the capacity of developing country governments and responding to the direct impacts of climate change. All these actions will require substantial financial support.

In 2009 the World Bank estimated that the costs of adaptation in developing countries would be US$75–100bn per year (World Bank, 2009; 2010). This amount is based on the assumption that global warming will be kept below 2°C (Oxfam, 2009). Oxfam and the Stockholm Environment Institute estimate that the non-binding emission reduction pledges made at Copenhagen and Cancun could steer the world towards a catastrophic 4–5°C (Oxfam, 2009). Adaptation in these scenarios would be exponentially more expensive, if not impossible. Furthermore, it is becoming clear that rich countries have not met their initial 'fast-start' commitments (Oxfam, 2012). In many cases the money they are providing is not new – it is recycled – and in other cases the 'fast-start finance' is not additional to the aid budget.

One of the positive outcomes of Copenhagen was that wealthy developed countries agreed to a fast-start fund of US$30bn, over the three years to 2012. The aim of this fund was to support early adaptation and mitigation efforts while agreement was still being sought in other aspects of the negotiations. Recently, the World Resources Institute released a report that suggested only around US$12bn of the US$30bn promised has actually been budgeted for by developed countries and in some cases as little as around 30 per cent has been delivered (Vidal, 2011). Australia's approximately $620 million in fast-start financing represented a fair share of the US$30bn global goal and is notable for the share allocated to adaptation (52 per cent of the total), the transparency of reporting, the priority given to Least Developed Countries and to Small Island Developing States and for being fully grants-based. While there has been a substantial increase over earlier levels, of the total pledge only US$366m was added after Copenhagen, and thus in Oxfam's judgement constitutes 'new' money. While part of a growing aid budget, given that Australia's Official Development Assistance remains well below the United Nations target of 0.7 per cent of Gross National Income, its commitment to climate finance cannot be regarded as additional to existing aid commitments (Oxfam, 2012).

In 2012 the UNFCCC annual conference in Doha confirmed the bleak picture for climate change adaptation financing. The Doha Agreement failed to commit developed nations either to scaling up climate financing from 2013 or to a dollar amount. This means that the initial commitment to fast start finance made in Copenhagen in 2009 is not being adequately progressed. Australia was one of a number of countries that gave no firm commitment to increase funding. More generally, there was no assurance given to developing countries that climate financing, be it for mitigation or adaptation, will increase in the immediate future. Given that global Official Development Assistance fell for the first time in a decade in 2012, the signs are not positive that additional funding will be put on the table.

Inadequacy of current adaptation financing mechanisms and frameworks

Current climate financing mechanisms are not working. Adaptation in the poorest, most vulnerable countries is being neglected. First, most climate finance is being spent on mitigation rather than adaptation. Oxfam estimates that less than one tenth of the climate funds to date have been spent on adaptation in vulnerable countries. Oxfam's position is that adaptation should be the focus of at least 50 per cent of all climate financing. The reality is that the impacts of climate change are being felt by some of the world's poorest communities now. While these communities have some scope for mitigation, their most pressing need is for assistance with adapting to the consequences of climate change.

Second, current mechanisms are neglecting the poorest countries. For example, one of the largest funds, the Global Environmental Facility (GEF), has delivered less than an eighth of its climate funding to the 49 poorest countries. One third has gone to China, India and Brazil (Oxfam, 2009b). One of the overarching problems with the current system is that there are too many funds with too little money. To date, the climate finance landscape has been characterized by a disparate jumble of sources, channels, institutions and governance arrangements, *and* a history of unfulfilled promises and demands.

There are currently over 20 established climate funds as well as a considerable number of additional non-climate-focused funds that support adaptation. Many of these funds have been woefully underfunded, and resource allocation and distribution has tended to be slow and unpredictable. For developing countries, fund proliferation undermines the effectiveness of finance and reduces the amount of support they receive. It increases the burden of transaction costs on countries that often have limited capacity to access funds, and fragments their ability to manage resources strategically (Oxfam, 2009b).

The difficulties for countries with relatively weak state capacity to access these funds is profound. As Espen Ronnenberg, the climate advisor of the Secretariat of the Pacific Regional Environment Program (SPREP), has noted:

The wide range of currently available climate change financing is cumbersome and difficult to work with for administrations with low technical and personnel capacities. We have found over the years many countries will only begin preparing project concepts if there is an assurance of funding, the window however between the assurance and the deadline of submission is usually short and many for this reason miss a deadline set by the funding agencies. The complexity of certain funding applications may also work against low capacity countries, as the focal point may be an expert on the adaptation needs of the country, but that person does not have all the financial and auditing information required by the application. Therefore, having an assured source of funding without time constraints and perhaps some technical support to write up applications would be of greater benefit that the current system.

(UNDP, 2012)

The mitigation crisis

As Chapters 1, 2 and 3 have suggested, we appear to be heading rapidly down the road to catastrophic climate change. Without urgent action to reduce greenhouse gas pollution, the world will face insurmountable adaptation challenges. Oxfam's experience is that it is the poorest who will be hit first and hit the hardest.

Global emissions have already overcome the 'blip' of the Global Economic Crisis and set a new record in 2010. The International Energy Agency (IEA) reported that global emissions in 2010 were five per cent higher than the previous record set in 2008 (IEA, 2011). This led the Chief Economist at the IEA, Dr Fatih Birol, to say:

Our latest estimates are another wake-up call. The world has edged incredibly close to the level of emissions that should not be reached until 2020 if the 2°C target is to be attained. Given the shrinking room for manoeuvre in 2020, unless bold and decisive decisions are made very soon, it will be extremely challenging to succeed in achieving this global goal agreed upon in Cancun.

(IEA, 2011)

The imperative for action on climate change has never been stronger. However, wealthy developed countries like Australia are falling behind the rest of the world – they are simply not contributing their fair share of the effort. As an example of rich emitters' modest actions, currently Australia's target range for emissions reduction is between 5–25 per cent (by 2020 on 2000 levels), but at present the stated position is that only the conditions for a five per cent target will be met. Oxfam's assessment is that Australia's fair share of global efforts to keep global warming below 2°C is an emissions reduction target of –40 per cent below 2000 levels by 2020.

The global dynamics of mitigation effort are shifting. No longer are developed countries leading the way on reducing greenhouse gas emissions and renewable energy. A new study by Oxfam, in collaboration with the Stockholm Environment Institute (SEI, 2011), reveals that developing countries are making more of an effort to cut their greenhouse gas emissions than developed countries. Oxfam/SEI estimates that over 60 per cent of emissions cuts by 2020 are likely to be made by developing countries. While all countries should do their fair share to tackle climate change, wealthy industrialized countries are not pulling their weight. Currently Australia is on course to actually increase its emissions by around 24 per cent on 1990 levels by 2020 (SEI, 2011).

The path forward

So far, this chapter has outlined a number of significant challenges for climate change adaptation in Australia's region. Oxfam believes that there are emerging solutions to these challenges that we can begin to implement now. The solutions also present opportunities to improve the long-term effectiveness of aid and development efforts. This concluding section will briefly outline Oxfam's views on 1) generating a sufficient volume of finance for adaptation, 2) establishing a fair, effective and transparent global climate fund and 3) Australia's role in reducing emissions.

New international sources of adaptation financing

The challenge of generating the needed volume of climate finance is significant, but not insurmountable. There are a range of opportunities to generate new, long-term and predictable sources of climate financing that do not draw upon general revenue. Often called innovative sources of revenue, these could be available in the medium to long term.

First, a financial transactions tax (also popularly known as the Robin Hood Tax and an adaptation of the Tobin Tax proposal developed by Nobel Prize winning economist James Tobin) could generate billions of dollars to tackle poverty and climate change while also providing increased stability to financial markets. A tax of only 0.05 per cent – which would only apply to transactions by investment banks, hedge funds, and other financial institutions, not every-day transactions conducted by individuals – would suffice. It has been estimated that depending upon the size of the levy, that approximately US$400 bn could be generated globally annually.

Second, aviation and shipping are significant contributors to greenhouse gas pollution and pay very little tax, as they operate outside national borders. A levy on emissions from international aviation and shipping, also known as bunker fuels, could raise revenue while also having a price effect that might help reduce emissions from these sources. It has been estimated that setting a carbon price for ships at around $25 per tonne can drive significant maritime emissions cuts. That is likely to increase the cost of shipping by just 0.2 per cent, or $2 for every $1,000 traded, but would raise $25bn every year (Oxfam/WWF, 2011).

New domestic sources of adaptation financing

Governments should redirect their fossil fuel subsidies to support renewable energy and assist developing countries to adapt to climate change. Recent analysis has shown that the Australian government currently subsidises fossil fuel use to the tune of Aus$12bn per year (ACF, 2011). The Australian government should dedicate a small proportion of revenue from any carbon pricing scheme towards supporting international adaptation finance.

Together, these innovative sources of adaptation funding have the potential to generate significant, new and additional financing for adaptation in developing countries. It is not a question of capacity – it is a question of will. But until these or similar measures are in place, formal budget contributions from developed countries will be crucial.

Making the global fund work

It is clear that the current system for financing adaptation in developing countries is not working. The world needs to establish a new global climate fund that can serve as a one-stop-shop for climate financing. We need a system that is effective in meeting the scale of finance that is required in developing countries and that is perceived as legitimate by civil society and governments alike. Oxfam has conducted substantial research on the topic of a new global climate fund. Its recommendations include ensuring developing countries and vulnerable groups are properly represented in fund-related decision-making. The entire governance structure of the finance system should reflect principles of gender equity, including striving for at least gender equitable representation on its governing boards and committees. The membership of governance bodies should also include dedicated representation from particularly vulnerable country groupings and civil society.

Second, a finance board should be established to ensure developing countries receive the funding they need. The board would have a central role in the measuring, reporting and verification of financial support, and it would oversee internationally agreed standards for what counts as climate finance against international obligations.

Third, a global climate fund must enshrine the principle of country ownership. Recipient countries should be required to establish inclusive national decision-making processes that are gender inclusive. Flexibility and financial support will be needed for countries that lack sufficient human, institutional or technical capacity. In addition, they should be able to access resources from the new fund directly, without an intermediary (Oxfam, 2010b).

Conclusion: contributing to a global deal

Professor Ross Garnaut has stated:

> The behaviour of Australia – the developed country with the highest per capita emissions … will have considerable influence. Australia will be influential because the developed countries with high per capita emissions will be expected by the rest of the world to fully contribute to the global effort. If they do not, this will materially weaken the commitments of others, especially in the developing world. We, and other developed countries, can through inaction exercise a veto over effective global mitigation. (Garnaut, 2011)

His comments underscore the logic and the imperative for strong action from Australia. Australia and its citizens are intimately connected – politically, socially and economically – to countries that are vital to achieving global agreement on climate change. However, while many of us want Australia to be a global leader in this domain, it is clear that we first have a lot of catching up to do. Many of our Pacific Island neighbours are on the front line of climate change. They are already feeling the impacts, and without urgent and concerted action from wealthy developed countries like Australia, their future – and ours – looks bleak.

Note

1   My thanks to Phil Ireland and Kelly Dent for their invaluable work on the original conference paper and to Kelly for her assistance in updating it.

References

ACF (Australian Conservation Foundation). 2011. Australia spends $11 billion more encouraging pollution than cleaning it up. http://www.acfonline.org.au/articles/news.asp?news_id=3308 [accessed 18 July 2013].

Christoff, P. and R. Eckersley. 2013. No island is an island: security in a Four Degree World. In P. Christoff (ed.), *Four Degrees of Climate Change: Australia in a Hot World*. Earthscan: London, ch. 11.

Crikey. 2011 From tiny Tuvalu: the island being destroyed by climate change. http://blogs.crikey.com.au/rooted/2011/03/07/from-tiny-tuvalu-the-island-being-destroyed-by-climate-change/ [accessed 26 July 2013].

Garnaut, R. 2011. Progress Towards Effective Global Action: Update Paper 2. Commonwealth of Australia. http://www.garnautreview.org.au/update-2011/update-papers/up2-progress-towards-effective-global-action-climate-change.pdf [accessed 18 July 2013].

IEA. 2011. Prospect of limiting the global increase in temperature to 2 degrees is getting bleaker. http://www.iea.org/newsroomandevents/news/2011/may/name,19839,en.html [accessed 18 July 2013].

Oxfam. 2009. Climate shame: get back to the table. Initial analysis of the Copenhagen climate talks. http://www.oxfam.org/en/policy/climate-shame-get-back-table.

—2010a. Climate Finance Post-Copenhagen. The $100 Billion Questions. http://www.oxfam.org/policy/climate-finance-post-copenhagen [accessed 18 July 2013].

—2010b. Righting two wrongs: making a new Global Climate Fund work for poor people. http://oxfam. org/en/policy/righting-two-wrongs [accessed 18 July 2013].

—2010c. The faces of climate change: Niu. https://www.oxfam.org.au/2010/12/the-faces-of-climate-change-nui/ [accessed 26 July 2013].

—2011. Growing a better future: a summary. http://www.oxfam.org/sites/www. oxfam.org/files/growing-a-better-future-010611-en.pdf [accessed 18 July 2013].

—2012. The climate 'fiscal cliff': an evaluation of fast start finance and lessons for the future. http://www.oxfam.org/sites/www.oxfam.org/files/oxfam-media-advisory-climate-fiscal-cliff-doha-25nov2012.pdf [accessed 18 July 2013].

Oxfam/WWF. 2011. Out of the bunker: time for a fair deal on shipping emissions. http://www.oxfam.org/en/grow/policy/out-bunker-shipping-emissions [accessed 18 July 2013].

SEI. 2011. Comparison of Annex 1 and non-Annex 1 pledges under Cancun Agreements. http://www.sei-international.org/mediamanager/documents/Publications/Climate/sei-workingpaperus-1107.pdf [accessed 18 July 2013].

Steiner, A. 2011. http://www.euractiv.com/en/climate-environment/un-chief-rattled-durban-climate-summit-prospects-news-505298 [accessed 18 July 2013].

UNDP (United Nations Development Program). 2012. Climate change and development, community, Pacific Solution Exchange. http://www.undppc.org.fj/userfiles/file/National_Climate_Funds_for_Pacific-Island_Countries-03072012-2.pdf [accessed 18 July 2013].

Vidal, J. 2011. Bonn climate talks: developing nations question funding commitment. http://guardian. co. uk/environment/2011/jun/06/bonn-climate-funding-commitment [accessed 18 July 2013].

World Bank. 2009. Adapting to climate change to cost to $US75–100 billion a year. http://web. worldbank. org/WBSITE/EXTERNAL/NEWS/0,,contentMDK:22332792~pagePK:64257043~piPK:437376~theSitePK:4607,00. html [accessed 18 July 2013].

—2011. Economics of Adaptation to Climate Change. http://climatechange.worldbank.org/content/economics-adaptation-climate-change-study-homepage [accessed 18 July 2013].

13 Can we successfully adapt to four degrees of global warming?

Yes, no and maybe ...

Jean P. Palutikof, Jon Barnett and Daniela A. Guitart

Introduction

Although global average warming of 2°C has been identified as the threshold for dangerous climate change, it is increasingly becoming clear that current mitigation efforts will miss this target by a substantial margin (Betts et al., 2011; Stafford Smith et al., 2011). Even if we contemplate 'overshoot' emissions trajectories, stabilization at or below 2°C is beginning to look like an impossible dream. Although we may hope for a world in which warming will be limited to 2°C or less, we should certainly plan for more, including average warming of 4°C by the end of this century ... a Four Degree World. In this chapter, we explore the potential for humanity to adapt to a world in which temperatures are much warmer than the present day. It is uncertain if, in this much warmer world, as many people will be able to live happy, healthy lives. We seek to explore this uncertainty in this chapter.

Can we adapt to a Four Degree World? We do not yet know if we can adapt to high rates and levels of warming. This is for two important social reasons. First, the answer depends on how 'adaptation' is defined. If adaptation simply means 'a response to actual or expected climate impacts', then we – as a society – most certainly can and will adapt. However, if adaptation is defined in terms of judgments about the outcomes of these responses as being *successful* in some way, then the answer becomes far more elusive, as such judgements are a matter of perspective and values (for reviews of the adaptation concept see Smit et al., 2000; Smit and Wandel, 2006). Adaptation for whom? Adaptation by whom?

The second reason is because adaptation is at its heart a process of decision-making. Whether or not adaptation is successful is determined by who has the power and responsibility to make decisions, the basis on which decisions are made, and the means of their implementation, as well as the material outcomes. In other words, the answer to the question is largely a matter of choices made across all levels of society and across many sectors, and the degree to which these are aligned. Central to our argument is that high-level institutions and values are powerful determinants of adaptation (Haddad, 2005; O'Brien et al., 2009) and it is the effects of variations in such institutions that we seek to explore through this chapter.

Efforts to explore the range of environmental and social impacts that might arise from high rates of warming have taken 4°C of warming as the measure of change (e.g. Stafford Smith et al., 2011). This research has largely been about the impacts of climate change and not about what adaptation can (and cannot) do to avoid these impacts. To extend this research endeavor, in this chapter we construct three storylines about future institutions, and explore what these imply with respect to adaptation to high rates of warming. To move beyond the character of past research about high rates of warming, we apply these storylines to a specific context, an approach which is reinforced by the recognition that the determinants and measures of adaptation success (or failure) are nationally and/or culturally specific (Adger et al., 2005; Haddad, 2005). In this chapter we take as an example Australia – a country that occupies a whole continent, which is culturally and ecologically heterogeneous, and whose vulnerability to climate change has been well documented (Hennessy et al., 2007; Braganza et al., 2013, Chapter 3 in this volume). As we shall demonstrate, national policy decisions are significant determinants of the capacity to successfully adapt (or not) to these risks, which amplify with increases in warming. We highlight the implications of the choices we make about the way we live for the degree to which we can adapt to high levels of warming.

Scenarios and storylines

This chapter uses storyline-type scenarios to explore the potential to adapt to climate change associated with high levels of warming. Scenarios are plausible and often simplified images of how the future might unfold based on a coherent and internally consistent set of assumptions about key driving forces and relationships (Nakićenović and Swart, 2000; Raskin et al., 2005). A variety of techniques have been used to construct scenarios in climate change research, varying from quantitative to qualitative, or some mix of these (Carter et al., 2007; Moss et al., 2010). Although there is no clear delineation of terminology in the climate change literature in particular, but also more generally (but see van Vuuren et al., 2012), the term 'storyline' is widely used to describe qualitative and descriptive scenarios, based on written narratives, which create images of future worlds (Rounsevell and Metzger, 2010; van Vuuren et al., 2012).

Some of the characteristics of the storyline-type scenarios identified in the Millennium Ecosystem Assessment include integration across social, economic and environmental dimensions, regional disaggregation of global patterns and numerous futures that reflect the deep uncertainties of long-range outcomes (Raskin et al., 2005). Some examples of studies that have created storylines can be seen in Table 13.1.

Table 13.1 Examples of recent storyline type scenarios across different scales

Study	Scale	Horizon	Storylines
IPCC-SRES (Nakićenović and Swart, 2000)	Global	2100	**A1**: rapid market driven growth, convergence in incomes and culture; rapid technological change. **A2**: Self-reliance and preservation of local identities; fragmented development. **B1**: similar to A1, but emphasizes global solutions to sustainability, relying heavily on technology. **B2**: local technological and policy solutions to economic, social and environmental sustainability.
Global Scenario Group (Raskin et al., 2002)	Global	2050	**Conventional worlds**: gradual convergence of incomes and culture toward dominant market model **a Market forces**: market-driven globalization, trade liberalization, institutional modernization **b Policy reform**: strong policy focus on meeting sustainability goals through technology. **Barbarization**: social and environmental problems overwhelm market and policy response **a Breakdown**: unbridled conflict, institutional disintegration, economic collapse **b Fortress world**: authoritarian rule with elites in 'fortress'; poverty and repression outside. **Great transitions**: fundamental changes in values, lifestyles and institutions **a Eco-communalism**: local focus and bioregional perspective **b New sustainability paradigm**: sustainable globalization, changing industrial society.
Millennium Ecosystem Assessment (Cork et al., 2005)	Global	2100	**Global orchestration**: a globally connected world with well-developed global markets and supranational institutions to deal with global environmental problems and inequity. **Order of strength**: a fragmented world concerned with security and protection of regional markets and with little attention for common goods. **Adapting mosaic**: a fragmented world resulting from discredited global institutions leads to the rise of local and regional initiatives supporting common goals. **TechnoGarden**: a globally connected world relying strongly on technology, seeking to solve environmental problems and global inequity.

Study	Scale	Horizon	Storylines
UK National Ecosystem Assessment (2011)	National	2060	**Green and pleasant land**: a preservationist attitude arises because the UK can afford to look after its own backyard without diminishing the ever-increasing standards of living. **Nature@work**: widely-accepted belief that the promotion of ecosystem services through the creation of multifunctional landscapes is essential for maintaining the quality of life in the UK. **Local stewardship**: a future where society is more concerned with the immediate surroundings and strives to maintain a sustainable focus on life within that area. **Go with the flow**: projection of current trends resulting in a future UK that is roughly based on today's ideals and targets. **National security**: climate change results in increases in global energy prices forcing many countries to attempt greater self-sufficiency (and efficiency) in many of their core industries. **World markets**: high economic growth with a greater focus on removing barriers to trade.
Shared Socio-economic Pathways (O'Neill et al., 2011)	Global	2100	**SSP1**: Sustainability. Low socio-economic challenges for adaptation and mitigation. **SSP2**: Middle of the Road. Intermediate challenges for adaptation and mitigation. **SSP3**: Fragmentation. High socio-economic challenges for adaptation and mitigation. **SSP4**: Inequality. Adaptation challenges dominate. **SSP5**: Conventional Development. Mitigation challenges dominate.
Resilience and water security in two outback cities (Albrecht et al., 2010)	Regional	2070	**She'll be right mate** **Chill out man! It's all sorted** **Mmmmmmm....it's not looking good** **We'll all be rooned/Up shit creek**

Source: Modified from Rounsevell and Metzger, 2010

Note
a For detailed summary of more global and regional storylines see Rounsevell and Metzger (2010).

Setting the scene for Australia

Australia is a country of 23 million people inhabiting the driest of the earth's continents. Of these 23 million, over a quarter (26 per cent) were born overseas, and 20 per cent (4.1 million) are the children of migrants but born in Australia (Australian Bureau of Statistics, 2012). It is a highly urbanized society, with 70 per cent of the population living in the six biggest cities, and a coastal society – 90 per cent of the population lives within 30 km of the coast.

The current climate is characterized by high year-to-year rainfall variability, influenced by the Southern Oscillation, with multi-year droughts interspersed by periods of high rainfall often leading to floods. The northern tropical regions experience cyclones. Even in southern mainland Australia, daytime temperatures will exceed 40°C for several days each summer, accompanied by high bushfire risk (Australian Government Bureau of Meteorology, 2012; Braganza et al., 2013 [Chapter 3, this volume]).

We assume that 4°C of warming will be reached sometime during the 2070s (see Betts et al., 2011; Christoff, 2013, and Whetton et al., 2013 [Chapters 1 and 2, this volume]). As earlier chapters suggest, for Australia, the principal impacts are taken to include:

- many severely threatened ecosystems; some, such as coral reefs and alpine communities, are in long-term decline and can be considered no longer viable;
- unpleasant and, in summer at least, life-threatening urban climates;
- more and more powerful extreme weather events; bushfires are more frequent and more intense, increased frequency and intensity of storms and flooding, and so on;
- more variable rainfall, with lower rainfall and more frequent, longer droughts in southern Australia;
- coastal developments more frequently inundated because of sea-level rise; coastal wetlands experience saline intrusion; shorelines erode and retreat.

The three scenarios

We imagine three scenarios for the 2070s, each with different assumptions about the nature of the state, including influences on public policy, social norms, adaptation policy, mitigation actions and international relations. We understand the state to be institutions that govern society and which in Australia arise from a social contract between individuals and governments. For each, we describe the implications of these assumptions for the future of cities, rural and regional areas, coasts, energy, water resources, ecosystems, agriculture, transport, tourism and human health under high rates of warming. Table 13.2 shows how the drivers of adaptation map onto the socioeconomic sectors adapting to climate change in the three storylines.

The three scenarios and their key assumptions are:

1 'Terror Australis' (minimal state / pro-growth), where the state is minimal and increasingly illegitimate; public policy is held hostage to the interests of capital; social norms include the values of growth, consumption and competition; and adaptation aims to secure growth through strategies such as the progressive privatization of essential services and public goods.
2 'Terroir Australis' (social development state / pro-equity), where the state is social democratic; public policy is made through negotiations between the

state, businesses, organized labour and localities; social norms include the values of equity and liberty; and adaptation is seen as a matter of adjustments to maintain regional growth through partnerships and joined-up government.

3 *'New Atlantis'* (purposeful state / pro global justice), where the state is purposeful; public policy is made by the state with respect to ensuring a balanced relationship between the needs of society, the environment and the economy; social norms include the values of justice, the good life and global citizenship. Adaptation policy is set in the context of international leadership on reducing emissions of greenhouse gases, deliberative processes of transformation of key sectors and places, and systematic and purposeful policies to build adaptive capacity across all sections of the population.

Scenario 1: Terror Australis

This wonderful climate – the envy of the world – seems to be turning on us. Terra Australis is becoming Terror Australis, a blast furnace of drought, heat and capricious tempests.

(Gleeson, 2008)

The state is rolled back in that it has transferred its responsibilities for the provision of public goods to the private sector. Machinery of the state is minimal, consisting of a well-funded judiciary, police and armed forces, with most other state functions reduced to small bureaucracies with weak powers. The state progressively loses legitimacy as effects of climate change and market forces, and their interactions, lead to retreating coasts, higher and more volatile prices for essential goods and services, increasing social inequality, and rising morbidity and mortality among some populations. As legitimacy erodes, so too does the ability of the state to perform even its minimal functions of maintaining law and order and to adjudicate among competing interests, such that corporate criminals are increasingly unconstrained and organized crime has increasing legitimacy among marginalized populations.

Public policy is influenced by capital. The power of labour is weakened by workplace reforms and decreased restrictions on the immigration of skilled workers, while civil society is consumed with the burden of providing those social services divested from the state. Public policy is a process of divestment of state responsibility for public goods through processes of privatization – for example, of management of public lands, education, transport and essential services such as water, energy and healthcare – and, more simply, through the curtailment of bureaucratic capacity. The sustainable use of resources is a matter of inter-temporal allocation through markets. After this process of rolling back the state, public policy ceases to be a meaningful category of activity, and instead becomes a matter of historical interest.

Social norms are dominated by a concern for the value and practice of freedom. As a result of social fragmentation, debates about attendant responsibilities to

Table 13.2 The drivers of adaptation and characteristics of the sectors adapting in the three storylines for the future of Australia with 4°C warming, as described in this study

	Storyline		
	1. Terror Australia	*2. Terroir Australia*	*3. New Atlantis*
Drivers of adaptation/context			
Nature of the state	Minimal	Social democratic	Purposive
Public policy	Influenced by capital, privatization.	Corporatist system of negotiation between the state, business and labour.	Convergence between the state, capital, labour, and civil society.
Social Norms	Values of growth, consumption, competition and freedom.	Values of equity and liberty.	Values of social justice.
Adaptation actions	Responsive adaptation, no effective action or policy.	Incremental adaptation.	Transformational adaptation.
Mitigation actions in Australia	Piecemeal and ineffective.	Moving to low-carbon economy based primarily around nuclear power; low community buy-in causing civil disturbance.	Highly effective, low-carbon economy achieved, on pathway to zero emissions.
Sectors			
Cities	High-density city centres; sprawling suburbs; poor air quality.	Universal high density living; high albedo, declining areas of green spaces leading to deteriorating air quality.	High density living, enclosed and roofed environments, multi-story cities; high-level parks.
Rural environments	Decline of rural communities driven by decline in agriculture and increased fire and flood risk; steep increase in property values in high-amenity locations driving out local population.	Decline of rural communities driven by shift to large highly-mechanized farms; steep increase in property values in high-amenity locations driving out local population; mandatory fire and flood insurance driving relocation.	Strong government support maintaining vibrant, safe and attractive rural communities; price controls and reserved housing in high-amenity areas; government grants and management of relocation of fire-prone and flood-prone communities.

| | Storyline | | |
	1. Terror Australia	2. Terroir Australia	3. New Atlantis
Sectors			
Energy	Fossil fuel-based energy still dominant; no effective national grid.	Strong shift to nuclear power; need for national energy grid recognized and planned.	Balanced mix of low carbon energy sources: nuclear and renewable, supported by effective grid.
Water resources and supply	Markets determine water allocation; environmental flows neglected; irrigated area in decline, rationing common.	Needs of urban areas and environmental flows prevail; desalination augments supply; occasional shortages.	Emphasis on rational and equitable distribution of water, with needs of all users including irrigation and environmental flows recognized and supported; use of water grids where feasible.
Agriculture and food security	Agricultural area in decline, irrigated agriculture severely threatened; food shortages and hoarding commonplace, prices rising.	Responsive-mode policies failing to keep track of shifts in climatic belts leading to food shortages.	Managed program of agricultural relocation as climate changes maintaining food security.
Transport	Effective public transport limited to inner cities, province of the rich; suburb-to-centre public transport links poor quality with commuters heavily reliant on cars; inter-city transport by air.	Effective public transport throughout urban areas; rural centres poorly served and reliant on cars; inter-city transport by air.	Effective public transport throughout urban areas; long-distance high-speed rail network well-developed and growing.
Ecosystems	Little recognition of ecosystem service; ecosystems severely threatened.	Recognition of ecosystem service; environmental flows maintained; strong emphasis on revegetation for carbon sequestration.	Green areas expanding strongly in urban areas; environmental stewardship financially supported as mechanism to sustain vibrant rural communities.

| | Storyline | | |
	1. Terror Australia	2. Terroir Australia	3. New Atlantis
Sectors			
Tourism	Rural tourism in decline in most areas due to low amenity; wetlands and coral reefs in decline.	Rural tourism in decline in most areas as rural population declines; wetlands protected with environmental flows; coral reefs in decline.	Rural tourism expanding in many areas as people escape urban heat; wetlands being restored; strategies in plan to protect reef biodiversity.
Human health	High mortality and morbidity from heat stress; asthma and allergic reactions to aeroallergens; dengue fever spreading south.	Effective response measures limit heatwave mortality; dengue fever control in place; allergen-related disease occurrence increasing.	Heatwave mortality very low; dengue fever and allergen-related disease controlled.

others and future generations are confined to obscure monthly journals and community radio stations. It then becomes impossible to speak meaningfully of community or communal values. Freedom remains the prevailing value of a small but influential upper class, which propagates the discourse and practice of unfettered consumption and mobility. At the other end of the social spectrum survival is the goal and opportunity is the desire, for there is little choice: market segmentation leads to redlining[1] from essential services such as insurance. Access to healthcare and education is restricted by the capability of civil society to provide, labour markets are dominated by employers and mobility is an unaffordable luxury.

Whether or not developments in Australia are mirrored in the outside world, *international relations* are characterized by isolation – refugees are strongly discouraged by the instruments the state has at its disposal and immigration is limited to just a few essential categories (where 'essential' may be defined as that necessary to ensure a compliant workforce). With a struggling agriculture sector, minerals dominate exports. With few allies and trading partners, when drought strikes and crops fail, Australia struggles to purchase grain on the international market. Partly in response to this risk, the nation seeks to maintain a stable or low-growth population. Efforts to limit greenhouse-gas emissions have largely failed, defeated by a growing demand for energy for cooling purposes and by industry interests. Dependent on the extent to which international efforts to reduce emissions have succeeded through mandatory restrictions, Australia may face penalties for failure to comply.

Consistent with the nature of the state and public policy, there is no *adaptation policy*. Rather, adaptation is a series of market opportunities: for insurers providing services to the affluent and extracting rents from residual markets; property developers for whom the turnover in stock caused by fires, floods and coastal erosion generates unprecedented demand, constrained only by a contraction of the market able to pay; for water traders selling water across sectors in an increasingly oligopolistic market; for food wholesalers able to manipulate expectations of scarcity and bottlenecks to gain higher prices with no changes in productivity. Yet there are market risks too: for suppliers of goods with high capital costs the costs of maintaining assets becomes too high, and a number of new entrants into urban water, transport and power markets go bankrupt, leaving customers stranded and causing large losses to shareholders. Community service providers seek to meet many social needs, for example for education, health care, housing, power, water and food, yet their ability to do this is undermined by higher costs, a contracting base of funders and a diminished willingness on the part of those who can afford to support their work.

Cities are increasingly characterized by a hyper-affluent inner city, rapid growth along the landward fringes and social marginalization increasing with distance away from the centre. Demand for inner-city housing rises as coastal properties are progressively devalued and some of the affluent classes seek urban lifestyles, at least during the working week. With a higher density of wealthy customers, private transport providers supply the inner urban market with trains, trams and buses, such that car ownership becomes a sign of poverty. Transport from middle and outer suburbs is met by private vehicle ownership for those who can afford the fuel and tolls. For those who cannot, a sparse and unreliable network of co-operatively owned bus routes is the only means of mobility. There is a contour of mortality and morbidity, which rises with distance from the centre. Fire proofing the fringes has turned green wedges into extensive fire breaks, heat absorbing surfaces abound, access to healthcare is minimal, heat stress increases as air conditioning and retrofitting houses are beyond the means of many people, and nutrition declines as people on lower incomes cannot compete with the wealthy in markets for healthy foods. Social problems abound with increasing homelessness leading to increased mortality during heatwaves.

Coasts are almost everywhere in retreat, and there is no planning response.

Regarding *rural and regional areas*, small towns continue to decline as some burn too often, others lose population due to the demise of irrigated agriculture and an increase in the size of dryland farms. Some areas with amenity and low fire risk grow as the rich seek to escape urban living which, in summer at least, reaches unbearable temperatures.

Concerning *utilities and water*, scarcity of water and an open market mean that cities buy water, and irrigated agriculture has largely ceased, apart from high-value commodities such as fruits, nuts and boutique dairy. Both domestic water and electricity are expensive for the consumer, exacerbating the health risks of heatwaves. Water rationing is becoming commonplace. Electricity is generated primarily by fossil fuels. A move to renewable energy was unsuccessful as the failure to create a viable carbon market drove investors and developers out of renewable developments.

In summary, this is an inequitable society, hopelessly incapable of managing the risks of climate change. Shortages of water and food are ever-present risks. Urban areas are poorly equipped to deal with heatwaves. Looking forward, without substantial policy intervention, this is a society where the gap between the rich and the poor will continue to grow, and where the poor will continue to be disproportionately impacted by climate change.

Scenario 2: Terroir Australis

The State is guided by the value of social justice, and derives its legitimacy from the degree to which it is able to achieve a fair distribution of wealth. Thus the state plays the role of economic manager, intervening to remedy unequal outcomes across the economy and seeking to minimize inequalities caused by climate change. The state is Keynesian in the sense that it is an active regulator of markets to achieve full employment. It is also a state that seeks to decentralize decision making to localities – a regulator, then, not just of markets, but of 'bottom-up' plans for change to ensure that such plans do not themselves create inequalities. But it is a vain state, in that its orientation is for the nation rather than the international community, and for the present more than the future.

Public policy is made through a corporatist system of negotiation between the state, businesses and labour, and frequently in association with regional entities seeking to pursue regional development goals. Regional planning contracts, which set goals and outline the roles and responsibilities of different arms and levels of government, capital, labour and civil society, are the centrepieces of policies.

Social norms include the values of equity and liberty. This is a caring society, as demonstrated by public discourses, government policies and tolerance in everyday encounters. Consumption is important: wealth is distributed but still measured in terms of material goods and services. Nationalism prevails, so that the community of concern is the population of the country, and not those in other countries.

Social justice prevails, at least with respect to consumption. Australia becomes more urbanized as the city turns its back on, and increasingly consumes the hinterland. However, this process of rural transition is smoothed, and relatively painless, due to the pacifying effects of the welfare state.

International relations – this is an inward-looking society. It continues the attributes of the Terror Australia storyline in seeking to limit immigration and hold population close to constant. This is in recognition of the threat of global warming, a sense that Australia is powerless to affect the outcome, and therefore the need to protect its own citizens. Seen from the inside, it is a society that strives to be fair, from the outside it is selfish and self-protecting. With a shift to nuclear power, this storyline has a greater likelihood of meeting any international requirements for emissions reduction.

'*Terroir Australia*' is structurally more resilient to climate change than the '*Terror Australia*'. In particular, it has a greater capacity to feed itself, and agricultural productivity is less prone to boom and bust. As such, it is less dependent on food imports. Nevertheless, there will be years when *Terroir Australia* will have to go to the international market for imports. The threats of food and water insecurity are not fully addressed by this storyline.

Adaptation policy is subservient to economic policy, and is approached through a series of adjustments to maintain regional growth over short time scales. Research, awareness raising and community engagement are central elements of the national adaptation strategy, but responses are unimaginative, largely determined by government, incremental in nature and poorly co-ordinated. Social policy is also central to adaptation policy, for in the absence of a more strategic approach impacts on some sectors of the population – delineated by sector or location – cannot be avoided, and reactive and remedial measures such as compensation, income support, skills training and housing assistances are used.

Cities are characterized by what Gleeson (2008) calls 'a social sensibility', where the suburbs are no less well served than inner urban areas. Nevertheless, as the climate continues to deteriorate, conditions in urban areas are at best unpleasant and in summer may be life threatening. Options to improve the urban environment are explored, with strong investment in public transport. Efforts to 'green' the city falter due to lack of water. Faced with unsustainable urban lifestyles, there is a move to higher-density housing with strong reliance on air conditioning and shading to create livable environments. City living is bearable, and only the most severe heatwaves lead to exceptional mortality – strategies such as door-knocking the vulnerable and opening air conditioned malls as refuges are, together with successful public awareness campaigns, generally effective.

In *rural and regional areas*, Fordism[2] dominates rural production, with large and highly mechanized farms operated by fly-in fly-out labour. There are various policy instruments to keep food prices low, rather than to sustain rural communities. As a result, many inland market towns have rapidly dwindling populations. Some, which lie in flood-prone areas, have either been relocated or, more commonly, their inhabitants merged with larger more viable neighbours. As with *Terror Australia*, unpleasant urban living conditions mean that those who can afford to, and whose job permits, move to high-amenity rural/seaside locations.

The magnitude of changes along the *coastal zone* cannot be forestalled by social policy: for example, salt water intrudes into Kakadu, and low-lying islands in the Torres Strait are abandoned due to erosion and inundation. Indigenous owners are compensated with new homes, jobs and communities, but sites of significance are lost, as are the aspects of culture they sustained. For small settlements along the coast adaptation is largely a reactive process: movements in response to sea-level rise are after the event, but social policy helps to minimize the psycho-social costs associated with such responses.

Regarding *utilities and water*, with the public acceptance of nuclear power, the large energy consumption implied by a high cooling requirement and possibly the need to pump water over distance is met. This took a long time to implement – public resistance was slowly worn down by years of rising fuel bills and, even then, lack of engineering expertise meant that progress was slow. However, expertise and investment from China now means that 80 per cent of Australia's electricity requirement is met by nuclear power, with a mix of hydro, gas, solar, wind and coal supplying the remainder.

Water is managed as an economic good, but with awareness of its environmental values. In the tradeoffs between water for small rural enterprises and cities, the rural enterprises lose. Environmental flows are a high priority and, where feasible, are increased. An affordable and sustainable water supply for all is a policy aspiration. Nevertheless, at least twice in the last decade water rationing has been imposed in the southern capital cities to address water shortages.

In *summary*, this is a highly urbanized, equitable society, at least from the inside. Nevertheless, not enough is being done to ensure food and water security, and this is a society that lives with the fear of shortages – of water and even of food. Increased risk of fire and flood is driving an ever-increasing proportion of the population to the cities. The government is able to contemplate building a water grid, given the large amounts of cheap power now available, which will build water security provided that northern Australia continues to be wetter than in the past. Investment in agriculture in northern regions is seen to be essential in the future to build food security.

Scenario 3: New Atlantis

The *state* is what Oakeshott (1975) calls 'purposive' in that it strongly pursues common objectives and outcomes, in this case to respond to climate change through domestic action and international leadership, in order to universalize the Good Life. This is not an across the spectrum 'war economy', as Spratt and Sutton (2008) argue, as the rapid responses that are needed for mitigation of greenhouse gases have been achieved with policy reforms only in the transport and energy sectors.

Large-scale investment in nuclear power and a suite of renewable energy technologies reduce emissions from the power sector. In this scenario, some 40 per cent of energy is generated from nuclear power, 50 per cent from renewable and 10 per cent from fossil fuels, mainly gas. This investment has been accompanied by large investment in transmission grids, allowing distant location of nuclear power stations to allay public concerns. Electricity from large solar concentrators in central Australia can be brought to the large coastal cities. These investments provide the large quantities of power required to maintain good health and an acceptable lifestyle in urban areas, especially for cooling. Similarly, large investments in high-speed public transport within and between cities and towns further contribute to significant reductions in emissions.

It is not a state that intervenes as a matter of course but, rather, to the extent necessary, as a matter of efficacy. Yet the nature of the state itself means such changes are accepted and legitimate because they are desired by citizens.

Public policy is a matter of convergence between the state, capital, labour and civil society at the behest of a public that is intolerant of the politics of fear, and desires a politics of hope. These partnerships converge on agreed policy goals of stability, global leadership, full employment, intergenerational equity, transparency and the Good Life. Governance is multilayered yet integrated across levels and sectors. The innovation, creativity and motivation for adaptation come from business more than government. Growth is a goal of policy, but it is modest, distributed and significantly dematerialized and decarbonized. Corporate laws are reformed so that corporations are more accountable to shareholders and the state, and employment is as important as profit as a measure of business success. Private property rights are not subordinate to policy, but they are reconfigured in important ways, including through changes in the duration of ownership (which is now subject to environmental triggers), and the degree to which property implies exclusive use. Policy instruments are not selected on the basis of ideology but likely efficacy, and the relationship between markets, planning and regulation is responsive and changes across spatial and temporal scales and sectors. Adaptation is mainstreamed across all sectors of policy and is designed to be robust with respect to a variety of possible futures (Lempert and Schlesinger, 2001).

Social justice exists, and indeed is fundamental to this society's approach to managing climate change impacts. These values underpin not only national policies, but also Australia's international relations. In a nation that recognizes the importance of forward planning to manage climate change, society as a whole becomes future oriented, with recognition of the responsibilities of present to future generations.

'New Atlantis' sees its *international relations*, especially in the Asia-Pacific region, as a critical component of policies to address climate change and build resilience. It leads in the introduction and negotiation of international agreements, and is on course to meet its own targets. It is a substantial aid donor, and has entered into trade treaties in an attempt to ensure food security. Agricultural production continues to contribute to exports, although wheat exports have fallen. Through agreements with a number of small island states, Australia is a world leader in facilitating labour mobility as a means to enhance the adaptive capacity of people in low-income countries that are vulnerable to climate change.

Adaptation policy is subservient to a larger climate change policy framework where less is made of the distinction between mitigation and adaptation. All climate change policy is purposeful and planned. Synergies between mitigation and adaptation are maximized: for example, in urban designs that reduce emissions and promote healthy lifestyles and aesthetically rich experiences, transport services that reduce emissions and promote social integration and agricultural enterprises that are emissions neutral and water efficient. The state plans for transformative change in vulnerable sectors, over appropriate timescales: for example, cities are planned so that sea-level rise, fire and heat stress are less risky despite a warming climate; agriculture is planned so that high production occurs in climatically appropriate zones, and shifts as these zones shift. Such plans are made on decadal time scales and are subject to environmental triggers, as appropriate.

Cities are revolutionized. The suburbs are the sites of transformation: where each house is a net power supplier, green spaces are water catchments and food producing precincts, public transport services are dense, cars are scarce, and people belong to localities. The suburban is dynamic, desirable and sustainable (Gleeson, 2008). Urban development occurs along more co-operative lines, where municipalities do not compete for capital, but collectively plan for change in partnership with the state, developers and civil society (Iveson, 2009).

In *rural and regional areas*, there is an emphasis on the maintenance of viable communities. There has been planned and government-supported relocation of agriculture to northern areas, which allows Australia to maintain some level of food exports in most years.

Coastal zones are planned so that settlements are able to adapt in ways that are fair and efficient, yet enable growth and the satisfaction of amenity values. There is far greater recognition of the cultural impacts of loss, and investment in documenting and keeping as much knowledge of Indigenous ways of living as possible, for while information alone cannot sustain a culture, it is the best that can be achieved once material practices can no longer be sustained (Garrett, 2009). The losses that cannot be avoided are memorialized through museums and popular narratives, and take the status of identity narratives that serve to remind about the price of failure to tackle climate change.

National grids for *water and electricity* exist and are a basis for rational and equitable resource allocation. Shortages only occur under the most extreme conditions. Irrigation is regulated with mandatory water-saving methods.

In *summary*, this is an outward-looking society, respected by its peers; resilient to the impacts of climate change through the implementation of policies embedded in concepts of equity and social justice.

Conclusion

The construction and evaluation of storyline-based scenarios can be a valuable tool in visualizing a world in which we live with a changed climate. Here we have constructed three future storylines about the institutions that are influential in determining adaptation responses, and we explore the nature of adaptation responses that flow from these diverse institutional configurations. These storylines demonstrate that, although the scale of climate change is an important determinant of the extent to which our environment and livelihoods will be affected, so too is the way in which we manage and interact with the changes at the national and local level. Although there may be little or no capacity at the national level to affect the scale of global climate change (Australia contributes around 1.5 per cent of global greenhouse gas emissions), there is the capacity to construct institutions and infrastructure, which protect the environment and enable people to lead meaningful and fulfilled lives to the maximum extent possible. Conversely, these storylines demonstrate that failure by the state to allow for climate change impacts can have disastrous consequences for the environment and society.

Three main conclusions can be drawn from the storylines presented here. First, the institutional framework of the state is key to adaptation success. The choices we are able to make about adaptation are a function of the institutions in which they are nested: in terms of governance, the highest order institution is the state. We show here how the state matters for adaptation, suggesting that given the current nature of the state, a transformation of the state itself may be required if we are to successfully adapt to high rates of warming. Transformability has been defined as the capacity to create a fundamentally new system when ecological, economic or social, including political, conditions make the system untenable (Walker et al., 2004). Indeed, as Giddens (2009) argues, it may be that the state transformed can avoid 4°C of warming. Even so, even at 2°C of warming, and with the most effective and purposeful state possible, some impacts of climate change cannot be avoided: ecosystems will change, some species will be lost, and places will change. Other studies have argued that in some places and for some systems, risks and vulnerabilities will be so major that they will require transformational rather than incremental adaptations (Kates et al., 2012). However, what the best of all possible states *can* do is to avoid the transmission of these changes in environments into social impacts.

Second, adaptation will require large amounts of power to be successful – to cool urban environments, to pump water to where it is needed, to power public transport systems. To avoid maladaptation, low-carbon (across the entire life cycle) generation is required. Planning and implementation of appropriate infrastructure takes time (of the order of decades), not least of which is the time to gain public acceptance if the solution is to be based around nuclear energy. State institutions need not only to be purposeful – they need to be wise if infrastructure solutions for adaptation are to be delivered in an appropriate and timely fashion.

Finally, Australia adapts to climate change within its international context. How it adapts, and how successfully, is conditional on the impacts of climate change on other nations and their responses. Most critically, this will affect food trade and security. Under changing rainfall patterns, it is not clear if Australia can grow enough to feed its own population and maintain exports. If it cannot, Australia will rely on others to be able to make up the shortfall to the extent necessary to prevent shortages, price increases and, potentially, civil unrest.

Notes

1 A discriminatory practice whereby institutions refuse to make loans/sell insurance because applicants live in an area deemed to be a poor financial risk, for example, because of exposure to flooding.
2 Named after Henry Ford, Fordism refers to a notion of modern economic and social systems based on an industrialized and standardized form of mass production.

References

Adger, N., N. W. Arnell and E. L. Tompkins. 2005. Successful adaptation to climate change across scales. *Global Environmental Change* 15: 77–86.

Albrecht, G., H. Allison, N. Ellis, M. Jaceglav. 2010. *Resilience and Water Security in Two Outback Cities.* National Climate Change Adaptation Research Facility, Gold Coast, Australia.

Australian Bureau of Statistics. 2012. Cultural diversity in Australia. Reflecting a nation: stories from the 2011 census. www.abs.gov.au/ausstats/abs@.nsf/Lookup/2071.0main+fe atures902012-2013 [accessed 18 July 2013].

Australian Government Bureau of Meteorology. 2012. Australia – climate of our continent. www.bom.gov.au/lam/climate/levelthree/ausclim/zones.htm [accessed 18 July 2013].

Betts, R., M. Collins, D. Hemming, C. Jones, J. Lowe and M. Sanderson. 2011. When could global warming reach 4°C? *Philosophical Transactions of the Royal Society A* 369: 67–84.

Braganza, K., K. Hennessy et al. 2013. Changes in extreme weather. In P. Christoff (ed.), *Four Degrees of Climate Change: Australia in a Hot World.* Earthscan: London, ch. 3.

Carter, T. R., R. N. Jones, X. Lu, S. Bhadwal, C. Conde, L. O. Mearns, B. C. O. Neill, M. D. A. Rounsevell and M. B. Zurek. 2007. New assessment methods and the characterisation of future conditions. In M. L. Parry, O. F. Canziani, J. P. Palutikof, P. J. van der Linden and C. E. Hanson (eds), *Climate Change 2007: Impacts, Adaptation and Vulnerability. Contribution of Working Group II to the Fourth Assessment Report of the Intergovernmental Panel on Climate Change.* Cambridge University Press: Cambridge, pp. 133–71.

Christoff, P. 2013. Australia in a Four Degree World? In Christoff, P. (ed.), *Four Degrees of Climate Change: Australia in a Hot World.* Earthscan: London, Ch. 1.

Cork, S., G. Peterson, G. Petschel-Held, J. Alcamo, J. Alder, E. Bennett, E. R. Carr, D. Deane, G. C. Nelson, T. Ribeiro, C. Butler, E. M. Mendiondo, W. Oluoch-Kosura and M. Zurek. 2005. Four Scenarios. In S. R. Carpenter, P. L. Pingali, E. M. Bennett and M. B. Zurek (eds), *Ecosystems and Human Well-being: Scenarios.* Island Press, Washington, DC, pp. 223–94.

Garrett, B. 2009. Drowned memories: the submerged places of the Winnemem Wintu. *Archaeologies* 6: 346–71.

Giddens, A. 2009. *The Politics of Climate Change.* Polity Press: London.

Gleeson, B. 2008. Waking from the dream. In J. Schultz (ed.), *Griffith Review 20: Cities on the Edge.* ABC Books, Sydney, pp. 13–49.

Haddad, B. M. 2005. Ranking the adaptive capacity of nations to climate change when socio-political goals are explicit. *Global Environmental Change* 15: 165–76.

Hennessy, K., B. Fitzharris, B. C. Bates, N. Harvey, M. Howden, L. Hughes, J. Salinger, R. Warrick, S. Becken, L. Chambers, T. Coleman, M. Dunn, D. Green, R. Henderson, A. Hobday, O. Hoegh-Guldberg, G. Kenny, D. King, G. Penny and R. Woodruff. 2007. Australia and New Zealand. In M. L. Parry, O. F. Canziani, J. P. Palutikof, P. J. van der Linden and C. E. Hanson (eds), *Climate Change 2007: Impacts, Adaptation and Vulnerability. Contribution of Working Group II to the Fourth Assessment Report of the Intergovernmental Panel on Climate Change.* Cambridge University Press: Cambridge, pp. 507–40.

Iveson, K. 2009. Responding to the financial crisis: from competitive to cooperative urbanism. *Journal of Australian Political Economy* 64: 211–21.

Kates, R. W., W. R. Travis and T. J. Wilbanks. 2012. Transformational adaptation when incremental adaptations to climate change are insufficient. *Proceedings of the National Academy of Sciences of the United States of America* 109(19): 7156–61.

Lempert, R. and M. E. Schlesinger. 2001. Climate-change strategy needs to be robust. *Nature* 412: 375.

Moss, R. H., J. A. Edmonds, K. A. Hibbard, M. R. Manning, S. K. Rose, D. P. van Vuuren, T. R. Carter, S. Emori, M. Kainuma, T. Kram, G. A. Meehl, J. F. B. Mitchell, N. Nakićenović, K. Riahi, S. J. Smith, R. J. Stouffer, A. M. Thomson, J. P. Weyant and T. J. Wilbanks. 2010. The next generation of scenarios for climate change research and assessment. *Nature* 463: 747–57.

Nakićenović, N. and R. Swart (eds.) 2000. *Special Report on Emissions Scenarios. A Special Report of Working Group III of the Intergovernmental Panel on Climate Change.* Cambridge University Press: Cambridge.

Oakeshott, M. 1975. *On Human Conduct.* Clarendon Press: Oxford.

O'Brien, K., B. Hayward and F. Berkes. 2009. Rethinking social contracts: building resilience in a changing climate. *Ecology and Society* 14: 12.

O'Neill, B. C., T. R. Carter, K. L. Ebi, J. Edmonds, S. Hallegatte, E. Kemp-Benedict, E. Kriegler, L. Mearns, R. Moss, K. Riahi, B. van Rujiven and D. van Vuuren. 2011. *Meeting Report of the Workshop on The Nature and Use of New Socioeconomic Pathways for Climate Change Research*, Boulder, CO, November 2–4, 2011. https://www.isp.ucar.edu/sites/default/files/Boulder%20Workshop%20Report_0.pdf [accessed 18th July 2013].

Raskin, P., T. Banuri, G. Gallopin, P. Gutman, A. Hammond, R. Kates and R. Swart. 2002. *Great Transition: The Promise and Lure of the Times Ahead.* Report of the Global Scenario Group, Stockholm Environment Institute: Boston, MA.

Raskin, P., Monks, F., Ribeiro, T., van Vuuren, D. and Zurek, M. 2005. Global scenarios in historical perspective. In S. R. Carpenter, P. L. Pingali, E. M. Bennett and M. B. Zurek (eds), *Ecosystems and Human Well-being: Scenarios.* Island Press: Washington, DC, pp. 35–44.

Rounsevell, M. D. A. and M. J. Metzger. 2010. Developing qualitative scenario storylines for environmental change assessment. *WIREs Climate Change* 1: 606–19.

Smit, B., I. Burton, R. J. T. Klein and J. Wandel. 2000. An anatomy of adaptation to climate change and variability. *Climatic Change* 45: 223–51.

Smit, B. and J. Wandel. 2006. Adaptation, adaptive capacity and vulnerability. *Global Environmental Change* 16: 282–92.

Spratt, D. and P. Sutton. 2008. *Climate Code Red: The Case for Emergency Action.* Scribe Publications: Melbourne.

Stafford Smith, M., L. Horrocks, A. Harvey and C. Hamilton. 2011. Rethinking adaptation for a 4°C world. *Philosophical Transactions of the Royal Society* A 369: 196–216.

UK National Ecosystem Assessment 2011 *The UK National Ecosystem Assessment: Synthesis of the Key Findings.* UNEP-WCMC, Cambridge. http://archive.defra.gov.uk/environment/natural/documents/UKNEA_SynthesisReport.pdf [accessed 30 July 2013].

van Vuuren, D. P., M. T. J. Kok, B. Girod, P. L. Lucas and B. de Vires. 2012. Scenarios in global environmental assessments: key characteristics and lessons for future use. *Global Environmental Change*, 22: 884–95.

Walker, B., C. S. Holling, S. R. Carpenter and A. Kinzig. 2004. Resilience, adaptability and transformability in social-ecological systems. *Ecology and Society* 9(2): 5. [online] URL: http://www.ecologyandsociety.org/vol9/iss2/art5 [accessed 30 July 2013].

Whetton, P., D. Karoly, I. Watterson, L. Webb, F. Drost, D. Kirono and K. McInnes. 2013. Australia's climate in a Four Degree World. In P. Christoff (ed.), *Four Degrees of Climate Change: Australia in a Hot World.* Earthscan: London, ch. 2.

14 Conclusion

Avoiding a Four Degree World – Australia's Role

Peter Christoff

Despite years of international negotiations and growing public and scientific concern, both global fossil fuel use and carbon dioxide emissions have continued to increase at an accelerating rate. In May 2013, atmospheric concentrations of carbon dioxide rose above 400 ppm for the first time in human history (see: keelingcurve.ucsd.edu). Similar levels were last experienced some 3.2 to 5 million years ago, when global average temperatures were between 3°C and 4°C warmer and as much as 10°C more at the poles and sea levels ranged between 5 and 40 meters higher than present.

The first 12 years of the 21st century were all among the top 13 warmest years since 1850, when records began, and 2012 was the 27th consecutive year in which the global land and ocean temperatures were above the 1961–1990 average (WMO, 2013). Such warming has contributed in the northern hemisphere to the record loss of Arctic sea-ice, intense drought in the United States and south-eastern Europe, and major storms such as Hurricane Sandy (WMO, 2013: 3).

Even at current low levels of global average warming of around 0.8°C, Australia is proving highly vulnerable to the impacts of climate change. The summer of 2012/13 was the hottest on record (BoM, 2013a). At the same time, in January 2013, extreme rainfall in Queensland and northern New South Wales resulted in severe flooding (BoM, 2013b). As the Climate Commission noted in its report *The Angry Summer*, 'Australia was hit by a series of extreme weather events, including heatwaves, bushfires, intense rainfall and flooding, that caused serious damage in many places … As a result, the resources required for our society to deal with extreme weather is increasing' (CC, 2013: 1).

Despite international agreement that global warming should be kept below 2°C, the voluntary national mitigation pledges in the Copenhagen Accord 2009, confirmed at Cancun in 2010, are insufficient to hold warming below the 2°C threshold, much less the safer target of 1.5°C. Recent negotiations have paved the way for a new international climate agreement to be finalized in 2015 and come into effect by 2020. However, such an agreement is neither certain, nor is it clear that its targets will be robust enough to keep warming below the 2°C 'guardrail'. In all, in the absence of a massive international effort and substantial additional action by individual nations to greatly reduce emissions during the next decade, we remain on a path to global warming of four degrees or more – a

Four Degree World (Schellnhuber et al., 2012: 23). This chapter reviews and summarizes the findings of this book and then considers how Australia should respond.

Australia in a Four Degree World

The authors of this book explore the likely consequences of a Four Degree World for Australia and its region. This section and Table 14.1 summarize their key findings.

What emerges is a disturbing and bleak vision of a continent under assault. Australian communities, Australia's economy and Australia's environment will confront raised temperatures and sea-levels, variable rainfall and accentuated droughts. They will be battered by heatwaves, fire, floods, storms and coastal surges, and a range of other pressures on urban and natural systems. Food production and water supplies, and transport, power generation and health systems will come under stress. Adaptation costs will rise in response to these pressures and impacts. Our everyday lives will change profoundly even if adaptation succeeds. Food will cost more. We'll work earlier or later, travel less and consume less. We'll go out less in the midday sun. Gardens will look very different, even if watered with expensive desalinated water. The Great Australian Summer will be transformed by the loss of iconic beaches. Places of great natural beauty such as the Great Barrier Reef, Kakadu and the Daintree will be degraded or destroyed.

Temperature, rainfall and extreme weather events

Inland, in summer, average temperatures may rise by between 3.5°C and 7°C, and by 3°C to 5°C degrees in winter. In southern and coastal regions, they would increase by 3°C to 5°C, and 2°C to 4°C degrees in winter. In the southern third of the continent, rainfall is likely to decrease, by up to 40 per cent. As a result, Perth, Canberra, Adelaide and Melbourne could possibly experience semi-arid climates now common to parts of inland Australia. Living in Melbourne could be like living permanently in Griffith in New South Wales. Sydney will be like Rockhampton, Canberra like Cobar, Adelaide like Kalgoorlie, and Alice Springs comparable to the Sudan. But some places – for instance, Darwin – may become, in terms of climatic extremes, unlike anywhere currently on the planet.

Species and ecosystems

A range of now-common Australian native plants and animals will become rare, endangered or extinct across both natural and already highly modified landscapes. Terrestrial ecosystems will change or disappear in response to altered rainfall, temperatures and the increased frequency of extreme events such as wildfires and flood. For instance, alpine ecosystems and wet tropical rainforests will be hard hit by declines in precipitation and by warming. Fish are of exceptional importance as a food source in the Asia-Pacific region, while certain

Table 14.1 **Australia in a Four Degree World**

Average temperature	Inland regions – summer warming of between 3.5 and 7 Celsius; – winter warming of between 3 and 5 Celsius Southern and coastal regions – summer warming between 3 and 5 Celsius; – winter warming of between 2 and 4 Celsius
Average rainfall	Very broad range of changes across continent – summer rainfall changing by between +50% and −50% across Australia Southern third of continent – likely decrease in rainfall, typically around −40% to +10%
Drought	Likely increased frequency, area and intensity (e.g. up to five times more frequent droughts in the south and west of Australia) By 2070, the 1-in-20 year drought pattern for the 20th Century will become a 1-in-10 year drought over the Murray Darling Basin, Victoria, east NSW, Tasmania and south-west Western Australia
Snow cover	Snow seasons greatly reduced, with falls possibly reduced to zero across much of the existing alpine range
Sea level rise	Increase of up to 1.1 metres by 2100 and more than 7 metres in the longer run even if no further warming. Increased inundation of low-lying coastal land and increased shore erosion
Extreme high and low temperatures	Substantial increase in frequency of high temperature days (over 35°C) by 2070: For instance the number of days over 35°C for: – Sydney would increase from 3.5 to 12 days, – Canberra 5 to 26 days, – Melbourne 9 to 26 days – Adelaide from 17 to 47 – Perth from 28 to 67 days – Brisbane from 1 to 21
Extreme rainfall	Increased rainfall variability; increase in frequency of extreme rainfall events
Sea-level surges	Storm surges that now happen every 10 years will happen every 10 days in 2100, and even more frequently around Sydney.
Tropical cyclones	Average tropical cyclone maximum wind speed is likely to increase, although increases may not occur in all ocean basins. It is likely that the global frequency of tropical cyclones will either decrease or remain essentially unchanged. Around Australia, there is a southward movement of 100km in the genesis and decay regions
Terrestrial ecosystems and biota	Gradual and abrupt changes to patterns and levels of temperature and rainfall will lead to changes to the boundaries of ecosystems. Some ecosystems – such as alpine systems and wet tropical rainforests – may disappear and be replaced with entirely new ones. Changes in drivers and stressors such as water availability and weather extremes (rain, snow, fire, flood) may significantly transform some ecosystems and influence the health, distribution, and survival, of plant and animal species

Marine ecosystems and biota	Increases in surface sea temperature, extreme warming events, and ocean acidification, cause the collapse, degradation or transformation of marine ecosystems, and the decline or extinction of a range of marine species. Degradation or collapse of regional coastal fisheries, and transformation of ocean fisheries. Widespread destruction and degradation of the Great Barrier Reef from bleaching and ocean acidification.
Agriculture	Change in the availability and productivity of farm land Large areas abandoned because of poor rainfall and temperature increase. Change in pattern and impacts of agricultural pests, weeds and diseases. Changes in faming location, methods and species, and decline in crop productivity and yields. Production in the Murray-Darling Basin may have declined by up to 90 percent. Possible food insecurity, enhanced by Australia's population growth (projected to increase to between 33.7 million and 62.2 million by 2101.)
Health	Annual temperature-related deaths are estimated to increase in Australia from 5800 in 1990 to 17,200. Dispersal of infectious diseases like malaria and dengue fever. Vulnerable groups – such as the aged; low-income households; and the ill - likely to be affected by compounding health effects of declining food availability and poor nutrition, inappropriate housing conditions, and insufficient medical services.
Cities	70 percent of Australia's population lives in six major cities and over 90 percent in cities plus regional centres. Increasingly frequent heat waves, storms, floods and bushfires, will affect transport, health, housing and disaster response services, and potentially also energy, water and food supplies. Coastal settlements will be vulnerable to the impacts associated with sea-level rise: up to 250,000 properties could be potentially exposed to inundation with a sea-level rise above one metre, with a replacement cost of up to AUD$63 billion.
Economy	Substantial and growing costs of dealing with adaptation, disaster relief and reconstruction as global warming increases. Threat to Australia's export capacity re farm produce – currently valued at AUD$30 billion in 2011-12. Decline in tourism employment and revenue. Growth in renewables sector and associated employment. Likely contraction or end of fossil fuels sector and associated employment, and export revenue.
Human security	In the Asia-Pacific, growing populations, coastal flooding in populous low-lying settlements, declining marine and terrestrial resources and increasing food insecurity, will in combination further destabilizing influences. Up to 250 million people in the Asia-Pacific may be displaced by drought and coastal inundation. Climate-induced migration will place additional pressure on infrastructure and services. Increased pressure on Australia to change its foreign aid, defence and border security policies.

marine ecosystems such as coral reefs are economically important as tourism destinations, including in Australia. Marine systems will be affected not only by gradual changes in surface sea temperature but also by temperature fluctuations, which can cause heat stress and bleaching in coral reefs. Ocean acidification will affect marine species reproduction and survival. As with terrestrial systems, where marine ecosystems and species have already been affected by human activity and their resilience compromised, their vulnerability to climate-related and other pressures will be increased. Australia's major reefs – the Great Barrier Reef and Ningaloo – will decline precipitously. And as with land-based plants, animals and ecosystems, changes and extinctions will result.

Agriculture

Over half of Australia is farmed for crops and livestock. Predicted changes to temperature and rainfall patterns, to weather extremes, and other aspects of climatic variability, will have profound effects upon agriculture. Droughts will likely increase in frequency, area and intensity, with the possibility of droughts becoming five times more frequent in the south and west of Australia. By 2070, what was a 1-in-20 year drought during the 20th century will become a 1–10 year drought for the Murray–Darling Basin, Victoria, east New South Wales, Tasmania and south-west Western Australia. These changes will alter the location and type of cropping. The Murray–Darling Basin, Australia's principal farming region, will be especially hard hit. Estimates suggest that farm production in the Basin will decline – the extreme estimates are for declines up to 90 per cent due to water shortages alone. Large areas will become unsuited to current farming use. The presence and impact of pests, diseases and weeds affecting production, and the yields obtained, will change. Some will likely decline in impact and some get worse. Australia, which has long been an exporter of surplus grain, meat and wool, could become insecure in its ability to feed its domestic population under certain combinations of high population growth and high climate change. For example, Australia's population growth is projected to increase from 23 million in 2013 to between 31 million and 42.5 million in 2056, and to between 33.7 million and 62.2 million by 2101 (ABS, 2008). Meeting these needs will reduce exports. While the impacts of global warming on farming might be ameliorated by changes in crop varieties, livestock breeds, farming locations and methods, these impacts would nevertheless have significant regional social and economic consequences. Farm produce was valued at some AUD$46 billion in 2011, and so economic losses could amount to some AUD$30 billion in export revenue alone, based on 2011–12 figures (ABS, 2012).

Health

The likely changes and disruptions to the natural environment, social conditions and effective governance in a Four Degree World will hugely escalate risks to the population's health, many of which cannot be yet clearly foreseen. The greater frequency and severity of extreme climatic events will intensify increasing and ongoing pressures on human health. For instance, yearly temperature-related deaths are estimated to increase in Australia from 5,800 in 1990 to 17,200 in a Four Degree World. Nevertheless, it is difficult to project the location, scale and intensity of the primary, secondary and tertiary impacts of a Four Degree World on human health in Australia. Much depends on where those changes manifest and on the level and quality of investment in health services, and capacities for increasing resilience to climate change's direct impacts such as heatwaves, floods and fires, and the ecologically-mediated dispersal of infectious diseases like malaria and dengue fever. Even so, vulnerable groups – such as Australia's ageing population, low-income households and those already ill – are more likely to be affected by direct impacts, and by indirect impacts such as declining food availability and nutrition, inappropriate housing conditions and medical services insufficient to these new challenges.

Urban Australia

Australia is one of the world's most urbanized societies: 70 per cent of its population lives in six major cities and over 90 per cent in these cities plus regional centres. The direct and indirect impacts of climate change will be exacerbated by the density of urban settlement and valuable infrastructure. Increasingly frequent heatwaves, storms, floods and bushfires will affect transport, health, housing and disaster response services, and potentially also energy, water and food supplies. Coastal settlements will be vulnerable to impacts associated with sea-level rise. Effective adaptation to preserve the complex interactions between these systems will become increasingly expensive as warming progresses. Some adaptive planning is underway in all States and some capital cities (Melbourne and Sydney), including changes in land use planning, building standards, 'weather-proofing' technologies and improved public education. However, adaptation planning is poorly integrated and action to reduce risk and ameliorate urban impacts remains limited, under resourced and largely ad hoc.

Human security and the region

Climate change poses a threat to regional human security, and to national security more conventionally defined. Australia's Asia and Pacific neighbours, already highly vulnerable to natural disasters, will be hard hit by global warming. The combination of growing populations, flooding in populous low-lying coastal settlements, declining marine and terrestrial resources and increasing food insecurity, will be further destabilizing influences. Indonesia, China, India and Bangladesh will suffer droughts, food shortages and possibly mass starvation. Up to 250 million people in the Asia-Pacific may be displaced by drought and coastal inundation. Climate-induced migration (much of it internal to the nations affected) will place additional pressure on countries' infrastructure and services. Australia's energy, defence, foreign aid and Asia-Pacific engagement policies currently largely ignore the problem of global warming for regional security. These transformations demand a rethinking of Australia's external relationships, its border security arrangements, and the pattern and level of Australian foreign assistance to cope with these pressures.

Compounding crises

The threats of a Four Degree World add to major problems already confronting the planet. Other pressures (such as population increase, ocean acidification, biodiversity loss resulting from other causes, and economic and political instability) will accelerate and intensify the already complex impacts of climate change – possibly distracting from efforts at mitigation and adaptation. Given the interrelatedness of these impacts across global as well as regional, national and local scales, it is likely that – as warming continues – profound, compounding global crises will have severe and unpredictable ramifications for Australia's economy and society.

Can we adapt?

Current mitigation efforts are insufficient to hold global average warming below 2°C and preparation for a Two Degree World is certainly required. It is uncertain how far adaptation could ever go towards successfully reducing our vulnerability to a Four Degree World with higher temperatures and wilder weather. A range of scenarios depending on different responses by the state, industry and individuals has been imagined for Australia. Australia has considerable economic and social capacities to facilitate adaptation to some shocks, as described above, but the more extreme the warming, the greater our vulnerability and the greater the certainty that adaptation will be insufficient to protect us from hard times.

How should we respond? Australia's responsibility

Global warming is a collective action problem requiring urgent, effective and equitable international co-operation. Article 3.1 of the United Nations Framework Convention on Climate Change (UNFCCC) requires Parties to the Convention to protect the climate system 'on the basis of equity and in accordance with their common but differentiated responsibilities and respective capabilities', but what this mean in practice remains uncertain. The fundamental question for Australia remains: what is our fair share?

Australia's current targets

In 2012, Australia emitted some 552 million tonnes (Mt) CO_2-e (DCCEE, 2012).[1] It ranks 12th among the planet's 195-plus nations for its domestic greenhouse gas emissions and contributes some 1.3 per cent of total global emissions (EDGAR, 2013).[2] It is 14th for domestic CO_2 emissions alone (Olivier et al., 2012: 12).[3] Its per capita emissions are among the world's highest (Olivier et al., 2012: 29). Further, when emissions associated with Australian coal and gas exports are added to its domestic greenhouse emissions, Australia is the source of over 4 per cent of total global emissions (see below). In all, Australia is a major national emitter, a very significant contributor to global warming, and should shoulder part of the additional reduction burden associated with bridging the 'ambition gap' and preserving the 2°C 'guardrail'.

In 2009 Australia adopted an unconditional short-term emissions target – to cut national greenhouse emissions by 5 per cent below 2000 levels by 2020.

The Rudd government also accepted the recommendation of the Garnaut Review (2008) that Australia adopt two additional, conditional 2020 targets, of −15 per cent and −25 per cent below 2000 levels.

Australia has pledged to increase its commitment to −15 per cent if there is a global agreement under which major developing economies commit to substantially restrain emissions and advanced economies take on comparable commitments. Further, Australia will increase its commitment to −25 per cent if the world agrees to an ambitious global deal consistent with stabilizing atmospheric concentrations of greenhouse gases at 450 ppm CO_2-e (DCCEE, undated). It can be credibly argued that the conditions for the −15 per cent by 2020 target have already been met.

'Conditionality' in climate negotiations is predicated on the idea that the conditional offer of greater mitigation effort will encourage greater cooperation and induce other states also to adopt more stringent targets, and that delayed action will cost less in the future. Will other parties respond to Australia's inducements? Both at and since COP 15 at Copenhagen, the setting of national targets has depended on the bottom-up nomination of effort by individual parties rather than a top-down negotiation based on commonly agreed formulae. There has been no sign, despite significant 'conditional' offers being made by a number of parties, including the European Union, that these offers of enhanced mitigation effort have had any effect on negotiations or, particularly, on the efforts of the two major actors, the United States and China. To date, contingent promises have proved insufficient to encourage a binding international agreement. By contrast, early exemplary and substantial effort *may*, in a 'bottom-up world', have a leadership effect and help to induce stronger efforts by other individual states and build the basis for strong international agreement built on already tangible outcomes.

'Conditionality' for Australia has also, in part, been based on the belief that delayed abatement will be cheaper if accompanied by a stronger, later international effort. This rationale is based on the flawed assumption that the costs of climate change is confined to the costs of mitigation alone, and that a future exists in which the aggregate costs of mitigation, adaptation and climate-related losses will be less if intensive mitigation is delayed. These are implausible expectations. A contrasting and convincing view is offered by the Stern Report, which recognizes that the social and ecological costs of climate change must include both adaptation and remediation costs, the costs of widespread damages associated with warming and the value of productivity foregone. These costs all will continue to mount if mitigation is delayed. By this broader calculus, early action will always cost less than delayed mitigation given the value of these other 'externalities', especially once warming of 2°C, 3°C and 4°C or more occurs. Accordingly, a 'conditional' approach should not be used in setting a revised 2020 target for Australia.

Principles to guide our actions

Political and academic debates over equity, responsibility and capacity have focused on the unequal contributions of different states to the accumulated atmospheric store of greenhouse gases, and the economic wealth and capacity that have accrued to developed states since the start of the Industrial Revolution. (A separate but related argument about responsibility applies to national actions since 1990, when the IPCC first provided an incontrovertible baseline for scientific and political acknowledgement of climate change as an international issue.)

Developing states emphasize that this (mis)appropriation of the atmospheric commons by developed states has infringed their sovereign right to develop via a path of fossil fuel-based industrialization and, further, that developed states bear a responsibility for the climate damage they have wrought. The principles underlying their claims have variously been termed the 'beneficiary pays' principle (referring to the benefits derived by states using the global atmospheric commons for their advantage) and the 'polluter pays' principle (referring to the future damage of global warming). These principles are reflected in the architecture of the UNFCCC and Kyoto Protocol, with their grouping of Parties based on development status – for instance, the Annex 1 and non-Annex 1 lists – and underpin assertions about the additional responsibilities of developed nations to take leading steps in mitigation.

Claims about climate change, wealth and inequity are often also founded on the egalitarian view that individuals have rights to an equal share of the atmosphere, sometimes termed the 'per capita emissions rights' principle. According to this view, the historical benefits of fossil fuel-based economic development are inequitably distributed because clusters of individuals have 'appropriated' more than their fair share of the global emissions space. Many developing states support the idea that, at minimum, future access to remaining emissions 'space' should be equally shared on a per capita basis, using a 'contraction and convergence' model that would allow them to increase or stabilize their emissions while major developed country emitters make considerable reductions, all converging at an equal per capita emissions level at some future point (Meyer 2000).

Such considerations have, in combination, led to a variety of arguments, claims, and formulae for how *mitigation and adaptation effort and costs* should best be apportioned to reflect equity, historical responsibility, development and capacity, and nominating how the *remaining quota of atmospheric emissions* should be shared (e.g. Hohne et al., 2003; Heywood, 2007; Baer et al, 2008; Gardiner, 2010). Depending on where the 'baseline' for historical responsibility, or the future point of convergence, is established, developed states owe more or less to developing states under a global budget model. Depending on whether and how carbon rights are accorded to individuals or states, more or less of that fossil-fueled development is 'owed' by and to specific states.

These arguments (and ones which follow) suggest three principles to guide the determination of Australia's short and longer term targets, which should:

- be consistent with internationally agreed efforts to limit global average warming to less than 2°C, or the safer lower goal of 1.5°C, above preindustrial levels;
- reflect the best available climate science with regard to the pace of mitigation;
- be equitable in committing Australia to its fair share of the international mitigation effort by taking into account Australia's historical emissions profile ('polluter pays' principle), its national economic wealth ('beneficiary pays' principle') and capacity, and the equal right of individuals to the global atmospheric commons ('per capita emissions rights' principle).

Australia's carbon budget and 'ambition gap'

Australia's national carbon budget

Climate scientists have proposed a global carbon budget which defines the maximum additional volume of emissions that still may accumulate in the earth's atmosphere if global warming is to have a chance of staying below the 2°C 'guardrail'. Research suggests that this 'budgetary limit' will be reached when approximately one trillion tonnes of CO_2 have been added to the amount already in the atmosphere at the start of this century.

Further, in 2009 the German Advisory Council on Global Change (WGBU) suggested that 'By the middle of the 21st century a maximum of approximately 750 billion tonnes CO_2 may be released into the Earth's atmosphere if the guardrail is to be adhered to with a probability of 67 per cent. If we raise the probability to 75 per cent, the cumulative emissions within this period would even have to remain below 600 Gt CO_2,' (WGBU, 2009: 2).

Human activities have already added some 420 ± 50 billion tonnes of CO_2 to the atmosphere since 2000 and we continue to add some 50 billion tonnes per annum (Olivier et al., 2012: 18). We have used half or more of our global carbon budget in 13 years. Only another 500 billion tonnes of CO_2 can be added if we are to have only a 50 per cent chance of staying below the 2°C limit and avoiding 'dangerous climate change', around 330 billion tonnes if we are to have a 67 per cent chance, only some 180 billion tonnes for a 75 per cent chance, and less again for a target of 1.5°C (Schellnhuber et al., 2006; Meinshausen et al., 2009; WGBU, 2009).

A national carbon budget can be determined by building on the concept of per capita emissions rights first proposed by Meyer (2000). As the WGBU puts it, 'The global CO_2 budget is distributed among the world's population on an equal per-capita basis so that *national CO_2 budgets* can be calculated for all countries, and adopted on a legally binding basis. These budgets provide an orientation for countries on how swiftly and substantially their CO_2 emissions need to be reduced' (WGBU, 2009: 3). This approach in part depends on the baseline for population – which can be set contemporaneously (say, at 2013) or based on projections (for instance, for 2050, when global population is commonly estimated to peak).

The global average per capita allocation, based on projected 2050 global population data and a budget of 500 billion tonnes CO_2-e divided by approximately 9 billion (roughly the UN's median projection), is 55.6 tonnes per capita for a 50 per cent chance of staying below the 2°C limit. For a global budget of 330 $GtCO_2$-e (67 per cent chance), it is 36.7 tonnes per capita, and for a global budget of 330 $GtCO_2$-e, (75 per cent chance) it is 20 tonnes per capita.

These outcomes translate into an Australian national carbon budget (meaning all the carbon we have left to emit) of 1.72 billion tonnes, or 1.13 billion tonnes, or 620 million tonnes, depending on the level of risk we adopt in relation to the 2°C limit. In other words, even before taking equity considerations (i.e. responsibility, wealth and capacity) into account, Australia's carbon budget will provide for only between one and three more years of emissions at its current annual emissions level.

Australia's 'ambition gap'

As noted earlier, current aggregated national mitigation pledges for 2020 fall well short of what is required to hold to that 2°C 'guardrail', much less a safer target of 1.5°C. This deficit in international effort is now commonly called the 'ambition gap'. The UNEP 2012 *Emissions Gap* report estimated the gap between current mitigation pledges and effort and the emissions level consistent with a 'likely' (greater than 66 per cent) chance of staying within the 2°C target, to be 14 billion tonnes per annum CO_2-e in 2020 (Höhne et al., 2012: 30).

Clearly, more is required of all parties to reduce emissions rapidly by that amount. At minimum, major emitters need to adopt a proportionate, science-based 'carbon budget' response to bridging the ambition gap of 14 billion tonnes per annum by 2020. Australia too will need to accept a proportion of this additional reduction. A minimally equitable approach would be to adopt further reductions proportionate to Australia's global emissions contribution, or 1.3 per cent of the 'outstanding' 14 billion tonnes.[4] This would add some 182 million tonnes to Australia's 2020 mitigation target of −27.8 million tonnes below its 2000 baseline or, put another way, require an increase of another −33 per cent to its present target of −5 per cent of total emissions by 2020, to at least −38 per cent below 2000 levels by 2020.

Wealth and economic capacity

Australia's comparative wealth, capacity and economic advantage – derived in part from its historical use of fossil fuels – need to be taken into account in determining a short term target that reflects the requirements of Article 3.1 of the UNFCCC and better enables Australia to participate in the international climate framework on the basis of equity and in accordance with its common but differentiated responsibilities and respective capabilities.

Australia is the world's 12th largest economy by aggregate Gross Domestic Product (GDP) and also by GDP per capita. It is second among nations on the

Human Development Index and has among the highest international rankings for gross national income and per capita wealth. This wealth reflects the accumulated outcome of economic success over the past 150 years, evident in its highly skilled and well-educated workforce, its productive resources and manufacturing sectors, and its well-developed welfare services and public and private infrastructure. Such collective enrichment also reflects processes of greenhouse emissions-intensive agricultural and industrial expansion and indicates Australia's significant material capacity to invest in mitigation via domestic action and also to contribute to international adaptation funding ahead of other, poorer countries.

A country's ranking on international indices of national and per capita development, wealth and GDP is taken into account in various approaches offering a development-weighted assessment of national 'mitigation responsibility'. Baer et al. (2008) take these considerations into account. Using their development-adjustment index and 2020 as 'baseline' dates for national development, Australia's 2020 target increases to, at minimum, −41 per cent.

It is impossible to be conclusive about the effort that an individual state should adopt. Even so, the approaches used above show the lower limits for Australia's 2020 target if this is to be equitable and scientifically responsible. Based solely on current emissions contribution, if Australia is to participate meaningfully and successfully to an international effort to keep warming below 2°C, its science-based target cannot be less than −38 per cent below 2000 levels. If its efforts are to reflect its wealth, historical contribution and capacity, and also make provision for uncertainty, its emissions should be no less than −41 per cent and, given the 'ambition gap' probably higher and at least −45 per cent.

By contrast, Australia's current unconditional 2020 target of −5 per cent fails utterly when assessed against the principles by which such a target should be set. It will fail to contribute to keeping warming below 2°C. It is in no way equitable. It fails to reflect Australia's substantial economic and technological capacities to do more.

Carbon, trade and responsibility

National emissions accounting, as enshrined in the rules of the UNFCCC, includes only emissions produced within state borders. It ignores the flows of carbon that are a major part of international trade and therefore is 'blind' to the global warming contributions and associated responsibilities of states, companies and consumers that sit 'before' or 'after' the point at which those emissions are released. As a result, consumers of imported manufactured goods, and exporters of fossil fuels, remain unaccountable for their roles in the co-production of greenhouse emissions 'released beyond the border'.

Conveniently for economic beneficiaries such as Australia, Canada, the Russian Federation and Saudi Arabia, little attention has been paid to trade in raw (or unburned) fossil fuels, which shifts responsibility for emissions from exporting nations and companies to the middle-consumers (the states and companies involved in producing emissions using these fuels for producing emissions using those fuels for energy).

While Australia's domestic greenhouse emissions represent some 1.3 per cent of the global total, its global carbon footprint – the total amount of emissions it contributes to the global economy – is much bigger. Australia is the world's second largest coal exporter by volume (EIA, 2010/2011; WCA, 2013).[5] When emissions embodied in Australian coal exports[6] are added to its domestic greenhouse emissions, Australia's greenhouse footprint increases to 3.5 per cent of global emissions. Australian coal exports alone now contribute at least another 2.2 per cent of global emissions. In aggregate, therefore, Australia is currently the source of in excess of 4 per cent of total global emissions once emissions embodied in natural gas exports are added.

When its present domestic and exported emissions are combined, Australia ranks as the planet's sixth largest emitter of CO_2, after China, the USA, the Russian Federation, India and Indonesia.[7] It is responsible directly and indirectly for well over a billion tonnes of CO_2 per year. If planned and projected increases in Australian coal and gas exports are realized, its carbon footprint will more than double by 2030. A third of its domestic emissions growth over this period would come from the production of fossil fuels for export. Australia would be directly and indirectly responsible for over two billion tonnes of exported greenhouse emissions per year.

This 'trade-adjusted' reframing of Australia's emissions profile makes it clear that the global benefits of Australia's domestic greenhouse mitigation policy are overwhelmed by the negative effects of its energy export policy. Australia sees itself as an energy superpower, a view based on its bountiful resources and growing exports of fossil fuels and uranium, and expressed in national energy policy settings that have been constant across governments of different political persuasions over recent decades (see Commonwealth of Australia, 2004; 2012). As Australia derives significant additional economic benefit from its trade in fossil fuels, it owes an additional responsibility for contributing to mitigation and international adaptation funding of vulnerable developing nations.

Technological opportunity

Two decades ago there was little confidence in renewable energy technologies providing a cheap replacement for fossil fuels. The recent, rapid and accelerating uptake of renewable energy now points to the existence of viable alternatives. Globally, total renewable sources now supply 16.7 per cent of global final energy consumption. 'Modern renewables' – of which the most important renewable energy sources, in terms of globally installed capacity, are hydropower, wind power and then solar photovoltaics – comprise about half of this amount (REN21, 2012: 13). Renewables accounted for almost half of the power generation capacity added globally in 2011 and by the end of 2011, renewable power capacity worldwide supplied an estimated 20.3 per cent of global electricity (REN21, passim).[8] For all that, the rate of uptake remains, in the words of the conservative International Energy Agency, 'alarmingly slow' in relation to the problem of cutting greenhouse emissions (IEA, 2013: 7).

At least 118 countries, more than half being developing countries, had renewable energy targets in place by 2013, and 109 had supporting policies (REN21, 2012: 7). For example, the European Union has a binding 20 per cent renewables by 2020 target, as has Australia. For at least 30 countries, renewable energy provides above 20 per cent of the energy mix. Germany, with its *Energiewende* (energy transition) programme, leads the world in the transition from fossil fuels. With renewable sources in 2012 providing 25 per cent of its electricity consumption and 20 per cent of electricity consumption (up from 6.3 per cent in 2010), it has a target of 45 per cent by 2030. In the United States, renewables provided 12.7 per cent of total domestic electricity in 2011, up from 10.2 per cent in 2010, and accounted for about 11.8 per cent of domestic primary energy production (a similar amount as nuclear power) (REN21, 2012). Renewable energy comprised 70 per cent of the new generating capacity added in Europe in 2012. China is now the world's leader in terms of totaled installed capacity of renewable energy (152 GW) and also the rate of growth, with 23.1 GW of clean energy generating capacity installed in 2012 and US$65 billion invested in 2012 (PCF, 2012: 13–19).

Total global wind power capacity was 238 GW at the end of 2011, an increase of more than 20 per cent over 2010. The average rate of increase in capacity has been about 28 per cent over the last 10 years (GWEC, 2012). In 2011, most wind power capacity was installed in Asia (52 per cent), ahead of Europe (25 per cent) and North America (20 per cent), and the EU stands to be overtaken by Asia in terms of total capacity. China is now the world's largest wind power market, where wind is some 1.5 per cent of total power generation. Meanwhile, solar photovoltaic (PV) energy has seen dramatic reductions in cost in recent years and has moved toward 'grid parity' in terms of its unsubsidized cost compared with alternatives in many parts of the world. Total global solar PV capacity increased by 75 per cent in 2011 (EPIA, 2012), and solar technology has been the major recipient of investment in recent years (PCT, 2012: 11).

These trends underline the opportunities for Australia where the majority of power generating plants, which are coal and gas fired, will be commercially ripe for retirement by 2030 and will need to be replaced by 2045 at latest. Bloomberg New Energy Finance reported in 2013 that for Australia the production of electricity from unsubsidized wind power is now cheaper than from new-built coal and gas stations (BNEF, 2013). Moreover, by 2020 energy from large-scale solar sources will also be cheaper than coal and gas, when carbon prices are factored in. According to Bloomberg New Energy Finance, 'The Australian economy is likely to be powered extensively by renewable energy in future, and investment in new fossil-fuel power generation may be limited, unless there is a sharp, and sustained, fall in Asia-Pacific natural gas prices' (BNEF, 2013). A carbon price of AUD$25–50 would ensure their replacement with renewable sources even sooner.

Recent data indicate that Australia's Renewable Energy Target, the carbon tax and various State-based feed-in tariff schemes have assisted in influencing a shift from coal-fired power to hydro, wind and solar. In 2012, supply from hydro rose from 7.6 to 9.6 per cent (reflecting an improvement in water flows), and wind from 5.5 to 5.6 per cent of total power generation (Pitt and Sherry, 2013). Nevertheless, Australia's renewable energy consumption – the source of around 10 per cent of electricity generation in 2011–12 (BREE 2013, 29) – remains low given its considerable natural advantages. Meanwhile, over 1 million rooftop solar PV systems have been installed in Australia since 2007, serving some 11 per cent of Australia's population, and providing over 16,700 fulltime jobs (CC 2013b: 13).

Recent Australian studies suggest that the demand of baseload power is no longer an inhibiting factor for a renewable energy transition (Elliston et al., 2012) and that it would be technically possible to move stationary energy production to 100 per cent renewables within a decade (thereby reducing aggregate national emissions by 50 per cent by around 2020). The *Beyond Zero Emissions Plan* would require investment of AUD\$37 billion per annum for 10 years, creating 30,000 jobs and offsetting losses in the fossil fuel sector. The costs of transition should be set against the costs of business as usual, which would involve some AUD\$135 billion in investment to replace ageing energy infrastructure and an additional estimated AUD\$300 billion in expensive fossil fuel costs (Wright and Hearps, 2012: xix).

Coupled with enhanced energy efficiency measures, existing renewable energy technologies – with their uptake assisted by an adequate regulatory regime, appropriate financing and the withdrawal of confounding subsidies – are sufficient for Australia to move towards a very substantial emissions reduction target by 2020. In this context and given the need to bridge the ambition gap, Australia's existing Large-Scale Renewable Energy Target to provide 20 per cent of total stationary energy by 2020 could be increased to at least 50 per cent by 2020 and 90 percent by 2030, and be achieved using additional measures that support investment during that transition period.

Economic costs and vulnerability

The costs of extreme weather are already expensive, socially and economically. Even in affluent Australia, households, businesses and insurers sometimes struggle to cope. The Queensland floods, the Victorian bushfires, and cyclones Yasi and Oswald are all examples of traumatic and expensive weather events which caused critical power generation and public transport infrastructure to fail, disrupted production, killed and displaced people and livestock and caused significant damage to property. For instance, flooding in Queensland in January 2013 claimed 4 lives, left 230,000 homes without power, closed roads, damaged the railway network, affected coal production and inundated thousands of properties.

Insurance costs only partially reflect the economic losses associated with disasters, but are nevertheless broadly indicative of their scale. Estimates put the insured losses of the Queensland floods of December 2010/January 2011 at

approximately AUD$2.4 billion (Insurance Council of Australia, cited in AON/
WSP, 2013: 2). Similar damages were expected for the 2013 floods. Ironically,
further losses were incurred as widespread rainfall in Queensland also flooded
coal mines and reduced coal production and export by some 40 million tonnes,
valued at $6 billion (QRC, 2011). Cyclone Yasi, one of the most powerful
cyclones to have made landfall in historical times, was estimated to have cost
some AUD$517 million in insurance damages (Insurance Council of Australia,
cited in AON/WSP, 2013: 2). In all, the losses for insurers from recent storms,
floods and fires – over AUD$4 billion from six catastrophes in Queensland alone
since 2010 – has raised insurance costs and premiums and most likely reduced
private insurance coverage.

Governments also contribute to disaster relief work and funding. In January
2011, Treasury estimated that the Commonwealth's contribution towards
rebuilding bridges, roads, railway lines and other infrastructure destroyed in
Queensland and Victoria during that year would costs in excess of AUD$5
billion. In 2011, the Gillard government established a once-off AUD$1.8 billion
flood and cyclone levy, applied to those with incomes over AUD$50,000, to
offset these costs.

Sharing the burdens of mitigation and adaptation fairly has been a central
concern in international negotiations, based on recognition that the impacts
of global warming fall first and hardest on the most vulnerable nations whose
populations have contributed least to the problem (in terms of emissions),
and also received the least benefit (via associated industrialization and wealth
generation). Equitable burden sharing of the costs of mitigation and adaptation
has generally been less prominent in discussions about domestic climate policy.
Yet inequality will be exacerbated geographically – between households, communities and States – by climate impacts. For instance, it has been estimated that,
around Australia, up to 250,000 coastal properties could be potentially exposed
to inundation with a sea-level rise above one metre, with a replacement cost
of up to AUD$63 billion (DCC, 2009: 7). Rural communities in increasingly
drought-prone regions will also be hard-hit. In the absence of appropriate assistance measures (such as those in place since 2012 to compensate low-income
households for energy price increases resulting from carbon pricing), the poorest
and most vulnerable households will suffer most in their struggle to pay for the
transitional costs of rebuilding their homes or Australia's energy sector, and for
more expensive food, transport, heating, adaptation, or repair of climate-related
damage. The Australian Council of Social Services has pointed to an increasing
and disproportionate risk to Australia's most vulnerable people because of the
failure of community and government organizations to plan for extreme weather
events (ACOSS, 2012).

These issues are magnified in a Four Degree World, in which damages and costs
will rise abruptly and in a non-linear manner. As extreme events intensify and
become more frequent, the pressures for and costs of adaptation of critical infrastructure, housing and essential services, and for emergency relief, will multiply
and grow quickly. The World Bank rightly notes that 'projections of damage costs

for climate change impacts typically assess the costs of local damages, including infrastructure, and do not provide an adequate consideration of cascade effects (for example, value-added chains and supply networks) at national and regional scales' (Schellnhuber et al., 2012: xvii). Across the country, areas exposed to frequent serious flood, coastal storms, and bushfires, will probably have to be abandoned. Reconstruction will become unviable. Communities will move or be uprooted. Weather-related insurance will be harder and more expensive to get – and more households, communities and businesses will be left vulnerable to having to meet the costs of damage and adaptation from their own resources. Australian governments will be called on more frequently to fund emergency relief and reconstruction at a time when revenues may remain under strain from a general global economic downturn and the additional economic impacts of global warming. Meeting these costs will require dedicated levies, steeper taxes to fund adaptation and disaster relief, compulsory insurance – or the acceptance that climate change will produce increased poverty and greater inequality in life chances. Moreover, as Stern and Garnaut note, the longer mitigation and adaptation are deferred, and the more that impacts are displaced on to future generations (and other species), the greater the costs they will have to bear.

State governments are financially vulnerable to catastrophic climate-related risks, while the Commonwealth is exposed through the Commonwealth's National Disaster Relief Recovery Arrangements. It has been said that this growing exposure points to the need for alternative 'risk transfer solutions', perhaps via capital markets through new instruments such as new securities, like a catastrophe bond (AOL/WSP, 2013: 6). One-off levies are ad hoc responses to a pattern of crisis. Increasing pressure on limited state finances also points to the need to create an additional source of funding – a Climate Adaptation Future Fund – which will enable governments to reliably assist households, businesses and communities with the future costs of adaptation, emergency relief and reconstruction.

Beginning the shift

This chapter has suggested that an Australian 2020 emissions target which is responsive to the findings of recent climate science and which reflects Australia's economic and technological capacities would need to be no less than –41 per cent below 2000 levels, and preferably closer to –45 per cent.

To achieve such a significant outcome, Australia needs simultaneously to pursue two complementary approaches towards emissions reduction. Recent research has indicated that, with a modest carbon price of around $25 per ton, Australia has the potential to achieve up to 170 Mt CO_2–e in emissions reductions through improved domestic, industrial, transport and agricultural infrastructure and energy efficient practices (CW, 2010). The second involves the replacement of at least half of its fossil fuel power generation – which *in toto* contributes approximately half of Australia's greenhouse emissions with renewable energy – by 2020, including by employing additional measures such as a stronger national Renewable Energy Target to reinforce this shift. Together, these measures could effect an emissions saving of around 170 Mt CO_2-e in greenhouse emissions by 2020.

However, it is unlikely that it is unlikely that a mitigation target of −45 per cent could be achieved based on domestic effort alone in the brief time remaining before the end of 2020. Therefore it is important also to consider supplementary measures that would make achievement of that target possible, while encouraging the development of a domestic trajectory of rapid decarbonization. The shortfall – up to half the proposed target – might need to be met through the acquisition of certified carbon credits from overseas markets. The price of carbon in the European emissions trading scheme has plunged in recent years and at time of writing was around AUD\$6.5/tonne. If fully half the total 45 per cent emissions reduction sought by 2020 were bought, this could cost between approximately AUD\$800 million and AUD\$2.45 billion per annum (averaged annual cost) by 2020, depending on the market – here estimated to be between AUD\$6.50 and AUD\$20. (This approach is not seen a longer term solution to Australia's mitigation challenge.)

Even so, Australia will only contribute effectively to keeping global emissions below the 2°C 'guardrail' if its total emissions do not exceed its remaining national carbon budget (derived from the global carbon budget). Australia's national carbon budget will be exhausted in approximately one to three years given current (estimated 2012) emission rates. Only by cutting its national emissions by around 20 per cent of total emissions each year could Australia to stay within this budget. Such a rate of reduction is clearly not feasible given the carbon-intensity of Australia's economy. Nevertheless, any discussion of an effective and equitable 2020 target must address this larger issue. The recommended mitigation target of −45 per cent, with equal annual reductions beginning in 2014, would see Australia overshoot its carbon budget by some 1.7 billion tonnes by 2020. The resulting 'carbon deficit' needs to be offset through the acquisition of carbon credits in a program separate from any acquisitions necessary to ensure the −45 per cent target is achieved. This program of 'budget-balancing' acquisition would need to continue while Australia continues to emit greenhouse gases in excess of its national carbon budget.

Separately, in order to reinforce this abatement trajectory, policies would need to be adopted which will eliminate a major source of projected emissions growth over the next few decades. Increased exploitation of coal and gas resources for export is projected to be the main source of emissions increase for Australia over coming decades. A cap on the development of these resources, and their rapid phase out, would not only stop additional emissions but also reduce Australia's economic vulnerability to the inevitable global shift away from fossil fuels, which will occur as international concern about global warming intensifies.

These measures would require considerable political courage and will, multi-party support and a vigorous campaign of public education to ensure their legitimacy and success. Together, they would enable Australia to meet an ambitious emissions reduction target of at least −250 million tons per annum CO_2-e in domestic greenhouse emissions, or −45 per cent below 2000 levels, by 2020.

Large, long-term, state-planned and funded national infrastructural development was once common in Australia. This approach is largely unfashionable these days. Nation-building modernization, of the sort epitomized by the construction of the Snowy Mountains Hydro Scheme in the 1950s, is now believed to be an inefficient extension of state responsibility and that such infrastructural development is best conducted through public–private partnerships if it is to occur. Nevertheless, the scope and importance of some projects are such that they still attract substantial government involvement, as evidenced by the proposed National Broadband Network. The same should be said of a national energy transition programme, and climate adaptation works, of the scale and urgency required for Australia.

Such an ambitious transition programme – including the acquisition of international carbon credits – could be funded in several ways. While a proportion of investment could come from the private sector, public investment will be required. Funding sources could include, either individually or in combination, using revenue raised through a national emissions trading scheme; funds from consolidated revenue; a direct levy on the public; issuing government bonds specific to this purpose and at attractive interest rates; or a modest levy on Australian fossil fuel production.[9] Funds could also be derived from savings associated with the elimination of perverse subsidies to the fossil fuel sector, which serve to inhibit the transition to renewable energy by distorting energy prices in favour of fossil fuels and undermining the impact of a carbon price. The IEA (2012) estimates that global subsidies to fossil fuels exceeded US\$520 billion in 2011, compared to roughly US\$90 billion in policy support for renewable energy. Such subsidies in Australia were projected to cost over AUD\$10 billion per annum (in 2012/13) (EV, 2012; see also Riedy, 2007).

Conclusion

This book is a wake-up call to Australian policy makers. It examines the likely consequences of current policy settings. It presents a story about where we might go and describes a destination that is not yet inevitable. To have a reasonable chance of holding global warming below 2°C and avoiding a Four Degree future, the international community must first bridge the 'ambition gap' between existing national abatement pledges for 2020 and the collective mitigation effort necessary to contribute to that goal and, second, also restrain total international emissions to a safe global carbon budget. If Australia is to contribute meaningfully to these goals, it is necessary to decarbonize Australia's economy, with a large part of this effort occurring within the critical next decade (CC, 2011). A 2020 abatement target of no less than −45 per cent from a 2000 emissions baseline fairly reflects Australia's national wealth and capacities in the context of broader scientific argument for increased international mitigation effort. By contrast, Australia's present unconditional 2020 target of −5 per cent below 2000 emissions levels is unjustifiably low. The current target fails to contribute sufficiently to the goal of holding average global warming to 2°C or less, and is also profoundly inequitable. (The same holds for Australia's conditional targets of −10 per cent and −25 per cent.)

Rising public concern about global warming, relating to the impacts of extreme weather, will heighten expectations of climate policy. Already there is evidence of such changes in the United States, which was hard hit in the past two years by extreme weather events. Such shifts will lead to a rapid global turn away from fossil fuels – the recent policy shift in China to cap its greenhouse emissions, and US President Obama's Climate Action Plan (EOP, 2013) are merely precursors. Only the timing is in doubt. Under these circumstances, it would be unwise for Australian governments to continue to boost the development of fossil fuels-based energy as a major source of Australia's future economic wealth.

We now need a national energy transition plan, which includes immediately capping and rapidly scaling back our dependency on coal and gas. The experience of leading nations – such as Germany, which in 2010 had cut its emissions by 24.8 per cent from its 1990 base (EEA, 2012) and has an emissions target of –40 per cent by 2020 – emphasizes the need for effective, stable institutions for assessing what climate science tells us, for determining national targets, and for ensuring strong policy settings and effective abatement. In Australia, some of these institutions are now in place. The Clean Energy Finance Corporation (CEFC) and the Australian Renewable Energy Agency (ARENA) are well placed to assist in the funding of Australia's energy transition. The Climate Change Authority can provide independent, scientifically informed recommendations on Australia's future targets and annual carbon budgets. Yet at time of writing, they appear to be under political threat, as is the practice of pricing carbon.

The *Clean Energy Act 2011 (Cwlth)* created a carbon pricing mechanism which will switch from a fixed price to a cap-and-trade scheme, which will be linked to its European counterpart, and will likely be governed by targets revised in an orderly manner every five years. Carbon pricing has been the focal point of heated debate in Australia and entrenched political opposition by the Coalition since 2010. Yet carbon pricing was accepted by all political parties prior to the 2007 election as a valuable policy instrument for achieving abatement targets (see Howard, 2007). The use of carbon pricing, carbon markets and emissions trading is now internationally accepted as a key measure to reduce emissions, including in the European Union, a range of states in the USA, New Zealand and in China.

While carbon pricing is important, policy and industry experts generally recognize the need for a broad suite of policy measures rather than reliance purely on this measure alone if rapid change is to occur. A full palette of measures (REN21, 2013) would include:

- legally binding targets and scientifically informed timetables for emissions reduction and the introduction of renewables;
- electricity market reforms for power generation and combined heat and power;
- publicly supported research, development and commercialization;
- feed-in tariffs, quotas and/or other finance-attracting policy regimes;

- subsidies, tax credits and abatements, and other cost-reduction incentives that promote renewables;
- energy efficiency standards for equipment, vehicles and materials;
- national and local building codes and standards;
- emissions trading and cap-and-trade schemes;
- industrial policies that target renewable energy for jobs and international competitiveness;
- social policies that address and ameliorate the impacts of the energy transition renewable energy for its social benefits;
- frameworks for energy prices that reflect the full cost of energy, including environmental and social costs; and phase-outs of perverse subsidies for fossil fuel.

Australia's policy palette has few colours by contrast.

Whether we like it or not, things will change. The issue for us is the extent to which future changes are of our choosing and in our control, and therefore the extent to which we are prepared to act now to preserve our social, economic and ecological wealth for the future. Public clamour for urgent action will increase in response to the threats of climate change. The cost of renewable energy technologies will continue to fall, especially as the world's two largest emitters – China and America – move to decarbonize their economies. The global market for fossil fuels will contract. These shifts will force change in Australia. This book has made it clear that we must now choose do as much as we can, as fast as we can, to cut our greenhouse emissions and assist in adaptation in Australia and abroad. The positive outcomes of exemplary action are never certain, but they are a vast improvement on the consequences of a powerful nation acting as a laggard.

Notes

1 This represented an increase in national emissions of around 5 per cent since 1990. When the Kyoto Protocol was negotiated in 1997, Australia argued for an exceptional emissions target of 108 per cent above a 1990 baseline during the Protocol's first commitment period (2008–2012). It was one of only three countries to be awarded targets that permitted an emissions increase during that period. It received this having also gained the inclusion of land clearing-related emissions in its baseline, to its great advantage. See Hamilton, 2001. Stationary energy contributed around half of Australia's emissions (its contribution has grown from 195 Mt CO_2-e in 1990 to 288 Mt CO_2-e in 2012), while agriculture accounted for 16 per cent and transport 15 per cent in 2012.
2 Including land use and land use factors (LULUCF).
3 Excluding the EU27 as one 'country'.
4 This approach assumes that all states undertook additional mitigation regardless of their development status whether they are highly developed or least developed states. This is equitable, therefore, only in terms of a strict apportionment. A fairer response would take national wealth, relative level of development and capacity to mitigate into account: this would lead to an even higher target for Australia.
5 Australia was overtaken by Indonesia as the world's largest exporter in 2011.

6   The volume of coal exported in 2011 was some 280 million tonnes (DFAT, 2011). This represents 728 million tonnes of embodied CO_2, based on 2011 figure for Australian coal export volumes multiplied by an aggregate emissions factor of 2.6.
7   Using trade-adjusted data for carbon flows.
8   The following data are drawn from Olivier et al., 2012, REN21, 2012 and UNEP, 2012.
9   In the absence of a domestic carbon price, a levy of $AUD1 per tonne of CO_2-e – effectively some 2 per cent of the expected production value of $AUD 53.3 billion in 2013/14 – could be placed on all coal produced by Australia for domestic use and export. This approach would, in the short term, contribute $AUD1.17 billion (projected production, 2013–2014 [DTE undated], 2.6 x approx. 451.6 tonnes coal) to the cost of buying international permits. A lower levy could be used if gas production was also included or if revenue was also sought from other sources.

References

ABS (Australian Bureau of Statistics). 2008. 3222.0 – Population Projections, Australia, 2006 to 2101. http://www.abs.gov.au/Ausstats/abs@.nsf/mf/3222.0 [accessed 31 July 2013].

—2012. 7503.0 – Value of Agricultural Commodities Produced, Australia, 2010–11.

ACOSS (Australian Council of Social Services). 2013. *Extreme weather, climate change and the community sector*. ACOSS submission to the Senate Inquiry into recent trends in and preparedness for extreme weather events. ACOSS Paper 197. January.

AON/ WSP. 2011. The Potential Impacts of Climate Change on the VMIA's Insurance Portfolio. Consultants' Report (unpublished).

Baer, P., T. Athanasiou, S. Kartha and E. Kemp-Benedict. 2008. *The Greenhouse Development Rights Framework: The Right to Development in a Climate Constrained World*. Heinrich Boll Stiftung (revised second edition).

BNEF (Bloomberg New Energy Finance). 'Renewable energy now cheaper than fossil fuels in Australia'. http://about.bnef.com/press-releases/renewable-energy-now-cheaper-than-new-fossil-fuels-in-australia/ [accessed 31 July 2013].

BoM ([Australian]Bureau of Meteorology). 2013a. Special climate statement 43 – extreme heat in January 2013. Retrieved from: http://www.bom.gov.au/climate/current/statements/scs43e.pdf [accessed 31 July 2013].

—2013b. Special climate statement 44 – extreme rainfall and flooding in coastal Queensland and New South Wales. Retrieved from http://www.bom.gov.au/climate/current/statements/scs44.pdf [accessed 31 July 2013].

BP (British Petroleum). 2012. *BP Statistical Review of World Energy 2012*. http://www.bp.com/en/global/corporate/about-bp/statistical-review-of-world-energy-2012.html [accessed 31 July 2013].

CC (Climate Commission). 2011. *The Critical Decade: Climate science, risks and responses*. http://climatecommission.gov.au/report/the-critical-decade/ [accessed 31 July 2013].

—2013a. *The Angry Summer*. http://climatecommission.gov.au/report/the-angry-summer/ Securing Australia's energy future.

—2013b. *The Critical Decade: Australia's Future – Solar Energy*. http://climatecommission.gov.au/wp-content/uploads/Australias-Future-Solar-Energy-Report.pdf [accessed, 5 August 2013].

CCA (Climate Change Authority). 2013. *Caps and Targets Review Issues Paper* (April 2013). http://climatechangeauthority.gov.au/sites/climatechangeauthority.gov.au/files/files/caps/13-030-CATRIP.pdf [accessed, 31 July 2013].

Christoff, P. 2012. Reframing Australia's climate responsibilities: from carbon footprint to international funding. Paper delivered at Symposium on Climate Adaptation and Vulnerability, University of Sydney, August.

—2013. *Australia's Ambition gap, national carbon budget and 2020 target.* Monash Sustainability Institute Working Paper 1/2013. At: monash.edu/sustainability-institute/carbon-budget-report/ [accessed 30 July 2013].

Commonwealth of Australia. 2004. *Securing Australia's energy future.* Energy White Paper.

—2012. Australia's energy transformation. Energy White Paper.

CW (ClimateWorks Australia). 2010. Low Carbon Growth Plan for Australia. March. http://www.climateworksaustralia.org/sites/default/files/documents/publications/climateworks_lcgp_australia_full_report_mar2010.pdf [accessed, 31 July 2013].

Davis, S. J. and K. Caldeira. 2010. Consumption based accounting of CO_2 emissions. *Proceedings of the National Academy of Science of the United States of America* 107 (2): 5687–92.

DCC (Department of Climate Change). 2009. The first pass national assessment of climate change risks to Australia's coast. Canberra.

DCCEE (Department of Climate Change and Energy Efficiency). 2012. Australian national greenhouse accounts. Quarterly update of Australia's National Greenhouse Gas Inventory. June.

DFAT (Department of Foreign Affairs and Trade). 2011. Composition of Trade Australia 2011. http://www.dfat.gov.au/publications/stats-pubs/cot-cy-2011.pdf [accessed, 31 July 2013].

EEA (European Environment Authority). 2012. *Annual European Union Greenhouse Gas Inventory 1990–2010 and Inventory Report 2012.* Submission to the UNFCCC Secretariat. EEA Technical report No 3/2012.

EIA (US Energy Information Administration). undated. International Energy Statistics – Coal. http://www.eia.gov/cfapps/ipdbproject/iedindex3.cfm?tid=1&pid=1&aid=4&cid=r7,&syid=2003&eyid=2011&unit=TST [accessed 21 April 2013].

Elliston, B., Diesendorf, M. and MacGill, I. 2012. Simulations of scenarios with 100% renewable electricity in the Australian National Electricity Market. *Energy Policy* 45: 606–13.

EV (Environment Victoria). 2012. Pre-Budget briefing paper: an analysis of Australian government tax measures that encourage fossil fuel use. http://www.marketforces.org.au/MF%20and%20EV%202013%20polluter%20handouts%20assessment%20FINAL.pdf [accessed 31 July 2013].

Gardiner, S. M. 2010. *A Perfect Moral Storm: The Ethical Tragedy of Climate Change.* Oxford University Press: Oxford.

Garnaut, R. 2011. *The Garnaut Review 2011: Australia in the Global Response to Climate Change.* Cambridge University Press, Cambridge, UK.

Hamilton, C. 2001. *Running from the Storm: The Development of Climate Change Policy in Australia.* University of New South Wales Press: Sydney.

Heywood, M. 2007. Equity and international climate change negotiations: a matter of perspective. *Climate Policy* 7, 518–34.

Höhne, N., C. Galleguillos, K. Blok, J. Harnisch and D. Phylipsen. 2003. *Evolution of Commitments Under the UNFCCC: Involving Newly Industrialized Economies and Developing Countries.* European Business Council for a Sustainable Economic Future: Germany.

Höhne, N., J. Kejun, J. Rogelj, L. Segafredo, R. S. da Motta and P. R. Shukla. 2012. *The Emissions Gap Report 2012: A UNEP Synthesis Report.* November.

Howard, J. 2007. Melbourne press club speech, Hyatt Hotel. 17 July.

IEA (International Energy Agency). 2012. *World Energy Outlook 2012*. Paris.

—2013. *Tracking clean energy progress*. Paris.

Meinshausen, M., N. Meinshausen, W. Hare, S. C. B. Raper, K. Frieler, R. Knutti, D. J. Frame and M. R. Allen. 2009. Greenhouse-gas emission targets for limiting global warming to 2°C. *Nature* 458: 1158–62. doi:10.1038/ nature08017.

Meyer, A. 2000. *Contraction and Convergence: The Global Solution to Climate Change*. Green Books, Totnes, UK (second edition).

Oliver, J. G. J., G. Janssens-Maenhout and J. A. H. W. Peters. 2012. *Trends in global CO₂ emissions: 2012 report*. The Hague, PBL Netherlands Environmental Assessment Agency; Ispra: Joint Research Centre.

Peters, G. P., J. C. Minx, C. L. Weber and O. Edenhofer. 2011. Growth in emission transfers via international trade from 1990 to 2008. *PNAS* 24 (108): 8903–8.

PCT (Pew Charitable Trust). 2012. *Who's winning the clean energy race?* The Pew Charitable Trust.

Pitt and Sherry. 2013. National Electricity Market emissions continue at lowest level for ten years. Electricity emissions update – data to 31 January.2013. At http://www.pittsh.com.au/documents/201302_ps_cedex_electricity_update.pdf.

PWC (Price Waterhouse Cooper). 2013. *Business resilience in an uncertain, resource-constrained world*. Carbon Disclosure Project. https://www.cdproject.net/CDPResults/CDP-Global-500-Climate-Change-Report-2012.pdf.

QRC (Queensland Resources Council). 2011. High cost of floods confirmed. 21 July. chttps://www.qrc.org.au/01_cms/details.asp?ID=2835. Retrieved 23 January 2013.

Raupach, M., I. Harman and J. Canadell. 2011. *Global climate goals for temperature, concentrations, emissions and cumulative emissions*. CAWCR technical report 042, September, Canberra.

REN21. 2012. *Renewables 2012: global status report*. Paris, REN21 Secretariat.

—2013. *Renewables global futures report 2013*. Paris, REN21 Secretariat.

Riedy, C. 2007. *Energy and Transport Subsidies in Australia: 2007 update*. For Greenpeace Australia. Institute for Sustainable Futures. http://www.isf.uts.edu.au/publications/riedy2007subsidies.pdf [accessed 31 July 2013].

Rogelj, J., D. L. McCollum, B. D. O'Neill and K. Riahi. 2013. 2020 emissions levels required to limit warming to below 2°C. *Nature Climate Change* 3: 405–12.

Schellnhuber, H. J., W. Hare, A. Serdeczny, D. Coumou, K. Frieler, M. Martin, I. M. Otto, M. Perrette, A. Robinson, M. Rocha, M. Schaeffer, J. Schewe, X. Wang and L. Warszawski. 2012. *Turn Down the Heat: Why a 4°C Warmer World Must be Avoided*. Report for the World Bank by the Potsdam Institute for Climate Impact Research and Climate Analytics. November.

Scotney, R., S. Chapman, C. Hepburn, A. Wyatt and C. Jie. 2012. *Carbon Markets and Climate Policy in China: China's pursuit of a clean energy future*. At http://www.climateinstitute.org.au/verve/_resources/ClimateBridge_CarbonMarketsandClimatePolicyinChina_October2012.pdf [accessed 31 July 2013].

UNFCCC (United Nations Framework Convention on Climate Change). 2005. Sixth compilation and synthesis of initial national communications from parties not included in Annex I to the Convention. FCCC/SBI/2005/18/Add.2. 25 October.

—2011. FCCC/SB/2011/INF.1/Rev.1. Compilation of economy-wide emission reduction targets to be implemented by parties included in Annex I to the Convention. http://unfccc.int/resource/docs/2011/sb/eng/inf01r01.pdf.

—2012a. National greenhouse gas inventory data for the period 1990–2010. FCCC/SBI/2012/31.

—2012b. Additional information relating to the quantified economy-wide emission reduction targets contained in document FCCC/SB/2011/INF.1/Rev.1. http://unfccc.int/resource/docs/2012/awglca15/eng/misc01.pdf.

UNPD. 2010. CO_2 emissions per capita in 1990, 2000 and 2011, in the top 25 CO_2-emitting countries.

WGBÜ (German Advisory Council on Global Change). 2009. *Solving the Climate Dilemma: The Budget Approach.* Berlin, German Advisory Council on Global Change.

WMO (World Meteorological Organization). 2013. *WMO Statement on the Status of the Global Climate in 2012.* WMO-No. 1108.

Wright, M. and P. Hearps. 2012. *Zero Carbon Australia Stationary Energy Plan.* Beyond Zero Emissions Project, University of Melbourne Energy Research Institute. http://media.bze.org.au/ZCA2020_Stationary_Energy_Report_v1.pdf [accessed 31 July 2013].

Appendix: Description of the Climate Models and Analysis Methods

The primary source of GCM results used is the CMIP3 multi-model ensemble (Meehl et al., 2008), but additionally results from a large multi-member perturbed physics ensemble (climateprediction.net, here referred to as 'CPDN') are also considered and compared (Sanderson et al., 2008).

Analysis of the CMIP3 model archive employs the probabilistic method, developed by Watterson (2008) and Watterson and Whetton (2011) and used in the last national projections for Australia (CSIRO and BoM 2007). Based on this approach, a probability distribution is fitted to the projected local changes for 4°C global warming from across the 23 climate models. This provides the 10th, 50th and 90th percentile thresholds for each case, with 90, 50 and 10 per cent (high, medium and low) chances of exceeding these thresholds. Watterson (2008) applies a weighting function based current climate performance of the models (although this is weak and has minor impact on the projected changes). In CSIRO and BoM (2007) and Watterson (2008), the probability distributions were scaled to match scenarios of global warming for various time slices and emission scenarios. Here the results are simply scaled by a global warming of 4°C (4GW). Note that Watterson (2008) also applied a log-linear scaling to improve the realism of scaled rainfall decreases where these might otherwise exceed −100 per cent for cases of large global warming.

Analysis of the CPDN model ensemble includes formation of raw frequency distributions for area-average temperature and rainfall changes for regions of Australia for those ensemble members that reach at least a 4°C global warming in the last decade of the simulations (around 1,000 ensemble members).

Index

1.5 Celsius 'limit' 6, 235
2 Celsius 'threshold 5, 6, 235

adaptation 141, 143; Australian
contribution to international funding
212, 213; capital cities 178–9;
city-based planning initiatives 178–80;
City of Melbourne Strategy 178;
domestic sources of funding 210; fast
start funding 209; global costs 180,
209; Global Environmental Facility
(GEF) 210; healthcare system 167; land
use planning 172ff.; legal challenges
183; limits of 144; planning processes
179–80; possible future roles for the
state 220ff.; retreat from State-level
adaptation planning 183; role of
markets 143; roles of government 145;
three scenarios for Australia 220ff.;
under-resourcing of agencies 182; *see
also* planning
Adelaide: adaptation planning 179; days
above 35C 48; extreme sea level events
53; extreme temperatures 47; fire
danger 38, 52; heatwave (2009) 158;
rainfall/temperature under Four Degree
scenario 22, 24, 26; bushfires (2003) 37;
Climate Change Strategy (2007) 179;
temperature 25
agriculture, Australian: adaptation
potential 113–15; likely impacts of
Four Degree World 106; pests, diseases
and weeds 111–12; production for
export 101; rainfall impacts 107–9;
temperature impacts 107; uncertainties
relating to climate change 106; water
availability and quality 110–11; *see also*
crop production
Akkadian Empire 121

Alice Springs: climate under Four Degree
scenario 24; days above 35C 48;
rainfall/temperature under Four Degree
scenario 26
Ambition Gap (emissions) 6–7, 244–5,
253; Australia's contribution 244;
Australia's targets 241; dimensions of
6, 244; UNEP *Emissions Gap* report
(2012) 245
Angry Summer, The (2013) (Climate
Commission report) 235
Antarctica 7, 10, 53, 127, 128
Anthropocene Era 122–3, 126
Arab Spring 196
Arctic sea ice 7, 10, 128
Asia-Pacific: climate impacts 191ff.;
coastal flooding 191; health impacts
of Four Degree World 166; marine
resources 85
Asian Century White Paper (2012)
(Australia) 197–8
Asian Development Bank 166, 191
Australia: 'Ambition gap' 244–5; carbon
budget 244–5, 252; carbon exports
246–7; coal and gas investment 248;
Defence White Paper (2009) 194, 197,
200; economic costs of extreme weather
249–50; emissions (current, projected,
rankings) 212, 241–2, 246–7, 253; energy
superpower 247; exposure of coastal
properties 250; fossil fuel subsidies 213;
Gross Domestic Product (GDP) ranking
245; Human Development Index ranking
246; Kyoto Protocol negotiations 255;
National Security Strategy (2013) 194;
principles for emissions target setting,
243; Renewable Energy Target (RET)
148, 247–8, 250; renewable energy
uptake 248–9; three climate adaption

scenarios 220ff.; trade-adjusted emissions profile 247; warmest summer (2012/13) 235; weakness of existing 2020 target 253
Australian Council of Social Services (ACOSS) 250
Australian Defence Forces (ADF) 199
Australian Renewable Energy Agency 254

Baer, Paul 246
Bali Action Plan (2007) 4
Bangladesh 147, 158, 191, 192, 240
'Beneficiary pays' principle 243
Beyond Zero Emissions Plan 249
Biodiversity: Australia as megadiverse continent 63–4; biogeographic context 63–4; tipping points 65; *see also* ecosystems
Biodiversity Conservation Strategy (Australia) 65
Biodiversity, terrestrial 63ff.; Australian impacts of Four Degree World 66, 68–9; conservation role of market mechanisms 146; *see also* extinction
Biodiversity, marine: human pressures and impacts on 85; impacts of Two and Four Degree Worlds 90; recent responses to ocean acidification 86–9; recent responses to ocean warming 92
Birol, Fatih (IEA) 211
Bloomberg New Energy Finance 248
Brazil 126, 210
Brisbane: City Council, adaptation actions 179; days above 35C, 48; extreme temperatures 47, 162; fire weather days 52; floods, 181; rainfall/temperature under Four Degree scenario 22, 24, 25, 43
Brown, Lester 190
Bush, President George W. 150
bushfires: Canberra (2003) 2, 37, 181; ecological susceptibility 37; planning responses 175–78; Tasmania (2013) 2, 33; Victoria ('Black Saturday' 2009) 31, 37, 38, 181, 184; Victorian Bushfires Royal Commission 176, 181, 182

Cairns: cyclones 42; days above 35C 48; rainfall/temperature under Four Degree scenario 22, 24, 25–6; regional biodiversity 67
Canada 149, 165, 246
Canberra: bushfire (2003) 2, 37, 181; days above 35C 47, 48; extreme fire weather days 52; rainfall/temperature under Four Degree scenario 24, 25

Cancun *see* climate negotiations
carbon budget: Australian 244–5, 252, 254; global 244; national 244
carbon price 146, 148, 150, 212, 248, 251, 252, 254
Chin, Elias Camsek (Vice President, Palau) 192
China 146: 12th Five Year Plan 152; climate negotiations 149; climate threat to agriculture and food availability, 8, 239; CO_2 emissions, profile and global ranking (2012) 4, 148, 247; Copenhagen negotiations 5; emissions targets and mitigation plans 151–2; energy sources 152; receipt of climate funding 210; renewables energy production/consumption 248; wind power 248
cities 173: adaptation options, Australia 220ff.; projected temperature equivalents for Australian capital cities 24–5, 162, 172
civilizational threats 122, 126, 141, 147–8
Clean Development Mechanism (CDM) 150–1, 153
Clean Energy Act 2011(Cwlth) 254
Clean Energy Finance Corporation 254
climate change: as threat multiplier 193, 199; threats to military assets 193, 198
Climate Change Authority 254
Climate Commission (Australia) 235
climate funding: financial transaction tax 212
climate negotiations: Bali (13th COP, 2007) 4; 'bottom up' and 'top down' target setting 149; Cancun (16th COP, 2010) 6, 9, 142, 149, 235; Copenhagen (15th COP, 2009) 4, 5, 6, 142, 149, 209; Doha (18th COP, 2012) 145, 206; Durban (17th COP, 2011) 6, 149; Paris (20th COP, 2015) 153
climate policy measures, 254–5
climate 'refugees' 130, 135, 159, 189, 190, 193, 195; *see also* displacement
coasts: adaptation scenarios 220ff.; intensive settlement, Australian 169; inundation of 168; property exposure, Australia 250; threats to Asian coastal settlements 187–8
compounding global crises 129–32
conditionality of emissions targets 242
conflict, violent, and climate change 196
'contraction and convergence' 243
cooling events, global 161; AD 536 event 161; Toba eruption 161; Younger Dryas 161

Copenhagen Accord 5
Copenhagen climate conference; *see* climate negotiations
Copenhagen Diagnosis 4
coral bleaching 88
coral reefs *see also* Great Barrier Reef
crop production 102–12: effects of climate variability 106; impacts of domestic demand on export 112; impacts of projected rainfall changes 107–8
Crutzen, Paul 123
Cyclone Yasi 42, 168, 181, 249

Darwin: cyclones 42; days above 35C 48; extreme rainfall 43–4; heat stress 162; rainfall/temperature under Four Degree scenario 24, 25
Defence White Paper (2009) (Australia) 194, 197, 198, 200
Development Adjustment Index (Baer et al.) 246
development assistance (Australia) 209
Diamond, Jared 122
disaster response 249
displacement, climate-related 194, 195
Doha Agreement 210
drought impact: on crop production in Australia 104, 108; on crop production in Europe, Russia and United States 109–10; on ecosystems 67; *see also* extreme weather

Earth System 123–8; planetary boundaries 132–5; tipping elements 126–8
East Australian Current (EAC) 85
economy, Australian: agricultural production, export value 101; contribution of marine resources 84; impact of Four Degrees on marine resources 95–6
ecosystems: transformation 6; tropical rainforests (Cairns region) 67; vegetation communities, Australia 67; *see also* biodiversity
El Nino-Southern Oscillation (ENSO) 40
emissions *see* ambition gap, greenhouse gas emissions, mitigation, targets
emissions trading 150, 252, 253
endemicity, Australian 64
energy, renewable *see* renewable energy
Energy White Paper (2012) (Australia) 198
environmental security 193 *see also* national security, human security

European Union: emissions performance 150; emissions trading scheme 150, 252; renewable energy target for 2020 248; wind power 248
extinction 65, 68, 71–2, 123
extreme weather: global projections 46–7; social instability 196
extreme weather, Australian historical: extreme sea levels 45; fire weather 37–9; rainfall and drought 39–44; temperatures 35–9; tropical cyclones 42–5
extreme weather, Australian projected: drought 48–50; extreme sea levels 53–4; fire weather 51–3; hail 50–1; rainfall 48; temperatures 47–8; tropical cyclones 53; wind 51

financial shocks of climate change 147
fire regimes: impacts on ecosystems 67; *see also* extreme weather
fire danger rating systems 37
fisheries: Asia-Pacific 85; Australian 84, 95–6; Four Degree World 94–5; impacts of pressures 85
floods: Pakistan (2010) 3; Queensland (2010–11) 33, 168
flood and cyclone levy (Australia) 250
food: consumption 108; crisis, Global (2008) 130; grain price spike and Arab Spring 196; health 165; prices 121; security 55, 85, 94, 102, 104, 114; sub-Saharan Africa 208; trade 101, 112, 144–5
fossil fuel subsidies 213, 253
Fordism, 227
Four Degree World: Asia-Pacific impacts 191ff.; economic impacts 151; emergence of concept 7; extinction 71–2; impact on Earth system 126–9; Miocene era 159, 160; population displacement 158, 166, 192, 194–5; projected global impacts 8, 10; projected impacts on human health 155ff.; sub-Saharan African food impacts 204; terrestrial ecosystems 65–7; unpredictable health consequences 164–5
Four Degree World, projected Australian impacts: Australian agriculture 105–15; biodiversity, marine 90–5; biodiversity, terrestrial 66, 68–9, 72–3; combined temperature and rainfall 23–4; drought 24–8; extinctions 71–2; hail 50;

health impacts 162ff.; healthcare 167; projected temperature equivalents for capital cities 24–5, 162, 172; rainfall change 21–3; sea level rise/coastal impacts 28–9; snow 28; temperature change 18–21

Four Degrees and Beyond (Oxford Conference 2009) 9

Four Degrees or More? (Melbourne Conference 2011) 9

Garnaut, Ross 214, 251

Garnaut Climate Change Review (2008) 12, 142, 146–7, 241

Garnaut Climate Change Review Update (2011) 148

General Circulation Models 90

German Advisory Council on Global Change (WGBU) 244

Germany: emissions performance 254; emissions targets 254; energy transition strategy (*Energiewende*) 248; renewables energy production/consumption 248

Gillard government (Australia) 197, 229

global climate models 17

Global environmental change 123

Global Environmental Facility (GEF) 210

Global Financial Crisis (2008-) 131, 147

global warming limits: 1.5 Celsius 'limit', 6, 234; 2 Celsius 'threshold' 5, 6, 235

Great Acceleration, the, 123

Great Barrier Reef 88–9, 90–1, 92–5, 130–1

greenhouse gas atmospheric concentrations: increase from preindustrial levels 7; 400 ppm 234; 600 ppm 106; doubling to 560ppm 91; stabilization at 450ppm 4, 142

greenhouse gas emissions performance: Australia 151; China 151–2; Europe 151; United States 151

Greenland Norse community 122

Growing a Better Future (Oxfam 2011) 208

health, human 155ff.: Asia-Pacific impacts 166; changes in nutrition 164–6; diffuse impacts 166; extreme weather events 163; heat stress 162; impact of cooling events 161–2; infectious diseases 163, 165–6; migration and displacement, effects of 167; risks in a Four Degree World 159ff.; risks to Australia in a Four

Degree World 162ff.; types of climate-related impact 158

heatwaves: Adelaide (2009) 158; Australia (2009) 1–3, 33, 154; Europe (2003) 3, 34, 104, 156–60; health impacts 156–9; impacts on marine systems 95; Melbourne (2009) 38, 158; Paris 156–9; pressure on terrestrial ecosystems 67; Russia (2010) 3, 34, 104, 196, 198; United States (2011, 2012) 3, 104; urban adaptive planning 177–8; *see also* extreme weather

Henry Tax Review 146

Hobart: days above 35C 48

Holocene Era 126

human security 193, 199–200

ice sheets, Greenland and West Antarctica 128

inadequacy 214; levy on international transport emissions 212; new Australian Climate Adaptation Future Fund 250; new global climate fund 213; new international sources 216–17; plethora of sources 214, 215; removal of fossil fuel subsidies 213

India: CO_2 emissions, global ranking (2012) 246; receipt of climate funding 210

Indian Ocean 43, 45, 87, 92, 106

Indonesia 192; CO_2 emissions, global ranking (2012) 246; coastal flooding 192; coastal population displacement 192; food security 192; population displacement 192

insurance 143–4, 249–50

International Energy Agency (IEA) 211, 248, 253

International Migration Organization 194

IPCC: *Managing the Risks of Extreme Events and Disasters to Advance Climate Change Adaptation* (2012) 34; 2020 targets (*Fourth Assessment Report*, 2007) 4; sea-level rise projections 172

Johnston, Chalmers 201

Kyoto Protocol 3–4, 149

land use planning 172–89

livestock production 101, 105

Lynas, Mark 8

Mackellar, Dorothea 155
marine resources, Australian: Report Cards
   of Marine Climate Change 88; scenarios
   for Two and Four Degree Worlds 92–5
markets, policy role 144–6
Mayan Empire 121
Medieval Climate Anomaly 122
Mekong Delta 160, 191
Melbourne: *Climate Change Adaptation
   Strategy* (2009) 178, 185; days above
   35C 48; fire weather days 52; projected
   extreme temperatures 47; projected
   rainfall/temperature under Four
   Degree scenario 25, 172, 177; record
   temperatures (2009) 38, 158
Meyer, Aubrey 244
Millenium Ecosystem Assessment 217
Miocene Era 159, 160
mitigation: conservative case 147; crisis
   211; developing countries 212; *see also*
   climate negotiations, targets
Murray Darling Basin 106, 161

National Broadband Network 252
national security 193ff.; *Defence White Paper*
   (2009) (Australia) 194, 197, 198; failure
   of policy integration, Australia 198;
   relationship to human security, *Strong
   and Secure: A Strategy for Australia's
   National Security (Australia)* (2013) 194,
   200; violent conflict and climate change
   196; 'whole-of-government' approach
   199–200; *see also* defence
nationalism, paranoid 195
Netherlands Environmental Assessment
   Agency 5, 6–7
New South Wales: drought 50; planning
   for Bush Fire Protection Guidelines
   184; sea level rise benchmark 174; Sea
   Level Rise Planning Guideline 183;
   temperature and rainfall 24–6
New Zealand 150, 253
nitrogen 123
Northern Territory: rainfall 43; sea level
   rise benchmark 174
nuclear power 222, 223, 224

Ocean acidification 10, 89, 94, 95, 131
Ocean warming 42, 86ff., 94
Oil price spike (2007–8) 130
Oxfam: Australia's emission targets 211;
   climate financing 210; new global
   climate fund 211

Pacific islands: sea water intrusion 192;
   threat of sea level rise 192
Pacific Ocean 45, 87, 92, 94
Papua New Guinea 159
per capita emissions, global allocation, 244
'per capita emissions rights' principle 243
Perth: Rainfall/temperature under Four
   Degree scenario 25; City of South
   Perth, Draft Climate Change Strategy
   179; days above 35C 48
Philipines 191, 195
phosphorus, peak 126
Plague of Justinian 161
planetary boundaries 133–4
planning: climate impacts 173ff.;
   incrementalism 182
'polluter pays' principle 242
population: displacement 142, 158, 166,
   167, 191, 192, 194–5; food security
   102, 103; global coastal settlement 84;
   growth pressures on food 122; health
   conditions 159ff.; Indonesian coastal
   population 85, 192
public education 179
public participation 180

Quadrennial Defense Review (US) (2010)
   199
Queensland: bushfire planning response
   176; costs of 2010/2011 floods 248;
   cyclones 42, 53, 168; drought 50;
   floods 33, 42, 168, 181; health services
   168; heatwave planning response 177;
   rainfall 39; sea level rise planning 175
Queensland Reconstruction Authority 181

rainfall: Australian agriculture 107–8; *see
   also* extreme weather
renewable energy: global rate of uptake
   247; hydro 247, 249; national
   renewable energy targets 248; solar
   photovoltaics (PV) 247, 248; supply of
   global final energy consumption 247;
   wind 247–8
Renewable Energy Target (Australia) 148,
   248, 251
Roman Climate Optimum 121
Roman Empire 121, 161, 166
Ronnenberg, Espen 210
Rudd, Kevin 197
Russia 3, 34, 104, 130, 196, 198, 246, 247;
   CO_2 emissions, global ranking (2012)
   247

sea-level rise 90; Australian planning responses 178–9; impacts on cropping 113; Indonesia 196; IPCC (2007) projections 176; NSW Sea Level Rise Planning Guideline 187; Pacific islands 196
sea urchin *Centrostephanus rodgersii* 93, 99
security 193ff. *see also* environmental security, human security, national security
Senegal 208
snow cover, Australia 28, 29, 68
Snowy Mountains Hydro Scheme 253
soil erosion 109
soil salinity 109
South Australia: crops 108; fire weather 38; heatwave planning response 177; sea level rise benchmark 174
Southern Oscillation 220
species, Australian terrestrial: extinction record and rate 65; human ecosystemic influences 65; low fertility soils, influence on vegetation 64; options for adaptation 69–71; pre-adaptation to climatic variability 64; topographic influences 64–5
Steiner, Achim 207
Stern, Nicholas 251
Stern Review 8, 241
Stockholm Environment Institute 209
Strong and Secure: A Strategy for Australia's National Security (Australia) (2013) 194
Story-lines, climate 217–19
Sudan 26, 208
Sydney: days above 35C 48; extreme sea events 53; fire weather days 52; hail 50; planning for climate change 178; projected climate 24; projected extreme temperatures 47; rainfall/temperature under Four Degree scenario 25

Tainter, Joseph 122
targets, mitigation 149: Ambition Gap 6–7; Kyoto Protocol 3, 4; principles for choosing 243; *see also individual countries*
Tasmania: bushfires (2013) 2; drought 24, 41, 50; marine biota 89, 95; planning 175; rainfall 23, 24, 43, 49; sea level rise 29; sea level rise benchmark 174; wind 28
tipping points 66
tropical cyclones: pressure on terrestrial ecosystems 67; *see also* extreme weather
Tuvalu 208

Typhoon Bopha (2012), 195

UNFCCC (United Nations Framework Convention on Climate Change) 3; architecture of 243; Article 3.1 241, 245
United Nations: General Assembly 192; UNEP *Emissions Gap* report (2012) 245
urban density, Australia 173
United States: climate negotiations 149; CO_2 emissions, global ranking (2012) 247; emissions performance 150; public opinion 254; rejection of Kyoto Protocol 4; renewables energy production/consumption 248

Victoria: bushfires 2, 33, 37, 176–7; crops 108; drought 24, 50; flooding 42, 43; heatwave 33; heatwave planning response 177; rainfall 22, 41, 49; sea level rise 29; sea level rise benchmark 174; snow 29; temperature change 19–20; water availability 110; *see also* Melbourne
Victorian Bushfires Royal Commission 180, 185, 192
Victorian Civil and Administrative Tribunal 184

warmest recorded decade 235
water: adaptation scenarios 220ff.; availability and quality for farming 110; China 160; desalinisation 144; South and South-East Asia 160; urban and rural supply 144; water trading and climate 144
Weaver, Ole 193
Western Australia: bushfire planning response 176; extreme temperature 47–8; rainfall and drought 24, 39–41, 43, 50; sea level change 53; sea level rise benchmark 174; temperature and rainfall 18, 24, 35; tropical cyclones 53; *see also* Perth
WGBU (German Advisory Council on Global Change) 244
Wildfires *see* bushfires
Wind power *see* renewable energy
World Bank: global adaptation costs 180, 209; global climate damage costs 250; projections of change in 21st century 9; *Turn Down the Heat* Report 9
Worldwatch Institute 190
World Resources Institute 209

Made in the USA
Coppell, TX
25 April 2023

16050495R00162